THE CIVILIZATION OF THE AMERICAN INDIAN SERIES

Maya Cities: PLACEMAKING AND URBANIZATION

Edzna—five-story pyramid and temple (*Templo Mayor*)

MAYA CITIES

PLACEMAKING AND URBANIZATION

George F. Andrews

University of Oklahoma Press : Norman

Library of Congress Cataloging in Publication Data
Andrews, George F   1918–
    Maya cities: placemaking and urbanization.
    (The Civilization of the American Indian series, v.
131)
    Bibliography: p.
    1.   Mayas—Architecture.   2.   Cities and towns,
Ruined, extinct, etc.—Mexico.   3.   Cities and towns,
Ruined, extinct, etc.—Central America.   4.   Mexico—
Antiquities.   5.   Central America—Antiquities.
I. Title. II. Series.
F1435.3.A6A52   301.36'3'09701   73-19390
ISBN 0-8061-1187-9

The publication of this book has been aided by a grant from the National Science Foundation.

TO

my wife, who took part in every phase of this project from the time we first climbed the stairway of a Maya pyramid in 1958 to the final typing of the manuscript.

I am greatly indebted to the Graduate School, University of Oregon, for financial support in the form of three research grants which enabled me to extend the scope of this study during five summer field trips to Mexico and Central America during the years 1958, 1959, 1961, 1964, and 1971. I am also indebted to the Institute of International Studies at the University of Oregon and its director, John Gange, under whose auspices funds were made available for the extensive field surveys which were made at Comalcalco and Edzna in 1966 and 1968. In these latter efforts, I was assisted by a number of graduate students from the University of Oregon, who worked long hours under very trying conditions while making the detailed maps of Comalcalco and Edzna which appear in simplified versions in this publication. I am well aware that their efforts far exceeded the call of duty.

I also wish to acknowledge the encouragement and assistance I received from numerous officials in the Instituto Nacional de Antropologia y Historia of Mexico, and in particular its directors, Dr. Davalos Hurtado and Arq. Ignacio Marquina, who made it possible for me to secure the permits required for the field work undertaken at various archaeological sites in Mexico, including Comalcalco and Edzna.

My thanks also to William Bishoprick, Brad Reed, Don Ashton, and Philip Crundall, fifth-year students in architecture at the University of Oregon, who assisted in the preparation of many of the drawings included in this volume. The list of other individuals who helped in various ways would be much too long to fit on this page; to them, special thanks for all favors received.

I also wish to thank the National Science Foundation for their generous assistance in the form of a grant-in-aid which made it possible for this book to go to press. Without their help, this book would never have become a reality.

GEORGE F. ANDREWS

University of Oregon
Eugene, Oregon

Acknowledgments

Table of
Contents

xi

Illustrations

xvi

*Unless otherwise noted, all drawings and photographs
are by the author.*

The drawings of glyphs accompanying each chapter head
or section head were chosen for purely decorative purposes
from J. Eric S. Thompson's *A Catalog of Maya Hiero-
glyphs* (Norman, University of Oklahoma Press, 1962)
and are not intended to convey any meaning.

Maya Cities: PLACEMAKING AND URBANIZATION

Detailed investigations of the Maya civilization, particularly Maya architecture and civic planning, are comparatively meager in relation to the exhaustive studies which have been made of the Egyptian, Greek, Roman, and other Old World civilizations. The fact that the indigenous peoples of the New World, at least in Mexico, Central America, and parts of South America, were indeed civilized and were then living in or adjacent to large numbers of cities throughout this area was well known to the Spanish Conquistadors, who were the first Europeans to make contact with Maya tribes, in Yucatan in the year 1517. Bernal Diaz' story of the conquest of Mexico by Hernan Cortez and a few hundred Spanish soldiers in the following two years contains glowing accounts of the cities of Tenochtitlan, Cholula, Cempoala, and many others which he describes as rivaling anything found in Spain.

But the Spaniards were interested in gold and the conversation of the natives to Christianity, rather than the preservation of the visible aspects of a pagan culture, so the first New World cities, wherever they were found, were ruthlessly destroyed with no thought of their value to future generations. Christian churches and monasteries replaced the "pagan" temples, houses of the Spanish settlers took the place of the old "palaces," and rows of shops and houses, arranged in a strict gridiron, soon erased whatever vestiges remained of the old order of the pre-Columbian city. Finally, most of these once elaborate constructions disappeared even from memory, save for the written record of their existence left by Bernal Diaz and Bishop Landa in the Yucatan. Even then, it was several centuries before these accounts became a matter of public record (Bishop Landa's book was not published until 1863) and by then the early explorers had already begun the laborious process of gathering and recording reliable data about the Mayas and their neighbors.

Fortunately, most of the Maya cities with which we are concerned escaped the depredations of the Spaniards. With the exception of a few settlements situated in the more accessible parts of the Yucatan Peninsula, the cities built by the Mayas lay crumbling in the remote jungle and rain forest areas of Mexico, Guatemala, and Honduras where they had been abandoned by their builders nearly six hundred years before Cortez set foot on Mexican soil, their existence unknown to even the few natives who still lived in this inhospitable region. No gold or other precious minerals were found in this area, and for a period of three hundred years the occasional reports of the discovery of remains of large stone buildings and carved stone monuments emanating from the natives or those Spanish settlers who inhabited isolated pockets of the rain forest were greeted with almost total apathy by the lay and scientific communities alike, who were more concerned with exploiting the riches of the New World than in reconstructing its past.

Thus, it was not until the year 1840 that widespread attention was drawn to the remains of scores of magnificent stone cities in the jungles of Mexico and Guatemala through the efforts of John Lloyd Stephens, an American explorer, writer, and sometime diplomat. Stephens, accompanied by Frederick Catherwood, an English architect, spent the better part of four years exploring the Maya area, and the results of his work were published in four volumes, profusely illustrated with Catherwood's drawings (Stephens: 1841 and 1843). These books proved to be tremendously popular, and because of them it became apparent that the early inhabitants of this continent had in many ways achieved a degree of civilization comparable to that of Greece or Rome. During the latter part of the nineteenth century, the interest aroused by Stephens' books attracted a growing number of curiosity seekers and amateur archaeologists, who added much in the way

I.

Introduction

3

of useful documentation in the form of drawings and photographs to the superb, but limited, record provided by Stephens' descriptions and Catherwood's earlier drawings. The giants among these early explorers were A. P. Maudslay and Teobert Maler, who compiled extensive records of Maya buildings and carved monuments under conditions that would be intolerable for any but the most venturesome of their counterparts today.

Simultaneously, however, other individuals, misguided by uninformed enthusiasm, played havoc in the ruins through abortive attempts to dig up the treasures they supposedly contained, and created great confusion in regard to the origins of the builders of these monuments by wild speculations which had them proceeding from areas as far removed as Egypt, Israel, or the lost continent of Atlantis. Stephens had already correctly postulated an *in situ* development by indigenous but unknown groups as early as 1840, but it was not until the early part of this century that carefully documented evidence was forthcoming which substantiated his views. Since the beginning of this century, numerous highly skilled specialists, representing educational and governmental institutions in this country as well as Mexico and Guatemala, have begun to recreate, through painstaking excavations, the true story of the life and death of this great civilization.

For the most part, these studies have tended to focus on the identification and classification of ceramic materials and ritual artifacts which represent the bulk of archaeological material obtained from excavation, and on certain unique intellectual and artistic achievements of the Mayas which centered around their preoccupation with measuring and recording time intervals. Much of the stone carving, particularly the delicate relief sculpturing found on the great stone stelae which abound at the larger Classic Maya sites, is in the form of hieroglyphic inscriptions which record periods of time elapsed from the beginning of the Maya calendar. The surface remains, which consist by and large of crumbling buildings and mounds of rubble where important stone structures once stood, give mute evidence of the high degree of social organization and technological advancement achieved by their builders. The destruction wrought on these structures by the omnipresent jungle and their sheer mass in numbers alone has precluded anything more than the merest scratching of the surface at most sites in an effort to remove accumulated debris.

Even after fifty years of extensive reconnaissance, mapping, and excavation, the largest number of Maya cities still lie buried deep in the jungle, their locations known only to a few *chicleros* who stumble over them in their search for the raw material of chewing gum. In recent years, thanks in part to the explorations carried out by oil companies and the ready access provided by airplanes, a number of hitherto almost inaccessible sites with extensive architectural remains have been carefully mapped and their central areas partially excavated and restored, thus adding substantially to our knowledge of the physical make-up of the city and its immediate environs. Considering the total amount of information now at hand, it seems feasible to undertake a comparative study of Maya cities in order to project meaningful generalizations regarding their basic physical organization and structure.

The material which makes up the bulk of the present work is largely concerned with an investigation of the spatial concepts evident in the positioning and siting of Maya buildings and building groupings, and in the planning and physical organization of the "city" or "ceremonial center" as a whole. (This ambivalence in terminology will be taken up in detail later.) The nature of such a study requires the analysis and comparison of a large number of building complexes and larger city schemes, which even in their ruined or partially restored state are still capable of revealing the underlying conceptual ideas which brought them into being.

Several important questions are inherent in such a study. (1) How did the architectural ideas which produced the ceremonial center evolve and what was the course of their development? (2) Is there evidence of generic forms appearing consistently at different centers, even though these forms are modified as a consequence of local or regional influences? (3) Can the specific nature of the activities which took place in various parts of the center be identified more clearly by a systematic study of the relationships among buildings and building groupings? (4) Can it be demonstrated that the center evolved from an essentially religious or ceremonial space into a more complex urban center, or city, which contained buildings and other spaces devoted to a wide range of secular acitvities? (5) Is there any consistency in the orientation and siting of individual buildings and complexes of buildings, and what, if any, meaning can be attached to the patterns of orientation? (6) To what extent did fortuitous features of topography play an important role in the physical layout of the city?

It would be presumptuous to assume that concrete answers to these and similar questions can be derived from the present study, which is necessarily limited to whatever material is available; there is no guarantee that this particular material includes a sufficient cross section of building types and arrangements to permit useful generalizations. But it is doubtful that there will ever be a time when all the pertinent information is available. This being the case, it appears that the time is now ripe for a closer look at a number of cities as "artifacts" in an effort to shed a little light on the questions outlined above.

The description and analysis which follows is restricted

to an examination of the building remains associated with the lowland Maya culture from the Classic period; i.e., the interval between the years A.D. 300 to 900.[1] During this six-hundred-year period, Maya cities or ceremonial centers took on their final form, piled layer upon layer over the remains of earlier prototypical structures. Within the limits of our present knowledge, it is virtually impossible to trace the full course of Preclassic development at any site, but sites showing evidence of very early and very late development have been included, provided a relatively firm basis for projecting a temporal sequence of development during the Classic period. The consistency in form of the basic building types and building groupings throughout the entire Maya area indicates a common cultural root, within which smaller spheres of influence appear as regional or local variations. These regional variations are manifest in changes in the specific architectural details of individual buildings as well as in the particular arrangement of building groupings.

Twenty major settlements have been included in the present study, ranging in location from the most southerly parts of the Maya area in Honduras and Guatemala to both the northern and eastern edges of the Yucatan Peninsula. This has made it possible to include at least one example from all the major regions which make up the total of the Maya domain, with the exception of the Rio Bec area. For purposes of comparison, two Postclassic sites in Mexico and one highland Maya site in the mountains of Guatemala have been included in the descriptions and analyses of individual sites which form the second section of this book. The twenty sites described in this section vary considerably in size and complexity, ranging from a minor center such as Bonampak, with its nine small buildings overlooking a single plaza, to major urban centers such as Tikal and Dzibilchaltun, each with hundreds of structures extending in all directions from a densely built-up central core. The discussion which follows represents an attempt to seek out and characterize the ordering principles underlying this diversity.

---

[1] The simplest scheme for the chronology of Maya history uses three main divisions: Pregclassic, 600 B.C. to A.D. 300; Classic, A.D. 300 to 900; and Postclassic, A.D. 900 to 1520. Each of these major divisions is broken down into substages, and the Classic period can thus be divided into Early (A.D. 300 to 550) and Late (A.D. 550 to 900). Because this terminology has been used in the majority of the references cited, it is used throughout this present volume, even though G. W. Brainerd (1958) and E. W. Andrews (1965) have proposed alternate schematics which are more detailed and probably more accurate, since they correlate known architectural and ceramic sequences. In all cases, there still remains the problem of the correlation of the Maya calendar with the Christian calendar, and the period A.D. 300 to 900 which is used here as representing the Classic period is based on the Goodman-Martinez-Thompson correlation (11.16.0.0.0).

5

Architecture, in its broadest aspect, is concerned with providing a formal setting for the organized activities of man. The earliest efforts of man to provide himself with protection from the elements in order to satisfy the demands of a relatively settled existence involved only minute modification of existing conditions, which does not yet introduce the idea of "building" and certainly not of architecture. Even when larger units of building material in a comparatively unshaped state were grouped together to form a semipermanent dwelling or agglomerate of dwellings, the essential idea of architecture is not yet fully visualized. The reorganization of the existing natural environment at a scale commensurate with multiple human needs imposes two basic conditions which must be satisfied before we can conceive of the notion of architecture.

The first condition is the conceptualizing of ideas of order and systems which have the capacity to differentiate the activities of man from the balance of nature. A second condition is the formulation of the technical means which will enable him to give practical expression to such space concepts as he postulates for the creation of useful and meaningful surroundings. The process of conceiving any such structural arrangement as something complete in the mind's eye contains the germs not only of architecture but what is understood generically as "classic" architecture. The notion of architecture, then, implies a predetermined end, a conceptual origin, of which the material or visible expression is only the completion of the process. The fulfillment of crystallized concepts, as indicated earlier, depends ultimately on the practical techniques of building and the mastery of whatever material is available for building purposes.

To even the most casual observer, Maya architecture, and by extension Maya cities, meet the two conditions stated above. This is manifest in the individual building groupings as well as in the city or ceremonial center as a whole. The smallest temple, including the platform which supports it, can be observed to be composed of a number of discrete parts, or elements, whose ordering appears to be dependent on a set of "rules" as explicit as those governing the Greek or Roman orders. The temple proper, as seen in elevation, consists of a base, lower wall, upper wall, and roof comb, and each of these elements is carefully articulated by means of projecting cornices or moldings which divide the façade into a series of horizontal bands. Nothing is accidental in this composition, the details of each part have been fully preconceived and the proportions and spacings of doorways and moldings carefully adjusted in order to produce a visual harmony, or unity, which again has its counterpart in the Greek or Roman temple. Here is "classic" architecture with all of its controls and determinants, its pristine order designed to delight the eye and mind alike.

To a lesser extent, this same sense of unity pervades the whole city and it can be seen that, in spite of certain concessions which were sometimes made to the fortuitous features of existing topography at particular building sites, the city appears as an organic whole in which the individual parts bear some relationship to one another. The unification of the disparate elements is achieved in part through the use of a single building material for all structures, regardless of function of form, and through the repetition of a limited set of decorative and symbolic motifs in association with these structures. The symbols are strange to our eyes and the hieroglyphic inscriptions which are sometimes painted or carved onto the walls of buildings defy translation; but the underlying sense of order is strong and impels us to look beneath the symbols and seek out the basis upon which the city is projected as a visible symbol of man in search of his own identity.

The city is normally considered as being concomitant with civilization. It gives visible expression to the fact that man has emerged from the primitive state and has joined with other men in creating a community apart from nature which is essentially human. The basis of man's transition from nature to the "city" is described by Jose Ortega y Gasset as follows:

> How is this possible? How can man withdraw himself from the fields? Where will he go, since the earth is one huge, unbounded field? Quite simple; he will mark off a portion of this field by means of walls, which set up an enclosed, finite space over against amorphous, unlimited space. Here you have the public square. It is not, like the house, an "interior" shut in from above, as are the caves which exist in the fields; it is purely and simply a negation of the fields. The square, thanks to the walls which enclose it, is a portion of the countryside which turns its back on the rest, eliminates the rest and sets up opposition to it. This lesser, rebellious field, which secedes from the limitless one, and keeps to itself, is a space *sui generis* of the most novel kind, in which man frees himself from the community of the plant and the animal, leaves them outside, and creates an enclosure apart which is purely human, a civil space. Hence Socrates, the great townsman . . . can say, "I have nothing to do with the trees of the field, I have only to do with the man of the city. (Ortega y Gasset: 1951)

As Ortega y Gasset has suggested, the concept of a bounded open space representing a specific place apart from nature is the essential ingredient necessary in any effort to humanize the natural environment. Maya cities consist of a series of such bounded open spaces, defined by great platforms or buildings and accented by temples raised high on pyramidal bases, marking the points at which the presence of invisible dieties is given visible form. The rooms inside the temples are small and dark, retaining the size and shape of small thatched-roof huts, which were surely their precursors. These small rooms have nothing of the cathedral about them; it is clear that they are not gathering places where the community of man can meet together in order to pay homage to the gods. The gathering place is the plaza below and its smooth paved surface contrasts sharply with the richly articulated and heavily ornamented mass of the temple-pyramid. This contrast between solid and void, or mass and plane, sets up a configuration that is truly monumental, a heroic form that dominates both man and nature alike. This aspect of monumentality is necessary before the full process of man's symbolization of his detachment from nature is complete. It creates a new scale of things which is capable of setting up a direct rivalry with nature. Here, then, is a suitable place for man to express his ideas of humanness and godliness in a setting apart from the jungle which surrounds and sustains him. But then it becomes fair to ask, "How did such a thing come about?"

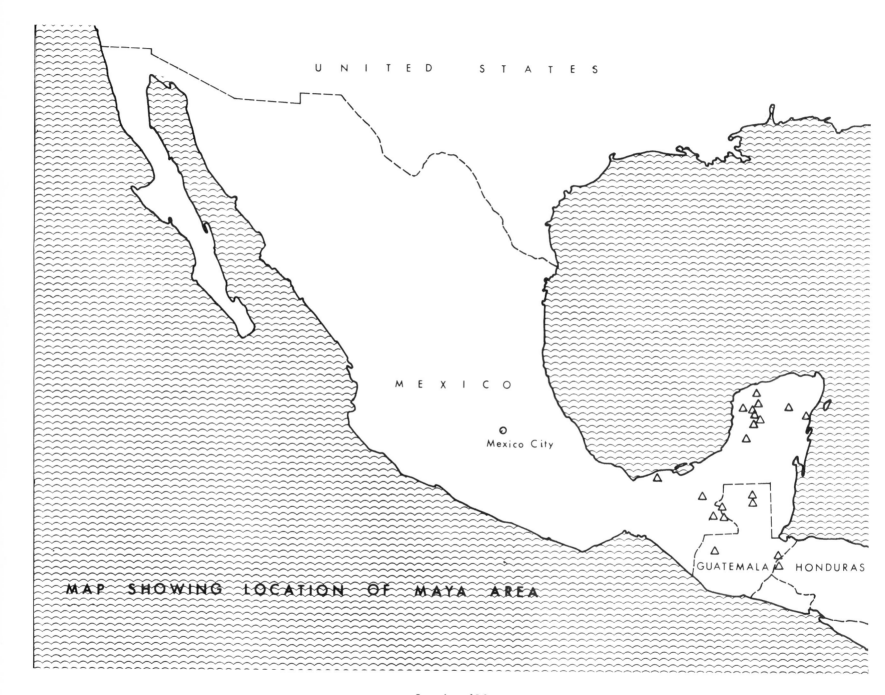

FIG. 1. Location of Maya area.

The area occupied by the lowland Mayas consisted for the most part of a dense rain forest stretching northward from the lower slopes of the Cordillera in Mexico and Guatemala to the tip of the Yucatan Peninsula. This area comprised those parts of Mexico and Central America which at present include the states of Tabasco, Yucatan, and Campeche, the eastern half of the state of Chiapas, and the whole of the territory of Quintana Roo in the Republic of Mexico as well as the lowland areas of Guatemala, British Honduras, and the western section of Honduras (Fig. 1). This is a warm, semitropical region, covered for the most part with a thick jungle made up of huge trees and luxuriant undergrowth, although the drier parts of the Yucatan Peninsula support only a scrubby growth of smaller trees and thorny plants.

To modern man, this is essentially a hostile environment and many parts of this same area are almost completely deserted today. Within the jungle, the great canopy of trees shuts out the sun and the ground below is dark and gloomy. The air is close, almost fetid, and the profusion of smaller plants and vines filling the spaces between tree trunks makes any movement impossible without the use of a machete. At intervals, the jungle gives way to *bajos*, or swamps, filled with a mixture of mud and water during the rainy season and covered with an almost impenetrable tangle of thorny plants during the dry season. Rivers are few and the main source of potable water is rainfall, which somehow must be collected and stored for later use. The soil is rich, but thin, and frequent rock outcroppings make much of the land unusable for agricultural purposes. To all of this must be added the hordes of stinging insects, snakes, and tarantulas, who make life in the jungle dangerous as well as uncomfortable. That a great civilization could have taken root and flourished for over six centuries in such an inhospitable environment is almost inconceivable to most of us who are used to the open spaces of farmlands and high deserts or the cool crisp evergreen forests which make up much of the rest of the North American continent.

To the Maya Indian, however, who was just one step removed from a nomadic hunting and gathering existence, the rain forest may have seemed like a veritable paradise where he found every reason to make his permanent home. Wild game and tropical birds, which served as a source of materials for garments and tools as well as for food, could be found in abundance on all sides. Other raw materials, which could be used to make anything from household implements to wooden houses or stone buildings, were also close at hand or directly underfoot. Maize, the staff of life to the Mayas, could be planted and harvested twice a year, its cultivation requiring nothing more complicated than a pointed stick with which to make a hole in which a few seeds could be dropped. Seasonal rains could be depended upon to ripen the crops; no artificial irrigation was required. Beans, chiles, and other delicacies could be grown alongside the corn, and other edibles grew wild. The climate was warm, requiring a minimum amount of clothing, and a thatched-roof hut, providing protection from rain and sun alike, was all that was further required to meet the demands of a reasonably comfortable existence. The fact that this same set of conditions would scarcely meet any of our own demands is beside the point. The physical remains of hundreds of Maya settlements in this area is sufficient proof that the Mayas were able to satisfy their own needs to the fullest extent.

It does not seem appropriate in this study, which is devoted to settlement patterns and urbanism, to dwell on a lengthy review of the origins and development of Maya culture as far as it is presently known. Morley, Thompson, Spinden, and many others have already supplied us with

3.
Origins

9

detailed accounts of all facets of Maya civilization, from its earliest known beginnings sometime during the first or second millennium B.C. to its sudden and still unexplained demise around the end of the ninth century A.D. (Morley: 1956; Thompson: 1954; Spinden: 1951). Our present concern is with the city-building, or Classic, period of Maya history, an interval which covers approximately six hundred years (A.D. 300 to 900). These six centuries witnessed the construction of over two thousand cities and ceremonial centers, scattered with surprising regularity throughout the entire Maya region.

The earliest known building remains dating from the Early Classic period indicate that the basic concept and main architectural outlines of the embryo ceremonial center, in the form of plaza, platform, and temple, were already fully developed at the outset of this period. This state of affairs can only be explained by assuming a long Preclassic period, during which the predecessors of the city builders originated and developed this generic form from much cruder prototypes, or by accepting the notion that this fundamental concept was imported full blown from elsewhere. In spite of the fact that few examples of this incipient form have been unearthed in stratified building remains, which argues in favor of the latter proposition, it must be remembered that Maya archaeology is still in its infancy and most of the known building sites still await excavation.

Large-scale excavations at the sites of Tikal and Dzibilchaltun, which represent ten years of intensive effort, have already pushed back the presumed beginning of the Classic period, and further work at these crucially located sites may yet produce the sought-after Preclassic prototype. Since this study was started, Preclassic prototypes have been uncovered at both Dzibilchaltun and Tikal, but there is some reason to wonder if these should be considered as Mayan. The diffusionist camp has its adherents, but the majority of Maya scholars favor an independent, or *in situ*, development. At this point it may be well to diverge from the mainstream of our discussion and try to visualize the manner in which the basic elements of the ceremonial center could have developed in place, even though this visualization is by necessity mostly speculative.

The Mayas, in common with their neighbors in other parts of Mexico and Central America, depended for their continued existence on a stable agricultural economy based on the planting and harvesting of corn, or *maize*. This process required the felling and burning of the forest which made up their surroundings, providing an open space, or clearing, in which the crop could be planted. This system of *milpa* farming, as it is called, requires the making of a new clearing every two or three years, as the soil throughout most of the region consists of a thin layer of earth over a limestone substratum, which is not capable of sustaining more than two or three crops in successive years. This fundamental need to continually create new open spaces in the jungle in order to survive must have been the most important fact of Maya life.

These clearings, which became the means of sustaining life in a dependable recurring cycle, are not in themselves evidence of architectural conceptualizations. Even with the small thatched-roof huts which were associated with them, they represent only a direct physical response to basic needs associated with biological survival. That is to say, the open field and the huts are neither abstract nor symbolic and have no implicit architectural content. But this clearing, and its associated hut or huts, is nonetheless the logical prototype for the more abstract notion of "plaza" and requires only the formalization of the man-made structures and open space into a specific, ordered arrangement to crystallize the concept of plaza and temple. The self-conscious realization of his ability to transcend and control the forces of nature, thereby setting himself apart from other living organisms, seems inevitably to have led primitive man in all parts of the world to symbolize this self-awareness in the form of architecture. How else can we account for the same phenomena taking place in widely separated parts of the world where there was no real prospect of diffusion due to differences in time and space? Perhaps this visualization is too simple-minded, as there are still many intermediate steps required before moving from corn field to paved plaza and from thatched-roof hut to stone temple, but it is certainly possible that the small ceremonial center, which ultimately led to the development of great cities such as Tikal, Copan, Dzibil-chaltun, or Palenque, could have developed *in situ* from such a humble and nonarchitectural beginning.

In order to test out this theory of *in situ* development, we have to look at the ceremonial center in its earliest known form. Unfortunately, it is not now possible to examine it in its embryo form, since most of these Proto-classic constructions have disappeared in the constant reconstruction and expansion of the city which marked the course of the Classic period. A few reported examples of Protoclassic remains from the northeastern Peten in Guatemala, the northern plains of the Yucatan Peninsula, and the Belize Valley in Honduras indicate that the earliest architectural agglomerations consisted of a group of three or four dwellings situated around a level plaza or courtyard. The conscious arangement of these dwellings around an open space as an expression of social order is a fundamental first step, leading toward the more formalized configurations to come later. Somewhat larger groupings of dwellings, containing the remains of a structure with presumed community functions, are also reported, and this suggests the beginning of organized ceremonial activity. But this larger grouping is still essentially residential and cannot be thought of as a ceremonial center. The creation of a discrete domain devoted exclusively to ritual activity is required before the notion of ceremonial center is crystallized, and the initiation of this final step is presumed to mark the opening of the Classic period.

Excavations at a number of sites indicate that the ceremonial center in its earliest form consisted of a single small plaza and its associated structures (Fig. 2).

The plaza is open space, cleared of trees and artificially leveled. It is paved with limestone cement and, by its visible negation of soil and plants, creates a specific, man-

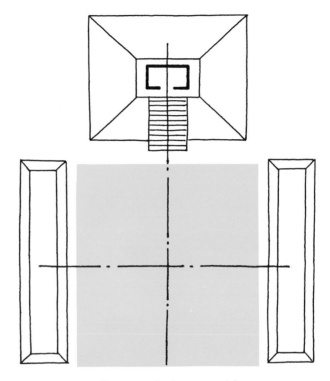

FIG. 2. Prototype, basic ceremonial group.

made domain. It must be emphasized that the leveling and paving of the plaza is an architectural conceptualization of the greatest importance. It represents a giant step beyond the crude clearing in the forest which is predicated solely on physical survival. The paved plaza is neither forest nor farmstead—the very act of its removal from fortuituous nature makes it unique and self-conscious, a fitting response to the need for self-determination which characterizes civilized man throughout the world.

One side of this plaza is occupied by a stepped platform or truncated pyramid, constructed of limestone blocks and rubble and surfaced with a thick coat of limestone cement. The platform is another unique part of this ensemble, a symbolic representation of the hierarchical ordering of the

Maya world. Even in its earliest known stage of development, this platform is a sophisticated and complex form (Fig. 3). Its smooth, multifaceted surfaces catch and reflect the bright sunlight in myriad directions. The geometrical precision of its stairways, balustrades, recesses, and projections contrast sharply with elaborate sculptural reliefs, in the form of giant masks, which border the stairways. Further elaboration may be found in the form of painted decoration, as traces of coloration can be found wherever sections of the original plaster remain. It is obvious that the nearest equivalent form to be found in nature is a mountain or hill, but we should not be too quick in verifying these natural forms as the source of inspiration for the platform or pyramid. It is equally obvious that any attempt to pile up loose material such as earth or stones produces a form which is roughly pyramidal or conical, a model of a mountain perhaps, but more readily amenable to the formal conceptualization of stylized platform than a mountain seen only at a distance. This transitional element, connecting the earth with the sky, is equal in importance to the paved plaza, and the small level space on top of the platform is sufficiently removed from the earth to be recognized as a new domain of special importance, a place suitable for the gods. Here stands the temple.

The temple is the final element in this ensemble, marking the place where man makes contact with the gods who control his universe. It is not a place for ordinary mortals and only the high priests are permitted to enter its portals in order to bring offerings and intercede with the gods on behalf of the uninitiated. Curiously enough, however, the temple in its embryo form is not significantly different from the wood-and-thatch huts in which the Maya peasant lived. Excavations have shown that the earliest temples were constructed of perishable materials and in size and form are not distinguishable from ordinary huts. As time went on, the wooden temple was replaced by a vaulted stone temple, although the enclosed space of this more permanent structure retained the same form as the earlier wooden structure.

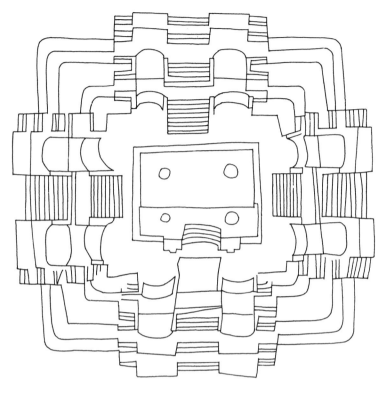

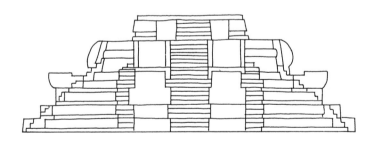

12   FIG. 3. Uaxactun—Structure E-Sub VII.

Even when the temples became much larger and more elaborate, they never completely lost their affinity to the small wooden hut. (More about this later.) From this it becomes clear that it is the position of the temple in space rather than its size or form that establishes its importance. Situated at the highest point in a man-made environment, it symbolizes those notions of hierarchies, or orders of importance, between man and the larger universe which dominated the thinking of the Mayas throughout the Classic period. While it will be shown that the plaza-platform-temple group is the basic prototype for the more complex ceremonial center, which consists for the most part of variations and elaborations of this basic form, other building types and building groupings soon appeared which combined to produce what we have called the Maya city. Before we look at the archetypical buildings and building groupings, however, it seems appropriate to look at the larger fabric of the city as a whole and to establish the legitimacy of the notion of "city."

4.
"City" or "Ceremonial Center"?

THE PREINDUSTRIAL CITY

It is not intended that this book concern itself with a detailed history of the origins of cities in general or even Maya cities in particular. The tangible evidence in support of the ideas being presented is limited almost entirely to the physical remains of a selected group of these cities which can be seen only in their final stage of development (A.D. 250–900). Any further development beyond this point was brought to an abrupt halt by the sudden collapse of Maya society which has been inferred from the cessation of building activity throughout the greater part of the Maya area near the end of the ninth century.

The evidence at hand, which consists of the ruins of scores of once great cities, forms the last chapter in a long series of events which probably extended back through several millennia. Excavations at several of these cities have uncovered evidence of Preclassic activity dating back to the first millennium B.C., but any clear image of Maya life or Maya cities, if such existed, during or prior to this period remains a vague shadow which cannot yet be filled in.[1] Nevertheless, within the limits of what can be deduced from standing remains or limited excavations below the surface of these remains, a somewhat cloudy picture does begin to emerge which suggests that the Proto- and Preclassic Maya settlement was probably little more than a small ceremonial center surrounded by scattered groups of houses. By the end of the Late Classic period, however, the process of urbanization had advanced to the point where real cities had begun to take form.

At this point it is only fair to ask, "Are the complexes of structures and open spaces referred to really cities, representing a full range of economic, political, commercial, social, religious, and educational activities which are normally associated with urban centers, or are they simply very large ceremonial centers, devoted exclusively to religious activities?" The answer to this question depends in part on whether you happen to be a geographer, historian, economist, sociologist, politician, archaeologist, or architect. Each of these specialists is inclined to view the notion of "city" from a different position, and great confusion results from any effort to find a definition which is acceptable to all. Is a city a physical conglomeration of streets and houses, or is it a center of exchange and commerce? Or is it a kind of society, or even a frame of mind? The difficulties involved in definition are countless and there is very little unanimity; we are almost left with the proposition that a city is anything that we choose to call a city. Part of the difficulty in definition comes from our tendency to think of cities in our own terms, i.e., we insist on measuring Maya or other prehistoric settlements against present-day cities, particularly Western cities, and thus confuse the issue even further. Both V. G. Childe and Gideon Sjoberg have developed several criteria for determining the extent to which prehistoric settlements could be called urban without falling into the trap of applying modern standards, and these criteria do help to clarify the issues under discussion.

In a survey of the main features of all the known cities of antiquity, including those of the New World, Childe suggested several criteria, some abstract, but all of them deductible from archaeological data, which distinguish

[1] The extensive programs of excavation and restoration which have recently been concluded at both Tikal and Dzibilchaltun should add substantially to our knowledge of the Preclassic period. The final reports covering this activity have not yet been published, but preliminary reports indicate a long Preclassic period at both sites during which the basic form of the Classic-period city was established. These reports also indicate that large ceremonial structures utilizing crude masonry construction were being built at a much earlier period than was previously suspected.

them as truly urban. *First*, the cities were very much larger, more extensive, and more densely populated than any previous settlements. These are relative terms, and they might not have ranked as large by modern standards. Sumerian cities were possibly between seven thousand and twenty thousand in population; those of the Indus civilization probably about twenty thousand. It is more difficult to estimate Egyptian or Maya cities, but they were probably of the same order. *Secondly*, the city had a different function from a village. Although most of the inhabitants might still be agriculturalists, there were large classes of specialists. *Thirdly*, a surplus was collected from each primary producer to form the basis of an effective capital. *Fourthly*, this accumulation was symbolized by a monumental structure(s) or public building(s). Sumerian cities had massive ziggurats with which were associated temples and graneries; the Nile Valley was studded with pyramids, the tombs of divine rulers; the cities of the Indus had their "citadels"; and the Mayan cities had their great stepped pyramids and temples. *Fifthly*, there was a class structure. Priests and leaders absorbed most of the surplus and, in exchange, arranged the entire routine of life and death. In the Mayan culture, the priests calculated the beginning and end of the year, the time for clearing trees, for planting, and for harvesting. To be able to construct a calendar was true power. The *sixth* criterion was, thus, the recording of the surplus, the measurement of the year, and writing, and, arising from these, the development of arithmetic, astronomy, and geometry. *Seventhly*, a new direction was given to artistic expression; sophistication replaced the naturalism of the hunter. *Lastly*, trade was a characteristic of all these urban civilizations, and consequently the manufacturer could become an integral part of this new community, his allegiance being transferred to the city, rather than residing solely in kin relationships. (Childe: 1950.)

Sjoberg goes a step further and makes a clear distinction between what he calls the "industrial city" of today and the "preindustrial city" of yesterday and postulates the following prerequisites for the emergence of the preindustrial city: "(1) a favorable 'ecological' base, (2) an advanced technology (relative to the preurban forms) in both the agricultural and nonagricultural spheres, and (3) a complex social organization—above all, a well developed power structure." (Sjoberg: 1960, 27.)

By a "favorable ecological base" is meant a set of conditions where climate and soil are highly favorable to the development of plant and animal life so that fairly large populations can be supported on relatively small cultivated land areas. An "advanced agricultural technology" assumes a condition wherein a sizable food surplus, over and above that required for sustenance between harvests, can be consistently maintained in order to feed an elite class who are not engaged directly in agricultural pursuits. This elite class includes not only those individuals who form the power group but those who are classed as artisans, craftsmen, warriors, and the like, who also spend little or none of their time in the direct production of food. A "complex social organization" implies that both the political and economic aspects of the society are developed to the point where certain specialized goods can be easily distributed within and among individual communities, agricultural surpluses can be moved to and stored in larger centers, and the activities of specialized workers can be sufficiently organized and integrated so that complex tasks, such as the construction and maintenance of large ceremonial complexes, can be carried out efficiently. Politically, the society must be organized in such a way that a small ruling group has both the power and skill to organize and direct the activities of the balance of the population. This latter condition assumes a certain degree of social stability in order that the system can function effectively over a long period of time.

With nothing more than the extant physical remains of scores of large centers such as Tikal, Uxmal, Dzibilchaltun, Palenque, and Copan as evidence, it is quite clear that Maya society must have met the conditions as outlined by both Childe and Sjoberg. Beyond this, however,

15

there is a growing body of evidence gathered from diverse sources which adds considerable weight to the assumptions in regard to Maya civilization that can be made solely on the basis of building remains. With regard to Sjoberg's first condition of a "favorable ecological base," it has already been pointed out that, while the jungles of the Peter and the Yucatan Peninsula are not at all favorable for modern man, they were highly favorable for the Maya peasant, who could plant and harvest two crops of corn each year and support a family of five persons on ten to twelve acres of land. The complete cycle of planting, harvesting, and growing required only fifty to seventy-five days of his time and effort, leaving the balance of the year free for other activities. All of this with no need for artificial irrigation systems, since nature was bountiful in terms of supplying an average of sixty to eighty inches of rain a year. These figures were derived from careful tests made between 1933 and 1940 near Chichen Itza as a means of proving the case for a favorable natural environment.

It can scarcely be argued in support of Sjoberg's second condition of an "advanced agricultural technology" that a pointed stick wielded by hand is either very advanced or very technical, but the whole system of slash and burn, or *milpa* agriculture, is advanced in the sense that it supplies the necessary food surplus with a minimum expenditure of effort and requires no draft animals, plows, or irrigation systems for its implementation. It must also be pointed out that the domestication of an unknown wild grain in the form of a stable crop like maize represents a technological advancement of the first order. In maize we have a concentrated food that can be stored for long periods of time without excessive deterioration, making possible a year-round food supply for an extensive urban population. Supplemented with small quantities of other plant and animal foods, it still forms the basic diet of the rural Maya Indian of today, who consumes it in the form of *tortillas* or *pozole*. It has been estimated that maize, in one or more of its prepared forms, represents upwards of 85 per cent of the total food consumed by the present-day rural Indian population of both Mexican and Guatemala, and this figure might have been greater for the Maya peasant, who had considerably less access to imported foods than his counterpart of today.

Sjoberg's third condition, which requires a "complex social structure" including a power group, was obviously met in full by the Mayas; evidence is available from a number of sources in support of this. Almost all scholars agree that Maya society was organized as an oligarchy, ruled by an elite priest class in whose hands rested all religious and secular authority. It seems pointless to indulge in speculations as to how or when Maya society first coalesced to the point where the priest emerged as the dominant figure, or to worry about how long this process might have taken. For our purposes, it is sufficient to recognize that the process did take place, and by the opening of the Classic period (A.D. 300) the basic outlines of the organization of Maya society, which were to control the course of its development for the next six hundred years, were fully crystallized. Some idea of the social and administrative structure of Maya society can be gained from the murals at Bonampak showing scenes within the ceremonial precinct of the city (Fig. 78). A fair cross section of the population is represented, ranging from the high priests through warriors, dancers, musicians, and the various minor "officials." The rank of each individual is made clear by his role in the scenes and by the degree of elaboration of his costume. This same idea is carried over into the figures shown on stelae and painted pottery, where priests are always delineated in elaborate ceremonial regalia.

In addition to the direct evidence of the manner in which Maya society was organized, as shown in the Bonampak murals, indirect evidence indicating the existence of an elite class is found in the systems of numeration, ritual calendar, and hieroglyphic writing developed by the Mayas. These intellectual achievements point directly to a leisured power group who kept unto themselves the accumulated knowledge of the society as a means of maintaining their authority. Inventions of this kind, which serve no immediate practical purpose, are only possible when a small elite group has the opportunity to devote their collective energies, over a long period of time, to some activity other than food production.

Finally, the physical fact of the city itself as represented by scores of large buildings, paved plazas, reservoirs, stone monuments, causeways, and terracing, together with a broad range of house types, is visible proof of a highly organized society at work, with an array of designers, artisans, craftsmen, and specialized building workers available at all times to take on the herculean task of continuously rebuilding and extending the man-made domain. Some of this might have been accomplished with part-time or even slave labor, but the highly specialized skills required for many building operations, including the vast amount of stonecutting and carving required, suggests a core of workers and supervisors who were completely disassociated from the agricultural sphere of operations and thus had to be supported by a larger body of peasants or farmers. The beginnings of both "industrialism" and "bureaucracy" are already present in this scheme of things and the city is well under way.

In spite of the arguments which have just been reviewed, many Maya scholars are reluctant to accept the existence of Maya cities. Gordon Willey and William Bullard, for example, apparently agree that Classic Maya society did in fact meet Childe's criteria, and by inference Sjoberg's as well, but they are troubled by the lack of archaeological evidence for large aggregates of houses in conjunction with the ceremonial precincts (Willey and Bullard: 1965). W. T. Sanders also insists that only communities with substantial numbers of nonfarmers (75 per cent or more) and with population elements of heterogeneous functions and interests qualify as urban. He would also place such criteria as size and monumental architecture as secondary. (Sanders: 1962.) George Brainerd states flatly that the settlement pattern in the northern Maya area is one of neither urban nor even village concentration (Brainerd: 1958). Thompson, Pollock, and others appear to hold much the same views. Thus, the most widely accepted image is one in which the Classic Maya ceremonial center is seen as a temple, palace, and public-building complex surrounded at some distance by widely spaced households and hamlets which extended many kilometers into the surrounding countryside. In short, it is believed that Maya civilization was achieved without the building of cities which normally accompanies the emergence of major civilizations.

As Willey and others have pointed out, the real problem in the question of city versus ceremonial center is in the lack of substantial archaeological evidence for fairly large and dense aggregates of dwellings in conjunction with the ceremonial precincts. It can be shown, however, that in most cases this apparent lack of evidence is not due to any actual lack of house remains as such but only the lack of detailed data pertaining to dwellings at most sites due to lack of comprehensive surveying. With few exceptions the available site maps, including many of those shown in the latter part of this volume, show only the remains of monumental structures in the central ceremonial area; the smaller structures, which represent the remains of houses, are normally not included, since they fall outside the areas surveyed. At the present moment, there are only three major sites where sufficient surveying, combined with extensive excavation, has been undertaken to make a good case one way or another. The three sites referred to are Tikal, Dzibilchaltun, and Mayapan. For the moment, Mayapan will have to be left out of the discussion, since it was a Postclassic site, founded somewhere around A.D. 1200. In addition to these three, six other sites have been the subjects of extended surface surveys, combined with some excavation. These are Uaxactun, Chichen Itza, Comalcalco, Edzna, Altar de Sacrificios, and Seibal. Thus, we have only nine sites out of a total of more than twenty-five hundred known Maya settlements where the maps are comprehensive enough to show any-   17 thing other than the monumental structures associated with the central ceremonial area.

It is well known that many other large sites are considerably more extensive than the existing maps would indicate; these include Palenque, Copan, and Uxmal. As early as 1889 Alfred Maudslay reported that the city of Copan extended well beyond the main ceremonial center and he observed hundreds of smaller mounds within this peripheral area (Maudslay: 1889–1902). Later explorations showed that there were at least sixteen subgroups associated with Copan extending outwards from the main nucleus to a distance of seven miles. A similar situation holds true for Palenque. Blom and La Farge reported in 1926 that the city of Palenque covered more than sixteen square kilometers and included large numbers of small, house-type mounds. The existing map shows only the main ceremonial area, which covers less than one-third of a square kilometer. The areas surrounding Uxmal, Labna, and Sayil are laced with smaller mounds (personal observation), and the same conditions must hold true for a number of other large centers.

Thus, the case for the "empty ceremonial center" is based largely on negative evidence; the majority of the existing maps show only major ceremonial structures, so it has been assumed that house mounds or other nonreligious structures simply do not exist. This is equivalent to arguing that present-day cities consist solely of "central business districts" by drawing maps that show nothing of the extensive residential or suburban areas surrounding these inner cores. In the cases cited earlier, where extensive areas surrounding the central ceremonial area have been carefully surveyed, the evidence is positive in favor of urbanization. House mounds exist in profusion and the spacing of the mounds is such that they could not have been immediately contiguous to extensive *milpa* plots. At both Tikal and Dzibilchaltun, houses represent 80 to 90 per cent of all the structures within the urban zone. This is equivalent to the condition in present-day cities where the bulk of the buildings are houses. Maya houses

vary in size and the degree of elaboration and show many of the basic characteristics associated with a stratified and diversified urban society. At this point, a close look at these urban centers is called for.

E. W. Andrews describes Dzibilchaltun in these terms: "Our survey described in Section 3 has shown that Dzibilchaltun in the Late Early period and the Early Florescent (500–800 A.D.) was a city in the strict sense of the word. It was enormous, a dozen times the size of Mayapan in geographic extent and much greater in population. Our most conservative estimates place the total number of structures in the 50-km archaeological zone at about 50,000. Excavation in seven hundred of these has indicated that 90 per cent were built or reused at the height of the city's expansion. If urbanism can be defined as the concentration of population beyond the possibility of agricultural subsistence on land close enough to be economically available for cultivation, Dzibilchaltun was heavily urbanized. It must have been supported almost entirely by tribute or trade with a large surrounding area." (E. W. Andrews: 1965.)

William Coe describes Tikal in very similar terms: "The main point is that central Tikal, or those 6.7 square miles of it that might have been mapped, unquestionably was more than a ceremonial center. A relatively dense population lived there. Though it may not *look* like a city, its population, at least by Classic times, was sufficiently dense and completely organized and functioning, to indicate an urban structure, and one dependent on the periphery for provisioning. Except for small attached gardens, the density of construction within central Tikal was too great to permit milpas, the agricultural plots cut from the forest by slash-and-burn methods. It is hard to believe that Tikal was not a great marketing center to which produce, pottery, and an extraordinary array of raw materials (obsidian, hematite, jade, etc.) were brought in." (Coe: 1965.)

William Haviland, who conducted the survey of Tikal house mounds, points out that while Tikal does not show a gridded and congested type of living condition which is typical of some Mexican sites such at Teotihuacan or Tenochtitlan, it was certainly more densely populated than the surrounding countryside and was a ceremonial, manufacturing, and trading center of considerable importance. He also suggests that it is not to be compared with less urbanized sites such as Uaxactun or Barton Ramie, where the conditions are substantially different. (Haviland: 1965.) The surveys at Comalcalco and Edzna also show that substantial residential areas lie just outside the main ceremonial precincts and there are numerous house-type mounds within the main ceremonial center itself (G. F. Andrews: 1967 and 1969).

It is interesting to note that the main physical features of a Maya city or urban center were projected as far back as 1932, although the concept of city in connection with Maya settlements has only recently been proposed. H. E. D. Pollock, who conducted the architectural survey of Coba in 1932, describes it as follows:

The area surrounding the lakes is literally covered with ruins. Between the main groups of Coba and Nohoch Mul there is an almost unbroken succession of mounds culminating just southwest of the latter in Group D, a group of considerable importance, which had probably best be considered as associated with Nohoch Mul. The shores of Lake Coba and Lake Macanxoc are surrounded by groups of varying size and importance, and this is probably true also of Lake Sacakal. In addition, from the Castillo at Coba, a number of mounds may be seen to the south. Excluding the ruins about Lake Sacakal as being somewhat distant and the intervening area not well understood, the proximity of all these ruins, one to another, would apparently necessitate the inclusion of the lake group into one great site about 3.5 km. east and west and 2 km. north and south, and certainly one of the greatest sites in the Maya area. The heart of the city, however, may be thought of as lying within an equilaterial triangle, roughly 2 km. on a side, formed by the three major groups of Coba, Nohoch Mul and Maxcanxoc. Oxthindzonot, Kucican, Nuc Mul and the small sites to the north and east should be considered as suburbs of the central city, connected to it by road and definitely belonging to the district, but not part of the main site. (Thompson, Pollock, and Charlot, 1932.)

This description corresponds in every way with E. W. Andrews' description of Dzibilchaltun, and I would suspect that these two great centers developed along parallel lines over the same time span.

The question which now remains is whether the heavily urbanized or citylike character of sites such as Tikal, Dzibilchaltun, Coba, and Edzna represent remarkable exceptions to an otherwise valid pattern of "empty ceremonial centers" or whether the accepted pattern has been based on less fortunate or incomplete observation. From the arguments presented in the foregoing paragraphs, it seems fairly clear that the present differences in interpretation are due in large part to differences in conditions of preservation of remains and differences in techniques of observation and surveying. For this reason, it seems reasonable to assume that many of the other larger Maya centers, which are presently thought to represent only ceremonial places supported by a dispersed population, were in fact as urbanized as Tikal and Dzibilchaltun.

Bullard's survey of the northeastern Peten in Guatemala would seem to refute this notion, since he says that house mounds are generally no more frequent in the immediate vicinity of major centers than they are in most other parts of the countryside (Bullard: 1960). It must be kept in mind, however, that Bullard was referring to a very small portion of the total Maya area, and most of the largest centers which are presently known fall outside of this area. His survey, when combined with data from Tikal, Dzibilchaltun, and elsewhere, does suggest that we may be confronted with a larger range of settlement sizes and forms than has heretofore been recognized, and it seems plausible that this extended list would include everything from very large urban centers with substantial resident populations to small villages and hamlets with little in the way of either ceremonial structures or permanent residents. Such a tentative scheme is projected in the following chart:

19

Class of Settlement	Common Designation	Estimated Population
1. Large Urban Center	City	8,000 to 40,000
2. Small Urban Center	Town	2,000 to 4,000
3. Major Ceremonial Center	Village	Less than 1,000
4. Minor Ceremonial Center	Hamlet	200 to 500
5. Housing Cluster	Farmstead	20 to 50

Based on present knowledge, the large urban centers would show the following characteristics:

1. *Population*: A resident population of 7,500 or greater. Present estimates place Tikal at 11,000 and Dzibilchaltun at 50,000 or more.[2]
2. *Architecture*: A great diversity of ceremonial and civic structures including large complexes of structures of the sort that we have called Acropolis Groups, Palace Groups, etc. Specialized structures such as ball courts, sweat baths, etc., would also be included.

3. *Residences*: A diversity of house types and locations. Houses would include masonry "palace"-type structures as well as small pole-and-thatch huts. Houses are located within main ceremonial precincts as well as in suburban or peripheral areas.
4. *Suburban Areas*: Presence of one or more "suburban ceremonial groups." These are ceremonial structures situated away from the main center but within the confines of the urban area. These suburban ceremonial areas are surrounded by residences.
5. *Satellites*: "Satellite" ceremonial centers found nearby. These would normally be located several kilometers, perhaps up to 10 kilometers, from the center of the city. They would be classified as "ceremonial centers" in the above classification, but in this case appear to be directly associated with a particular large urban center.
6. *Density*: The density of houses within the urban areas is too great to allow *milpa* farming in the same area. The density of houses is also significantly greater than general density of houses in the rural areas.
7. *Water Resources*: Sufficient water resources at hand to supply the domestic needs of the resident population during the dry season. This includes water for building construction as well as for drinking, cooking, bathing, etc. Water resources would include *chultunes, cenotes*, artificial reservoirs, rivers and streams, lakes and aguadas, but normally only one or two of these sources would be present at any given site.
8. *Physical Form*: Dispersed physical form when com-

[2] These figures are arrived at by counting house mounds and multiplying by the number of persons in each house. However, any attempt to use house mounds as the basis for projecting population has to take into account several variables. First, how many people are represented by a single house? Second, how many of the houses are contemporary, and third, how do we know that all the mounds actually represent houses? Finally, how do we know that we have actually located the remains of all the houses that might have been located in any given area? That is to say, how accurate is our map? All of these present problems, and the estimates of population for Tikal and Dzibilchaltun have been based on adjustments which try to take these variables into account and thus tend to be conservative. On this basis, the projected population of Tikal within the 16 square kilometers mapped is 10,000 to 11,000 and the population of Dzibilchaltun within approximately 20 square kilometers mapped is 50,000. It must be emphasized that both of these are estimates and could be pushed either up or down as new data is accumulated allowing for more accurate estimating. Nevertheless, both of these are sizable figures and point up the fact that houses represent 80 to 90 per cent of all the structures within the large urban centers. Thus, while house mounds are of the least interest to the casual visitor, being little more than amorphous lumps on the jungle floor, they are of very great interest in our efforts to understand the nature of Maya cities, including some clear view of how and where the people lived.

pared with cities in the Valley of Mexico or Old World cities. A Maya city would not show a gridiron organization or other rigid circulation patterns. The physical plan is largely the result of fortuitous ground form with only the higher portions of land being used for buildings.

9. *Architectural Style*: Distinctive architectural style. The large urban centers are the most likely places for regional styles to be initiated. The basic style would be exported to smaller urban centers within the same region and to ceremonial centers adjacent to urban centers.

10. *Lifespan*: Long period of occupation. This might vary from 1,000 to 2,500 years. The large urban centers undoubtedly represent accretions over a long period of time and at earlier stages of their development would have been classified as ceremonial centers.

11. *Stelae*: Presence of carved stelae or buildings with hieroglyphic texts. These might also be found at the smaller urban centers or at large ceremonial centers, but it is hardly conceivable that a major city would not have become involved in the stela cult.

12. *Location*: Major urban centers would be found along important communication routes, both internal and external. The general spread of what we call Maya culture undoubtedly moved from one major center to the other and from these to the smaller centers. Intracultural connections with Guatemalan highlands and Mexican plateau also would most likely involve the major centers.

The above list of criteria is obviously subject to modifications and additions as more data becomes available, but the characteristics as noted do single out certain sites as being significantly different from others on the basis of presently known characteristics. A tentative listing of the most likely possibilities of large urban centers is shown in the accompanying chart.

Admittedly this list is arbitrary, but it is based on size and complexity of known centers which have been carefully mapped, at least in part, and where they are known to meet many of the requirements outlined for major urban centers. Most of the large urban centers included in the above list are discussed in detail elsewhere in the text, but some mention must be made of Mirador, Rio Bec, and Santa Rosa Xtampak, since they have not been included among the twenty sites selected for detailed analysis. According to Ian Graham, who mapped the central portion of Mirador in 1962, Mirador is one of the largest centers in the Maya area and has the most massive

	Name	*Location*
1.	Dzibilchaltun	Northern Plains Area, Western Section
2.	Coba	Northern Plains Area, Eastern Section
3.	Oxkintok	Puuc Area
4.	Santa Rosa Xtampak	Chenes Area
5.	Edzna	Edzna Area
6.	Rio Bec	Rio Bec Area
7.	Tulum	East Coast Area (Postclassic)
8.	Mirador	Central Area, Northern Peten
9.	Tikal	Central Area, Northeastern Peten
10.	Yaxchilan	Upper Usumacinta Area
11.	Palenque	Lower Usumacinta Area
12.	Copan	Southeastern Area
13.	Benque Viejo?	Belize Valley Area

structures (Graham: 1967). Graham's map shows that the main structures cover an area 2.5 by 1.5 kilometers (no effort was made to show the small mounds, either within the central area or in the peripheral areas). It is linked by causeways to two other sites, both of which have tall pyramids, and one, at least, shows the same distinctive assemblages of mounds (large acropolis-type groupings). Other causeways stretch toward unknown destinations. These Acropolis Groups are noteworthy for their number, height, and extent, and one of them measures 55 meters (183 feet) above the flat ground on which it stands, even though the temple building it supported has disappeared. Unfortunately, Mirador is in an advanced state of ruin and there are no standing building remains. Even so, the above description suggests that it can be considered as a prime candidate for our large urban center category.

The archaeological site called Rio Bec is probably the least well known or understood of all centers we have considered for urban status. According to Karl Ruppert and John Denison, who spent several days mapping the site in 1934, the city appears to consist of ten or more individual complexes of structures spread out over a large area (Ruppert and Denison: 1943). One of these, which contains the remains of a beautifully preserved building in the Rio Bec architectural style, has been lost for over thirty-five years. The dispersed character of the building remains over a large area is consistent with conditions at other large urban centers which consist of a central area surrounded by suburban centers some distance away. Ruppert also reports that there are many smaller mounds between the large complexes which do not show on any of the existing sketch maps, as they do not include standing building remains. Since Rio Bec is located only a few miles south of the new highway from Escarcega to Chetumal, it should not be too long before new information is forthcoming in regard to its true organization and size. This data is badly needed, as clarification of the status of Rio Bec appears to be crucial to our understanding of the whole Rio Bec area.

Santa Rosa Xtampak is a very large site with the remains of a number of large structures including pyramid-temples, palace-type buildings, a three-story structure similar to the palace at Sayil, a ball court, numerous quadrangular groups, carved and dated stelae, and a variety of smaller structures. The existing sketch map shows a central area measuring 400 by 600 meters in extent, but Teobert Maler, who visited the site in 1902, reported that it was a full kilometer from the western edge of the site to the center. During my own brief visit to the site in 1969, I noted many small mounds in the peripheral areas on all sides. In spite of the limited data available, it is clearly larger than any of the other well-known Chenes sites, and for this reason must be thought of as the major regional center within the Chenes area.

As more data becomes available, the tentative list of large urban centers is subject to considerable revision. The point in attempting to make such a list in the first place is to indicate that, even with incomplete data, there is good reason to assume the existence of at least a dozen major urban centers within the Maya expanse, which, if true, would go a long way toward refuting the "empty ceremonial center" notion which is currently in vogue.

It does not seem appropriate to attempt to describe the characteristics of the other categories of settlements in the same detail as the major urban centers, but they can be briefly summarized as follows.

Small Urban Centers

The main difference between the large and small urban centers is one of size. Thus, a small urban center might have only one or two suburban centers connected with it and perhaps no satellite centers at all. Both large and small urban centers would have the same general characteristics and physical form and both would be distinguished from the smaller centers on the grounds that the density of population within the urban area, even though this might be small compared to present-day urban centers, would be substantially greater than anything associated with villages or a rural area. Size, in cities, is a relative term and what seems big for one period of history or one part of the world is small for another. The intent here is to make a clear distinction between rural and urban on the basis of both physical and social characteristics. As Jane Jacobs suggests, a town is not a small city. A town has no real potential for substantial growth, since it lacks the economic base and differentiated structure which promotes the growth of cities (Jacobs: 1970). Thus, there is a functional as well as dimensional difference between cities and towns and these differences hold true for the present-day cities and towns as well as those existing in prehistoric societies.

It would be possible to draw up a list of twenty to thirty known centers which might be classified as small urban centers, but here again the list would be very arbitrary, since we have so little data available in the form of comprehensive surveys. This list might well include sites such as Comalcalco, Kabah, Uxmal, Uaxactun, Chichen Itza (Classic Maya period), and Seibal, where we already have some evidence of sizable resident populations.

Major Ceremonial Centers

This category is represented by a cluster of ceremonial structures with some diversity and a small number of associated houses. In this kind of center, there will not likely be a great difference in density of housing between the residences found within the center and those in the rural areas. In some cases, the rural density may even be higher. *Village* seems to be a suitable description of this class of settlement, since it includes some of the elements associated with urban centers but differs substantially from the urban centers both in function and size. The number of houses is not great and the area it serves is also not likely to be great. The people who normally make the greatest use of this class of center live too far from the large urban centers to go there except on very special occasions. The limited resident population projected would be largely confined to religious and administrative personnel, since it is assumed that its function is basically religious in character.

Minor Ceremonial Centers

The difference between major and minor ceremonial centers is largely one of size, although minor centers would not likely include specialized structures such as ball courts and would have few, if any, stelae. The minor centers are usually found in very close physical proximity to housing clusters, and we have already suggested that the suburban ceremonial centers and their accompanying houses which lie within the large urban centers are fairly similar to those found in the rural areas. The minor ceremonial centers are just that: hamlets which serve most of the fairly immediate needs of a small surrounding rural population but are lacking in almost all the distinguishing characteristics which have been predicated for urban centers.

Housing Cluster

A housing cluster is represented by a group of houses, perhaps five to ten, which are sometimes arranged in a fairly orderly way around a court or plaza. They may occupy an area of 200 to 300 square meters and are generally separated to some extent from other housing clusters in the same general area. In some cases, the house cluster includes a larger and apparently more important structure which is thought to represent the remains of a family shrine or temple. The cluster probably represents some kind of kinship group or extended family who worked *milpa* plots within walking distance of its abode. It is the equivalent of the large rural house groups found in many parts of rural Mexico today, where the actual plots of farmland are held in common by a group who live together in small aggregates some distance away from the land under cultivation. In the case of the Mayas, the land might have been a considerable distance away, since a single *milpa* plot had to lie fallow for upwards of twenty years before the subsequent growth could be recut and the same land used again for growing corn. House clusters have been found in nearly every part of the Maya area; 23

the basic pattern was established rather early and appears to have maintained itself throughout the Classic period.

It must be admitted that all of the preceding discussion involving the classification of various kinds of Maya settlements is based on a minimum amount of physical evidence, but, in spite of this, all of the positive evidence at hand tends to support the notion of urbanization as it has been projected. There is a great enough difference between the large and small centers in terms of size, make-up, and configuration to indicate functional differences warranting some specific differentiation. It is also clear that many of the conventional notions of what constitutes a city will have to be modified if we are to accept the evidence for Maya cities. They are more dispersed than most cities as we think of them and, as has been pointed out in reference to Tikal, they don't *look* like cities as we know them. This is due in large part to the fact that there are no observable street patterns within Maya cities, gridiron or otherwise. We have become so accustomed to looking at cities in terms of street patterns that we tend to think of a city as a network of streets; the buildings merely fill up the spaces between the streets. A present-day map of a city is an abstraction which shows street patterns and gives the numbering system for the various buildings but shows us almost nothing of the actual spaces and buildings which make up the city. One intent of this book is to clarify the nature of Maya cities as an organization of places—places in the form of open spaces and buildings which were built and used by people as a means of asserting their humanness. We will still have to spend much time talking about patterns of various kinds, but it is hoped that these can be used to demonstrate something about the quality of life as it might have existed in Maya cities rather than leaving them entirely as abstract symbols in the form of maps.

LARGE SETTLEMENT PATTERNS

In the preceding section we diverted from our central theme of placemaking in order to establish the legitimacy of the notion that the larger Maya settlements were essentially urban and should be considered as cities if the general conditions as postulated for the preindustrial or prehistoric city are accepted. Our real concern, however, is with the structure and form of the city as a physical entity, and the administrative, social, economic, and political aspects of city life will be referred to only to the extent that they can be seen as forces giving rise to or influencing its physical form. Before proceeding on to a more detailed examination of the physical fabric of these cities, further effort should be made to place them in space and time. This involves us with questions of settlement patterns at the largest possible scale and the spatial distribution and organization of the larger urban centers with respect to the smaller or subsidiary centers as evidenced by these patterns. The temporal sequence in terms of the evolution of larger patterns should provide us with additional insights in regard to the growth of any of the smaller parts, such as city, ceremonial center, town, or hamlet.

It must be recognized from the outset that any effort to describe the larger pattern(s) of settlement for the Maya area as a whole is fraught with uncertainty. Several factors combine to produce this uncertainty and all have to do with a lack of adequate data. The most important gaps in our present knowledge can be summarized as follows: (1) While the total number of settlements which have been reported from the entire lowland area numbers somewhere between twenty-five hundred and three thousand, the majority of these can best be described as "unspecified groups of mounds" about which we have no real data of any kind. By this is meant there are no maps, no drawings of buildings, no photographs, or even adequate verbal descriptions beyond a report indicating that mounds were observed in such-and-such a location. In my own travels through the Maya area I have encountered many such small groups of mounds and have no idea which, if any, represent archaeological sites with names that are shown on some maps. (2) Taking into account only those sites which have at least been partially explored and described, we are left with no more than two hundred and fifty, and of these, just over a hundred have even been partially mapped. Thus, we know next to nothing about the size, spatial organization, make-up, or details of over 90 per cent of all lowland sites which have been reported. (3) Of the hundred sites for which we do have maps, only forty of these have been carefully mapped using approved surveying techniques,[3] while seventy others have been sketch-mapped using compass and pacing methods.

In addition to these problems, there are large areas within the total Maya expanse which have scarcely been explored at all, including much of the territory of Quintana Roo and parts of Yucatan and Campeche in Mexico as well as some sections of the department of Peten in Guatemala. As certain parts of these sparsely populated areas have become more accessible in the last few years due to new road construction, hitherto unknown sites continue to be reported, but it will still be many years before we have any clear idea as to the over-all distribution of sites in these largely unknown areas. In short, we simply have very little to go on in terms of reliable data, so all discussions of large-scale or even small-scale settlement patterns must be considered as highly speculative. This is certainly true of the discussion which follows, even though there is *some* evidence to support the conclusions drawn.

The Maya area is divided into two major physiographic regions which by common consent are called the Northern Lowlands and the Southern Lowlands. This division occurs along the line where the Yucatan Peninsula joins the main mass of Central America and runs from the Caribbean coast of northern British Honduras along the northern frontier of the department of Peten in Guate-

mala and then directly across to the Laguna de Terminos of the Bay of Campeche in Mexico. The Yucatan Peninsula is a relatively flat limestone shelf which is generally no more than a few meters above sea level, while the area to the south is generally very hilly with an average elevation of about two hundred meters above sea level. Within these two major regions several smaller regions can be observed which are based in part on geographical or ecological conditions and partly on cultural considerations.

Within the Northern Lowlands area, five major regions can be described: the *Northern Plains Area*, which can be further subdivided into a western and eastern section (Yucatan and Quintana Roo); the *Puuc Area* (south of Puuc hills in Yucatan); the *Chenes Area* (southeast Yucatan); the *Rio Bec Area* (southern Campeche); and the *East Coast Area* (east coast of Quintana Roo and British Honduras). It is also possible to speak of the *Edzna Area* (northwest Campeche), but our knowledge of this area is so minimal that it cannot be specified as a major cultural or ecological area at the present time. The Southern Lowlands include the *Central*, or *Northern Peten, Area* (Peten in Guatemala and part of southern Campeche in Mexico), and this area can be further subdivided into northern and southern sections; the *Western Coastal Area* (parts of Tabasco, Campeche, and Chiapas); the *Lower Usumacinta Area* (lower Usumacinta and Candeleria river drainages); the *Upper Usumacinta River Area* (upper Usumacinta and Pasion River drainages); the *Southeastern Area* (Motagua and Chamelecon river drainages in Guatemala and Honduras); and the *Belize Valley Area* (Belize River drainage in British Honduras).

In most cases the borders of these regions cannot be sharply defined except where they correspond to river valley and drainage systems or where there are pronounced changes in topography, such as the low range of hills which divides the northern plains area of Yucatan from the Puuc and Chenes regions further south, or where the flat coastal areas of Tabasco and Chiapas meet the hills to the south. In other instances, the divisions between regions

[3] It should be noted that there is a considerable difference among these maps in regard to the extent to which they include more than the central precinct of the city and the extent to which the smaller house mounds are shown. Only the newer maps, such as those of Tikal, Dzibilchaltun, Mayapan, Comalcalco, Edzna, and Seibal include the mounds in the peripheral areas as well as the main center. Many of the older maps, while showing the central area in some detail, do not recognize the existence of the suburban zones.

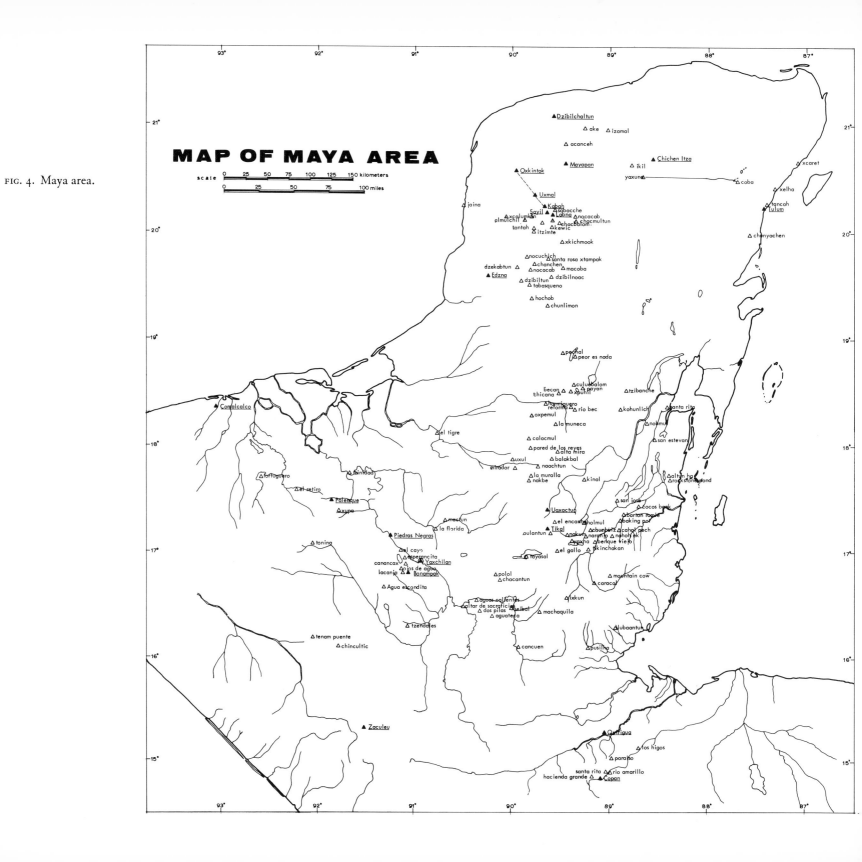

FIG. 4. Maya area.

are based on cultural differences which are manifest in archaeological remains. While the borders are hard to draw precisely, the differences between regions appear to be significant and have considerable relevance to the discussion of the spatial patterning of the various classes of centers which were described earlier.

Some idea of the over-all distribution of Maya settlements can be seen in Figure 4. This map shows approximately one hundred and fifty sites representing all the regions described above. Included are the twenty sites discussed in detail in this book, together with the balance of those which have been partially mapped, and twenty others which have been more carefully mapped. In addition, forty to fifty other sites are shown, most of which appear to be large enough to be considered as ceremonial centers. Even though these sites represent only a small percentage of the total number which have been reported, it is likely that they include most of the larger settlements, since these are the least likely to have escaped notice.

Perhaps the most striking pattern which can be observed on this map is the very uneven distribution of sites at the scale of the whole Maya area. It can be noted that there are several dense concentrations of sites which correspond to the Puuc, Chenes, Rio Bec, and Northern Peten areas and somewhat less dense concentrations in the Usumacinta and Belize river areas. Vast areas of southern Campeche, northeast Yucatan, and the inland portion of Quintana Roo in Mexico are virtually empty, as is part of the northwest area of the Peten in Guatemala. It is the writer's opinion that additional important sites will be found in these areas once they are more fully explored, but for the moment they must be left out of our considerations. It can also be noted that several of the large urban centers, including Dzibilchaltun, Coba, and Edzna, appear as somewhat isolated elements in otherwise sparsely occupied areas, while other major centers such as Tikal, Mirador, Rio Bec, and Copan are surrounded by numerous smaller, but still sizable, centers. Finally, it can be observed that the majority of all the sites shown fall within a very narrow north-south band between the latitudes of 89°30' and 90°. A significant number of the balance are located just to the east or west of this narrow strip. There is no obvious explanation for this concentration of sites in a thirty-five mile-wide strip, as it does not correspond to the natural phytogeographical divisions of the Yucatan Peninsula or to any other known ecological divisions. It may well be nothing more than an accident due to uneven exploration.

At first glance, the specific locations of the large urban centers which have been tentatively postulated do not seem to correspond to any pattern derived from consistently applied criteria. We would normally expect to find the largest centers in the most densely settled regions, but we have already noted that Dzibilchaltun, Coba, and Edzna appear as isolated elements in rather sparsely settled areas. We might also expect that the larger centers would be sited on the basis of a dependable year-round water supply, but this is not always the case, as several of the largest centers were completely dependent on man-made water-storage elements such as reservoirs and *chultunes*. Tikal is a good case in point. It is not far from the sites of Tayasal and Yaxha, both of which enjoyed favorable situations on the shores of large inland lakes. Yaxha was a very important center and includes the remains of several structures which were larger than any at Tikal. In spite of this, Tikal developed into the most important site in this region, even though a great amount of energy had to be expended in building water-storage devices. In addition, both Yaxha and Tayasal had substantial natural food resources available from the lakes they were sited on while Tikal was entirely dependent on artificial cultivation of crops such as maize and *ramon*. Mirador, which may prove to be even larger than Tikal, appears to have been located in an even more unfavorable situation, since it is surrounded by *bajos* on three sides; *bajos* were normally avoided by the Mayas for either building or agricultural purposes.

These conditions suggest that the largest urban centers

were located on the basis of their strategic positions with respect to communication and trade routes and that each of the large urban centers could be thought of as a regional center within this pattern. We should then expect to find at least one large urban center within each of the dozen regions postulated earlier, and this appears to be the case. In a few instances, where archaeological sites are found in dense concentrations, there might be two fairly large urban centers in the same region. Uxmal and Oxkintok, Yaxchilan and Piedras Negras, and Tikal and Yaxha are cases in point. While we actually know very little about the specific locations of the communication routes used by the Mayas, either internally or externally, it is fairly clear that they were established prior to the beginning of the Early Classic period.[4] From this we can assume that the major cities grew to their ultimate size largely in response to their positions along these routes.[5]

Assuming the validity of regional urban centers or cities, which represented the largest known Maya settlement, it is logical to assume that the smaller urban centers would be found in favored locations within the sphere of influence of the larger centers and would be located along secondary communication routes which served each of the large centers. The term *communication route* does not necessarily imply anything similar to the old Roman roads or present-day highways, although there are a few instances where paved roadways, or *sacbes*, did connect one Maya center to the other. The best-known example of this is the raised roadway which connected Coba to Yaxuna, but it is not clear that this was built for purposes of trade or for everyday communication. It may well have had more symbolic importance in connection with ceremonial processions. The communication routes had to exist, however, even though they did not take the form of a paved and graded roadway.

Within this pattern, the smaller urban centers might be seen as provincial cities in relation to their more important neighbors. The number and specific location of these provincial centers within any region was partially a function of the location of the major and secondary communication routes and partly a function of subregional conditions of soil and climate. Parts of the Maya area are marked with natural savannas and *bajos* (swamps), which were not suitable for *milpa* farming. Since the small urban centers would also have required a considerable sustaining area, they would tend to be located only in those areas highly favorable for agriculture. The differences in soil and climate among the various regions may account in part for the uneven distribution of sites as shown in Figure 4.

The general pattern which emerges from the foregoing is one in which the largest urban centers are viewed as regional centers occupying strategic positions along the major internal and external communication routes. These regional centers exerted considerable influence over fairly large areas and this influence shows up in specific cultural manifestations such as architectural style, sculptural style, types of ceramics, and regional customs in matters of speech, dress, etc. This kind of influence can be exerted even though it is not accompanied by direct administrative or political control; there are many examples of this in various parts of the world today. The smaller urban

---

[4] There is ample proof of continuous communication between all parts of the Maya area throughout the entire Classic period and there is also proof that long-distance trade was important to them during this same period. Long-distance trade would most likely be confined to the large urban centers, as luxury goods were wanted by the elite classes who resided there. Trade goods would then move from regional to other centers within their sphere of influence. (Willey and Shimkin: 1971)

[5] Dennis and Olga Puleston have postulated that the Maya area was initially populated by river and estuary agriculturalists who moved into the Maya Lowlands from the Pacific Coast of Guatemala and from the coastal plains of Tabasco. This assumption is based on recent evidence which suggests that the earliest Maya settlements were located along the river systems in the Southern Lowlands. From there, latter-day "pioneers" moved northward into the forested interior. (Puleston and Puleston: 1971.) Since there is some reason to believe that the large urban centers in the Northern Lowlands (Dzibilchaltun, Coba, Oxkintok, Edzna) were established as early as the large centers in the Southern Lowlands (Tikal, Mirador, Copan), the basic communication routes within the larger Maya area must have been developed sometime during the first millennium B.C.

centers, which might be called provincial cities, would logically be situated along the secondary communication routes within each of the major regions, and the number of these centers within any region is a function of soil and climate as well as over-all distribution of population within the region. These conditions might vary considerably from one region to another, so there is no reason to assume an even distribution of small urban centers. Below this come the ceremonial centers, each serving a smaller local population, and finally come the rural house clusters which represent the lowest end of the scale. As we go down the scale in reference to both size and complexity, the specific locations and physical structure of ceremonial centers and residential clusters become more and more dependent on local conditions, and certain areas which were very undesirable from the Maya point of view were avoided entirely for settlement purposes.

It has been suggested by several scholars that the Maya area, particularly toward the end of the Classic period, was made up of a number of city-states, and the picture we have just drawn in regard to settlement patterns tends to reinforce this notion. The inference can be drawn from a number of sources that the Maya sociopolitical structure attained its most complex development at the end of the Classic period. This structure included a hierarchy of social classes as well as an emerging hereditary aristocracy, which normally accompanies the beginning of "state" as an administrative unit. It must be pointed out, however, that the evidence for this kind of political or administrative organization is very slight. It appears to have greater validity in the northern Yucatan area during the Postclassic period, where the seat of power seems to have shifted from Dzibilchaltun to Chichen Itza and finally to Mayapan. Beyond this, a recent study has suggested that the figures on certain stelae at Yaxchilan actually represent members of a ruling family, where the authority to rule was passed on from father to son (Proskouriakoff: 1963). If this is not an isolated case, it tends to support the city-state concept, which assumes that local chieftains

resided in the regional capitals and extracted tribute from the area under their control. At this point in time we actually have little more than the over-all pattern and physical structure of various settlements to go on, and the intercity administrative organization which accompanied these settlements must be left in limbo pending further data.

The pattern of settlement and the relationships between the large urban centers and the smaller ceremonial centers which has just been outlined is obviously different from the one which has generally been accepted up till now and for this reason is likely to be subject to considerable criticism and revision. As noted earlier a number of Maya scholars have projected a settlement pattern which does not recognize the existence of urban centers or cities (Bullard: 1960; Sanders and Price: 1968; Willey and Bullard: 1965). Bullard describes only three classes of settlements, which he calls large ceremonial centers, small ceremonial centers, and house groups. The large ceremonial centers are seen as forming the nucleus of a "district," which in turn was made up of smaller "zones," each of which included a minor ceremonial center. Individual dwellings were dispersed around these minor ceremonial groups in "house groups" of five to twelve and these groups included an unidentified structure with presumed community significance. A zone might include anything from fifty to one hundred houses, while districts might vary considerably in size but might average something like one hundred kilometers in extent. (Bullard: 1960.) Bullard's three categories correspond very closely with the three smaller kinds of centers which we have called major ceremonial center, minor ceremonial center, and housing cluster. The pattern he describes obviously has considerable validity when applied to a province or subregion within one of the larger regions, such as the northeastern section of the Peten which Bullard surveyed, but fails to take into account patterns at the regional scale which involve the two classes of urban centers which we have postulated.

The large urban centers, using our tentative list, are   29 generally between one hundred and two hundred kilometers apart and might have had an immediate sustaining area of three or four hundred square kilometers. This is the area required for the production of food used by the nonagricultural residents of the urban areas. Depending on the density of occupation of any given region, the smaller urban centers might be fairly close to the larger centers. This would hold true in the Puuc, Chenes, Rio Bec, and northern Peten areas, where several important sites are found within ten to twenty kilometers of one another. In other less densely populated areas, such as the northern plains area of Yucatan or the Usumacinta areas, the smaller urban centers might be upwards of forty to sixty kilometers from their larger counterparts.

All of the above lends us to wonder what the total population for the whole Maya area might have been at the height of the Classic period. Any estimate of this kind is bound to be largely guesswork, as it has already been pointed out that we know very little about the three thousand Maya settlements which are known to exist. We also have no way of knowing if all of these settlements were occupied simultaneously, although most of the exposed building remains at all sites do date from the Late Classic period when Maya civilization reached its apogee. But, lacking data on the size and make-up of over 90 per cent of the settlements, we have to turn elsewhere to find a plausible basis for arriving at a figure.

Another approach to the question of population potential is based on assumed estimates of population using agricultural considerations as the control. On this basis, we can assume anything from ten persons to two hundred persons per square mile, depending on the specific conditions of soil and climate within the area under consideration. This would allow a total population of several million at the height of the Classic period, but this seems too high in view of the population of the same area today, which is less than one person per square kilometer in the more remote parts of the Peten, Campeche, and Quintana Roo. The figure of several million also seems high in view of the population figures which were projected for the Yucatan Peninsula shortly after the Spanish conquest. These figures suggest that the entire Northern Lowlands area at the time of the conquest had a population of no more than half a million and that the Southern Lowlands area was much less densely populated during this same period. Perhaps the best we can say is that it took a large population to construct the number of known Maya settlements, and the term *large* can be interpreted to mean anything from half a million to perhaps two or three million. Much more data will have to be gathered from both the urban and rural areas before more accurate figures can be projected.

REGIONAL STYLES

Much has been made in the past of the several distinctive architectural styles developed by the Mayas which have come to be associated with particular geographical regions. On this basis, the terms *Puuc, Chenes, Rio Bec, Usumacinta, Peten*, etc., are used both as names of regions and of styles of architecture. The term *architectural style* as used here has to do with the specific treatment of the decorative zones of the exteriors of buildings (moldings, cornices, friezes, etc.) as well as the location and details of roof combs. Similar stylistic differences can be noted in the sculptural elements and hieroglyphic inscriptions between the same regions. This scheme, in which styles are associated with fixed geographical regions, has led to a considerable amount of confusion when attempts are made to establish a temporal sequence of Maya architectural development. Many questions arise, such as whether the Rio Bec style is earlier than the Puuc style or if the Chenes style is contemporary with both, and panic ensues when Chenes-style buildings are found in the Puuc area or vice versa. This state of confusion seems to call for a general reassessment of the question of style to see if it can be made to fit into a larger pattern which has validity for the whole Maya area. Such a scheme is outlined below.

Earlier in this section it was suggested that the two main

30

divisions of the Maya Lowlands area (Southern and Northern Lowlands) could be broken down into several smaller regions, some of which were based in part on visible cultural manifestations which tend to set the regions apart. These differences show up in the architectural style associated with building remains as well as sculptural and decorative elements found in association with buildings. We have also suggested that one of the distinguishing features of a large urban center would be the presence of a distinctive architectural style. From this it would seem to follow that geographical regions as postulated earlier are represented by a single architectural style and that this style would be most prominent at the largest urban center within each region.

This is not necessarily the case, however, since this proposition fails to take into account any kind of time scale. It assumes that the same style was present at any given place for an extended period of time and that the various regions suggested are associated with a given style. The view we have presented differs from this in that we have suggested that the various regions are associated with major urban centers, i.e., that the regions represent areas coming under the influence of major cities and that certain cultural traits move from the larger centers to the smaller centers under their influence. In this scheme, style does not represent a fixed condition. At any given period of time, the architecture at any particular place would tend to be consistent and would be in a particular style, but the style might be different at different times. What we see exposed at any archaeological site today is the latest series of buildings, many of which may have been built within a short period of time. What is underneath is likely to be different, particularly the architectural style represented. At the same time, while we have assumed that styles emanate from the larger centers and make their way to the smaller centers in the same region, there is likely to be a time lag involved in this process and we could then expect to find more than one style present in the same region at the same time. This is a fairly likely possibility,

since it normally takes some time for provincial centers to catch up with the latest styles already in vogue in the capital.

Thus, it would appear that the question of style has to be put on a time scale in order to test out the validity of styles in relation to geographic regions. Once this is done, we would likely find that certain smaller centers showing a pronounced architectural style were built during a fairly short period of time when that particular style was popular, while other centers in the same region might show a different style because they were built in a different time period. By the same token, the large urban centers which we have postulated as having a very long life span should show evidence of the presence of several styles if enough layers of the outermost structures could be peeled off to reveal the earlier structures underneath. The most recent evidence pertaining to this latter proposition comes from extensive excavations carried down to bedrock at both Tikal and Dzibilchaltun. The decorative styles associated with structures from the Early Classic period are very naturalistic and much use was made of stucco-relief sculptural elements showing lifelike human and animal forms. By the end of the Classic period, the styles had shifted to more abstract geometrical patterns, and cut-stone mosaic work was used in many places instead of the earlier applied plaster decoration. The basic architectural style of the earlier structures in reference to details of bases, moldings, etc., also differed from the later styles; this has been carefully documented during the excavation of the North Acropolis at Tikal (Coe: 1965.)

In addition to the present confusion in regard to time scales and architectural styles, there is also some confusion in regard to the number of styles which can be differentiated out and the criteria which can be used in making meaningful classifications of styles. It cannot be overemphasized that we still have very little concrete data from the vast majority of known sites, which represent only a random sampling; several large areas are scarcely represented at all. Given a larger cross section of examples

31

from the entire Maya area and more specific criteria, it might be possible to draw finer distinctions between various styles, which could then be fitted into a time sequence. This would serve as one kind of check in regard to the theory we have advanced with respect to the spread of styles from major centers to the smaller centers. It would also allow us to check the spread of styles from one major center to another if in fact this actually took place.

Beyond this, it can be argued that style is a secondary indicator of cultural tradition, since the larger Maya area appears to be fairly homogeneous when more basic factors are considered. Style as such has very little to do with determining the physical organization and spatial order of the center as a whole and can be thought of as a superficial overlay which is subject to change at will; it has no real operational function. The same thing can be said of hieroglyphic writing. While the styles of glyphs might vary from region to region, anyone who was familiar with the basic structure of the glyphs would have had no difficulty reading glyphs in an unfamiliar style; the underlying operational function of the glyphs is not dependent on style. The fundamental similarities which can be observed at all Maya centers, large and small, have to do with formal relationships between elements and with the basic forms which provide the structural framework for buildings and building complexes. These are generic concepts which tend to be maintained in spite of shifts in architectural or sculptured style or methods of building construction. For this reason, questions of style will be played down in the balance of the discussion in favor of spatial relationships and basic forms which are consistent throughout the entire Maya area. This consistency is readily apparent in the basic building elements and basic building groupings, or complexes, which will be described in the next chapter.

GROWTH AND DEVELOPMENT

One of the objectives of the present study is concerned with clarifying the main outlines of the evolution of specific architectural or placemaking ideas from the Early to Late Classic periods wherever it can be shown that there is some plausible basis for assuming a chronology of development, or that a sequence is implied by the presence of a series of forms which logically derive one from the other. In attempting to do this, we are sometimes aided by chronological evidence obtained from hieroglyphic inscriptions carved into the lintels or walls of certain buildings which give specific dates when correlated to our own calendar, and by radio-carbon dating methods, which can be used whenever organic material was used in the construction of buildings and substructures. On other occasions, we are dependent on ceramic materials incorporated into the heartings of walls or fill under the floors of various structures which can be correlated with long-dated sequences of ceramic development obtained by other means, or by stylistic changes in the decorative elements associated with buildings. In some cases, the basis for sequential development is purely architectural and stems from evidence of improved building technology which can be demonstrated to have occurred in a logical sequence. It may also rest on even more subjective evidence which assumes that complex building forms and building groupings derive from simpler models. It can hardly be argued, for example, that buildings such as the Governor's Palace at Uxmal or the Acropolis Groups at Copan and Piedras Negras did not result from a long series of earlier and less complex visualizations which passed through many intermediate stages before culminating in these highly sophisticated conceptions. Finally, there is irrefutable evidence of a sequence of ordering ideas which followed one another at any particular place which can be obtained only from excavation. Here is a stratigraphic record of successive layers of building which can be traced down to bedrock. The extent of this kind of evidence is still fairly limited but forms a growing body of reliable data wherever it is available.

In spite of the support which can be obtained from these sources, much of what follows must, of necessity, be partially speculative; the stones cannot really speak for themselves, but, nonetheless, they are there by intent and their arrangements and relationships do speak a language which is still comprehensible in terms of design and form. This is an abstract language of solids and voids, verticals and horizontals, openness and enclosure, volume and mass, length and width, axis and cross axis, module and rhythm, light and shade, shape and size. This is the basic language of architecture which has been used throughout the world wherever human beings have developed the capacity to reorganize the existing environment on a large scale and give it meaning in their own terms. This is the language which can still be read in a Maya city; the hieroglyphic inscriptions, other than calendar notations, are still mute and the abstract symbols on buildings and stelae have no real meaning for us and serve only to impress us by sheer weight of numbers. What can be learned, then, from this so-called universal language?

The evidence thus far obtained from extensive excavations in the central portions of a number of Maya cities included in this study indicates that they were built and occupied over periods of many hundreds of years. Recent excavations in the North Acropolis at Tikal, for example, suggest an unbroken sequence of building activity extending over a period of nearly fifteen hundred years (Coe: 1965a). Dzibilchaltun appears to have been occupied for nearly twenty-five hundred years, although the

5.
The
Structure
of the City—
Forms and
Functions

33

first millennium of its existence cannot be assigned to the Mayas (E. W. Andrews: 1965b).

Since Maya cities, like most modern cities, grew by accretion over a very long period of time, it must be recognized that whatever order we can observe in its final form does not stem from a preconception of the whole complex of structures and open spaces as a single visualization by a lone architectural genius, but is rather an attempt by many generations of designers and builders to expand and refine their own ideas of system and order while retaining those parts of previous schemes which were still useful to their purposes. In some cases, this resulted in the addition of new construction directly over an earlier structure without changing the basic form of the earlier structure or its relationship to contiguous elements. This procedure results in a physical enlargement of certain parts of the city but introduces no new concepts. In other cases, earlier structures were razed to the ground in order to permit the construction of new building elements or the creation of open spaces which differed conceptually from their predecessors. In this connection it must be remembered that any change in physical form, whether we are speaking of a single building or a whole settlement, is a visible expression of cultural change involving feelings, aspirations, and ways of looking at the world.

The city took on its final form some time during the eighth century A.D. More settlements are known from this period than from any other period. Virtually all major settlements which had been occupied in Preclassic and Early Classic times were now built over. Total construction volume was enormous compared with earlier or later periods and most of what is visible at any of the sites discussed in the latter part of this book was built during an eighty-year period (A.D. 711 to 790). As the city expanded, adjoining areas of the jungle were destroyed and brought into the domain of the city, but even these outer sectors were ultimately rebuilt by later generations of more knowledgeable builders who were eager to erect their own monuments to the greater glory of the gods, thereby bringing glory to themselves. Any modern city is subject to the same cycle of building, rebuilding, and expansion, which differs from the cycle of a Maya city only to the extent that the increase in our technological capabilities has reduced the time required to complete the cycle.

Thus far we have seen the Maya city in its incipient form as consisting of two essential kinds of places: open spaces, leveled and paved, in which the populace gathered together for collective and formalized activities; and singular or enclosed places, highly particularized and differentiated out from surrounding context by means of an intermediate element in the form of a raised platform. These two kinds of places combine into the plaza-platform-temple group which has already been described in chapter 3. Surrounding this nucleus were the clearings in which corn was planted, together with small clusters of huts in which the general population lived. Most of the ordinary events of life took place outside the precincts of the ceremonial area, and the bulk of the rural population repaired to the center only for those collective activities which, in themselves, mark the difference between civilized society and primitive man. The center served as a market place and meeting place in addition to its function as a religious or ceremonial precinct, though it cannot be demonstrated that any special places were set aside for purely secular activities, such as trading. If the present pattern of open-air markets in the plazas in front of churches is any indicator, the Maya peasant who bought or sold goods in the plaza in front of the temple would see no essential conflict of interest when the same space was later used for a great ceremonial pageant.

Even though the city was still in its embryo form, the general population was already under the sway of a small group of priests who kept unto themselves the accumulated knowledge of Maya society, including a system of numeration, which they were able to record and pass on to successive generations by means of hieroglyphic inscriptions. Only the initiated could translate these ideograms, and therein lay the source of the power wielded by this elite group. The rituals or ceremonies, conducted by the priests, were designed to curry favor with the gods and involved the mass of the population, who carried out their parts in the open space of the plaza, while only the priests had access to the temples or other sacred places. Unquestionably, those periods which marked the planting and harvesting of corn, the onset of the rainy season which would ripen the corn, births and deaths, the phases of the moon, the coming of the new year, or any of the natural phenomena associated with the most visible facts of Maya life must have been cause for rejoicing or prayer, procession or dance. In time, as the priests were able to observe and measure the basic cycles of nature with greater accuracy and correlate them with the activities of man, the rituals must have become both more elaborate and more frequent, with the result that more gods were added to the existing pantheon, which could now be counted on to act in regard to even the smallest details of community life.

This increase in ritual activity, together with the inevitable necessity for greater specialization among those individuals most directly connected with the functioning of the center, brought about a corresponding increase in building requirements both qualitatively and quantitatively. From this it follows that the process of urbanization represents both a simple addition of the city's most basic ingredient, plaza and temple, plus the addition of new elements which were necessary to accommodate the more specialized functions then taking place, including living places for the growing elite and middle classes who now had no time to take part in agricultural or other everyday affairs. The height of the Classic period, as far as building is concerned, is marked by a sharp increase in what have been called "palace"-type buildings together with the introduction of specialized building types such as observatories, bathhouses, and ball courts. It is virtually certain that the large number of structures which have been grouped together under the general heading of "palaces" actually represent a number of different func-

tions, including residences, even though most of these functions cannot be clearly identified at present.

This expanded urban center, or city, consists of numerous plazas, terraces, courtyards, and platforms together with their associated structures in the form of pyramid-temples, palaces, shrines, ball courts, utility buildings, and storehouses. Somewhere in the near vicinity are the houses of the high priests and other members of the elite class, who are in charge of all activities taking place within the center. Beyond this central nucleus are the suburban residential areas, which probably housed the growing middle class of artisans and traders as well as the skilled building workers. Each of these suburban areas has its own community center, containing temples and other civic structures. The houses continue out into the countryside and in some places there is no sharp break to tell us when we have left the urban area and entered the rural zone.

If we assume a vantage point in front of the doorway of one of the great pyramids, we can survey the fully developed city and mark out its essential features. The sunlight gleams on the smooth plaster surfaces of plazas and terraces, which contrast sharply with the bold reliefs in stone or stucco which fill the upper zones and roof combs of temples and palaces. Broad stairways connect plazas, terraces, and platforms, and raised causeways connect those portions of the city which are separated from one another by low-lying ground, which occasionally fills with water. The whole assemblage is unified with a coat of plaster, punctuated at certain points by numerous stelae, which stand in rows at the foot of broad stairways or adjacent to important structures or, more rarely, appear as "exclamation points" in the open spaces of plazas or courtyards. Rising high above everything else are the great temples; resting securely on their massive pyramidal bases, they can only be reached by stairways which are so steep that today's casual visitor hesitates to make the climb. The temples may include an altar or sanctuary, but more frequently the walls are bare of any ornamentation and the

35

enclosed spaces are small and dark, seemingly unsuited to any high purpose. Each temple may be dedicated to a single god and must compete for attention with other temples which appear to vie with one another in terms of height and majesty. It is tempting to think that the differences in elevation among the various temples symbolizes the relative position of different gods within the larger pantheon of gods, but this is mere speculation.

From this same vantage point we can note that the city consists of a number of discrete assemblages, or complexes, within which the individual buildings and open spaces form a coherent and strongly organized whole. The temple in front of which we are standing belongs to such a group and it is not difficult to distinguish the other buildings which are directly associated with it. We may also be able to discern a larger order within which the individual groups are related to other groups both physically and visually. Axes and cross axes establish quadrilateral organizations, plazas lead into other plazas, broad stairways lead through archways or doorways which in turn take us into hidden courtyards, and elevated causeways form physical links between otherwise isolated groups of buildings. Some parts of the city do not seem to fit into any larger order and it is possible to pick out random groupings which cannot easily be charged to fortuitous features of topography. This condition might represent either a conscious effort to establish independent zones of activity, i.e., residential versus ceremonial, differentiated out by design, or merely a lack of ability on the part of the builders to conceptualize ideas of order at a large-enough scale to include these elements. Certainly the individual "architects" who were in charge of building efforts at specific sites differed in their creative capabilities when confronted with situations outside the existing traditions. (Real creativity was probably no more widespread among the Mayas than it is in our own society.)

An examination of a large number of cities from the same kind of vantage point suggests that the organization of the city as a whole is dependent in large measure

upon the specific features of existing topography. Where the existing terrain is very irregular, building groupings themselves are carefully disposed with regard to the best utilization of existing ground form. Wherever sites are relatively flat or lacking in fortuitous spatial definition, the over-all scheme becomes more deliberately geometric and, in a formal sense, more unified. The individual complexes are also more formally ordered and deviations from approximate right-angular relationships and cardinal-point orientations appear to be deliberate rather than accidental, as is the case where the ground is very irregular and problems of cut and fill limit the amount of reshaping which can be done economically. Further evidence in support of these notions will be introduced in the discussion of individual sites. For the moment, it seems more useful to suggest that the general nature of the differences in over-all organizations at various sites appears to be the consequence of specific factors of geography associated with three distinct types of building sites.

These basic site types include: (1) the irregular ground formations which are characteristic of the Peten area in Guatemala and parts of the states of Chiapas and Campeche in Mexico, which are marked by low hills, ridges, and depressions; (2) those sites which lie immediately adjacent to large rivers, such as Yaxchilan, Piedras Negras, and Altar de Sacrificios, which also tend to be fairly irregular in ground configuration; and (3) the relatively flat sites which are characteristic of Tabasco, Campeche, and the northern part of the Yucatan Peninsula and the lower Motagua Valley in Guatemala. Within any of the general areas indicated, certain exceptions can be noted, but the three main types of site location are fairly distinct. It must be pointed out that the river-front sites are restricted to the Southern Lowlands, since no large rivers are found in the northern area. While there is a large number of river-oriented sites, most are quite small, owing perhaps to the fact that the levee system of agriculture as practiced at riverine sites was fairly restrictive in terms of the amount of usable land available. Ridged-field systems, which have recently been discovered on the Candelaria and Usumacinta rivers, did increase the acreage of productive soil at some riverine sites, but these enlarged fields were still too small to support the large populations postulated for the urban centers.[1] The river must have served as an important means of communication, however, and to some extent was recognized as a unique element, which influenced the form of those cities built along its banks.

Each of the three basic types of site just described led to a somewhat different resolution of the city scheme, which will become more apparent later on when we consider the specific organization of individual cities. It must be emphasized, however, that these differences are not differences in form or basic structural relationships, but only differences of shape and arrangement, which are dependent on local conditions of topography and geography. We will try to demonstrate that all Maya settlements, large or small, were made up of the same basic forms, which can be thought of as large-scale building blocks and which vary from one another physically in terms of the number of components utilized and the way the components have been used to reorganize the existing natural environment. The specific arrangement and detailed design of the components varies considerably from place to place, but the generic forms remain constant. It is the repetition of these "ideal" forms throughout the Maya area that gives Maya cities their consistency and special character.

BASIC ELEMENTS

It was pointed out in chapter 2 that the making of "places," whether these are in the form of open spaces such as squares, plazas, courtyards, and terraces or take the form of essentially solid masses representing buildings and substructures, constitutes the conscious reordering of the na-

---

[1] Dennis and Olga Puleston have suggested that once the potential of the riverine sites had been exhausted, the movement to the forested interior was inevitable and ultimately led to what has been called Maya civilization. They have also outlined the basis upon which a forest-based agricultural system developed in place of the earlier river-based system. (Puleston and Puleston: 1971.)

tural environment leading to the notion of architecture. The basic elements of Maya architecture, which are the building blocks used in the making of the city, consist of several fairly distinct categories of open spaces, which can be distinguished from one another on the basis of how they are defined and by their positions in space, together with several categories or types of buildings and substructures. Admittedly, clear distinctions are sometimes hard to draw between similar categories, but in most cases there are sufficient differences to be meaningful. It should also be emphasized that the differences referred to represent basic differences in conception, rather than mere changes in size or style, and thus imply differences in function or meaning. For purposes of discussion and analysis, the following terminology has been adapted to describe the basic categories of open spaces.

Plaza

An open space, artificially leveled and paved, which generally conforms closely to the natural ground level. Plazas tend to be rectilinear in shape but may be irregular where the natural terrain is very broken. In most cases, the actual paving has disappeared, but the position, shape, and size of the plaza can be inferred wherever the ground has been carefully leveled. The edges of the paving are in themselves sufficient to establish the boundaries of the plaza, but it is generally given further definition by means of one or more buildings situated around its periphery. It cannot be overemphasized that the open space of the plaza is one of the essential ingredients of Maya cities. They are public places above all and must have served as a focus of community life. (By contrast, in our society a considerable amount of community life takes place inside of buildings.) Plazas also performed a vital function at some sites in collecting rainwater, which was drained into reservoirs, or *chultunes*, for use during the long dry season.

Terrace

An open space, leveled and paved and in many ways similar to a plaza, but built up artificially above the na-

37

tural ground level. Its boundaries are described by the edges which mark the intersection of the sloping sides with the upper level of the terrace, and its uniqueness lies in the fact that the level open space created has been differentiated from the general ground level by a change in elevation. At building sites where the natural topography was very irregular, hills and ridges were terraced by a process of cutting and filling, but the resulting space is the same as an artificially built-up terrace. As in the case of a plaza, the edges of a terrace may be reinforced with buildings, and in some cases buildings are situated within the open space of the terrace itself.

Platform

An open space which is represented by the upper level of a masonry mass in the form of a stepped and truncated pyramid. These so-called pyramids might also be thought of as a series of progressively smaller terraces placed one on top of another. In many cases, temples or other buildings are situated on the upper level of these platforms, but there are numerous examples where they were conceived and utilized as open places which were never intended to support buildings. The distinction between platform and terrace is sometimes difficult to draw but is partially one of origin. The mass of a platform is normally visualized and accepted as a completely man-made structure, while a terrace tends to be perceived as a manipulation of the natural ground configuration.

Courtyard

Also an open space, leveled and paved, but created and defined solely by virtue of the buildings or walls which surround it. In this sense, the open space of the courtyard cannot be thought of as separate from the structures which define it. A courtyard may be situated either above or below the natural ground level and its real distinction lies in its specific relationships to the surrounding building elements. Courtyards vary considerably in size but must be small enough, and sufficiently well defined, to be comprehended at a glance. A more detailed discussion of courtyards is included in the description and analysis of quadrangles which appears in this chapter in the section entitled *Basic Building Groupings*.

Causeway

A graded and paved open space in the form of a roadway, or walkway, which is raised above its immediate surroundings. In many cases, the causeway is given further definition by low parapet walls along its edges. Since the Mayas had no wheeled vehicles or domesticated animals, these spaces must have functioned as processional ways rather than roads, permitting large numbers of people to proceed in mass from one sector of the city to another. This function is substantiated by the fact that most causeways terminate at either end in important plazas associated with important buildings, and tend to be found only where the terrain between major sectors of the city was too irregular to provide a suitable ground-level connection. Extended versions of causeways, called *sacbes*, were occasionally used to connect different cities in the northern parts of the Yucatan Peninsula but are rarely found elsewhere in the Maya area. It is unfortunate that so little can be said about streets or other pathways which served for general circulation purposes within Maya cities. Much of the open space in the center of present-day cities is in the form of streets, roads, or walkways, which can make up as much as 40 per cent of the total available ground area. In a like manner, the Mayas must have needed some kind of circulation network which was kept clear at all times. Lacking evidence to the contrary, we must assume that the basic circulation system, beyond the system of plazas and causeways, consisted of unpaved paths, or trails, which left no trace of their existence.

Ball Court

A ball court is a highly particularized open space which generally has the plan shape of a capital *I*. The playing alley, which is represented by the upright part of the *I*, is bounded on either side by a low wall and sloping bench, which in turn supports another, and generally higher, wall. Stone rings or markers were mounted on this upper wall and it is assumed that the games played in the ball court required the players to hit the markers with a rubber ball or pass it through the hole in the ring. In many cases, the main playing alley extended into a wider paved space at either end, bounded occasionally by low walls or buildings, which then form the top and bottom legs of the *I*, but apparently this additional space is not a basic requirement, since many ball courts are restricted to the narrow playing alley. Ball courts are generally associated with important plazas, and the playing surface of the ball court tends to be at the same level as the plaza.

It might be possible to make further distinctions between the various formalized open spaces found in different centers, but it seems reasonable to insist that these would only be variations of the basic spaces just described and would not represent distinct or useful categories.

BUILDING TYPES

The categories used in characterizing the various building types represented in the center present many difficulties, since it is virtually impossible to make distinctions between them on the basis of known differences in function. The terminology used here is based in part on conventional usage which has been adapted in most of the references cited. These terms have become so ingrained in the literature that it is virtually impossible to change them, even though they tend in some cases to confuse rather than clarify the problems at hand. I have gone a little further in trying to define the different building types on the basis of their general form characteristics, but it must be kept in mind that these represent formal rather than functional distinctions. At this point in time it is simply impossible to ascribe particular functions to certain buildings, particularly those which have been put under the heading of *palaces*.

In spite of the difficulty in regard to function, it is clear that there are a very limited number of basic building types, or forms, which are common to all building sites throughout the Maya area. There is even less variety in the rooms or enclosed spaces within these buildings, which consist, for the most part, of endless repetitions of hutlike spaces and, more occasionally, long galleries where the cross walls between individual rooms were omitted. Exceptions to these general categories will be noted later at certain sites where unique forms are found. The major building or structure types are as follows:

Temple

The simplest description of a temple would be limited to characterizing it as a small building used for ritual or ceremonial purposes. Unfortunately, this same description might also be applied to a number of other buildings, some of which are obviously not temples and others which are merely indeterminate. This difficulty is partially resolved, however, by the fact that temples are always situated on top of large substructures which have the form of stepped and truncated pyramids. As suggested earlier, the substructure is an integral part of the temple concept, symbolizing as it does the removal of the temple building from the ordinary events of life taking place on the ground below. Temple-pyramid might be a more appropriate designation for this building type, as it would eliminate those buildings which are templelike in size or form but lack the required substructure.

The earliest temples were undoubtedly constructed of wood and other perishable materials, although proof of this is only indirect. Archaeological evidence also indicates that temples passed through an intermediate stage in which the lower walls were built of stone while the roof continued to be made of poles and thatch. (Figs. 167, 168.) The final stage in the development of temples was reached when the wooden roof was supplanted by masonry corbeled vaults; the temple buildings with which we are concerned are all of this type. The evolution of the corbeled vault and the structural principles involved will be discussed in detail in chapter 6, Building Technology. For

39

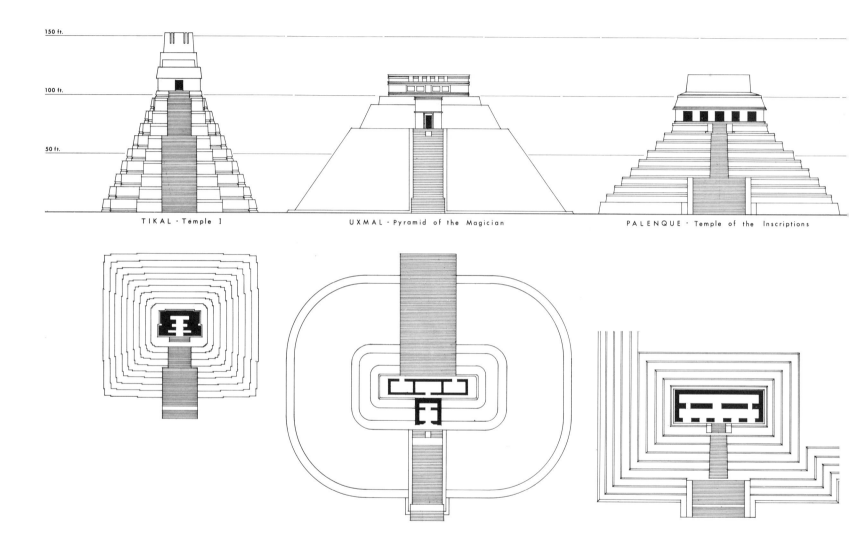

150 ft.

100 ft.

50 ft.

TIKAL · Temple I   UXMAL · Pyramid of the Magician   PALENQUE · Temple of the Inscriptions

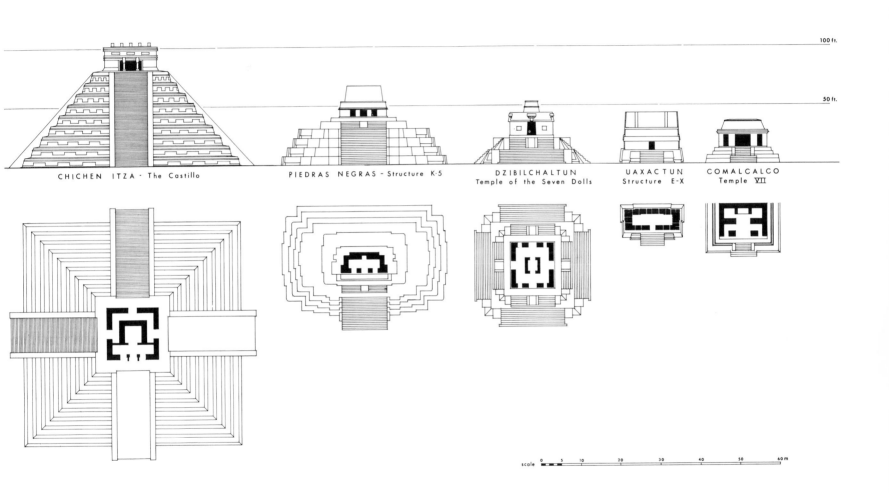

CHICHEN ITZA - The Castillo

PIEDRAS NEGRAS - Structure K-5

DZIBILCHALTUN
Temple of the Seven Dolls

UAXACTUN
Structure E-X

COMALCALCO
Temple VII

scale 0 5 10   20   30   40   50   60 m

FIG. 5. Comparison of temple structures.

the moment, we are more concerned with the general outlines and plan arrangement of the typical temple form.

The stone temple consisted of one or more small rooms which could normally be entered from one side only. These rooms were sometimes arranged side by side in a row of three or five but more often were positioned one in front of the other and entrance into the inner rooms could be gained only from the outer, or front, room. Due to the limitations imposed by corbeled vaulting, the rooms tended to be very high and narrow and in no case did they ever exceed ten feet in depth. The interiors of the rooms were cramped and dark, and in many cases completely devoid of decoration save for crude graffiti which were sometimes scratched into the plaster on the walls. In other cases, the inner rooms contained shrines, or sanctuaries, which were decorated with elaborate sculptural reliefs and hieroglyphic inscriptions (Fig. 105). Very rarely, the interiors were painted, and in one instance all of the walls of a small three-room temple (Bonampak) were completely covered with frescoes in full color, depicting scenes of ritual ceremonies (Fig. 78).

The specific plan arrangement and over-all size of temple buildings vary considerably from site to site, but in general they are rather small (25 to 50 feet long and 15 to 25 feet in depth) and tend toward square shapes in plan. In most cases they are highly directional and exterior doorways are found only in the front wall. These doorways always occur in odd numbers of one, three, or five, but three seems to have been most popular. In these instances, the central doorway was normally wider than the other two. Doorways were generally framed with wooden lintels, although stone was sometimes used if they were very narrow. Because the doorways were limited to a single side, temple buildings are very directional and it is obvious that they are meant to relate in a special way to the plaza below. The physical connection between the temple and plaza consists of a broad but very steep stairway on the plaza side, and its steepness attests to the fact that it was not meant to provide ready public access to the temple

from the plaza. In those instances where the temple building had doorways on two or more sides, additional stairways were provided on those sides of the substructure corresponding to the location of the additional doorways. These instances are fairly rare, however, and the normal pattern is the unidirectional temple with a single stairway.

As a means of giving added visual importance to the temple, wall-like elements called roof combs were frequently added on top of the temple proper. In most cases this extension was positioned directly over the front or rear wall, but on those buildings having two rooms, one behind the other, it would more likely be positioned over the central dividing wall between the two rooms. Roof combs were many times pierced with openings in geometrical patterns and, failing this, were covered with stone or plaster decorative elements (Figs. 42, 100, 259). The combination of temple and roof comb appears to be limited exclusively to Maya architecture and provides one of the most dependable means of distinguishing Maya buildings from those belonging to other cultures. These appendages have no structural function and, in fact, add considerable dead weight which must be taken up by the vaults and lower walls. They might best be described as being analogous to a headdress: physically superfluous but highly desirable as a status symbol.

Viewed from the level of the plaza, the temple is an imposing and monumental structure. The smooth surfaces of its lower walls contrast sharply with the decorated portion of the upper walls and the roof comb. Each of these zones is clearly marked out by the strong horizontal bands of the projecting cornices which divide the façade into three sections. The sloping surfaces of the supporting substructure are carefully articulated so that they, too, create strong horizontal bands, interrupted by the broad stairway which moves in a single sweep from the plaza to the small terrace in front of the temple. Standing free of jungle and ground alike, its great supporting mass giving it a sense of permanence, the temple asserts its dominance of both man and nature and thus achieves true monumentality. A number of examples of temples and their supporting substructures are shown in Figure 5. They are drawn to the same scale in order to facilitate comparison of dimensions and details.

Palace

The term *palace* has been used to describe a variety of structures with different ground plans which can be distinguished from other known building types on the basis of their size, ground plans, and relationships to other structures. Within this general category two subtypes can easily be distinguished: *gallery-type* structures and *multichamber-type* structures. Gallery-type structures can be described as long, rectangular buildings with one or two interior spaces in the form of colonnaded galleries roofed over with masonry vaults. Buildings of this kind are found in both the Northern and Southern Lowlands areas and differ from each other only in terms of style and detail; the basic form is maintained in all cases. Multichamber-type structures can be broken down into several subtypes, each with its own distinguishing characteristics. One of the major subtypes can also be described as a long, rectangular structure, but in this case the interior consists of two parallel ranges of small rooms which are also roofed over with masonry vaults. Buildings of this type are very common in the northern area, and somewhat more complex varieties of the same form are characteristic of the southern area. Beyond this, there are many other multichamber structures exhibiting a great variety of ground plans and over-all shapes, including *L* shapes and *U* shapes, and multistory structures are fairly common.

In short, there is really no archetypal form which can be associated with the term *palace*. The closest approximation of this would be a building which consists of two parallel rows of rooms, one behind the other, which can be entered by means of a series of doorways centered in the rooms along one side only. Large numbers of buildings with plans of this kind can be found in the Yucatan area (Figs. 191, 230), but they are found less frequently in the southern area.

It seems fairly certain that the palace, in any of its forms, came into being sometime after masonry temples were fully developed, and it is possible that the palace form evolved directly from a large version of the temple.[2] This possibility is suggested by the fact that it is very difficult in some cases to make a clear distinction between certain buildings which might be classified either as temples or palaces. Generally, the distinction is made on the basis of size, but there are examples of fairly large multichambered temples as well as rather small palace-type structures. An additional basis for distinguishing palaces from temples is found in the size and shape of their supporting substructures. Palaces tended to be supported on low substructures which can best be classified as platforms, rather than pyramids, because of their proportions of length to height. Again, there are many cases where it is difficult to distinguish between platform and pyramid.

The actual functions of any of the so-called palaces is still unknown. It has been widely postulated that many of them served as living quarters for the high priests who ruled Maya society, but most palace-type structures which are still in a good state of repair show little or no evidence of having been lived in. The spaces are not really suited to living purposes and anyone who has spent even a few hours in one of these damp, dark cells or exposed galleries would gladly settle for a thatched-roof hut as being vastly superior as a dwelling. It is still possible that some of them served as temporary living quarters on those occasions when large numbers of important visitors were present in the center. They might also have been used for various purposes in connection with the training of neophytes, for administrative or commercial activities, and for storing

[2] The earliest masonry buildings which have been found near the bottom layers of stratified superimpositions are all of the temple type. Palace-type buildings are generally Late Classic constructions, although data from recent excavations in the Central Acropolis at Tikal may push back the dates of the earliest palace construction to sometime in the Early Classic period.

43

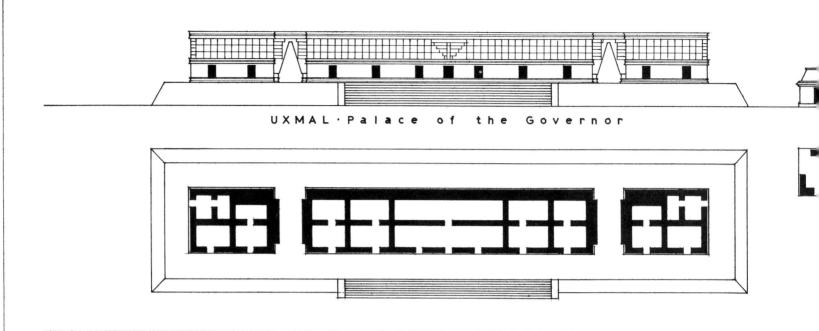

UXMAL · Palace of the Governor

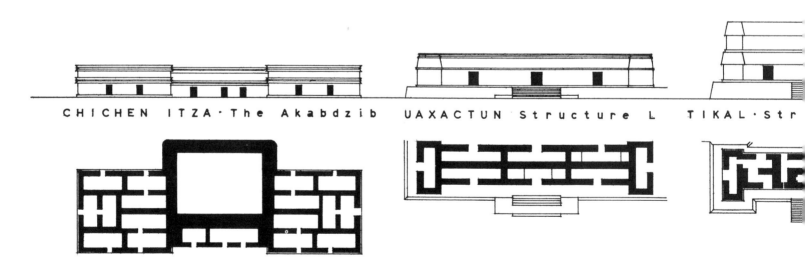

CHICHEN ITZA · The Akabdzib   UAXACTUN Structure L   TIKAL · Str

FIG. 6. Comparison of palace structures.

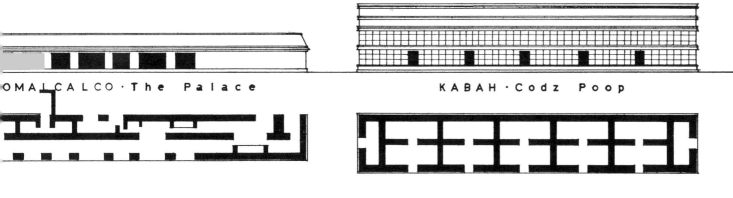

OMALCALCO · The Palace

KABAH · Codz Poop

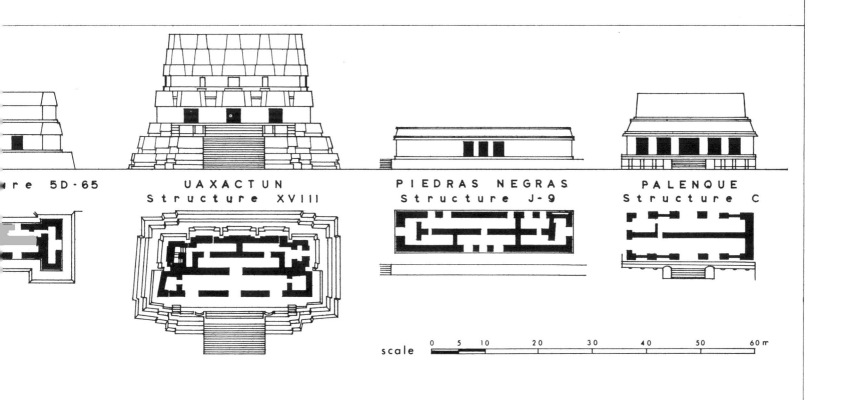

re 5D·65

UAXACTUN
Structure XVIII

PIEDRAS NEGRAS
Structure J-9

PALENQUE
Structure C

scale   0   5   10   20   30   40   50   60 m

ritual objects and clothing. As more detailed information becomes available as a result of excavation, it is to be hoped that the very large group of structures which have been lumped together under the heading of *palaces* can be sorted out into several smaller categories representing specific functions. For the moment we are simply stuck in a situation where most of the basic data is still missing.

In basic construction and details, palace-type buildings do not differ substantially from temples. In both cases the length, width, and height of the inner spaces are nearly identical, due to restrictions imposed by the overhead vaults. Many palace-type buildings support roof combs which are similar to the roof combs on temples in all respects except for their greater length. Treatment of façades, cornices, and decorative features are also very similar, so we are forced to accept size, complexity of plan arrangement, and position in space as the primary distinguishing feature of this building category. A number of palace-type structures from different sites are shown in Figure 6. Most of the basic plan types are included and these occur with numerous variations at different sites.

Altar and Ceremonial Platform

At a great many sites, low platforms with stairways on one or more sides are situated in important positions in the open spaces of plazas or courtyards. In many respects, these small structures can be seen as small-scale versions of the larger platforms, or pyramidal substructures, which serve as the supporting bases for temples and palaces. If any real distinction were to be made between altar and ceremonial platform, it would have to be on the basis of size; altars would tend to be smaller. Some of these freestanding platforms are fairly large and might have supported perishable buildings, while others are clearly too small to have served this purpose. In all cases, however, it is clear that structures which fit into this category were not actually intended to support buildings.

The smaller platforms, which are assumed to be altars, tend to be aligned with the central doorways of temples and palaces, while those that are called ceremonial platforms are found in many different positions with respect to other building elements. Whether any of the altars were used for sacrificial purposes is a matter of conjecture, but this is a distinct possibility. The larger platforms were certainly used for ritual activities, including ceremonial dances, as witnessed by the wall paintings at Bonampak. The most unique examples of this kind of structure are represented in the twin-pyramid complexes at Tikal, which will be discussed in greater detail under the heading of *Basic Building Groupings*.

Shrines, or Sanctuaries

This category includes a number of very small templelike structures which are usually built inside of the inner rooms of temples or palace-type buildings or, more rarely, built into the stairways of substructures supporting these same buildings. Some are large enough to admit one or two persons in a standing position, while others are too small to hold anything larger than a ritual offering. In a typical situation, the shrine is built against the back wall of a temple. It is covered with a corbeled vault, making it a room within a room. The floor of the shrine is raised above the general floor level, further distinguishing it from the balance of the space. The wall of the shrine facing the spectator is covered with relief carvings of priests or gods in human form, centered between panels covered with hieroglyphic inscriptions. (See chapter 7, Palenque and Comalcalco, for examples of sanctuaries in temple buildings.) The care devoted to the details of these small spaces indicates that they served some very important ceremonial function whose specific nature can only be guessed at. Perhaps they can best be thought of as the "holy of holies," although this would hardly be the case when they are associated with palace-type structures or external stairways.

Ball Courts

Ball Courts have already been discussed as open spaces but must also be included as a building type, as the elements which define the space of the court represent specific building forms. The vertical and sloping surfaces of these masses form the enclosure of the court but contain no enclosed space in themselves. Small buildings of the palace type are sometimes situated on top of the ball-court structures, which suggests that the court was used for ceremonial or religious purposes in addition to any recreational function it might have had. Ball-court structures vary considerably in size and cross-sectional configuration, but the basic form remains constant. It was also pointed out earlier that ball courts vary considerably in terms of their positions with respect to other structures, indicating that they are not functionally related to any one building type or building complex. In spite of this, they must have played an important role in Maya life, as virtually no city or ceremonial center of any importance was without at least one of these specialized structures. A selected group of ball courts is shown in Figure 7. Three basic-plan types are included: those consisting of an alley with open ends, those with one end closed, and others with both ends closed.

Dwellings

The earliest written record we have of what Maya houses were like was provided by Bishop Landa who described a Maya city in these terms: "Before the Spaniards had conquered that country, the natives lived together in towns in a very civilized fashion. They kept the land well cleared and free from weeds, and planted very good trees. Their dwellings place was as follows:—in the middle of the town were their temples with beautiful plazas, and all around the temples stood the houses of the lords and the priests, and then [those of] the most important people. Then came the houses of the richest and those who were held in highest estimation nearest to these, and at the outskirts of the town were the houses of the lowest classes." (Landa: 1941.) It must be remembered that Landa was speaking of a sixteenth-century Maya city rather than a Classic Maya city from the eighth or ninth

century, which may have been substantially different from its successor, particularly in regard to the concentric organization of the various house types. Nevertheless, the most recent excavations of house mounds at both Tikal and Dzibilchaltun have tended to substantiate Landa's general description; at both sites there actually are a large number of different house types and the smallest houses do tend to occupy the least favorable positions. This can be seen more clearly by looking at some of the specific house types in greater detail.

Excavations of house mounds at a number of different sites (Tikal, Barton Ramie, Dzibilchaltun, and Uaxactun) indicate that the Mayas built and lived in a variety of house types, ranging from one-room pole-and-thatch huts to large masonry structures containing several rooms. The priests and nobles apparently had all the best of it and lived in permanent dwellings which were not substantially different from the ceremonial structures which they emulated. Below this group came the artisans, builders, warriors, scribes, and other specialists, who can be thought of as representing a middle class. They lived in somewhat less elaborate houses, which might have had two rooms and a separate kitchen. Ordinary workers or peasants lived in one-room huts made of poles and thatch. Within the three major categories of houses as briefly outlined, there were many variations, but the basic types appear to be fairly well established, as they appear in all parts of the Maya area.

The smallest houses were situated on a square or rectangular platform with masonry foundation walls retaining an earth and rubble fill. The platform was surfaced with a plaster floor and supported a thatch-and-pole hut which was probably very much like the houses built by present-day rural Maya Indians. The houses included both rectangular and apsidal plan shapes and in some cases the lower walls were made of rough-block masonry rather than poles and mud. There is also some evidence that houses were occasionally built directly on the ground with no supporting platform. Both at Tikal and Dzibilchaltun

47

FIG. 7. Comparison of ball courts.

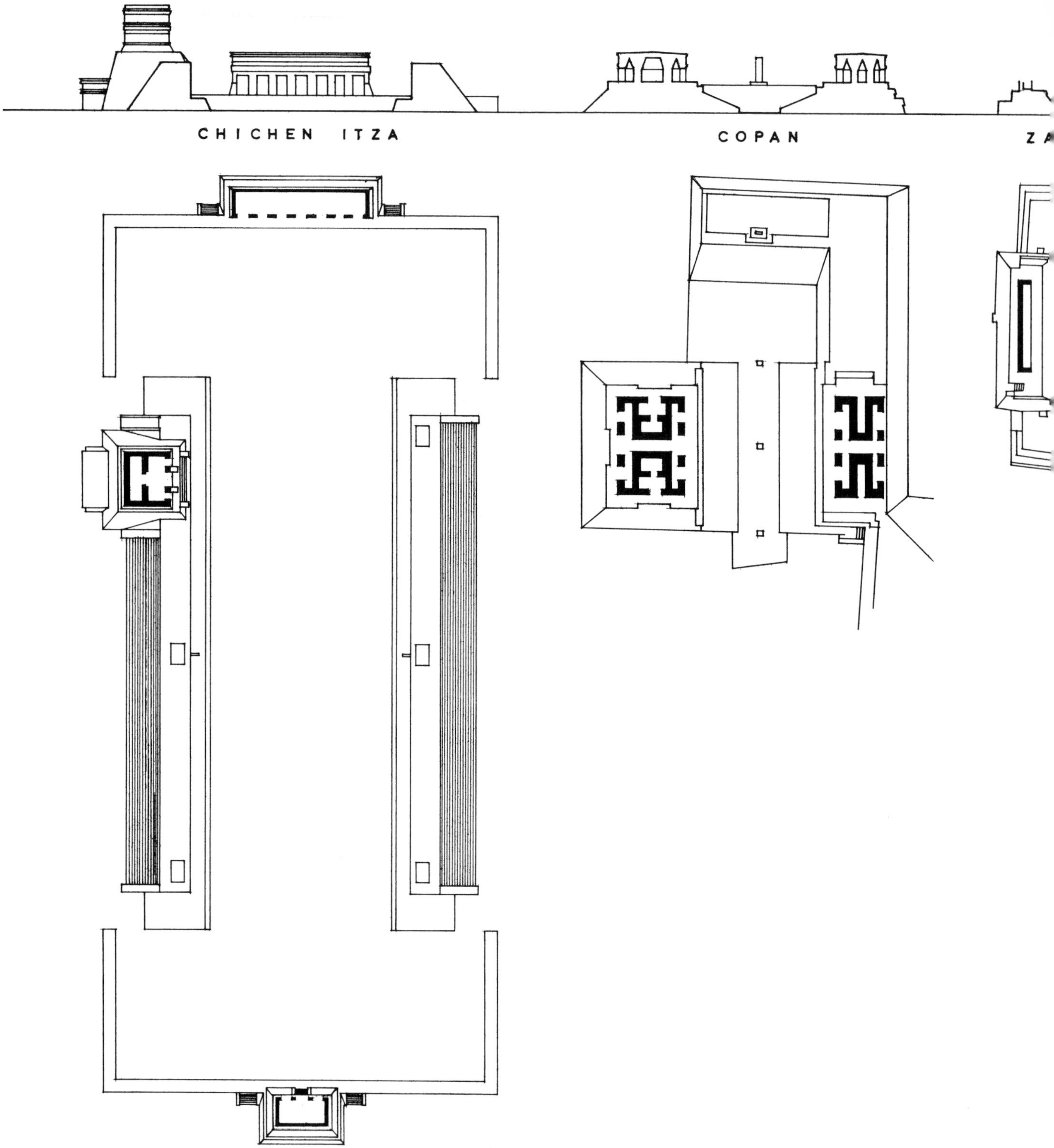

CHICHEN ITZA   COPAN   ZA

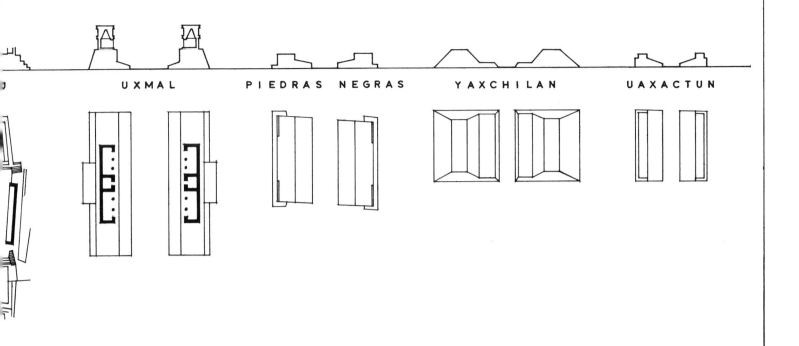

UXMAL PIEDRAS NEGRAS YAXCHILAN UAXACTUN

scale 0 5 10 20 30 40 50 100 m.

the remains of small structures, which were represented by post holes set at the natural ground level, were found in the same areas containing house platforms. Whether these post holes represent houses or small utility buildings is a matter of conjecture, however.

Another house type is represented by somewhat larger platforms, with two or three slightly higher platform levels which supported two or three houses or perhaps a house and a separate kitchen. These houses were also mostly of the pole-and-thatch type, but some houses with masonry walls are also represented. The houses tend to be larger than the single-room huts, and occasionally low walls are found which divided the single room into two smaller spaces. House platforms of this type were also arranged around two or three sides of a small level plaza, forming a discrete cluster. It seems reasonable to assume that this type of house was built for use by the so-called middle class.

The largest and most elaborate houses were built of masonry and contained a row of rooms with low platforms or benches along one side. Some of these had pole-and-thatch roofs, while others were roofed with masonry vaults. These "palace"-type structures are smaller than the huge multichamber palace-type structures found within the main ceremonial center, but the difference is one of size rather than form. Burials associated with these structures are more elaborate than those found in association with ordinary houses, but they are still less elaborate than those found in tombs or graves associated with major ceremonial structures, which must represent only the nobles or high priests. The evidence of class distinction within the residential area is clear, however, and the individuals living in the large masonry structures must have had a higher social status than those living in the smaller houses.

All of the above-mentioned house types are frequently found in groups which are represented by three or four dwellings situated around a plaza or courtyard. In some cases there may be a ceremonial-type structure on one of

the sides, indicating the presence of a family shrine or a private temple. These groups of houses might represent the abode of an extended family group in which several generations are represented. The patriarch who lived in the largest house was surrounded by sons, or other family members, living in smaller houses. There are many variations of these house clusters, in terms of the size and complexity of the individual units represented as well as the manner in which the units are related to one another. These variations are also indicative of a structured society in which the upper strata could enjoy the advantages of specialized masonry structures in which sleeping, cooking, and worshiping were separated out while the lowest class had to make out with a one-room multipurpose building made of perishable materials.

In the discussion of building types earlier in this section, reference was made to the possibility that some of the palace-type structures in the heart of the main ceremonial area might well have been used as residences for the high priests and nobles who ruled Maya society. Firm evidence of this assumed residential function is hard to come by, and the case rests largely on the fact that there is a considerable difference in over-all size, details of interior layout, and construction between the very large palace buildings with their endless ranges of rooms and the smaller structures with only a few rooms. Many of these smaller structures have benches, cupboards, provisions for sealing off doorways with curtains, and other details which are indicative of a residential function.

The case has yet to be proved, however, and we might still wonder if the elite class would be willing to sacrifice comfort in favor of appearance, since the thatched-roof hut is much better suited to a warm humid climate than a cold and damp stone chamber with no ventilation and little daylight. In spite of its lack of pretense, the thatched-roof hut is still an ideal solution for a semitropical climate. The building materials required are ready at hand and can be put into usable form with a minimum of effort. The dwellings are easy to construct, can easily be repaired or replaced, and provide whatever protection from the elements is necessary. Under these conditions, a masonry dwelling becomes an undesirable luxury.

In addition to the basic building types as just outlined, there are many others which can only be considered as variations of the generic types rather than distinct categories or species. Beyond this, there are other fairly unique building types which, in many cases, are confined to a single site and cannot therefore be considered as representing basic classes or types. The walled compounds found in association with the twin-pyramid groups at Tikal are an interesting example of a unique form which has not yet been found at any other site (Fig. 25). Tombs are found at many sites but not as free-standing structures. In most cases tombs are small subterranean structures of simple slab construction, although vaulted chambers are not unknown. (See discussions of Palenque and Comalcalco in chapter 7 for descriptions and photographs of very special vaulted tombs.) Free-standing arches, towers, sweat baths, and other specialized structures have been found at various sites but occur so infrequently that they can hardly be classified as representing important categories. Further reference will be made to these unique building forms in the descriptions of the sites where they occur.

Stelae

One further space-defining element of the ceremonial center should be included in this discussion, even though it cannot actually be classified as a building. Numerous stelae, or large vertical stone monuments, are found in association with buildings and various open spaces in nearly every Maya city of any importance (Figs. 28, 76, 77, 142, 149). The stelae range in size from six or seven feet to nearly twenty-six feet in height and may be as much as four feet square at the base, though a typical stela is somewhat smaller. Each is made from a single block of stone, the largest weighing upwards of thirty tons. These stelae vary greatly in their details but in most cases

include shallow relief carvings on at least one side, normally considered to be the front, and very frequently are carved on three or four sides. The front side is usually taken up with the stylized figure of a priest or god in human form, while the sides and back contain rows of hieroglyphic inscriptions (Fig. 8). The bulk of these inscriptions refer to calendar dates as determined by the Maya system of chronology, and when correlated with our own calendar provide a fairly reliable means of establishing a rough date of erection for the buildings with which the stelae are associated. Similar calendric inscriptions are sometimes found carved into the lintels over doorways in temples and palaces, providing a more accurate dating possibility. In a good many cases, stelae are accompanied by stone altars, generally round in shape, which are also covered with relief sculptures and hieroglyphic inscriptions (Fig. 26).

The majority of stelae are positioned in relation to stairways of substructures which support temples or palaces. In other cases, they are situated in the open spaces of plazas in well-defined groupings. These markers were important to the spatial ordering of the center and their spatial connotations will be discussed in greater detail later. It is perhaps unwise, however, to attach too much importance to the space-defining characteristics of these monuments, since they must have had greater symbolic value to anyone who understood the inscriptions carved into their surfaces. In spite of their greater symbolic significance, their positions in space are not accidental and it is clear that this positioning was accomplished with an eye toward visual enrichment and differentiation of special places.

BUILDING ORIENTATION

An examination of a large number of maps and site plans of Maya settlements, including those illustrated in this study, indicates that the Mayas consistently oriented major structures with regard to the cardinal points of the compass. Deviations from magnetic north are generally no

51

FIG. 8. Typical stela—Stela P,
Copan (after Gomez).

front   side   rear

more than eight to ten degrees, and in many cases the orientations come close to true north, since the average magnetic declination from true north is around seven degrees in most parts of the Maya area. Since it is unlikely that the Mayas had even a crude form of magnetic compass, it is possible that orientations were established by taking sightings on the North Star. It is a fairly simple matter to lay out north-south lines using direct line-of-sight methods once the importance of the North Star is understood. Another possibility is suggested by several assemblages of buildings in the Peten area, where it is clear that monuments and buildings were so arranged that line-of-sight readings could be used to determine the equinoxes (21 March, 21 September) and also the winter solstice (Fig. 18). Such knowledge would also permit the laying out of accurate east-west and north-south lines.

Whatever the methods employed, within any particular site the majority of buildings tend to be oriented consistently with regard to one another and with the cardinal directions. Deviations from this practice are fairly rare and tend to occur only in those places where the natural terrain is very irregular and hills and ridges were chosen as the locations for important structures. Under these circumstances, buildings might deviate from the normal orientations in order to take better advantage of fortuitous outlooks, or in order to reduce the amount of cut and fill required when reshaping hills. Thus, in spite of anomalies which can be observed at certain sites, the general pattern is all in favor of rectilinear configurations in which great care was taken to assure consistent orientation.

While major buildings and building complexes are generally positioned with regard to predetermined orientations, there does not appear to be any preferred orientation for either temples of large palace-type structures. At any given site there may be a preference for a particular orientation, as is the case at Edzna, where all the major temples face west, but at other sites this is not the case. At Tikal, for example, three of the five great temples face east, one faces west, and one faces north. Patterns at other sites are even more confused. It does not seem unreasonable to assume that there was some symbolic significance to the orientation of major temples. In many primitive societies (and some not so primitive) there is an assumed "world order," and certain gods are associated with different quarters of the world. It is possible that the general practice of quadrilateral building groupings is an expression of a Maya notion of world order, but, if this is so, the specific nature of the symbolism is not clear. Order was certainly wanted, however, and this was obtained by consistent orientation and cross-axial relationships.

From what is presently known, the orientation of houses was not as precise as the larger ceremonial structures and was likely predicated on a different set of factors. These would include matters of comfort and convenience, and it has been suggested that western orientations for houses were avoided in order to avoid the excessive heat which accompanies the late afternoon sun. Questions of wind direction, rain, drainage, shade, and shadow also enter into the positioning and orientation of houses and these can be thought of in very practical terms. In those cases where shrines or temples were included in house groupings, they were generally situated on the eastern side of the group, but this is not always the case. It stands to reason, however, that the assumed symbolism associated with orientation of important ceremonial structures would not find its way down to the level of ordinary houses, or that if some symbolism was connected with their orientation it would have been of a different order. Ordinary daily events such as the rising and setting of the sun have practical as well as symbolic overtones and it is hard to know which might be considered most important where houses are concerned. Perhaps this question should be left open until we know a good deal more about Maya houses than we do at the present time.

BASIC BUILDING GROUPINGS

We have already postulated that a Maya city, or more particularly the main ceremonial precinct of the city, consisted of a series of building complexes or groupings, each of which have distinctive form characteristics. In the case of a modern city, these groupings, or subsets, consist of aggregates of buildings and their associated open spaces, devoted to similar functions such as residential, commercial, industrial, or recreational, and we can recognize the particular uniqueness of each set partly because of the repetition of specialized forms of which it is composed and partly because of the way individual elements of the group are related to one another. (The zoning ordinances in modern cities reinforce this kind of differential distribution of building types, but there is a tendency toward this even in more primitive societies.) In addition, the physical boundaries of each set are further defined by visual barriers such as walls, streets, and highways. In some cases the boundaries between subsets are difficult to perceive and one blends into the other, particularly when they are devoted to similar functions, as in the case of two contiguous residential neighborhoods. But almost any city can be visualized to some degree as being made up of districts and neighborhoods, which in turn are composed of even smaller discrete units. The city block, defined by streets on all four sides, is the most easily recognizable unit of this sort in the typical American city. Within the block, the houses or other buildings are arranged in a more or less orderly manner and we are acutely aware of any deviation from this norm.

In contrast to this, the Maya city, while consisting of even more strongly differentiated subsets of building elements, has no boundaries between sets in the form of streets and cannot, at the present time at least, be said to be zoned on the basis of function. While some differences in function may be inferred on the basis of building types, as discussed earlier in this chapter, these are only tentative and may lead to great confusion if we attempt to rely on functional differences between building groupings as a basis for analysis. In spite of this difficulty, it is possible to identify and characterize a number of archetypal building groupings or complexes of structures on the basis of

both form and organization. This can be done with no initial consideration of function or symbolic meaning.

Before attempting to describe what appear to be archetypal groupings, it may be useful to clarify the terminology which must be used in making clear distinctions between groupings. The term *form* is generally used to describe the general characteristics which are common to any class of objects or set of objects. For example, all chairs or tables can be said to have the same basic form, even though they may differ considerably in their specific details. (All tables have tops and supports and all chairs have seats, backs, and supports.) In a like manner, building types can be identified on the basis of form rather than function; we have already differentiated Maya temples from other buildings on the basis of a fundamental difference between a Puuc-style building and a Chenes-object or building as a way of describing the difference in its details from another object or building having the same form. *Style* is a more detailed aspect of design; the difference between a Puuc-style building and a Chenes-style building lies in the manner in which certain decorative elements are handled, but no essential difference in design or form exists.

At a larger scale, sets or groups of objects and structures can be said to have the same form on the basis of their spatial relationships to one another. Thus, for example, *quadrangles* constitute a specific category of architectural forms which may differ in design from one another and, in addition, tend to maintain this generic identification without regard for function or cultural content. The Nunnery Quadrangle at Uxmal has the same basic form as any quadrangle on a modern college campus, but it would be a mistake to assume any similarity in function or meaning because of this. The notion of form, then, has reference to structural relationships among the individual parts of a larger entity which we perceive as something more fundamental than design or style. Furthermore, we can grasp the notion of form without any initial reference to function or to any specific meaning we may choose to associate with it. This makes it possible to analyze Maya cities on the basis of form once we are able to set aside temporarily questions of function or symbolic meaning. The formal relationships which give them their order are abstractions which do not belong to any particular time or place. They may not have the same meaning to us as they did to their builders, but the basic order is still comprehensible.

If it is meaningful to use the word *form* to describe our way of recognizing the essential unity of groups of objects or buildings, it is also useful to use the term *organization* to represent the specific relationships among a number of these individual groups or forms. It might be argued that organization is simply the notion of form extended to a larger scale, but there does seem to be an essential difference which can be described in this way: We tend to think of physical organizations, such as cities, as being linear, radial, concentric, cellular, axial, omnidirectional, dispersed, etc., all of which refer to the notion of composition rather than form. This may be a fine distinction, but very necessary, since we tend to speak of large aggregates of buildings such as a Maya ceremonial center or city as being *composed* of certain basic forms. It also can be seen that decisions in regard to composition depend on a different set of factors than those which generate form ideas, giving added weight to the necessity of making a distinction between them. Compositions can be predicted on considerations as diverse as a concern for making a good "fit" to existing topographical features, arbitrary aesthetic notions, or simply making good use of whatever elements we happen to have on hand at any given moment. In the last instance, the number or kind of elements is not very important. Forms, on the other hand, are very much concerned with numbers and kinds and have nothing to do with accidental or fortuitous relationships. In the discussion of basic groupings which follows, it will be necessary to concentrate on questions of form, leaving questions involving organization to the discussion of individual cities.

What we have called *Basic Building Groupings* are those archetypal forms of building complexes which tend to be repeated with minor variations throughout the entire Maya area. This leads us to believe, among other things, that they proved themselves to be exceptionally useful either on functional or symbolic grounds. Under the heading of *Basic Elements* we have also described the generic building forms such as temples, palaces, ball courts, etc., and the basic forms of open spaces such as plazas, platforms, terraces, and courtyards, which have been combined together in particular ways to produce the larger forms we are now considering. A careful examination of the twenty site plans included in the present study indicates that there are four of these groupings which occur so frequently and whose forms are so unique that they deserve special attention. For purposes of discussion these will be called *Temple Groups, Palace Groups, Quadrangle Groups,* and *Acropolis Groups.* In addition to these four major categories, there are two other distinctive groupings: the twin-pyramid groups at Tikal and the special astronomical assemblages at Uaxactun and other sites in the southern areas, both of which represent important but restricted additions to this fairly limited vocabulary of forms. (See description of Tikal in chapter 7 for a discussion of twin-pyramid complexes.)

It must be kept in mind, however, that any particular form is not necessarily limited to a single function, and a quadrangle at one site may have a different function than the same form at another site. Still, it is possible that an analysis of a number of similar forms will yield some clues in regard to function, since the actual decision to use a form is based on some idea of appropriateness in relation to use. Quite apart from contemporary notations of *functionalism*, it is clear that any form is restricted in terms of its usefulness, which depends to some extent on the minimum physical or visual requirements associated with any specific activity or set of activities. This reduces the range of possible functions with respect to any particular form but still leaves open the question of which spe-

55

cific function is most probable. It must also be kept in mind that differences in design within any form category may suggest further division into subcategories, but the whole notion of form rests on very general characteristics, which is self-limiting. Perhaps this will become more clear in the discussion of each of the basic groupings which follows.

Temple Groups

It was postulated earlier that the basic prototype for the more complex ceremonial center consisted of a single temple and pyramidal substructure in association with a level plaza. Evidence from a number of sites indicates that very early in the Classic period individual temples gave way in favor of groups of temples, although isolated temples still continued to be built. For the most part, however, building remains from the height of the Classic period indicate that temples were commonly constructed in groups of three in conjunction with a plaza or low platform. The frequency with which this grouping is encountered at various sites suggests that it should be considered as a generic form with specific functions and symbolic significance. If we include the possibility of substituting a small palace-type building for one of the temples without insisting that this substitution represents a new form idea, the number of these groupings increases to the point where they represent the largest class of forms among the four basic categories. In some cases, numerous variations of this grouping make up the greater part of the whole ceremonial precinct. (For example, see descriptions of Edzna and Oxkintok in chapter 7.)

In the discussion which follows, the term *temple* is used to represent the combination of temple building and supporting substructure, since other expressions such as pyramid-temple are awkward and may even be misleading. With this qualification, we can now look at an idealized Temple Group, which is shown in diagrammatic form in Figure 9.

In its simplest form, the Temple Group consists of a

set of three temples situated on three sides of a rectangular plaza, the fourth side being open. It must be emphasized immediately that the one open side to the plaza is critical to this form, since it established a unique set of relationships among the several elements of the group which would be altered significantly if all four sides were closed. A minimum of three temples (perhaps *ceremonial buildings* would be better) are required to complete this form, but additional structures may be added to any of the three sides of the plaza already occupied by buildings. It can be seen that in such an arrangement one of the temples faces toward the open end of the plaza while the other two face toward one another across the open space of the plaza below. A number of important relationships are built into this scheme, which establishes a clear hierarchy, or order of importance, among the three temples. This results from the position of the temple facing the open side of the plaza, which is singled out as being the

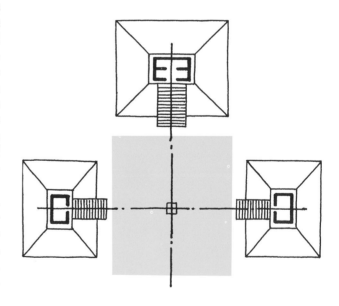

FIG. 9. Basic Temple Group.

most important. The pairing of the other two temples places them in a subordinate position. In addition, the open side of the plaza permits movement into and out of the inner, or private, open space belonging to this form. This "inside-outside" aspect is greatly reinforced by the solid masses of the temple substructures which bound the plaza.

Since the plaza is not completely shut off from its surroundings, either physically or visually, it maintains other relationships to a larger context in addition to the circulation connection provided by its open end. These basic relationships can be modified, giving emphasis where it is wanted, by manipulation of the detailed aspects of the various elements forming the group, and these alterations can be made without destroying the basic form. Changes in height, size, spacing, and degree of complexity or visual interest among the individual temples, together with changes in size or shape of the plaza, all have some effect on how we respond to this form or interpret it. The introduction of altars or stelae within the larger space of the plaza may in turn create subordinate open spaces associated with only one structure.

The flexibility inherent in this form, owing to the built-in controls just described, makes it ideally suited to a variety of ritual or ceremonial activities involving large numbers of participants or spectators. If the spectators take positions around the periphery of the plaza with their backs to the temple substructures, their attention is focused on any activity taking place in the open space of the plaza. In contrast to this, the spectators may occupy the greater part of the open space of the plaza and direct their attention toward one of the temples where the activity is localized. It is also possible for several groups of individuals to be engaged simultaneously in separate activities involving all of the temples at the same time, since each group can be differentiated out by open space between and could face in different directions. Great processions can proceed into the plaza through its open end while only the select few move up the stairways and enter

the sacred precincts of the temples. The temples dominate the plaza below and proclaim their dual allegiance to earth and sky; below is the finite world of man, marked out by his own hands, while above is infinity, the realm of the gods.

It would be possible to outline even more elaborate visualizations of the various activities which could take place within the spaces of this idealized Temple Group. Our purpose, however, has been to dramatize the fact that this basic form has great possibilities of satisfying a variety of different needs, due to the fundamental relationships among its parts, and that changes in emphasis or details of the parts further extend the possibilities of diversification. The widespread elaboration of the basic Temple Group throughout the course of the Classic period suggests that ritual practices continually took on new forms as a means of pacifying or currying favor with the gods. These changes were then given visible form through changes in the specific design of temples or plazas with the hope of increasing the efficacy of the rituals. As these ideas made their way from one city to another, where they were subject to a variety of interpretations by groups of individuals who were normally isolated from one another, it is only natural that no exact carbon copies would be created in different locations. Under these circumstances, only the general form could be maintained, and it is the formal unity of placemaking ideas which gives all Maya cities their special character.

Four Temple Groups from different sites are shown in Figure 10. For purposes of comparison they have been drawn at the same scale and the plazas with which they are associated are shown in yellow. Among other things, these four Temple Groups demonstrate rather clearly the difference between form and design as defined earlier in this chapter. The groups at Piedras Negras and Palenque are much more irregular than the groups at Copan and Comalcalco, and the temple buildings in all four groups are different, both in size and plan arrangement. Both at Copan and Piedras Negras, the open side of the plaza is

57

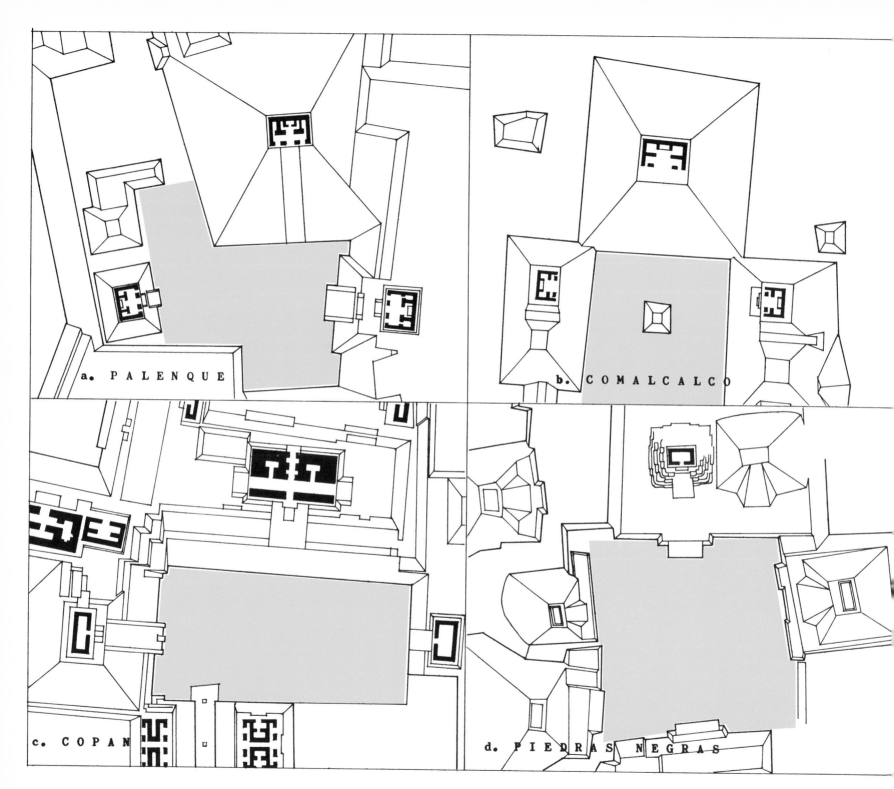

FIG. 10. Comparison of Temple Groups (Palenque, Comalcalco, Copan, Piedras Negras).

partially blocked off by a ball court, while the open side at Palenque is bounded by low terraces. There are also great differences in details of substructures, size and shape of plaza, positioning of stelae and altars, and height relationships among different temples, but in spite of these and other differences, the basic form is maintained. The greater irregularity of the groups at Palenque and Piedras Negras as compared with the more precise geometry of Copan and Comalcalco is due to the fact that the existing topography at the former sites is very irregular and the man-made structures have been fitted into existing hills and shelves, while the ground is essentially flat at the latter sites. (The tendency toward more precise geometric arrangements appears to be generally characteristic of all sites where the existing terrain is relatively flat.) While there may be no extant example at any site of a Temple Group in its pure or idealized form, the four groups illustrated are obviously efforts to maintain that ideal within the limits imposed by local conditions of terrain and architectural tradition.

Palace Groups

The term *Palace Group* has been selected to describe a complex of structures, generally of the palace type, related to one another in such a way as to form a nearly continuous wall of buildings around its outer periphery, behind which are other structures, positioned so as to create a series of inner courtyards, separated spatially by intervening buildings. This kind of complex is situated on a raised platform, which may consist of a number of different levels. The platform serves to differentiate the complex from the open spaces and structures surrounding it and acts as a strong unifying element for what might otherwise be a disorderly collection of buildings. Access into the inner buildings and courtyards is gained by passing through the peripheral buildings, which in turn are connected to the surrounding plazas by broad stairways.

In its simplest form, the Palace Group would consist of four palace-type buildings situated around the periphery

of a rectangular platform. These structures might be either gallery- or multichamber-type buildings, and there appears to be no strong preference. Behind the buildings forming the exterior of the complex are other palace-type structures and, occasionally, one or more temples. These additional structures are positioned roughly parallel or at right angles to the outer ring of structures so as to form a number of small rectilinear courtyards, some of which may be at a lower level than the main platform. Each courtyard is a discrete space, and access to any individual courtyard can normally be gained only from the structures immediately surrounding it. Various structures and courtyards are connected to one another by means of passageways, doorways, and stairways, facilitating movement within the complex, but there is no order of importance among the various paths of movement. In a like manner, there is no single building which can be singled out as being more important than the others (Fig. 11).

The lack of any implied hierarchy of spaces and structures is one of the unique aspects of this form and helps

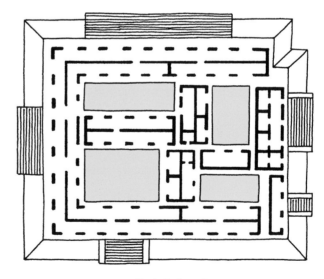

FIG. 11. Basic Palace Group.

59

to distinguish it from Acropolis Groups, which are characterized by a clear hierarchic ordering of specific spatial sequences. It is also important to recognize that the buildings situated on the outer periphery of the complex maintain a dual set of relationships with both the inner and outer spaces. Doorways and stairways connect these buildings to the plazas or open spaces external to the complex, while other doorways and stairways connect the same buildings to the inner courtyards, which are removed both physically and visually from the surrounding environment. The polarity created by these internal-external relationships also distinguishes the Palace Group from the Quadrangle Group, which is essentially inner-oriented.

The actual function, or functions, of a Palace Group are somewhat of an enigma. On one hand, it is strongly related to the public spaces of plazas or terraces which it confronts along one or more of its sides, which suggests public ceremonial activity involving both the plazas and the peripheral buildings of the palace complex. On the other hand, the inner courtyards and buildings of the complex are fairly private and not readily accessible from the outside. The semipublic character of this group suggests that it might have functioned as a work and living place for neophytes, who were trained in the arts of astronomy, numeration, and hieroglyphic writing. The temples within the complex would have served admirably as private places of worship for this elite group, and some of the lesser, or minor, buildings might well have been used for the preparation of ritual materials or equipment used in connection with its assumed school function. It is not yet a cloister, entirely detached from the world of man and nature alike, yet its inner spaces are cut off from contact with the outside world, creating places suitable for the more abstract world of the mind: a primitive form of university, perhaps.

The picture we have just drawn of the idealized Palace Group is, of necessity, oversimplified, and it must not be assumed that the development of this form is the consequence of a premeditated design in which "form follows function." Palace Groups as we know them (Middle and Late Classic periods) represent accretions which took place over long periods of time; a group's form underwent many changes as buildings were added or remodeled and its supporting platform was raised and extended. Excavations within several of these complexes indicate clearly that the Palace Group evolved from the basic Temple Group and therefore appears later in the history of Maya placemaking than the prototype Temple Group.

Proof of this assertion is found in the data obtained from careful excavation of a Palace Group at Uaxactun which was given the prosaic designation of Structure A-V. In its earliest form, this group consisted of three temples situated on a low platform, as shown in the upper drawing in Figure 12. This is the generic Temple Group in its simplest form. Over a period of nearly four hundred years, this small Temple Group evolved into the Palace Group shown in the lower drawing in Figure 12. Seven distinct construction stages are represented in this transition and it is clear that the Palace Group represents an entirely different set of functions than the Temple Group. Among other things, this indicates that during this four-hundred-year interval great changes had taken place within the structure and organization of Maya society as a whole. These changes are in the direction of greater specialization and differentiation of function and greater emphasis on secular activity over purely ritual activity. In time, further changes might have led to even more specialized forms, but the collapse of Maya society shortly after the flowering of the Palace Group leaves us with a complex form whose specific functions are still largely unknown.

Three Palace Groups from different cities are shown in Figure 13, including Structure A-V at Uaxactun, which was referred to above. The complexes at Palenque and Uaxactun are considerably more compact than the group at Tikal, but all show the same form characteristics as outlined earlier, despite their differences in size and specific make-up. It is not possible to reconstruct the step-by-step evolution of the final forms at Palenque and Tikal as

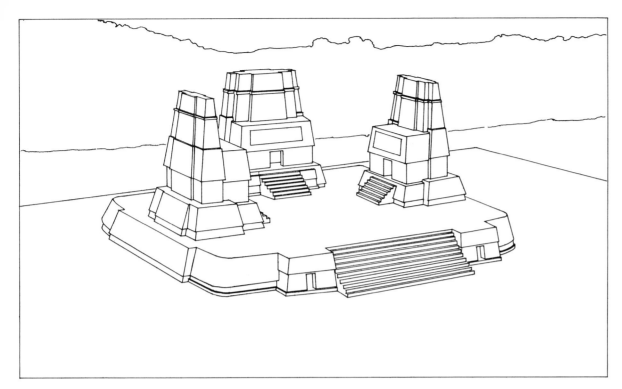

FIG. 12. Evolution of Palace Group
from Temple Group—Structure A-V,
Uaxactun (after Proskouriakoff).

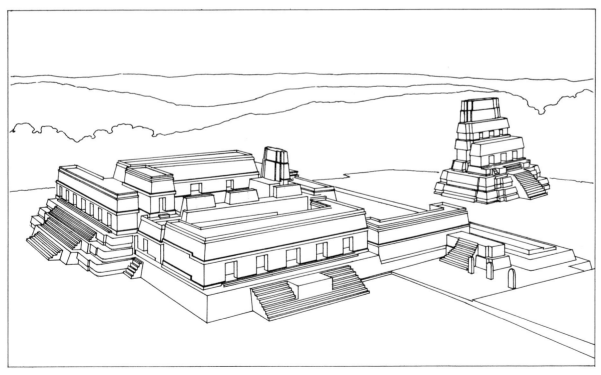

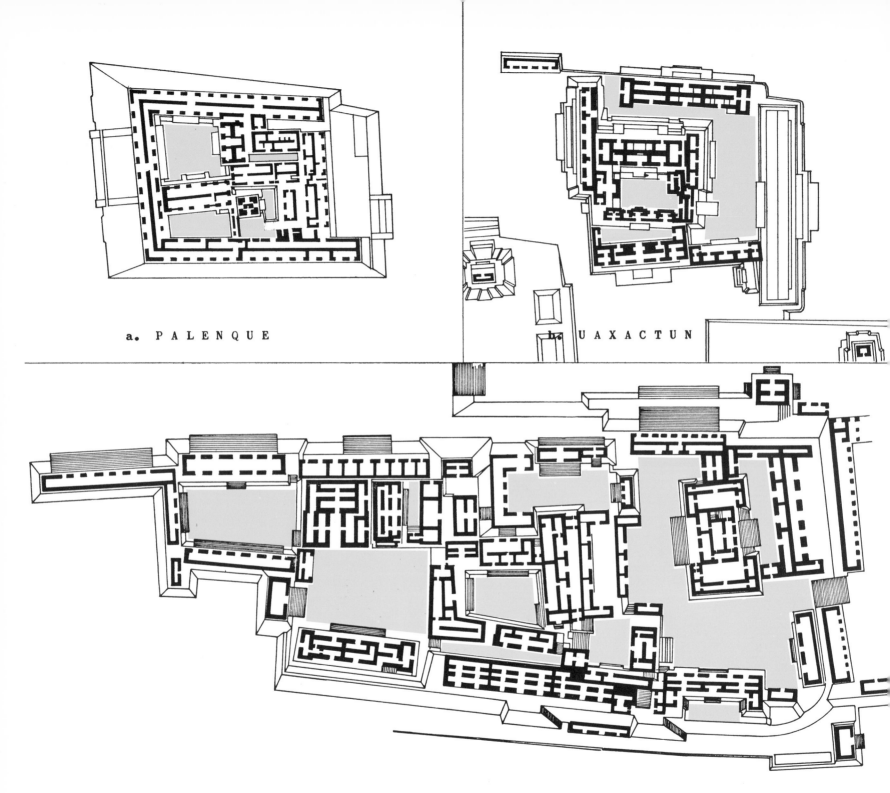

a. PALENQUE

b. UAXACTUN

FIG. 13. Comparison of Palace Groups (Palenque, Uaxactun, Tikal).

has been done at Uaxactun, but it is clear from even a cursory examination of the standing remains at these latter sites that they also represent accretions over a long period of time.[3] It is also clear, however, that considerable effort was made to retain some unity in the enlarged schemes as new elements were added, even though the relationships among the individual elements changed appreciably. In all three examples we are confronted with a variety of building types, including a tower in the case of Palenque, as well as temple-type structures, gallery-type structures, and multichambered, multistoried buildings of several kinds. One of the buildings on the south side of the group at Tikal is actually five stories high.

A closer look at the group at Tikal seems in order, inasmuch as it is the most complex group illustrated and embodies so clearly the general characteristics which have been specified for Palace Groups in general (Fig. 13). Several features in particular are worth noting. First, the polarity between interior and exterior orientations is very pronounced. The majority of the structures along the north side of the group are connected with two separate external plazas by means of monumental stairways. The buildings on the east side also connect to plazas or courts lying outside the complex, but in a less monumental fashion. At the same time, several of these same structures open to interior courtyards, but the specific nature of these connections varies considerably. It can also be noted that several of the structures on the south side open toward a large reservoir, and it is tempting to think that the "view" obtained was important in the siting of these buildings.

Second, most of the buildings are organized around eight interior courtyards, and each of these subgroups

forms a slightly different arrangement. In some cases the individual structures are situated on raised platforms with respect to the courtyard, while in other instances they are on the same level. There are differences in degrees of privacy attained within different buildings and within different courtyards. No two elements are alike and it is this marked differentiation of elements, coupled with the lack of a clear internal circulation system, which suggests the multipurpose character of the whole complex. For the moment, we can only reiterate the suggestion that a Palace Group most likely represents a combination of administrative, educational, and residential functions. A more definitive case must await further excavation.

Quadrangle Groups

The term *Quadrangle Group*, when used to describe an architectural form, refers to any grouping of buildings which form a more or less continuous enclosure around all four sides of an open courtyard or square. It is not necessary that the open space of the quadrangle be completely enclosed, nor is it necessary that each side consist of a single building, but in its simplest form it does consist of four long buildings which are sometimes joined at the corners. In the case of Maya quadrangles, the individual buildings do not engage each other at the corner intersections, although the spaces left between the buildings do not serve as entryways. Entry into the open space of the courtyard is accomplished through one or more of the peripheral buildings by means of doorways or archways cut through these buildings at their center points. The whole complex is situated on a large platform, which removes it both physically and visually from the surrounding terrain (Fig. 14).

The sense of removal is further heightened by the fact that the enclosed spaces of the peripheral buildings tend to be oriented toward the inner space of the court rather than the exterior. This is not exclusively the case, however, and some doorways may be found in the exterior walls facing outward. In spite of this, the distinguishing hall-

---

[3] Additional excavation and restoration of the Palace Groups at Tikal and Palenque were being carried out as this was being written. A more definitive sequence of construction has been worked out at Tikal and it appears that there was a general extension of the group from west to east during the late Classic period (A.D. 550 to 900). The plans as shown here will have to be revised once this work is completed.

mark of the Quadrangle Group lies in its quality of being exclusive, or inner-oriented. It turns its back, so to speak,

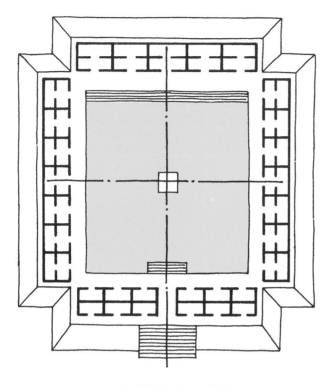

FIG. 14. Basic Quadrangle Group.

on its surroundings and focuses its attention on its own private world. In this sense it functions as a cloister, a place set apart from the ordinary events of life, where all activity can be regulated according to a predetermined order. The internal environment within the quadrangle is pervaded by a sense of quiet repose, which is expressed in the geometrical precision of its plan arrangement and the implied symmetry of its form. The plan shape of the quadrangle tends toward a square, as any excessive elongation of one of its dimensions produces a void space

which is highly directional or mall-like; with any further elongation, the open space would become a street. The open space of the courtyard is truly a man-made space and even if it is planted as a garden it is not really part of nature. (The courtyards of Maya quadrangles were always paved.) Multiple doorways in the surrounding buildings open toward the courtyard and broad terraces in front of the buildings encourage the user to proceed along the pathway formed by the terraces rather than cross through the open space of the courtyard. We may be drawn out into the open space by means of ceremonies taking place in connection with an altar or stela, but the open space is a powerful abstract symbol, complete in itself, and requires no activation beyond its physical presence.

In Maya cities, Quadrangle Groups are found as discrete elements, related to, but isolated physically from, other building elements, or as parts of an even larger complex such as an Acropolis Group. The Nunnery quadrangle at Uxmal, shown in Figure 15, is an example of the first condition, while the Acropolis Group at the same site is partially composed of several quadrangular forms. The remains of Quadrangle Groups can be observed at many sites, but most of these are in such an advanced state of ruin that only their general outlines can now be perceived. A quadrangle at Tikal, which is better preserved than most, is also shown in Figure 15. Using these two examples, a more careful analysis of the internal and external relationships of a Quadrangle Group can be made.

It can be noted from the plan drawings in Figure 15 that the buildings of both Quadrangle Groups are situated on high platforms, with access to the upper level of the platform effected by means of broad stairways situated on the south sides. The inner courtyard of the quadrangle at Tikal is raised only slightly above the surrounding ground level, while at Uxmal it is nearly thirty feet above the level of the plaza to the south. At Uxmal, the courtyard can be entered directly by means of a vaulted archway which passes through the south building, while at Tikal it is necessary to pass through two successive rooms of the

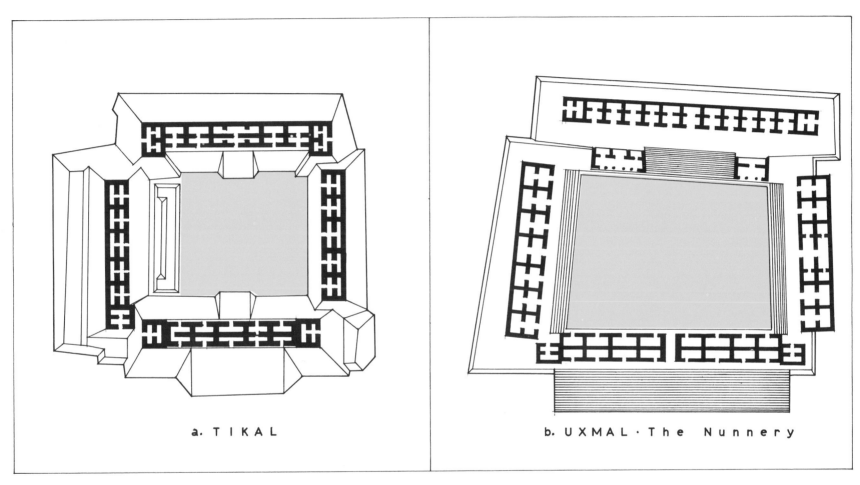

a. TIKAL

b. UXMAL · The Nunnery

FIG. 15. Comparison of Quadrangle Groups (Uxmal and Tikal).

south building before gaining entrance into the inner court. At both sites the buildings forming the quadrangle consist of long palace-type structures, each of which is made up of two parallel rows of small rooms. Most of these rooms are in pairs, one room behind the other, which can be entered only from the inner court, but again in both cases the buildings on the south side have doorways opening both to the court and to the exterior. This gives special emphasis to the entrance side without taking too much away from the cloister effect. Having passed through the archway at Uxmal, it is possible to proceed directly into the open space of the court at the same level, while at Tikal the level of the courtyard is appreciably lower than the level of the main platform and a further stairway is required.

While the plan shapes of both groups are essentially square, both manage to become very directional, although the inherent tendency toward symmetry is overcome by different means in each case. At Uxmal, the directionality has been accomplished in part by raising the north building considerably higher than the east and west buildings, both of which are at a slightly higher elevation than the south building, and by emphasizing its façade over the other façades through changes in decorative detail. At Tikal, there appears to be little difference in height between the individual buildings, and the directionality is due to the emphasis placed on the north-south axis by the positions of the two stairways leading down into the courtyard. The main entrance stairway from the exterior is also on this same axis. The low platform on the west side of the courtyard, which has no counterpart on the east side, further destroys the potential symmetry. A more complete description and analysis of the quadrangle at Uxmal will be found in the description of that site which appears in a later section. Our immediate purpose in going this far with issues involving symmetry and directionality has been to point out once more that differences at the level of design do not destroy the integrity of basic forms

and the two Quadrangle Groups illustrated tend to bear this out.

It is still on open question as to what functions took place in these and other similar quadrangles. The term *Nunnery* has been used to describe the quadrangle at Uxmal on the basis of the almost endless repetition of cell-like spaces surrounding the inner courtyard. These cells are highly reminiscent of the small living spaces found in nunneries or monasteries throughout the Old World. Unfortunately, there is no real evidence to support this presumed function; the reasoning is only by analogy. Still, the rooms *are* cell- or hutlike, and, in spite of the fact that they are not really suitable for ordinary living functions, it is difficult to suggest alternative possibilities which are more logical. The fact that all of the rooms are nearly identical suggests a common function, shared equally by all, though there is some implied order of importance among the individual sets of rooms due to the conscious effort to avoid the equalizing effects of mirror-image symmetry. The relationship of the rooms to the open space of the court suggests activities involving both spaces simultaneously, and this involvement was more likely visual rather than physical. It is easy to imagine some important ceremonial activity taking place in the open spaces of the courtyard involving large numbers of spectators, who are then forced to leave the enclosure while the priests or active participants retire to the small rooms surrounding the court for meditation and prayer. But to use the same spaces as permanent living quarters is another matter.

In spite of the uncertainty which we are forced to accept with respect to its function, the Maya Quadrangle Group, in common with any quadrangle, expresses certain notions of withdrawal, privacy, and introspection by means of the formal language of architecture. The community which is created within its walls is a private one and its conscious removal from the larger community which surrounds it speaks of some special purpose to which it is devoted. The basic language of form has no boundaries in time or place and the scores of quadrangular forms which continue to be built in our own time attest to this. We may question whether many of these serve any special purpose of the sort we have postulated for the Mayas, but the intention is the same symbolically. What is wanted is a cloister, a place to carry on our affairs in seclusion from the ordinary events of life. The quadrangle has the formal capability of providing this atmosphere in full measure.

Acropolis Groups

The term *Acropolis Group* is somewhat misleading when applied to certain building groupings in Maya cities if we project the image of the Acropolis in Athens as our model for this complex. The Greek Acropolis is, in fact, a citadel, and the great wall which surrounds it is an essential part of the concept, giving form to and providing protection for the space within. A more general definition of an acropolis describes it as "a settlement located on an eminence," which does not imply that an enclosing wall is a necessary part of the form. If we accept this more general definition, the term *acropolis* can be applied to a number of building complexes, in certain Maya cities, which exhibit a range of similar characteristics, even though none of them have enclosing walls. Some Maya scholars have been inclined to use the word *acropolis* rather freely, and it has been applied somewhat indiscriminately to a number of aggregations of buildings which do not constitute a class based on similarity of form. A more limited view of the notion of acropolis as used in this discussion is based on the following general form characteristics.

The Maya Acropolis Group consists of a number of related structures of the palace or temple type, which are situated at various levels on a large platform or, more precisely, a series of platforms. In general, the sides of these supporting structures are articulated into a series of steeply sloping steps, which is characteristic of nearly all Maya substructures, large or small. Access to the upper levels of the acropolis is by means of stairways located at strategic points, thus establishing very controlled paths of movement into the complex from the plaza or terrace at the base of the supporting platform. The major stairway(s) gives access to a series of courtyards and their associated structures, which are organized sequentially; movement from one space to another can only be accomplished along a predetermined path. The sequence culminates in the most important building within the complex, usually a temple, and this building occupies a position which is the farthest removed from the plaza below both in terms of height and distance. The pre-eminence of this singular building is reinforced by the fact that it is likely to be at the highest point within the entire city as well as within its own context.

From the doorway(s) of the all-important temple we can look down into the cascade of courtyards and structures below and retrace the upward path which traverses the open spaces of the courts before passing through the archways or doorways of large palace-type structures which divide one court from the other. Beyond are other large complexes of structures; those lying closest to the acropolis are linked with it by means of great plazas which tie them together both physically and visually. An explicit sense of order pervades this environment—a purposeful order which sets up a hierarchy of places, and it cannot be overemphasized that the distinguishing form characteristic of the acropolis is its insistence on the order of importance among the various elements of which it is composed. This ordering system depends on position rather than size or building type for its effectiveness, and the position of any element or subgroup within the sequence establishes its relative importance to the whole. The subgroups may take the form of Temple Groups, Palace Groups, or Quadrangle Groups, but the unique relationships among them gives rise to a larger and more complex form in which the smaller groupings are useful only to the extent that they reinforce the central idea of progression from public to private, or secular to sacred. The basic elements of the acropolis and the manner in which

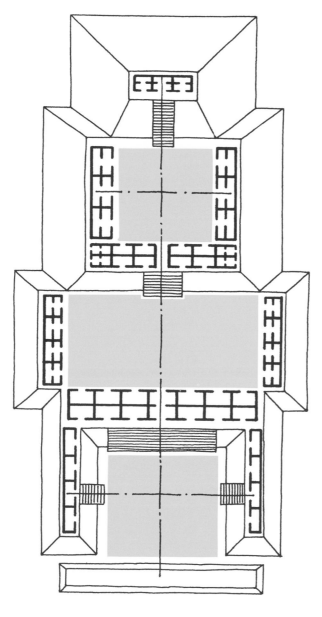

FIG. 16. Basic Acropolis Group.

they might be arranged is shown in the accompanying diagram (Fig. 16). The diagram has been simplified in order to show the formal organization more clearly, but it is based on the Acropolis Group at Uxmal.

It might be useful to draw some comparisons between the four Acropolis Groups shown in Figure 17 as a means of further clarifying the nature of the acropolis concept. The plans of these groups have been drawn to the same scale to facilitate direct comparison of dimensions and building types. Four distinct geographical regions are represented by these complexes, and the basic-form notion of acropolis has been modified to some extent in each case by topographical or other local conditions. Uxmal is situated in the state of Yucatan, Mexico, an area which is characterized by very rocky, though relatively flat, terrain covered by scrub jungle. Piedras Negras is located adjacent to a large river in the department of Peten, Guatemala, and this river at present marks the boundary between Mexico and Guatemala. The Peten region is characterized by many low hills and ridges interspersed with rivers and swamps. Edzna is located in the state of Campeche, Mexico, near the head of a large valley surrounded by low hills. The existing terrain is slightly irregular and one side of the Main Acropolis is adjacent to a large *aguada*. Comalcalco is situated in the state of Tabasco, Mexico, not far from the Gulf of Mexico. Here again, the land is very flat and subject to partial inundation during the rainy season. This area is also totally lacking in limestone, which is found so abundantly in the balance of the Maya area.

The preceding digression into questions of geography and topography has been necessary in order to set the stage for a closer look at the four groups being considered. The differences which can be noted among them in terms of plan organization, geometrical configuration, building types, and architectural style are indicative of the degree to which the basic form ideas which were current throughout the Maya area were modified by local conditions of

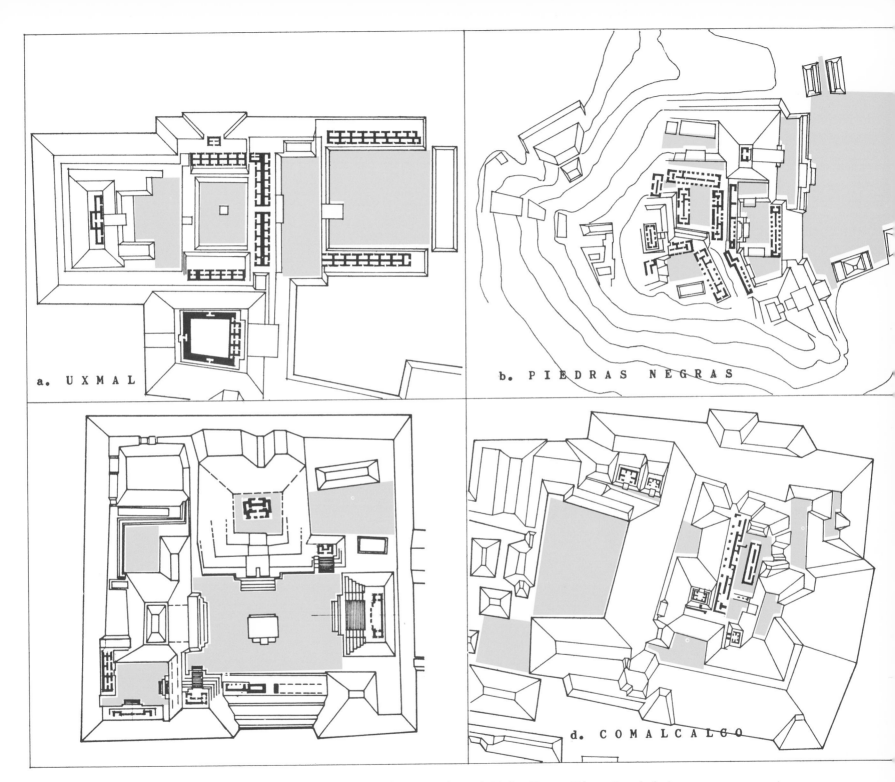

a. UXMAL

b. PIEDRAS NEGRAS

d. COMALCALCO

FIG. 17. Comparison of Acropolis Groups (Uxmal, Piedras Negras, Edzna, Comalcalco).

topography and climate as well as local traditions involving decorative details. The complexes at Uxmal, Edzna, and Comalcalco appear to be entirely man-made constructions, built up on fairly level existing ground planes, while the group at Piedras Negras has been built on an existing hill which has been reshaped into a rising series of courtyards and terraces by a process of cut and fill (Fig. 56). In order to avoid excessive cutting and filling at this latter site, buildings have been positioned so as to take best advantage of existing contours, and the shape and size of courtyards have been modified on the same basis. The greater irregularity of the scheme at Piedras Negras might better be termed *organic*, since it is an obvious effort to respond to the existing environment, while the other schemes can be called *formalistic*, in the sense that they are impositions on the existing environment and their ordering is external to the fortuituous features of nature. In all cases, however, the basic-form notion of acropolis has been maintained and each group achieves a degree of monumentality that sets it apart from the balance of the city or center in which it appears.

The groups at Edzna and Comalcalco are considerably less complex than those at either Uxmal or Piedras Negras, but both are fairly elaborate when compared with typical Temple or Quadrangle groups. The sequential ordering of spaces is also less clear at Comalcalco, though this is due in part to the total disintegration of the stairways, which would otherwise indicate the path(s) of movement within the complex. It is clear, however, that the main approach to the upper levels was from the large plaza described by the two arms extending out from the main mass and forming a space enclosed on three sides. Undoubtedly there were other secondary points of access, but these are even more difficult to locate. It is also interesting to note that palace-type buildings rather than temples appear to be the most important structures in all of these groups, but this does not disturb the basic hierarchy which we have already pointed out as being based on position rather than building type.

The more elaborate Acropolis Groups at Uxmal and Piedras Negras are considerably alike in basic conception, although this is not readily apparent at first glance. The contrast between the rigid geometry of Uxmal and the organic irregularity of Piedras Negras tends to set up an artificial polarity which has to do with pattern and shape rather than spatial organization and form. A closer look reveals that both conform very closely to the ideal acropolis form as described earlier. That is to say, the central organizing idea for these two groups produces a scheme in which the individual open spaces and buildings are arranged in a continuous succession of solids and voids which moves in a progression from most accessible and most public to least accessible and most private. The progression is controlled by distance and height; the higher we are allowed to go and the farther away we move from the open public space, the closer we get to the realm of the gods, where only the privileged may enter. The courtyards are shut off from one another and from the plaza below by intervening buildings or high terraces, which heightens the effect of the progression (Fig. 222). The same concept has been utilized in building groups throughout the world wherever societies have been organized on the basis of rank and privilege, and the Maya Acropolis Group is a powerful statement which gives visible form to the established hierarchic order at a grand scale. The temple at Karnak or the palace at Versailles are hardly more impressive.

The continuous rebuilding and enlargement of the Acropolis Groups which have just been discussed are evident even from unexcavated surface remains and suggest that as time went on the organization of Maya society became increasingly more complex, calling for a succession of more sophisticated versions of the acropolis concept as a means of expressing these changes in organization. These great complexes are still impressive, even in their ruined state, and serve to remind us once more of the extent to which societies are willing to invest their surplus energy in constructing monuments that have no practical value, but answer instead to a deep-rooted need to alter, and thereby humanize, the natural environment at the largest possible scale. The specific functions which took place in the acropolis can only be guessed at, and only in our mind's eye can we visualize the activities which at one time breathed life into the empty plazas and ruined palaces which still remain. Nevertheless, the symbolic value of the spatial form has lost none of its force and we are inclined to tread lightly as we walk through the sacred precincts lest we disturb the old order. The conceptualization and development of this sophisticated form is surely a true measure of the degree of civilization attained by the Mayas.

Special Astronomical Assemblages

Before we bring this section to a close, some mention must be made of the building groups which have been called *special astronomical assemblages,* even though they occur too infrequently to be added to our list of generic building groupings. The basic grouping consists of four terraces, or substructures, arranged in quadrilateral form around a small plaza. The western side of the plaza is occupied by a pyramid-temple while the terrace on the eastern side supports three temple-type structures with stairways leading up from the plaza. In front of the eastern terrace are three stelae with altars, all of which are associated with the central stairway and temple. From the stairway of the pyramid on the west side of the plaza, line-of-sight readings could be taken on the three temples across the plaza at the times of the solstices and equinoxes, as illustrated in Figure 18. There are twelve known examples of this

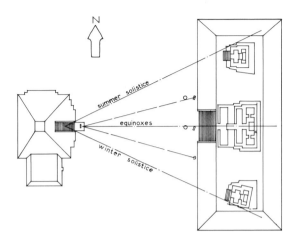

FIG. 18. Special astronomical assemblage—
Uaxactun (after Ricketson).

kind of grouping, but they are confined to the northern Peten and southern Campeche areas. While a good case can be made that Group E at Uaxactun (shown in Figure 18) had some astronomical significance, Karl Ruppert has pointed out that there is no significant correlation between the geographic locations and orientations of these groupings at the different sites, which negates the possibility that they were erected for making a common set of astronomical observations. He also suggests that, while the original model (Uaxactun) may have been for astronomical purposes, the others at more provincial centers might have become merely symbolic. (Ruppert and Denison: 1943.)

6.

Building Technology

Any discussion of Maya city building would not be complete without some description of the technological means which were employed in carrying out these conceptions. The earliest buildings of any sort constructed by the Mayas were undoubtedly made entirely of wood and other perishable materials. There is no way of knowing at what point the wood-and-thatch-roofed hut first made its appearance within the Maya area, nor is there any way of estimating how long it might have taken for this generic form to evolve from a cruder prototype model. A good many centuries must have been required, however, before the fairly refined version of the hut, as reconstructed from excavations at several important sites, was finally crystallized. The use of stone for building purposes was initially confined to the construction of very low platforms. Loose stones held together with mud could be used for this purpose and tamped earth served as a fill. In time, the platforms became larger and more complex, requiring the use of larger quantities of stone, which also had to be roughly shaped. These constructions were still very crude by any standards, however, and involve only an incipient notion of architecture. The dawn of Maya architecture begins with the late Preclassic or Early Classic period.

Very little is known at present regarding the developmental, or Preclassic, phase of Maya building, during which the ceremonial platform first came into being, but excavations have revealed that prior to the beginning of the Classic period the Mayas had already mastered the technique of quarrying and shaping the soft limestone which lay just under the surface of the soil throughout much of the area under their control. They had also learned the art of burning this same limestone in order to make lime cement and could raise and cement into place sufficient quantities of rubble and rough-cut limestone to form the large platforms or masonry substructures which mark the beginning of the formalized ceremonial center.

Recent excavations at Dzibilchaltun and Tikal indicate that low platforms faced with mud and loose rock and covered with plaster were being built prior to 600 B.C. By 300 to 250 B.C., large ceremonial platforms and terraced pyramids were being built, where walls were formed of rough-cut stone blocks, also covered with plaster. At this time, superstructures appear to have been made of poles and thatch. Within a short space of time, perhaps as early as A.D. 50, the builders were able to extend the use of masonry into the erection of massive corbeled-vault buildings, which became the hallmark of Maya building efforts during the course of the classic period. These two versions of the same basic material (limestone and limestone cement), together with small quantities of wood which were sometimes employed in making lintels over doorways or cross ties in vaults, constituted the entire catalog of building materials employed by the Mayas for major building purposes. Earth and rubble were used for fill purposes, and wooden huts continued to serve for residences and minor structures, but the basic building technology was confined to limestone masonry as described. The only notable exception to this occurred at the site of Comalcalco in the state of Tabasco, Mexico, where burned-clay bricks were used in place of the traditional limestone. This represents a special case, however, which will be discussed more fully in the description of that city.

The quarrying and shaping of limestone was accomplished entirely by means of stone tools, as metals of any kind were unknown to the Mayas. Local flints and cherts as well as obsidian imported from other areas were used in making the tools required for stonecutting and for the axes needed in felling and cutting trees. The process of quarrying limestone using only stone tools was not as difficult as it might seem, since the stone is rather soft while it is in the ground and hardens upon exposure to the air.[1] All building operations were limited to hand labor, as the Mayas did not understand the use of the wheel in making vehicles or mechanical lifting devices and had no domesticated beasts of burden. In spite of the inherent limitations imposed by indigenous building materials and hand-labor building techniques, the Mayas were able to construct thousands of buildings and substructures, large and small, with a degree of precision and refinement that rivals anything from the Old World.

The total expenditure of human effort involved in this construction is staggering,[2] and we are led to wonder if slave or conscripted labor was required to perform the more menial building tasks, such as transporting and lifting cut stones or rubble-fill material. A smaller corps of skilled building workers of all kinds would have been required for the more exacting tasks, and they undoubtedly worked at their occupations on a full-time basis. But, regardless of how the labor was supplied, the great pyramidal substructures and temples were built, and the extremely laborious methods of transport and building procedures employed must have stretched out the time required for the erection of large complexes of buildings to

periods of many years. Even when a large number of people can be employed simultaneously in building operations, there comes a point where any increase in numbers reduces the efficiency of the process, since they tend to get in each other's way. Details of the specific processes employed in building are not our real concern, however, and have been touched on only to indicate the magnitude of the problems involved.

The general technology employed in the construction of stone-masonry buildings is of greater interest, however, since the technology employed at any given moment sets certain limits on what can actually be built as opposed to what might be desired. Individual building forms and, by extension, the city as a whole are both limited to the availability of building materials and to the extant knowledge in regard to how these materials can be put together to form structural or decorative components. The development of masonry buildings, roofed over with a corbeled masonry vault (one of the distinguishing features of Maya architecture), appears to have taken place shortly before the beginning of the Early Classic period, as building remains from the Preclassic period show little positive evidence of the presence of stone vaults.[3] It seems most likely that temple buildings, in their earliest form, were little more than formalized variations of the wood-and-thatch hut which was normally used for dwelling purposes. There are many instances of substructures dating from the late Preclassic and Early Classic periods which show clear evidence of having at one time supported wooden buildings which were essentially the same size and shape as dwellings. The corner post holes of those buildings, which can still be found intact where they were preserved by later superimposition, give us firm evidence of their location and size and point clearly to the hut form. This prototype can still be seen in the stone mosaics of Puuc-style

---

[1] In an experiment carried out in 1964, it was found that one man, using a hardwood post as the only tool, excavated 1,700 kilos of stone in a five-hour work period. Since about 1,440 kilos of rock are used in a cubic meter of masonry, this means that one man could excavate sufficient rock in one five-hour day to provide the material for nearly four square meters of finish wall, assuming the wall to be about a foot thick. (Erasmus: 1965.)

[2] As a result of the experiment referred to earlier, it was calculated that the total labor input for the major ceremonial structures at Uxmal including fill, masonry, stonecutting, and stone sculpturing totaled seven and one-half million man-days of labor. Stretched out over a period of two hundred and fifty years, the length of time assumed for the occupancy of Uxmal, this figure is not so overwhelming, as it comes to only thirty thousand man-days of labor per year. (Erasmus: 1965.) It must be pointed out that these figures do not include the labor required in razing old buildings and rebuilding new structures in the same location several times. A good guess would be that the total amount of labor required would be tripled or quadrupled if these superimpositions were taken into account.

[3] There is some reason to believe that buildings roofed with crude corbeled vaults were being erected at Tikal as early as A.D. 50, but this is not yet fully verified (Coe: 1965).

73

building is represented by a thatched-roof building whose models of wooden huts (Fig. 255).

It is not yet possible to determine at precisely what point in time the corbeled masonry vault first made its appearance at some unknown place within the Maya expanse, but it appears no later than A.D. 300 in both the southern and northern areas. It is clear that the concept of the vault was developed *in situ*, since none of the adjoining cultures preceding or contemporary with the Mayas ever used similar vaulting. For this reason, the presence of corbeled or concrete masonry vaulting provides a positive means of identifying building remains as being Maya in origin.

The physical fact of the post holes, as described in the preceding paragraph, indicates that the first stage leading to the development of the Classic Maya corbeled-vault building is represented by a thatched-roof building whose lower walls were constructed of poles, covered with mud or lime plaster. The structural system employed in making the roof over these walls requires a structural frame supported on four corner posts which are independent of the walls. The corner posts are joined together by horizontal beams which, in turn, support a series of sloping members serving as rafters. In order to prevent the rafters from pushing out the horizontal beams or the walls, they are tied together across the bottom by horizontal members which span the short dimension of the enclosed space. To prevent the sloping rafters from sagging too much under the weight of the imposed thatching, they may be tied together horizontally at the half or third points as well as at the bottom with additional poles. The joints, where one member meets another, are tied together with vines or other pliable material, and the whole frame forms a stable skeleton which may be reused many times by replacing the more perishable materials which are used to cover the roof and walls (Fig. 19-a).

Many variations in size or shape are possible, utilizing the basic system of construction just described, and fairly long buildings can be obtained by increasing the number of poles used as vertical supports and by enlarging the size of individual framing members. There is no evidence of very large buildings ever having been constructed by the Mayas in this manner, however; the small, single-room hut with rounded or square ends is the basic model.

The next step beyond this wooden model in the making of a masonry building consists of replacing the wooden lower walls with masonry walls of the same height. Since the roof structure is independent of the walls, this step can be accomplished with no basic change in building form or size. Masonry walls of this type would not have to be very heavy, since they support none of the roof load (Fig. 19-b). The wooden corner poles used to support the roof can be omitted, however, and the weight of the roof transferred directly to the walls, as shown in Figure 19-c. The lower portions of walls or buildings of this type have been uncovered in excavations at a number of sites, and a very large structure of this type has recently been reconstructed at Edzna (Figs. 167, 168). This intermediate type of construction represents an important technological advance over the wooden building, as the walls are now much more permanent and may be used as a base for decorative elements, which can be painted or otherwise applied on, or carved into, the surface of the stonework. Again, it is clear that this construction technique could not have been introduced simultaneously throughout the entire Maya area, but the specific place at which it originated is still unknown.

The final stage in the development of a building that is constructed entirely of masonry consists of erecting a corbeled stone vault on top of masonry walls that previously supported a wood-and-thatch roof. We can only guess whether the concept of the corbeled vault was the result of a single stroke of genius on the part of some unknown architect or craftsman or whether it resulted from a long series of experiments carried out consciously in an effort to devise a more permanent roof construction. In either case, the corbeled vault proved itself to be a huge success, and stone vaults became the order of the day throughout the entire Maya area. The structural prin-

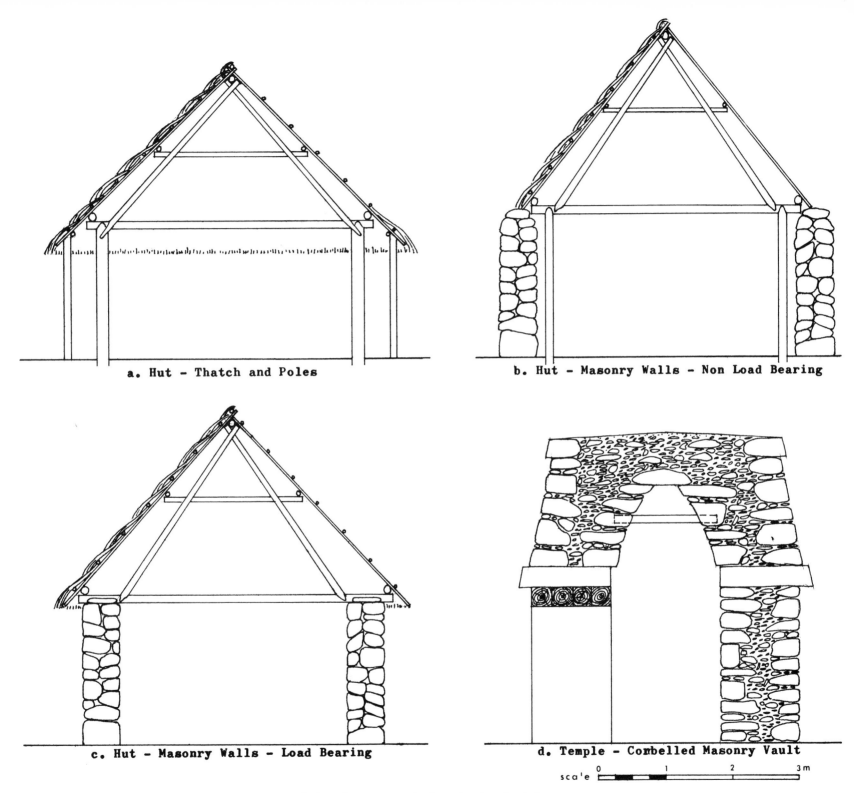

a. Hut – Thatch and Poles

b. Hut – Masonry Walls – Non Load Bearing

c. Hut – Masonry Walls – Load Bearing

d. Temple – Corbelled Masonry Vault

scale 0   1   2   3 m

FIG. 19. Evolution of masonry vaults from thatch-and-pole hut.

ciple involved in a corbeled vault is fairly simple.[4] A narrow space can be roofed over in stone by the process of allowing each succeeding course of stone in two parallel walls to project slightly beyond the course below, thus forming an inward-angled, or sloping, surface. If this is done until the two sloping surfaces come together, a corbeled vault is formed. The two halves of the vault are structurally independent, as they exert no thrust on one another as is the case in masonry arches. The whole system is stable due to the dead weight of material which is piled on top of the projecting stones, and great care must be exercised to keep everything in balance. It should be noted, however, that not all vaults constructed by the Mayas conformed to this ideal condition, and many of them were shaped in such a way that their center of gravity would tend to overturn them if they were not held up by the other half vault. The strength of any vault depends in great measure on the strength of the cement used, and this also varied considerably from place to place.

The clear span which can be obtained from this kind of vaulting is extremely limited, as the slope of the vault must be kept as near vertical as may be practical in order to avoid overbalancing. There are no recorded cases of Maya vaults exceeding twelve feet in span, and the majority are in the neighborhood of five to eight feet. The walls supporting the vaults have to be very thick in order to hold up the dead weight of the superimposed stonework and range from two and one-half to nearly five feet in depth. The combination of thick walls and short spans tended to produce long, narrow rooms, which were also very high in relation to their width due to the steep slope of the vaults (Fig. 19-d).

[4] The development of the corbeled vault appears to have resulted in a tremendous upsurge in building activity throughout the Maya area. At Tikal, much of what had been built before was torn down and replaced by larger structures using the improved technology. At Dzibilchaltun, building activity resumed after a long period when almost nothing had been built. Less well-substantiated evidence from other sites indicates a similar outburst of activity which is one of the natural consequences of the introduction of improved technology.

In the majority of cases, the vaults were spanned at the half or third points by wood tie beams in the same fashion as the pole-and-thatch roofs which were described earlier (Fig. 19-d). These wooden members actually have no real structural function, since the vault is a stable structure and the two half-vaults require no tying together, as they exert no outward pressure. Even during the period of construction, when the vaults were incomplete, it does not seem likely that these cross members served any useful purpose, since more elaborate, temporary wooden formwork would have been required to hold the masonry in place while the mortar dried. Since the stone-masonry building in its entirety appears to be a direct translation both in size and form from the wooden hut, it is probable that the wooden cross ties are carryovers from the wooden model, even though they are structurally redundant. The historical precedent for this is found in Greece, where it is quite clear that many of the details of stone temples that have no apparent function are likewise translations into stone of wooden members that are no longer needed. It is likely that the Maya builders did not fully understand the structural behavior of the corbeled or concrete vault and used wooden cross ties in the mistaken belief that they actually did serve some structural purpose. We should not be very surprised by this lack of understanding, since it is still virtually impossible to make a rigorous structural analysis of the stone vaulting in a Gothic cathedral even with the sophisticated mathematical tools available to us today.

Excavations of building remains at a number of sites indicate that the development of stone-masonry technology from the Early to Late Classic period can be divided into three major phases. In the earliest phase, both walls and vaults of masonry buildings were constructed of crudely shaped limestone blocks set in a thick bed of mortar. The stones were laid in rough horizontal courses and the exposed faces covered with a thick layer of plaster. These surfaces tended to be fairly uneven, since no amount of plaster could completely cover up the irregularity of

a. Slab Masonry Type – Peten

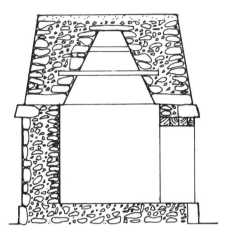

b. Intermediate Type – Peten

c. Veneer Type – Peten

d. Veneer Type – Yucatan

FIG. 20. Masonry vault type (slab masonry type, intermediate type, veneer type—Peten, veneer type—Yucatan).

the stonework (Fig. 20-a). This kind of slab stonework was employed in both substructures and superstructures during the early part of the Classic period. In the second phase, the exposed faces of individual stones were cut and dressed much more accurately, and numbers of small stones were employed in the hearting to fill in the voids between the larger stones. The exposed surfaces were much more even and could be made relatively smooth with a thin coat of finish plaster (Fig. 20-b). In the final stage, the hearting or structural part of walls and vaults were made of a kind of crude concrete, finished with a thin veneer of cut stones. The vault stones and the projecting cornice stones were tenoned into the hearting. It is fairly evident that the veneer stones were actually used as forms and the concrete hearting was placed behind the veneer stones, which were held in place temporarily by some kind of wooden framework. The very smooth stone surface produced by this veneer technique required very little plaster to complete the finished surface (Fig. 20-c).

The change from true corbeled vaults to concrete vaults represents a fundamental change in technology but did not result in a significant change in the size or basic form of vaults, which retained their hutlike character throughout the entire sequence as outlined above. The elaborate cut-stone mosaics in the upper walls of Puuc-style buildings and the further elaboration of the entire wall in Chenes- and Rio Bec-style structures required the cutting, carving, and fitting of veneer stonework of the highest order of precision. Some of this stonework could be produced on a mass production basis, as it involved repetitive patterns, but each stone had to be fitted and put into place individually (Fig. 20-d).

The exposed patterns of stonework in building walls and substructures which the visitor presently sees at the ruins of any Maya city are very misleading, as the exposed stone surfaces were invariably covered by a finish coat of plaster or stucco at the time of their construction. It is unlikely that the elaborate stone mosaics in the upper walls of Puuc- or Chenes-style buildings were plastered, but the lower walls, together with the walls and sloping faces of vaults on the interior, were plaster coated, and many buildings are found with the plaster on the interior still intact. The exposed surfaces of plazas, terraces, courtyards, substructures, and ball courts were also plaster coated, which tended to unify these diverse forms into a larger and visually comprehensible whole. It is easy to imagine the smooth surfaces of floors and walls gleaming white in the sun against the dark green background of the surrounding jungle. The over-all whiteness was relieved by occasional touches of color, which may still be found in a few places where the plaster is well preserved.[5] Elaborate bas-reliefs in stucco were used on pilasters, upper walls, and roof combs in parts of the Usumacinta and Peten areas in much the same manner as stone mosaics were used in the Puuc and Chenes areas.

It must be said that the Mayas made little progress technologically beyond the initial conceptualization of the corbeled vault. In spite of the change from rough coursed stone to veneered concrete structures as described above, which permitted the use of large amounts of rubble concrete in place of dressed stones, the basic design and form of buildings were not affected to any great extent. Vaults were widened slightly toward the end of the Classic period and cross walls were omitted between rooms, forming long galleries, but these changes represent minor modifications within the existing technology. Post-and-beam-framing systems were introduced into the Maya area by the Toltec invaders from the Valley of Mexico during the Postclassic period, but there is some question as to whether this system represents a real improvement over the veneered concrete vault. It is true that larger spaces could be created by using a series of posts and beams running in two direc-

---

[5] It is very possible that the use of color on buildings was more widespread than is presently believed, since it occurs fairly frequently wherever the remains of plaster are found in place on building exteriors. In 99 per cent of the cases, however, the exterior plaster has entirely disintegrated, so there is no way of really knowing how extensively color was used.

78

tions, but it is also true that all roofs constructed in this fashion have entirely collapsed, while many of the earlier stone vaults are still intact, as strong today as when they were first built. Wooden lintels over doorways and the wooden cross ties in vaults have also rotted away without disturbing the structural integrity of these massive roof structures.

Many writers have postulated that it is unfortunate that the Mayas never learned the use of the keystone arch in place of the corbeled vault, or so-called false arch. The appellation *false arch* suggests that a fraud has been perpetrated or that this vault is somehow less worthy of notice than a true arch, but this is a mistaken belief. It cannot be denied that the rooms covered by corbeled vaults have to be high and narrow and the walls must be thick in proportion to the void spaces created. But it is not necessarily true that these limits in any way prevented the Mayas from building structures that were ideally suited to their purposes. The climate throughout their territory was warm and humid and most activities could be carried on out-of-doors during the greater part of the year; protection from sun and rain is the prime problem under these conditions. No large enclosed spaces were required for any of the activities associated with daily life, and most ritual or ceremonial activities involving large numbers of participants or spectators could also best be carried on in the open spaces of plazas and courtyards. Since we have assumed that the interiors of temples and most palace-type buildings were accessible only to the high priests, there was no necessity for these spaces to accommodate more than a few people at one time. The symbolic value of the temple is not, after all, a function of the size of the space it encloses. In fact, a good case can be made that the reverse is true; its value goes up as the degree of privacy is increased.

Even though no individual enclosed space in a Maya building ever became much larger than the interior of a small hut, it was recognized that numbers of these spaces could be joined together in long rows, placed one behind the other, or arranged one on top of another. With the addition of a roof comb, these multichamber or multistory structures became very imposing masses, and the desired effect was in no way diminished by the small size of the spaces inside the masses. Monumentality was wanted, but not large enclosed spaces. The keystone arch and the great vaulted interiors which it is capable of producing had no place in Maya society. The building technology employed seems entirely consistent with their purposes, and one can only marvel at the range of architectural forms and space-ordering ideas which resulted from such limited technical means. The stone cities, now in ruins, are not really permanent, but the fact that a large number of buildings have survived over twelve hundred years of destruction by the combined forces of man and nature suggests that the technological capabilities of the Mayas, in terms of producing lasting physical monuments, far exceeded their capacity to establish a lasting framework for a viable "community of man."

79

7.

**Descriptions
of Individual
Cities**

GENERAL

The selection which follows is devoted to a description and analysis of twenty Maya cities. The salient features of each site are discussed in detail in an effort to identify and characterize the unique features of its basic spatial structure and form. Archetypal building forms and building groupings, as identified earlier in the text, are singled out for special attention and compared with similar forms at other sites. Since our main concern is with the structure of the city as a whole, rather than individual buildings, details of building construction and architectural style have generally been passed over in favor of spatial relationships and formal order, as evident in the siting and arrangement of groups or complexes of buildings.

The description of each city is accompanied by a site map, or site plan, together with a large number of photographs which have been selected on the basis of their ability to aid the viewer in visualizing the form of the city and its components as described in the text. It must be emphasized again that most of the maps show only the main ceremonial areas of these sites, as definitive data in regard to the peripheral areas is not available. The exceptions to this are Dzibilchaltun, Mayapan, Edzna, Comalcalco, and Tikal, where extensive surveys of the areas surrounding the central ceremonial nucleus have been carried out. A number of restoration drawings are included with the photographs; these have been constructed from enlargements of the photographs which accompany them. Every effort has been made to assure the accuracy of these restorations, but certain details have had to be filled in on the basis of assumption where reliable information was lacking. The basic forms are correct, however, and it is only small decorative features that may be questionable.

The choice of sites to be included in this section was

limited on the basis of several considerations. First, it seemed highly desirable to include representative examples from all parts of the Maya area. Thus, the sites chosen range in location from the Motagua Valley in Honduras to the Peten and Usumacinta areas in Guatemala, and from Chiapas to the Yucatan Peninsula in Mexico. All important regions, based either on style or geographical considerations, have been included, with the exception of the Rio Bec area, where insufficient information was available for any site in this region to warrant its inclusion. At the present moment, however, rather extensive surface surveys accompanied by excavation and restoration are being carried out at the sites of Becan and Chicana in the Rio Bec area. Both of these appear to be ceremonial centers rather than urban centers, but Becan is particularly noteworthy because it is surrounded by a moat, a feature which is almost unknown at other sites. No reports have yet been issued covering the recent work at these sites, so they have to be omitted from our discussion.

Second, the choice of sites was further restricted by eliminating those which had not been accurately surveyed using approved mapping techniques. (It has already been noted that in some cases the areas surveyed may represent only the main ceremonial area.) A number of important cities with extensive architectural remains were thus omitted on the grounds that the available maps lacked the accuracy required for critical analysis. Finally, there was the question of accessibility, since it was of vital concern that any description or analysis of physical remains be based on firsthand knowledge of the city under study, fully documented with up-to-date photographs and drawings. A few exceptions to this requirement were made in those cases where reliable data was available in quantity and the sites in question had been carefully mapped and partially excavated.

Of the twenty sites considered, seventeen were constructed and occupied during the Classic period, and in two cases occupation and construction continued on into the Postclassic period following invasion by a group from the Valley of Mexico (Dzibilchaltun and Chichen Itza). In order to draw further attention to the unique aspects of Classic Maya construction, as contrasted with later developments in the same areas, two Postclassic sites and one highland Maya site were also investigated. The two Postclassic cities, Mayapan and Tulum, are both surrounded by walls, and at this writing represent the only well-known examples of walled cities from either the Classic or Postclassic periods. Zaculeu is a highland Maya city whose lifespan appears to have extended from the early part of the Classic period, measured by lowland standards, up to the time of the Spanish invasion. Most scholars believe that the highland and lowland Maya cultures represent two separate lines of development, even though they were contemporary in time and not far removed from one another in space.

Further attention should be drawn to the site maps, since they form the most important documentation presented in support of the present study. The graphical representation of the various man-made elements in the cities as shown presents many difficulties, and a conscious effort has been made to simplify the smaller details in order to concentrate on the basic spatial scheme. Many structures which are presently nothing more than rough mounds of rubble have been shown with sharply defined edges and surfaces. This stylization has been used consistently in all plans as a means of indicating the basic three-dimensional form of rough mounds where no other information about them is available. In some cases, these mounds may actually represent the remains of vaulted stone buildings in an advanced state of collapse, while others may represent nothing more than low platforms or terraces which at no time supported buildings.

Plans of individual buildings are shown where they are still standing or where sufficient information is available to make reconstruction possible. Stairways are indicated where they are exposed or where it is clear that steps did exist even though they can no longer be seen. Pyramidal substructures, terraces, and platforms are shown as having stepped faces wherever the size and shape of these steps can be ascertained, while others are shown with smooth sloping faces when this information is lacking. It should be pointed out, however, that in almost all cases it can be assumed that substructures did have stepped outer faces, even though most of these facings have been stripped off by the action of tree roots. Contours are shown, where known, in order to show the relationships between natural and man-made forms. *Cenotes*, or natural wells, are indicated at these sites where they are known to exist and artificial reservoirs are also shown wherever they can be positively identified.

The basic graphic symbols used in these drawings are as follows:

1. Plazas and courtyards which appear to be of major importance are shown in yellow. Secondary plazas, or other leveled areas, are shown in light gray. It is assumed that all plazas, courtyards, terraces, and platforms were paved in addition to being carefully leveled.

2. Floor plans of temples, palace-type buildings, etc., are shown as they would have appeared in their original state, even though many of them are now badly deteriorated.

3. Dotted lines have been used to suggest important alignments between buildings and stelae where it is believed that the alignments or axes were of some importance in determining functional or symbolic relationships among these elements.

4. The sloping sides of pyramidal substructures, platforms, and terraces have been shaded in two tones of gray in order to emphasize the three-dimensional quality of these forms in contrast to the flat planes of the open spaces.

81

5. Stelae are shown as very small rectangular shapes, while altars are indicated by small circles.

6. Names of buildings or building groupings and other identification have generally been omitted in order to emphasize spatial arrangement and form.

7. Contour lines are generally shown, particularly where the ground is very irregular, and have been omitted only where they are unknown or where the existing ground plane is relatively flat.

Every effort has been made to insure the accuracy of the over-all city layout as shown and all elements have been drawn accurately to scale. In many cases, the plans have had to be constructed from a variety of source materials and certain details cannot be verified. Parts of many sites are almost completely overgrown, which made it impossible to check out certain visual alignments or verify dimensions of some structures. It must also be kept in mind that there is presently no way of knowing what parts of the area in the immediate periphery of the central precincts of the city were kept cleared of trees or how natural landscape elements were treated within the central precinct itself. The same kind of difficulty is encountered in regard to the locations of the plots of ground in which maize was planted. Some of these may well have been situated in the immediate environs of the smaller cities, but again, this is only an assumption. We actually know very little about the distribution of *milpas* in the rural areas either, except that their specific locations were dependent on local considerations of soil and drainage rather than formal planning notions.

All of the site maps must be considered as being partially incomplete on the basis of these unknowns, although the site maps of Tikal, Comalcalco, Edzna, Mayapan, and Dzibilchaltun are more detailed than the others and do show even the smallest known subsidiary mounds. I believe that the basic plan arrangements are essentially correct, however, and that the plans as delineated give a reasonably accurate picture of the central portion of the city at the time it was last occupied. Deviations from the controls or symbols as noted earlier will be pointed out in the discussion of individual sites.

The ruins of the city of Tikal are located in the northeastern sector of the department of Peten, Guatemala, about thirty miles northeast of the city of Flores, the capital of this department. With the possible exceptions of Dzibilchaltun and Mirador, Tikal is the largest Maya city which is presently known, and its full extent is still not clearly established, even though the central area, covering sixteen square kilometers, was carefully mapped over a period of three years, and much exploring was done outside this area.

The area shown on the small-scale map drawing covers only the central portion of the center, which was linked together by four raised causeways, but there are literally hundreds of other structures extending outward from this nucleus in all directions (Fig. 21). The larger-scale plan drawing shows the Great Plaza and central area in greater detail (Fig. 22). The area shown on the small-scale map is slightly over two miles from east to west and one and one-half miles from north to south. Within this area, all of the larger structures of Tikal are found, including the five great pyramid-temple structures, which are the highest ever constructed in any part of the Maya area. Temple IV, the highest of this group, measures 224 feet from the level of the plaza to the top of its roof comb, while Temple II is the lowest at 143 feet. Other large pyramid-temple structures are situated in outlying sectors of the city, but the five great temples towered over all else and clearly dominated the city in all directions (Fig. 23).

A detailed contour map of the greater Tikal region would indicate that there are no large hills in this area, but the ground is very broken locally, as indicated on the site plan, and the location of major building groupings has been strongly influenced by details of natural topography. The largest plazas, Temple Groups, and palace complexes occupy a high broken ridge, running generally east and west, with Temple IV at the westernmost and highest point. From Temple IV, an artificial causeway runs northeast, following the crest of a narrow ridge, and terminates in the North Zone complex, which occupies a large knob at the end of the ridge. In general, the larger structures are located on the tops of ridges or small hills with lesser structures situated on smaller ridges below. Low areas have been avoided as building sites, as they are apt to fill with water during the rainy season. The pattern of building on the higher points of ground was followed consistently at other sites in the Peten area where the topographical conditions are generally similar to the conditions at Tikal. While the positioning of buildings and building groups has generally been determined by topography, the specific orientation of these structures is remarkably consistent, and nearly all structures are oriented within a ten-degree variation of true cardinal points. This pattern is also consistent with other sites in both the southern and northern areas.

It can be noted in the site map (Fig. 21) that the largest number of individual structures tend to occur in groups of three or four, and these structures are generally situated around a level plaza or courtyard. This holds true even where the natural topography makes this kind of grouping extremely difficult to construct. For example, where these groupings occur on steep slopes, it is necessary to build up the terrace on the downhill side and cut it into the uphill slope. There are many exceptions to this simple quadrilateral grouping, and this is particularly true of the large ceremonial complexes such as the North Group, the North Acropolis, the Central Acropolis, and the great sweep of structures which run on an east-west line south of the Great Plaza. But even these more complex groups tend to be made up of a number of small quadrilateral groupings built around interconnecting plazas or court-

Tikal

83

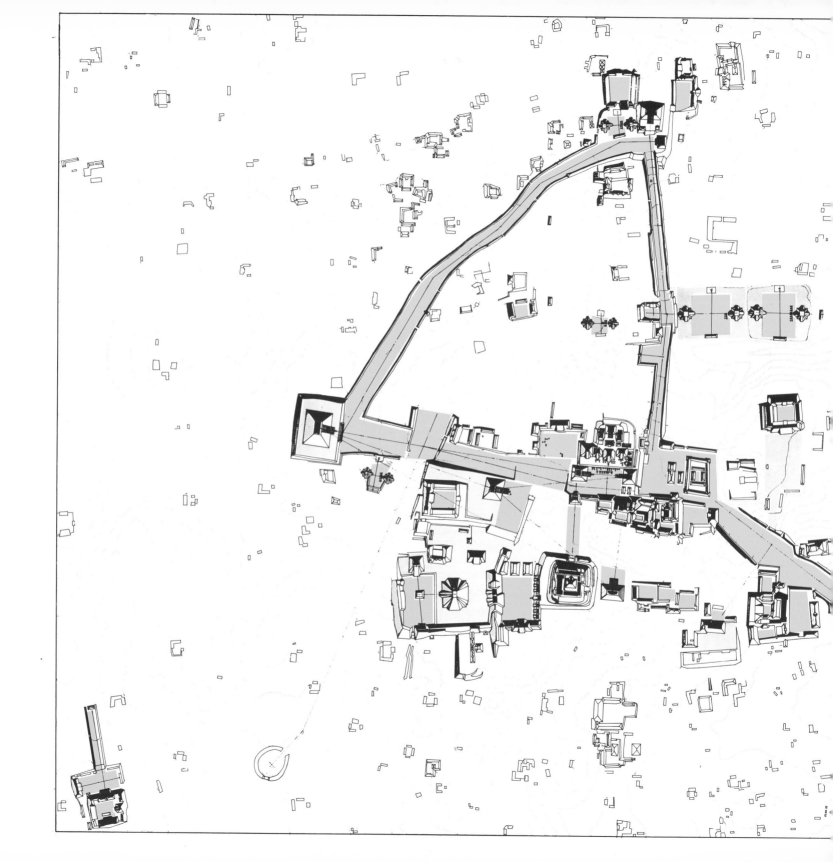

FIG. 21. Tikal (after Carr and Hazard).

GREAT PLAZA & CENTRAL AREA

TIKAL

PETEN, GUATEMALA

SCALE 40 20 0   50   100   150   200
METERS

FIG. 22. Tikal—central area
(after Carr and Hazard).

yards. Temple III, Temple IV, and the Temple of the Inscriptions are exceptions to this rule, since they appear as isolated elements with no other structures directly related to them.

Among the most interesting variations on the basic quadrilateral scheme are the seven twin-pyramid complexes which are located in different sectors of the city. Each of these groupings consists of two truncated pyramids facing each other across a level plaza, together with a small palace-type building and a walled courtyard facing one another on the other two sides (Fig. 21). This kind of complex is unknown at other Maya sites, and walled compounds of the kind associated with these groups are also unknown. Two of these unusual complexes are situated just east of the Maler causeway, which connects the North Group to the plaza immediately behind Temple I (Figs. 24, 25, 26). A third, and much smaller, group of this sort is situated slightly west of the same causeway. The fourth is part of the North Group, and a fifth lies just south of the plaza in front of Temple IV (Figs. 27, 28). Another somewhat unusual grouping can be found in the southwest corner of the site map. This group consists of a dead-end causeway which opens at the other end into a large plaza, behind which is situated a more typical quadrilateral grouping. This compact and highly articulated assemblage is entirely unrelated to any other important group in the site and has the appearance of a suburban ceremonial center in relation to the central area.

While the largest number of structures appear in well-defined but seemingly unrelated groupings, the largest and most important ceremonial complexes are connected together by means of four graded causeways. The causeways expand into larger plaza areas at the points where they intersect, and these plazas form the nucleus of more extended building complexes. In some cases, fairly large building groupings are situated immediately adjacent to the causeways, and access to these groups is gained directly from the causeway. There are some exceptions to the rule that all of the important ceremonial groups are related to

the causeways, notably the large quadrangle northeast of the Great Plaza and the linear chain of structures situated south of the east-west, or Tozzer, causeway. Access to some of these latter structures appears to have been from the causeway, but the nature of these connections is not clear.

The positions of the large ceremonial groups, their individual internal organizations, the distances between them, and the character of the intervening terrain all suggest that the same basic pattern of growth took place at Tikal as had earlier been postulated for Uaxactun and other cities in the same region. This pattern indicates that the individual groups began as discrete, isolated elements, which were only casually connected to one another by means of small trails along the higher sections of ground. As the city expanded, and ceremonial activity became more important and more formalized, it was necessary to provide adequate means for large processions to move from one sector of the city to the other, and graded and raised causeways replaced the earlier trails. As the more important ceremonial groups were remodeled and expanded over the course of time, the causeways themselves were undoubtedly raised in height, and perhaps widened, assuming their present form. At the same time, other elements were being constructed adjacent to the causeways, adding to the grandeur of these processional ways. The foregoing description is obviously speculative, since no temporal sequence has yet been established for the construction of the causeways in relation to the building groups associated with them, but almost all aspects of the arrangement of these elements tends to substantiate this kind of growth pattern.

It can also be noted in the site map (Fig. 21) that three of the causeways form a large triangle, while the fourth runs in a southeasterly direction from one apex of this triangle and dead-ends in a plaza in front of a large pyramid-temple structure called the Temple of the Inscriptions (Fig. 29). One of the causeways forming the triangle runs on a north-south line from a plaza immediately east of the

Great Plaza, terminating in a small plaza associated with the North Group. From this same plaza, another causeway, called the Maudslay causeway, follows the crest of a ridge in a southwesterly direction, terminating in a plaza in front of Temple IV (Fig. 30). From this plaza, the Tozzer causeway moves eastward, terminating in the Great Plaza, around which are situated Temple I, Temple II, and the North Arcopolis.[1]

While it is evident that the causeways form a strong physical connection between these otherwise disassociated groups, it is also clear that there is no formal conceptual order underlying this arrangement. Fortuitous features of topography have dictated the positioning of major elements, and the causeways are afterthoughts generated by specific physical needs rather than abstract notions of order expressed in more formal terms. In spite of this accidental ordering, the organic quality of the causeways, which fit closely to the natural terrain, produces a scheme which is readily comprehensible, since it involves no necessity for abstracting on the part of the user. The intended relationships are perceived directly and the disparate parts form a coherent whole because of this direct perception. The same level of perception does not hold true, however, for the organization of the ceremonial groupings themselves, which depend on more sophisticated notions of orders of importance, expressed in specific geometrical relationships. The discussion which follows will attempt to identify and clarify some of these relationships.

The various structures related to the great Plaza can best be used to illustrate the nature of these formal conceptualizations, since they were thoroughly excavated and partially restored during the ten-year period from 1955 to 1965, thus making visible certain details which are important to an understanding of the whole. The plaza, which is very level and at one time was paved, measures 280 feet from east to west and 220 feet from north to south. The north side of the plaza is bounded by a broad stairway, stretching the full width of the plaza, giving access to a platform or terrace, upon which are situated fourteen pyramid-temple structures (Figs. 31, 32, 33).

The platform and its associated group of temples is called the North Acropolis, but, as noted earlier, this group of structures does not correspond to the concept of an Acropolis Group as developed earlier in the text. It can be noted that the fourteen temples are arranged in three smaller groups. One group, containing four temples, is ranged in a row set well back from the edge of the terrace and faces south toward the plaza (Figs. 34, 35). Near the southeast corner of the terrace is another row of three temples which face west. Immediately behind the row facing the plaza is a group of six temples arranged in a quadrilateral form. The largest, and most northerly, temple of this group faces south into a very small courtyard, while two smaller structures face into the same court on the east and west sides. There is no apparent access to this latter group from the plaza except through very narrow alleyways at the base of the structures fronting onto the plaza.

The relationship among the three groups of temples, and their relationship to the plaza, suggests several possible interpretations. At first glance, it might be assumed that the rows of temples facing directly onto the plaza should be considered as the most inportant, since the other two groups occupy subordinate positions with respect to the plaza. On the other hand, it might be argued that the quadrilateral group behind this row is more important, since it is less accessible from the plaza and therefore more private. The notion of privacy, or degree of removal from direct public access, has been shown to be extremely important to the concept of an Acropolis Group and may equally well apply here. A third explanation will be shortly forthcoming when the full report of the extensive excavations recently carried out in this group is published. The

<hr>

[1] In this discussion I have used the terminology which has generally been adopted to describe various buildings and building complexes at Tikal. Nevertheless, the group of temple-type structures which is commonly called the North Acropolis does not fit our definition of Acropolis Group and should be considered as a unique form, particular to Tikal.

preliminary report indicates that the North Acropolis represents nineteen separate superimpositions which took place over a period of nearly one thousand years. Buildings were replaced, enlarged, or added on numerous occasions and only when the full temporal sequence of building is clearly established will the conceptual order become clear.

The second group of structures associated with the Great Plaza consists of the two great temples, Temple I and Temple II, which confront each other across the plaza. Temple I is the highest, measuring 187 feet from the plaza level to the top of its room comb (Fig. 36), while Temple II is somewhat lower, measuring 143 feet in height (Figs. 37, 38). These two structures are situated near the base of the terrace on the north side of the plaza, creating a secondary space within the larger plaza. This secondary space has been given further recognition by virtue of two long rows of stelae and altars, which are ranged in an east-to-west row between the two great temples near the base of the stairway leading to the North Acropolis (Figs. 39, 40). Other stelae are more closely associated with the temples of the North Acropolis, but the row of stelae in the plaza appears to be associated with the large temples.

Two extensions of the main plaza are formed by the spaces which lie between the great-temple substructures and the base of the high platform on the south side of the plaza. Access to the main part of the plaza from the east and west is through these spaces, and it is interesting to note that the space south of Temple I has been partially filled in by a ball court, making access into the plaza from this side extremely difficult, since any path of movement from the east would have to circumvent the ball court (Fig. 43). It is tempting to assume that the ball court represents a late addition to the scheme at a time when there was some reason to emphasize the western entry into the plaza, but this is obviously speculation. In support of this contention, however, it can be noted that a small temple-type building faces north toward the plaza exten-

sion at the base of Temple II, giving added importance to this space as the main entry point.

From almost any position within the Great Plaza, Temple I and Temple II dominate the scene, both in terms of mass and height (Figs. 41, 42). While the difference in height between the two structures suggests some rank order of importance, the fact that they face toward one another produces a mutually reinforcing effect rather than one of competition. If the notion of reinforcement is not clear, simply imagine these structures in the same position but facing in the same direction rather than toward one another, and the struggle between them for dominance becomes apparent. As it stands, each bears the same relationship to the plaza and the North Acropolis, and together they complete the definition of the plaza, which is the most important space of the whole complex. In spite of the energy and care which has gone into the construction of the great temples and their supporting substructures, the inner spaces of the temples are mean and dark, and the total floor area is only a few hundred square feet. These spaces are extremely important symbolically, but functionally the Great Plaza and the open space of the North Terrace play the most important roles, as it is here that the population gathers to take part in the sacred rites. Only the initiated may mount the steep stairways leading to the great temples (Fig. 44), or penetrate the inner sanctums of the temples of the North Acropolis, but without the participation of the masses gathered in the plazas the rituals conducted in temples are private events, witnessed only by the direct participants.

Above all, this particular complex demonstrates clearly the dual role that buildings play in giving form to urban spaces. On one hand, each building is perceived as a free-standing object or monument, dominating its own immediate surroundings and simultaneously enclosing its own private spaces. On the other hand, the same buildings serve as abstract space-defining elements, giving form and meaning to the open spaces between. The dialogue between these two roles gives the spaces of a Maya ceremonial center their particular character, and variations on the basic dialogue create great variety between individual groupings. A brief look at several of the other large complexes at Tikal will help to bear this out.

Immediately south and slightly east of the Great Plaza complex is a large group of structures which is called the Central Acropolis. Here again the use of the term *acropolis* in describing this group is a misnomer, since its spatial organization corresponds very closely to the notion of a Palace Group as described earlier in the text. The internal organization of this complex has already been described under the heading of *Palace Groups*, and a detailed plan is shown in Figure 13. In the context of the present discussion, the question arises as to what functional relationship, if any, existed between this great complex and the balance of the structures associated with the Great Plaza. It is evident that some important connection did exist, as monumental stairways lead up from the plaza to the long palace-type structures on the southern side of the platform supporting the palace complex (Figs. 45, 46). Multiple doorways in the façades of these structures face toward the plaza, reinforcing the notion that ceremonies taking place in the plaza involved both the temple structures and the palace structures.

Once again we are confronted with the enigma of the function of Palace Groups in general as well as of the particular group now being considered. In spite of the lack of supporting data, we are still inclined to postulate a combination of administrative, educational, and residential functions as being most likely. The existence of a large administrative center is entirely consistent with our assumption that Tikal was a regional urban center which functioned as the capital of a large district. Administrators and other specialists trained here would be sent out to the provincial centers, carrying with them the accumulated secrets of the elite ruling group. Within this kind of image it is only fitting that the great Palace Group should share the center of the stage at Tikal, which is represented by the larger complex of structures surrounding the Great Plaza (Figs. 47, 48, 49, 50).

Another grouping of special interest, which is called the Group of the Seven Temples, is situated about two hundred yards south of Temple III (Figs. 51, 52). This group gets its name from the row of seven temples which faces west toward a large plaza or courtyard measuring about 220 feet from east to west and 350 feet from north to south. The west and south sides of the courtyard are bounded by long, steeply sloped platforms supporting the remains of several masonry buildings, while the north side is defined by a triple ball court. This is the only known example of a triple ball court and deserves more attention than can be devoted to it here. The row of seven temples is also a most unusual feature, and again there is no corresponding group to be found at other sites.

The variety of building elements which make up this group provides us with a convincing reminder that the quadrilateral grouping depends on the clear definition of the open space of the plaza for its comprehensibility and order rather than the specifics of the defining elements. The cities of Europe are full of similar plazas in the sense that the elements defining the plaza may be of almost any sort so long as they form a nearly continuous wall of buildings which gives form to the open space of the plaza. A careful examination of the map of Tikal reveals that most of the large quadrilateral complexes are very similar in their basic organization and vary only in regard to the more detailed make-up of the surrounding elements. One such grouping can be seen in the complex immediately east of the row of seven temples. In this case a further variation has been introduced, since a large pyramidal structure is centered in a courtyard surrounded by long palace-type structures.

The North Group, which is situated at the juncture of the Maler and Maudslay causeways, consists of five separate subgroups, which collectively form a rather disjointed whole. In spite of this, it undoubtedly was an important ceremonial precinct, since it is linked to two other sectors of the city by large causeways. The Maler causeway, which runs north and south, is terminated at the North Group by a large platform supporting a group of three pyramid-temple structures. The largest temple faces south toward the causeway, while the two smaller temples face north toward the large temple. This arrangement is an unusual variation on the basic Temple Group, where the two small temples generally face toward one another rather than toward the main temple. Northwest and northeast of this Temple Group are two small quadrilateral groupings of structures, each representing further variations on the basic theme of building and plaza as outlined earlier. In addition, a twin-pyramid complex is situated directly east of the main Temple Group, and an additional quadrilateral group is positioned directly south of this complex, separated from it by the causeway.

Many other smaller groupings are scattered around this nucleus, but there is no apparent pattern to their positions with respect to the North Group or to each other. Taken as a whole, the North Group lacks the coherence which is characteristic of many of the other major complexes at Tikal but illustrates very graphically the tendency toward disorganization which characterizes most accretions of the sort represented in this complex. The fact that other complexes within the same center exhibit larger notions of order is an indication of the application of a conscious act of will which manifests itself in symbolic rather than organic relationships. The conceptual differences in organization between various parts of Tikal are real, but there is no basis for assuming one is necessarily better than the other.

It would be possible to devote further discussion to other specific groupings of structures, but such discussion could only be repetitious, since both the typical and most unique groupings have already been described. Beyond this, it might be worthwhile to look for even larger patterns among the many hundreds of individual structures represented as a means of describing the organization of the city and its environs at the largest possible scale. It

was postulated earlier in this study (chapter 4) that Tikal, together with other large centers in various parts of the Maya expanse, belong to the largest class of known Maya settlements, to which we have given the designation *city* or *large urban center*. In this same chapter we described the basic characteristics of a large urban center and used Tikal as one of the examples where the maps are sufficiently comprehensive to demonstrate the presence of these characteristics. Since the general case for the urbanization of Tikal has already been presented, it does not seem worthwhile to reiterate it here. It does seem worthwhile, however, to look more carefully at the actual physical structure of the residential areas as a means of establishing their relationships to the central ceremonial area in greater detail. The physical structure of these areas should also tell us something about daily life in a Maya city, even though this image can be created only by inference.

The urban zone of Tikal, as represented by the 6.7 square miles of it which have been mapped, consists of a major ceremonial center surrounded by several suburban, or neighborhood, centers, around which are found numbers of houses or housing clusters. The full extent of these suburban areas is not presently known, although it seems fairly certain that they extend some distance north and south of the area mapped. The areas to the east and west are marked by large *bajos* and it is unlikely that the city extended any distance in these directions. Beyond the confines of the city, other satellite centers are found which are independent of the city itself but probably related to it administratively. The general pattern is not essentially different from modern cities, which consist of a central business district which in turn is surrounded by numbers of local, or neighborhood, centers, each of which is the focus of a residential district. At Tikal, some ten to twelve of these local, or suburban, centers can be found; these are distributed somewhat unevenly within the urban zone due to the character of the existing terrain, which is very broken. Only the higher portions of land were used for building purposes and the local centers occupy the best pieces of land available.

The houses are grouped around these local centers in varying densities, which may be due in part to certain details of the landscape which have now been obscured by the jungle growth. It may also be due in part to a condition where certain sectors of the city represent areas devoted to specialized activities, such as stone carving, ceramics, weaving, etc., but there is no evidence as yet for this kind of "zoning," which is so prevalent in modern cities. It is also possible that the various suburban districts were given over to specific classes of Maya society; this again would not be very different from modern cities, which generally show class differences in different parts of the city. While the general pattern of relationships among the various parts of the city seem fairly clear, the actual physical pattern as it appears on the map is somewhat confused, as there is a kind of randomness to the over-all distribution of structures which obscures details of the larger pattern. This may be nothing more than an indication of our lack of ability at the present time to comprehend the order present, but the feeling of disorder persists nonetheless.

Perhaps the outstanding characteristic of suburban Tikal is its seeming lack of premeditated order at a scale larger than an individual house cluster. The housing clusters, which are represented by quadrilateral groupings of house platforms around a central plaza, are not essentially different in concept from the larger ceremonial groups in the central portion of the city. The general pattern of orientation is maintained in these housing groups, and to this extent there is some order among them. Beyond this, however, the small clusters or individual house platforms seem to be scattered throughout the landscape and there is no observable patterning to their positions. This is in sharp contrast to the main ceremonial area, where we have already noted a high degree of order among the large aggregates of ceremonial structures, which are arranged in traditional, formal configurations.

It is clear that to some extent the lack of formal order-ing ideas in the suburban zone is a consequence of building only on the higher portions of ground. Since the ground is fairly irregular, the space available for building is composed of fortuitous shapes, which makes formal planning difficult even if it is desired. This still does not account entirely for the randomness of the plan, however, as it would have been possible to impose some kind of premeditated scheme on any piece of ground, regardless of its irregularity. The missing element, which might tell us a good deal about how these areas were really organized and used and how they related to the main center, is a circulation system. Without some knowledge of the character of such a system, we are simply lost.

We have already suggested that maps of cities as we know them today are devoted for the most part to a description of the circulation system(s) of the city. We assume that buildings are situated along the various circulation routes, and the pattern of building is then a direct translation of the street pattern. Where the street pattern is a gridiron, the buildings take on the same kind of pattern. If the streets are arranged in circles or like the spokes of a wheel, the buildings follow this pattern. In some cases, the street patterns are nongeometric and tend to follow contour lines, where the ground is very irregular. In this case, the pattern of buildings is also irregular, but it is still linear; i.e., the buildings simply follow the shape of the streets and tend to make two parallel rows, even though the rows are curvilinear. The relationship between street patterns and building location in contemporary cities is so intimate that we could reconstruct the circulation patterns just by looking at the locations of buildings.

To come back to Tikal, it is this very lack of observable circulation systems outside of the great causeways in the central ceremonial area that confuses us in our efforts to understand its physical structure. We would expect that this system would include some way to get from critical points along the great triangular causeway system to the secondary, or suburban, ceremonial areas and from there to the houses themselves. Since we have assumed that the

93

resident population was made up of nonfarmers, they would go about their normal daily business within the urban area, and, depending upon the nature of their work, this might take them to almost any part of the urban zone. Hence, the necessity of a workable circulation system. We might expect that these pathways would tend to follow the tops of ridges somewhere in the midst of the houses, but any attempt to reconstruct the specifics of such a system on the map is pure guesswork. As it stands, we can only assume a pattern which would allow easy movement throughout the city, even though this might not involve anything more than cutting narrow trails through the jungle where the land was not cleared.

The manner in which the housing clusters are spaced out at varying intervals leads us to believe that small portions of land were assigned to individual families or kin groups and that some of this land was used for garden plots to grow foods to supplement the main crop of maize, which was grown in the rural areas. There is obviously not enough space for *milpa* farms in the leftover space between houses, particularly when the low-lying land which is not suitable for *milpa* farming is taken into account. Thus, we get a more dispersed pattern of urban living than we normally associate with densely built-up cities; there is a considerable amount of open space in the form of garden plots and natural landscape. What this openness seems to suggest is that the process of urbanization at Tikal involved the gradual infilling of houses into areas that at one time might have been *mipla* plots when the city was very small. As the city grew in population and size, and more permanent residents were added, the open spaces gradually filled up, but not on the basis of a predetermined plan.

Lacking any detailed knowledge of the administrative control exercised by the high authorities in matters of land use, and lacking any real knowledge of the question of private ownership of land by families or kin groups, we can only speculate as to how much land was actually available for building purposes at any given time. Thus,

the apparent randomness of the housing layout appears to be a consequence of a slow, unstructured growth process coupled with a nongeometric circulation scheme which does not produce any kind of formal order. This process was abruptly terminated some time around the end of the ninth century when the greater part of Tikal was abandoned. Had the process continued, we might have seen a different kind of order emerging as urban space became more restricted and formal planning was required to make the best use of whatever space was still available.

From all of the above, it is patently clear that we still do not know very much about the details of a Maya city like Tikal in terms of the daily life of its inhabitants, but it is no longer a completely abstract pattern of mounds of rubble as it was just a few years ago. Its urban form is now evident, even though the edges are still blurred. W. R. Coe, who spent the better part of ten years working at Tikal, summarizes this view as follows: "By Late Classic times at least, Tikal was a completely organized and functioning city with a large resident population. It was a great marketing center to which produce and a large range of other raw materials were brought for processing and distribution. It was an administrative center for a large region and was completely dependent on a rural sustaining area for provisioning. That it was also a cultural center of great importance is self-evident from the character of its monuments and the richness of the materials included in burials. Whether its rulers gained their power by force or persuasion is still not known, but they succeeded in maintaining and expanding Tikal for a period of nearly a thousand years till it became one of the truly great cities of the New World." (Coe: 1965.)

Note: Staff members of the University Museum, University of Pennsylvania, together with representatives of the I.N.A.H. in Guatemala, have recently completed a ten-year program of excavation and restoration at Tikal. Work is now in progress on the final reports covering this monumental effort, but much information is already

94

available to interested readers in the form of preliminary reports, issued by the museum during the time work was in progress, as well as articles in various professional journals, including *Expedition*, the quarterly journal published by the museum itself. (See bibliography under Tikal.) The site is now included in a national park which is maintained by the government of Guatemala.

FIG. 23. Tikal—view looking east from Temple IV, Temples I, II, and III showing above treeline.

FIG. 24. Tikal—pyramid and stelae, Group E (twin-pyramid complex).

FIG. 25. Tikal—courtyard, stela, and altar, Group E (twin-pyramid complex).

FIG. 26. Tikal—detail of Altar No. 10 and Stela No. 22, Group E.

FIG. 27. Tikal—Altar No. 5,
twin-pyramid Complex N (left).

FIG. 28. Tikal—Stela No. 16,
twin-pyramid Complex N (right).

FIG. 29. Tikal—Temple of the Inscriptions, rear view showing glyphs on roof comb.

FIG. 30. Tikal—Temple IV, highest structure at Tikal (212 feet).

FIG. 31. Tikal—North Acropolis, view looking northeast.

FIG. 32. Tikal—Temple I (Temple of the Giant Jaguar).

FIG. 33. Tikal—Temple I and part of North Acropolis.

FIG. 34. Tikal—Structure No. 32, North Acropolis
(after partial restoration).

FIG. 35. Tikal—stelae at base of stairway to North Acropolis.

FIG. 36. Tikal—Temple I as seen from doorway of Temple II.

FIG. 37. Tikal—Temple II as seen from North Acropolis.

FIG. 38. Tikal—Temple II as seen from Temple I.

FIG. 39. Tikal—Temple I as seen from North Acropolis.

FIG. 40. Tikal—Temple I (restoration).

FIG. 41. Tikal—Temple I and Temple II as seen from West Plaza.

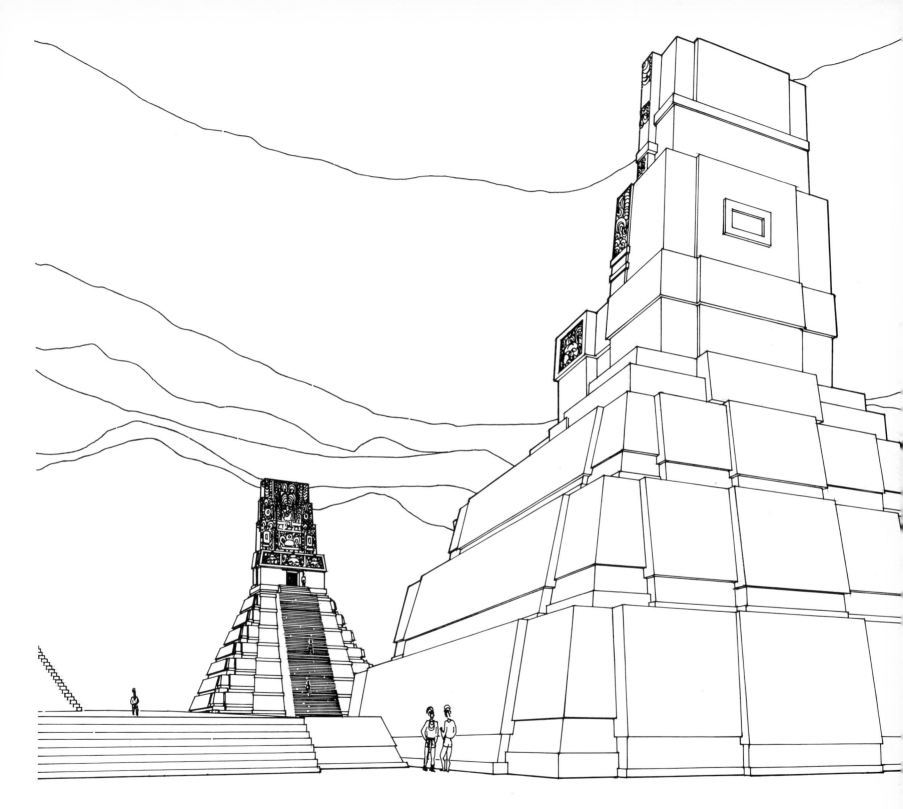

FIG. 42. Tikal—Temple I and Temple II (restoration).

FIG. 43. Tikal—Temple I and ball court.

FIG. 44. Tikal—Temple I
and Central Acropolis
(Palace Group)
as seen from
North Acropolis (right).

FIG. 45. Tikal—Great Plaza and Central Acropolis (Palace Group).

FIG. 46. Tikal—ball court and part of Central Acropolis (Palace Group).

FIG. 47. Tikal—Structure No. 65, Central Acropolis (Maler's Palace).

FIG. 48. Tikal—Court No. 6, Central Acropolis, view looking southwest.

FIG. 49. Tikal—Part of Five-Story Palace
(Structure No. 50), Central Acropolis.

FIG. 50. Tikal—interior of palace structure showing wooden cross ties.

FIG. 51. Tikal—Group of the Seven Temples, rear view.

FIG. 52. Tikal—Structure No. 96, Group of the Seven Temples.

Uaxactun

The site of Uaxactun is located near the center of the northeast quarter of the department of Peten, Guatemala, about twelve miles north of Tikal. While it was not as large as Tikal, Uaxactun was an important center and, because it was constructed and occupied over a long period of time, has provided much valuable information in regard to the patterns of growth and development of ceremonial centers in general. Extensive excavations were carried out at Uaxactun during the years 1926 to 1937 by archaeologists representing the Carnegie Institution of Washington, and complete details of their efforts may be found in the two reports issued by the Carnegie Institution in 1937 and 1950.[2] The discussion which follows draws heavily on material contained in these monographs, since the site is once more overgrown with jungle and it is no longer possible to obtain first-hand information by direct observation.

The main ceremonial area of Uaxactun consists of eight distinct groups of structures, each of which occupies the top of a natural hill or ridge, separated by ravines or low areas (Fig. 53). The upper parts of these hills have been artificially leveled and terraced so that little or nothing of their natural form remains. The practice of locating important groups of buildings on the tops of hills or highest points of ground within the center was followed consistently by the Mayas, even at sites where the natural terrain was considerably less irregular than at Uaxactun. The individual groups thus show little formal relationship to

one another, with the exception of Groups A and B, which are shown in the detailed site plan (Fig. 54). These two groups were begun as separate entities but at a later period were connected by a raised causeway, creating in effect a single large complex of plazas, terraces, and structures.

The other groups appear as discrete, isolated elements and, with the exception of a narrow causeway which starts at the east plaza in Group A and moves in the general direction of Groups D and E, there is nothing to suggest that these outlying groups are linked to the main center by formal circulation elements, as is the case at several sites in the Yucatan Peninsula. Each of the individual groups presents an orderly arrangement of buildings situated around a major plaza or courtyard. This configuration is basic to all Maya ceremonial centers. The larger groups contain one or more secondary plazas, with other structures forming subgroups within the larger complex. In other cases, structures are related to one another by virtue of the fact that they are situated on the same platform or terrace rather than forming groups around plazas or courtyards. Groups A and B were selected for illustration, since they contain the largest and most imposing structures within the entire site and because they include representative examples of all the typical building types and building groupings which are repeated with minor variations in other parts of the site.

The orientation of most buildings is fairly uniform, corresponding roughly to the cardinal points of the compass. The deviation from true north is about the same as Tikal, approximately 6°45′. Many of the larger temples, particularly those that were constructed during the early part of the Classic period, face south in the direction of Tikal, but there appears to be no single orientation that is predominant. As noted earlier, in Group E special effort was made to orient all structures to the true cardinal points

[2] Excavations were carried out almost continuously at Uaxactun from 1926 to 1937 by archaeologists representing the Carnegie Institution of Washington. The results of their efforts were published in two monographs issued by the C.I.W. The first of these, issued in 1937, is *Uaxactun, Guatemala, Group E, 1926–1931*, by O. G. Ricketson, Jr., and E. B. Ricketson. The second report, issued in 1950, is *Uaxactun, Guatemala: Excavations of 1931–1937* by A. Ledyard Smith.

and the alignment of buildings and stairways was predicated on specific lines of sight which could be used in making astronomical observations (Fig. 18).

Group A, which is the large complex of structures shown in the southern portion of the plan drawing (Fig. 54), occupies the top of a large hill, which was cut and filled on many different occasions in order to provide the necessary level spaces for plazas and structures. It contains the remains of thirty-four structures, and at the time the site was abandoned was the largest single complex at Uaxactun. In its earliest stage of development, Group A consisted of nothing more than a few small house platforms associated with level floors extending beyond the houses for a short distance. At this same point in time, Group E had already begun to function as a ceremonial group of some importance, but as Group A expanded, the importance of Group E declined, and by the end of the Classic period Group E was a minor center while Group A had become the largest and most important precinct in the entire city. It does not seem worthwhile to trace the course of development of Group A in great detail, since this has already been covered by A. Ledyard Smith in his monograph describing the excavations of 1931 to 1937 (Smith: 1950). Our main concern is with the center in its final form, although some references will be made to earlier stages of development as a means of explaining certain spatial concepts.

In its final stage of development, Group A included three distinct subgroups, each of which was related in one form or another to the major grouping of structures which focuses on the main plaza. This plaza in turn is connected to Group B by means of the large graded causeway running northward from the plaza. The plaza measures approximately 108 feet square and is bounded on the west side by a large pyramid-temple structure, on the south by a smaller pyramid-temple building which is situated on a platform raised above the general level of the plaza, and on the east by one of the Palace Group. As mentioned earlier, the plaza opens on the north side, giving access to

the causeway, but it is partially enclosed on this side by a small palace-type structure situated at right angles to the large palace building on the east side. The elements just described form an interesting variation on the archetypal Temple Group which is basic to all Maya sites, including Uaxactun. This basic group consists of three temples located on three sides of a level plaza and has been described in detail earlier in the text under the heading of Temple Groups. In the case under discussion, a palace-type building has been substituted for one of the temple buildings, but the basic spatial relationships are the same.

The case for the Temple Group as a generic form is clearly demonstrated by reviewing the history of the palace complex which bounds the east side of the main plaza. This structure was thoroughly excavated between 1931 and 1937; these excavations proved conclusively that in its first phase what is now an elaborate palace complex began as a group of three small temples situated on a low platform (Fig. 12-a). Over a period of five hundred years this group was altered and expanded into the palace complex as shown in the plan drawing and in Figure 12-b. A full description of this transition from Temple Group to Palace Group can be found in Smith's report on the excavations of 1931 to 1937 (Smith: 1950). There seems to be no question that the change in form from Temple Group to Palace Group was accompanied by a basic change in function, although there is still some doubt as to the specific nature of the functions which were accommodated within a palace complex. (See discussion of Palace Groups in chapter 5).

The three subgroups mentioned earlier, which are related to the main group just described, lie to the east, south, and west of the main plaza and represent three distinctly different spatial concepts. East of the Palace Group is a large plaza, somewhat irregular in shape, which is bounded on the north side by a two-story palace-type building facing south into the plaza and on its south side by a low platform with a small pyramid-temple structure situated toward its eastern end (Fig. 54). The east side of

FIG. 53. Uaxactun (after Ricketson and Smith).

GROUP C

GROUP B

GROUP A

GROUP 'D'

GROUP 'E'

GROUP 'F'

UAXACTUN

PETEN,   GUATEMALA

scale
0   25   50   100   150   200   250   300 meters

0   100 200 300 400 500   750   1000 feet

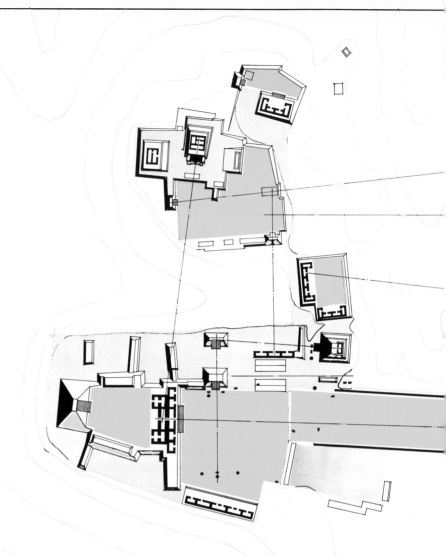

GROUPS A & B

UAXACTUN

DEPT. OF PETEN, GUATEMALA

SCALE   0 10 20 30   60   90   120   150   180

METERS

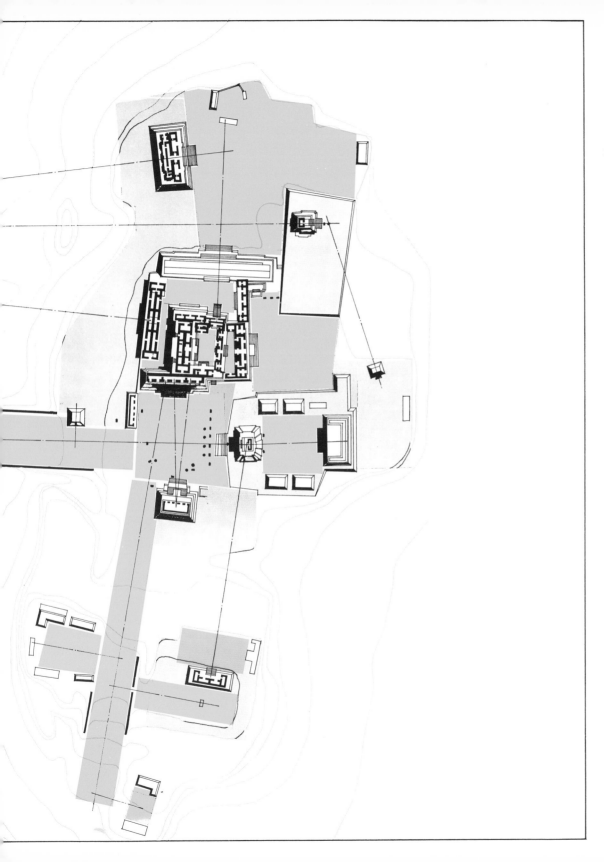

FIG. 54. Uaxactun—detail plan,
Groups A and B
(after Ricketson and Smith).

the plaza is not clearly defined and it is difficult to tell exactly where the plaza paving ended. The two buildings just described together with the long platform which terminates the east side of the palace complex constitute a somewhat disorderly group focused on the east plaza. The second subgroup lies immediately behind the temple on the south side of the plaza. It consists of a small courtyard bounded on the east and west by low platforms, on the south by a somewhat higher platform, and on the north by the pyramidal substructure supporting the temple which faces the main plaza. The whole ensemble is situated on a low platform with a lower terrace or platform just to the south. It can be observed that this same grouping of elements is repeated in Group B. The third subgroup is situated on a slightly higher rise of ground west of the main plaza. This group is connected to the main plaza by means of a short causeway which actually divides it into two smaller clusters.

Just north of the causeway is a small plaza surrounded on three sides by low platforms. Directly opposite, on the south side of the causeway, is a somewhat larger platform supporting a small building which appears to be an intermediate type between a temple and a palace. It can be noted in the plan drawing that this building faces directly toward the small temple on the south side of the main plaza. Whether this is a deliberate attempt to set up a special relationship between these two buildings or an accident due to the maintenance of a particular compass orientation is a matter for conjecture.

Taken as a whole, Group A exhibits most of those characteristics which we have come to associate with Maya notions of spatial organization. That is to say, the basic spatial structure is based on the grouping of several building elements around a plaza or courtyard. These quadrilateral complexes are based on cross-axial alignments and leave no doubt as to the designer's intentions, even though the various elements within the group may have been built at different times. The larger group exhibits no specific notion of geometrical order and depends for its coherence on smaller relationships between various subgroups. This kind of informal planning is a natural consequence of a situation where construction was carried on over an extended period of time and notions of order changed as the work progressed. Even so, it is apparent that some effort was made to maintain a comprehensible over-all order within the larger group as new structures were added and plazas and terraces were raised and extended. This is more evident in Group B, where it is obvious that considerable effort was made to develop a larger complex which included both Groups A and B.

It can be noted in the plan that Group B occupies the top of a second, and slightly lower, hill directly north of Group A. At one time the two groups were entirely separate, but early in the Classic period a graded causeway was constructed which joined the main plazas of the two groups. At a later date, the causeway was remodeled and the parapets added. The most striking aspect of the causeway is the fact that a line drawn between the central doorways of the two buildings which face the causeway across the main plazas of Groups A and B very nearly corresponds to the long central axis of the causeway. Perhaps we should only be surprised that the alignment is not perfect, but considering all the difficulties encountered in reshaping very irregular terrain and the lack of any instruments for making accurate measurements over long distances, it is clear that visual relationships between these two structures and the causeway are entirely satisfactory. The distance between the two buildings mentioned is nearly eleven hundred feet, and small deviations from precise geometry cannot be perceived at that scale.

As is the case of Group A, Group B consists of several subgroups which are associated with, or related to, a major plaza. The main plaza of Group B opens toward the causeway leading to Group A and is bounded on the west and north side by palace-type buildings set on raised platforms and on the east side by a narrow extension of this platform, together with a small pyramidal platform and the outer wall of a ballcourt. The organization of the elements around this plaza is less precise than is the case for the main plaza of Group A, but the same basic relationships are maintained and the two plazas are similar in many respects. Group B is the second largest group at Uaxactun in area but the largest group in terms of number of structures. It can also be noted that this group is divided into two sectors, the first consisting of the main plaza and its associated elements, while the second, situated on a higher rise of ground east of the main plaza, consists of a series of platforms or terraces supporting several small buildings. The eastern subgroup can be reached from the causeway by means of a narrow neck which runs at right angles to the causeway just as it enters the main plaza.

The main plaza and its associated structures was undoubtedly the most important part of Group B, both because of its size and by virtue of its relationship to the causeway. It is interesting to note, however, that the building which faces south across the plaza toward Group A is a large palace-type structure rather than a temple. The plan of this building is such that it opens both to the main plaza and to the small courtyard to the north. This courtyard is bounded on the east and west sides by low platforms and on the north side by a large pyramidal structure. The whole ensemble is situated on a large platform, making the level of the courtyard higher than the level of the main plaza. As noted in the discussion of Group A, this subgroup is related to the main plaza of Group B in the same fashion as the south court and its associated elements are related to the main plaza of Group A. The significant difference between them lies in the fact that it is possible to enter the palace building of Group B from the main plaza and then pass into the courtyard behind by means of three successive doorways, while entry into the south courtyard behind the temple fronting the main plaza of Group A could only take place at the base of the temple substructure, giving entry into the courtyard from the side.

Just east of the main plaza of Group B are a series of small plazas, or courtyards, bounded on the west side by elements associated with the main plaza and further defined by a number of low platforms, pyramidal substructures, a ball court, palace-type structures, and one large pyramid-temple. This temple faces north toward the narrow alley which connects the main plaza with the east group and probably was the most important temple in Group B. Just east of this temple are two small palace-type structures situated on a raised platform which opens to the east and south. Northwest of this temple, and contiguous with the main plaza on one side, is a small ball court which is the only ball court in Uaxactun. It is difficult to say if the open spaces on either end of the ball court served as end zones or if it was limited to the playing alley between the two sloping benches, but the space was available if needed. The position of the ball court at the head of the causeway, close to an important temple and adjacent to the main plaza, reinforces the theory that the ball games played in these courts were ceremonial in character rather than recreational. It might be argued that the whole set of elements just described forms a number of discrete subgroups, and this is quite clear in some cases—for example, the two palace buildings at the eastern extremity which are situated on a raised platform—but in other cases the relationships are ambiguous and the whole assemblage lacks the clarity and order that is readily apparent in the elements associated with the main plaza.

One further feature should be noted in connection with Group B. It can be noted in the plan drawing that there are two artificial reservoirs associated with this group (Fig. 54). The smaller of these is situated northwest of the opening in the parapet wall of the causeway and the larger lies just beyond the southwest corner of the main plaza. Since there is no river near the site, it was necessary for the inhabitants to collect and store water for use during the dry season. The large paved areas of plazas and causeways are admirably suited to the collecting of rain water which would otherwise run off and sink into the porous ground, so it was only necessary to slope the plazas in the

129

right direction in order to direct it into the collecting basins. On the east side of the larger reservoir, there appears to be a spillway to take the general drainage of the main plaza. It is obvious that additional sources of water were required, since these two reservoirs could not hold enough water to serve the whole population of Uaxactun, either for domestic or construction purposes, but they represent further evidence that the builders of Maya cities were capable of comprehensive planning which extended well beyond those needs associated solely with ceremonial activities.

A brief résumé of the growth and development of Uaxactun seems in order, since the extensive excavations which were carried out in various parts of the site over a period of eleven years have revealed that the growth of Uaxactun can be divided into a number of fairly distinct phases, each of which is represented by building remains embodying specific architectural and planning ideas. Obviously, the lines drawn between each of these phases is somewhat arbitrary, since we are actually describing a continuum, but the differences between the remains associated with each phase are great enough to make the divisions meaningful. The earliest phase, which Smith has called the Early Development period, began sometime in the first or second millenium B.C. and lasted until A.D. 100±. During this period, the inhabitants of Uaxactun and the surrounding region lived in wood-and-thatch huts without masonry foundations. As these huts were likely to be located on the higher points of ground, it is possible that some of them were situated on the same hills which later became the sites of ceremonial structures. In any case, there are no formal ceremonial structures associated with this period and whatever religious activity took place, if any, must have been in association with dwellings or in open spaces with no permanent formal setting.

The second phase, called the Late Developmental period, ended just prior to the beginning of the fourth century A.D. During this period the use of stone-and-mortar masonry was developed and the first formal ceremonial structures were constructed around paved and leveled plazas. During this period, the most important part of Uaxactun was Group E. At that time it consisted of a single level plaza with low platforms on three sides and a small truncated pyramid constructed of masonry and stucco on the fourth side. The remains of post holes on the upper level of this pyramidal structure indicate clearly that at one time it supported a building made of wood and thatch, hardly distinguishable from small huts that served as dwelling places for its builders (Fig. 3).

Because this pyramidal structure had been covered over by a larger structure at a later period, it was perfectly preserved when first excavated and its design and form raises several questions. In the first place, if we assume a long developmental period during which the concept of the pyramidal substructure was developed, why were no archaic versions of such a structure uncovered during the extensive excavations of this and other groups? If, on the other hand, this concept was imported full blown from elsewhere, what is the original source? Finally, is it possible that Uaxactun must be considered as a satellite or provincial center in relation to Tikal, and that the ceremonial structures at Uaxactun were built by émigrés from this larger and more important center? Perhaps these questions will be answered when the full reports of ten years of excavation and restoration at Tikal have been published. While this small pyramid was the most imposing structure of the period, there is some evidence that an additional ceremonial assemblage was constructed in Group A during the same period. There is no real evidence of similar building activity in the other groups during this period, so it can be assumed that the real "city building" phase began with the opening of the Classic period.

The Classic period at Uaxactun is assumed to have extended from about A.D. 280 to 890 and is divided into two major phases, Early and Late Classic. The Early Classic period lasted about three hundred and twenty years. At the beginning of this period, Group E was the dominant

130

ceremonial area, since a group of three vaulted masonry temples situated around a paved plaza were constructed here prior to the time when a similar Temple Group was constructed in Group A. During the early part of this same period, building activity commenced in earnest in all of the other groups and a fairly important pyramid-temple was built in Group B. As the Early Classic period progressed, Group E was completed and the focus of activity shifted to Groups A and B, where additional structures appeared around the main plazas and the plazas were connected by the first causeway. Groups C, D, and F also assumed their final form during the latter part of this period; the available evidence suggests that all building activity which took place during the Late Classic period was confined to Groups A and B.

The Late Classic period began around A.D. 590 and lasted until 890 or perhaps somewhat later. The last dated stela anywhere within the site carried the date A.D. 889 and was erected in Group A. If the assumption is correct that stelae were erected in conjunction with the dedication of new buildings, then we can assume that the year 889 marks the end of any important building activity at Uaxactun. During the Late Classic period many new buildings were constructed, plazas and terraces were extended in both Groups A and B, and the causeway was raised and parapets added along the edges. The great palace complex in Group A assumed its final form, making the transition from Temple Group to Palace Group complete. Various kinds of houses, including masonry as well as thatch-and-pole types, were erected in the suburban areas adjacent to the main center and some were located within the main ceremonial center itself. From a very humble beginning, Uaxactun had grown to become a center of real importance. While much of the ceremonial activity was confined to Groups A and B toward the end of the Late Classic period, it seems likely that the other groups continued to get some use until the final abandoning of the site, when all building activity ceased and the jungle soon reclaimed the great plazas and monuments representing the accumu-

lation of six hundred years of architectural evolution.

Before closing this discussion of Uaxactun, further mention must be made of the residential areas surrounding the main ceremonial area. While these peripheral areas were not surveyed in the same manner as at Tikal or Dzibilchaltun, a cruciform area centered on the main plaza was surveyed in order to verify the existence of house mounds. Within the area surveyed (approximately one million square meters of habitable land), seventy-eight house mounds were located. Since many of these were multi-platform mounds representing a housing cluster, the total number of houses represented might well be one hundred and fifty to two hundred. Assuming that only 25 per cent of the mounds were occupied simultaneously, a minimum figure of two hundred and seventy persons per square mile was obtained, assuming that the entire area devoted to housing conformed to the pattern as found in the area mapped (Ricketson and Ricketson: 1937). This is substantially lower than the figures obtained for Tikal or Dzibilchaltun, but the density might well be higher if the same mapping techniques had been used here as were used at the latter sites. Nevertheless, the lower density of housing combined with the size of the ceremonial center itself suggests that Uaxactun should probably be considered as a small urban center according to the list of categories as outlined in chapter 4. The density of houses in the peripheral areas indicates that a resident population of several thousand can be postulated, which is well above the population we have assumed for ceremonial centers.

The question as to why two centers the size of Tikal and Uaxactun should be found in such close proximity is hard to answer. Everything indicates that they were occupied at the same time and both had fairly long life spans, although it now appears that extensive ceremonial assemblages were being built at Tikal at a time when Uaxactun was nothing more than a small cluster of houses. There is some indication that during the Late Classic period there was some kind of rivalry between the two sites, as a defensive ditch, or moat, several kilometers in length has recently been located at a point approximately midway between Tikal and Uaxactun. The full implications of this assumed defensive element are not clearly understood, but it suggests that Uaxactun grew large enough to be considered as a threat to its more important neighbor. We have assumed that Tikal was a large regional center which exercised administrative control over a large surrounding area which would have included Uaxactun, at least up to the time when Uaxactun apparently asserted its independence.

The proximity of these two centers also suggests that conditions in this part of the Peten were extremely favorable for *milpa* agriculture, as the density of population in this region appears to have been much higher than in other parts of the Maya area where the larger centers are generally farther apart. Other large sites such as Nakum and Naranjo are not more than twenty miles from Uaxactun and Tikal, and there are countless smaller centers on all sides. The only other areas with comparable densities are the Puuc and Rio Bec areas to the north, where settlement appears to have been equally dense and numerous large centers are found within a few miles of one another. Further light may be shed on this question when the final reports on Tikal have been issued, since one of the last undertakings was the mapping of a test strip some sixteen hundred and forty feet wide to a point seven and one-half miles south of the Great Plaza. The information gained from this survey should do much to clarify the nature of the larger settlement patterns in this region and, hopefully, will clarify the position of Uaxactun both in relation to Tikal as well as to its own suburban and satellite centers.

The site of Piedras Negras is located in the department of Peten, Guatemala, on the east bank of the Usumacinta River. In this region the river forms the boundary line between Mexico and Guatemala. The area shown in the plan drawing extends nearly half a mile from north to south, and about a third of a mile from east to west (Fig. 55). A considerable amount of excavation was undertaken at the site during the early 1930's by archaeologists representing the University Museum, University of Pennsylvania, and most of the information available in regard to its over-all plan and details of buildings is due to their efforts. The site of Yaxchilan, which is on the southwest bank of the Usumacinta River and therefore located in the state of Chiapas, Mexico, lies about thirty miles downstream from Piedras Negras, and it might be expected that the two sites would show certain affinities due to their close proximity, but such is not the case. While they lie adjacent to the same river and were built and occupied during the same period, their plan organizations are significantly different. These differences will be discussed in greater detail in the description of Yaxchilan.

The site plan shows that the natural topography is very irregular and there is a series of hills rising close to the river (Fig. 55). As has already been pointed out in connection with other sites, the common practice followed at most Maya sites was to select the tops of hills or highest points of ground as the location for important ceremonial groups. This practice was also followed at Piedras Negras, even though this meant that most of the buildings had almost no visual or physical relationship to the river front. In fact, the entire scheme shows little concern for the presence of the river, although it must have been an important means of transportation and communication within the Usumacinta Valley. It is true that the general distribution of structures follows an arc, running from the lower

part of the site on the south to the highest point in the northwest quadrant, which roughly parallels the bend of the river, but there is no evidence of a causeway or roadway which might have connected the city with the river. The only logical point of entry into the city from the river would appear to be through the small draw which runs down to the river from the southwest corner of the east plaza. Further excavations will be required to verify such a connection.

The central ceremonial area of Piedras Negras consists of three distinct groupings of structures, each of which is associated with a large plaza area. For purposes of discussion these can be called the South Group, the East Group, and the Northwest Group. The South Group is the largest and contains several subgroups related to secondary plazas in addition to the structures grouped around the main plaza. The East Group is the smallest and consists, for the most part, of two large pyramid-temple structures which face into a large plaza at right angles to one another. The Northwest Group consists of two parts: the group of structures which opens directly into the large plaza, and the acropolis, which rises in a northwesterly direction to the top of the highest hill within the site (Fig. 56).

Each of the three main groups forms a discrete entity, although some effort was made to link them together. The East and South Groups are related by means of an intermediate or transitional plaza, although this plaza can also be thought of as being part of the South Group. The Northwest group is linked to the East Group. The transition between the two plazas is accomplished by means of a broad terrace at the foot of the stairway. In spite of the somewhat random positioning of the three major groups with respect to one another, there is a clear path of circulation between them and it would have been possible

Piedras
Negras

FIG. 55. Piedras Negras (after Parris).

PIEDRAS NEGRAS

PETEN, GUATEMALA

N

SCALE
0   25   50   75   100   125
METERS

to move from the small plaza at the far end of the South Group up the main plaza of the Northwest Group over a continuously paved surface, unbroken except for stairways or ramps. The plazas or courtyards are differentiated from one another by corridorlike spaces or narrow openings and the whole sequence of events culminates in the acropolis, which is the most monumental ensemble of the entire scheme. The clarity of the internal circulation scheme which is apparent at Piedras Negras is not found at most other sites, where they appear to have been no specific circulation connections between many of the major groupings.

The orientation of structures in all three groups is generally consistent, although the orientation varies about thirty-five degrees from the cardinal points of the compass. There is no obvious explanation for this deviation; at most other sites great care was exercised in orienting buildings within a few degrees of true east-west or north-south directions, and this is particularly true in the Peten area. It might be argued that the orientation of buildings at this site was determined by the shapes of hills, and the builders selected those orientations which required the least amount of earth moving, but this is a shaky assumption, since the reshaping of hills at many other sites was undertaken for the specific purpose of establishing predetermined orientations. Neither can it be demonstrated that building orientations were determined by the river. Many important buildings face away from the river and there is little about the scheme to suggest that it was a strong determining factor for either orientation or positioning of building elements. For the moment, then, the question of orientation must be left open.

The South Group, which occupies the top of an elongated hill running north and south, consists of two subgroups in addition to the group of structures organized around the main plaza. The main plaza is bounded on the northwest side by a large pyramid-temple structure, on the southwest side by a pair of similar structures situated on a raised platform, on the southeast side by an-

other pair of pyramidal structures, and on the northeast side by a long platform which also serves as the boundary for the ball court just behind it. Because of the advanced state of ruin of several of the pyramidal structures, it is difficult to determine if they supported masonry buildings; at the present time only the smaller pyramid on the platform on the northwest side of the plaza supports exposed building remains—in this case, a small one-room temple. The presence of stairways on three of the other substructures is a good indication that they also supported temple-type buildings, even though they may have been made of perishable materials. In spite of the presence of pairs of structures in place of the usual single structures on two sides of the main plaza, it seems reasonable to characterize this group as a typical Temple Group, which has been described in detail in chapter 5. The presence of a row of stelae at the base of the temple on the northwest side of the plaza, together with its size, suggest that it was the most important element of the group, though traditionally the temple facing the open side would occupy the key position.

Southwest of the main plaza is a secondary plaza which is connected to it by means of a narrower transitional space. A fairly large pyramidal structure bounds this transitional space on the southeast side, while the balance of the plaza is bounded largely by low terraces. A series of small terraces cascade down the slope from the southeast side of the plaza, but there are no buildings associated with these terraces. North of the main plaza is another small plaza, which also serves as a transitional space between the main plaza and the east plaza. A large ball court, with well-defined back courts, bounded this plaza on the southeast side, together with two low platforms situated just at the edge of the plaza. Several other platforms are associated with the ball court, together with a small one-room building which faces into a small courtyard southeast of the ball court proper. Directly opposite the ball court on the northeast side of the plaza is a large pyramidal structure which differs markedly in its orientation from most of the other structures in all three groups. While its position in plan suggests that it is related to the secondary plaza, it actually faces directly toward one of the pyramidal structures fronting the main plaza. Just north of this structure are two small single-room buildings which face into an enclosed courtyard. Since these buildings are not situated on pyramidal substructures, they cannot be considered as being temples, even though they have the same size and shape as temples.

The East Group is much less complicated than the group just described and consists primarily of two pyramid-temple structures which are situated on the northeast and southeast sides of a large plaza. A narrow neck of the plaza extends in a southeasterly direction and is terminated by a platform built into the side of a hill. A masonry building with an unusual ground plan faces toward the plaza extension from the northeast side. The pyramid-temple structure on the northeast side of the main plaza is worthy of special mention, since it probably was the most imposing single structure in the city. The temple itself is a large multichambered building with five doorways facing onto the plaza. The pyramidal substructure which supports the temple is partly a natural hill, which has been extended and terraced to form a typical stepped pyramidal base where it is exposed to the plaza. The importance of this structure is further attested to by the fact that there are ten stelae and one altar associated with it. Most of these stelae are situated in the plaza, close to the base of the pyramid, but two of them flank the stairway on the first step of the pyramid. Because of its height, a magnificent view of the river could have been obtained from any of the doorways of this temple, but there is still some doubt if this was an important consideration in its location. The pyramid-temple on the southeast side of the plaza is somewhat smaller than the one just described. The temple is a one-room building with three doorways. It faces toward a large stairway which leads to a low platform on the southeast side of the acropolis plaza, and this relationship is too precise to be acciden-

tal. It also helps to explain the presence of this stairway next to a much larger stairway which also leads to the acropolis plaza.

The Northwest Group, which includes the acropolis and the other structures associated with the acropolis plaza, culminates the entire scheme of Piedras Negras. The large plaza at the base of the acropolis measures approximately 400 feet by 250 feet in size. As indicated earlier, this plaza can be reached from below by means of two stairways which terminate in a small terrace raised slightly above the level of the east plaza. The largest stairway is about 130 feet wide, making it truly monumental in size. The acropolis plaza is bounded on the southwest side by a series of platforms, terraces, and pyramidal structures, on the northeast side by a large pyramid-temple structure, and on the northwest side by a series of elements which form the base of the acropolis proper. In front of the temple on the northeast side of the plaza is a small ball court with open ends. The central axis of the temple bisects the playing alley of the ball court and this axis is terminated on the far side of the plaza by a terraced platform. There appears to be no special position for ball courts with respect to other structures, when a large number of cases are examined. In most cases they are adjacent to, or part of, major plazas, but their specific locations and relationships to surrounding structures vary. In the case being discussed, the ball court is obviously related to an important temple, but this is an exception rather than the rule. A more thorough discussion of ball courts may be found in chapter 5.

By far the most interesting and imposing group of structures at Piedras Negras is the Acropolis Group, which begins on the northwest side of the acropolis plaza and terminates in a temple which is situated at the highest point of ground within the city (Fig. 56). Acropolis Groups in general have already been discussed in chapter 5 and some reference was made to the acropolis here, but it is deserving of a more careful examination. The structures which comprise the Acropolis Group can be divided

137

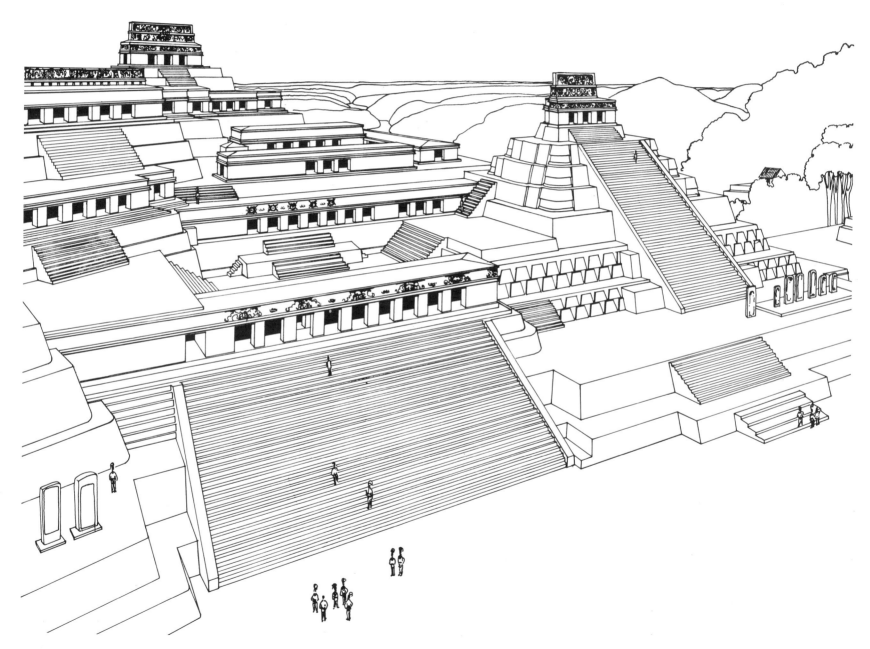

FIG. 56. Piedras Negras (restoration, after Proskouriakoff).

into three main subgroups. The first group, on the southwest side of the acropolis mound, is associated with a broad terrace which is reached from the main plaza by means of a short stairway. Behind this terrace, the hill has been reshaped in a pyramidal form and a large stairway leads to the top of this platform which, in turn, supports a smaller pyramidal platform. There are no building remains indicated on the top of this platform and it is possible that it was left unfinished or was never intended to support a building. On the northeast side of the acropolis mound is a similar, but much larger, group of elements. Here again a broad terrace is situated above the level of the main plaza, which is reached from the plaza by a set of two stairways. This terrace must have been of considerable importance, since it supports a row of eight large stelae. Rising behind this terrace is a large, wellshaped stepped pyramid which supports a small singleroom temple. From this temple much of the rest of the city could be seen and it dominates the acropolis plaza. Between these two sets of structures lies the main part of the acropolis, a unified series of courtyards and palacetype structures, which embodies the most sophisticated architectural ideas developed by the builders of Piedras Negras.

From the level of a major plaza a broad stairway leads up to a long palace-type structure which in plan consists of two long galleries. Passing through this building, we enter a small enclosed courtyard. Stairways to the left and right lead from this courtyard to small terraces on either side, but the main path is straight ahead, where another stairway leads to a second palace structure. Behind this building is another courtyard, situated at a higher level, surrounded on three sides by large palace-type buildings. Behind the northwest building of this group is an even smaller courtyard, which gives access to a large temple building situated on the crown of the hill nearly three hundred feet above the river. South of this temple, and at a lower level, is an additional courtyard, bounded on two sides by large palace-type buildings. The lower slopes on the northwest side of the acropolis mound have also been partially leveled and terraced in several locations, but there are no building remains associated with these terraces.

The importance of the Acropolis Group lies in the clarity of expression of an ordered sequence of spaces and events in which an obvious hierarchy is established. Stated more simply, the farther one moves through the sequence, the more private the spaces become, and it is obvious that only the members of the elite class were permitted to penetrate into the inner spaces far enough to enter the temple which terminates the sequence. It is also clear that the basic spatial concept utilized here is the same as was used at Uxmal (discussed later in the chapter), but in this case the regular, and almost symmetrical, geometry which characterizes Uxmal (Fig. 191) has given way to a more irregular configuration which has been determined in large part by the original shape of the hill. The fact that this irregularity in no way detracts from the clarity of the conception is a measure of the degree to which the architects of Piedras Negras recognized the nature of organic planning as opposed to rigid formalism. The distinction between these approaches lies in the fact that an organic scheme is able to accommodate to the existing conditions of its context, while the formalistic approach imposes its own rigid internal order without regard to the conditions of the natural environment. Certainly the Acropolis Group here takes full advantage of the existing topography and attains true monumentality on the basis of its conceptual order rather than formalized geometry.

Yaxchilan

The site of Yaxchilan is located in the state of Chiapas, Mexico, on the southwest bank of the Usumacinta River, about thirty miles downstream from Piedras Negras. A preliminary survey of the site was made early in this century by Teobert Maler, but his rough-sketch map gave a very distorted view of the relationships between the various building elements (Maler: 1903). The site plan shown in Figure 57 is based on a much more accurate survey map made later by John S. Bolles. Yaxchilan is best known in the literature for its outstanding collection of well-preserved carved stone lintels and stelae. Since our concern is with architecture and city planning, no reference will be made to these monuments, but interested readers will find a large collection of good photographs of the best-preserved carvings in Maler's monograph on Yaxchilan (Maler: 1903). Unfortunately, no large-scale program of excavation and restoration has ever been attempted at this important site because of its extreme inaccessibility, but this circumstance may soon be remedied, as a road is presently being built from Palenque to Bonampak and from there to Yaxchilan.

The site was obviously selected with great care, as it is located at the tip of a great bend in the river (Fig. 57). The major part of the city extends as a linear chain of plazas and structures for over half a mile along the bank of the river. Several other groups of structures are situated on ridges or hilltops behind this lower section, and, while these groups are rather isolated from each other, some effort has been made to connect them to the main group along the river. It can be noted in the plan that there is very little consistency in the orientation of various buildings and no real effort has been made to recognize the cardinal points of the compass. Many of the buildings face toward the river, but the specific relationships between these buildings and the river are not clear.

It is worthwhile to compare the site plan of Yaxchilan with that of Piedras Negras (Fig. 55), since they are situated on the same river, and the existing topography, which is very irregular in both cases, appears at first glance to be quite similar. It has already been pointed out in the discussion of Piedras Negras that the three groups of structures which comprise the central portion of that city are situated on high points of ground and, in general position and orientation, tend to ignore the existence of the river. At Yaxchilan, however, the largest number of structures lies close to the river and many of the important temples on higher points of ground appear to have been deliberately oriented toward the river. A closer examination of the natural contours surrounding the build-up areas of Yaxchilan suggests that the great difference in plan organization between the two cities is due in large part to specific differences in natural topography. At Yaxchilan, it is apparent that a natural shelf running parallel to the river was exploited by its builders to produce the long narrow plaza of the main group. This has given the city a very unusual form, but the generating force behind this decision, i.e., a desire to capitalize to the fullest extent on usable features of existing terrain, is consistent with the practice followed at other Maya sites in this region. Some effort has been made to retain the traditional forms of building groupings, but in many cases these have been considerably distorted in order to adjust to existing ground configuration. Once again we have a good example of organic planning as opposed to formalistic planning.

As already indicated, the main group of structures forms two rather irregular rows on either side of the long plaza which runs parallel to the river. The natural shelf has been reshaped and a retaining wall built along the river in order to make the plaza level, but even these adjustments have failed to produce the typical plan scheme

140

in which compact groups of structures are situated around rectilinear plazas in discrete clusters. The long plaza forms a continuous paved surface, which is partially interrupted in several places by platforms projecting into it; but in a very real sense the whole agglomerate must be considered as a single complex. With this complex, three major subgroups can be defined, but these groups are rather loosely knit and the boundaries defining them are indefinite. The first subgroup lies at the southeast end of the plaza and is defined on the upper side by a series of platforms and terraces which step up the hillside. The river side is partially defined by retaining walls and a row of very low platforms toward the northwest end of the group. A ball court, with the playing alley parallel to the long axis of the plaza, terminates this group at the same end. The southeast end of the plaza is loosely terminated where the terracing dies into the existing contours. Three small platforms are situated toward the center of the plaza, including one well-shaped pyramidal structure with the remains of a stairway on the northwest side. There are no masonry-building remains associated with this group and, with the exception of the ball court, it appears to consist of only minor elements.

The second subgroup, which includes the central portion of the long plaza, is bounded on the southeast by the ball court mentioned above, on the northwest end by a narrowing of the plaza at the point where the second ball court occurs, and on the other two sides by almost continuous rows of terraces, platforms, and buildings. On the river side, the plaza has been built up by means of a high retaining wall, while it has been slightly cut into the contours on the hillside. The central plaza is roughly diamond-shaped and at its widest point opens up toward a small ravine on the hillside. Two platforms project into the central plaza at right angles to the river, differentiating it into three smaller courts.

The southeast court appears to be limited to activities associated with the ball court, as the central axis of the platform on its northwest side bisects the playing alley of the ball court. In common with many ball courts that are situated in the open spaces of plazas, it has no well-defined back courts. The central court is the largest, and was obviously a place of considerable importance, since two large temple buildings face into it and it gives access to the head of the ravine where a group of subsidiary mounds is situated (Fig. 58). Another small building is situated on the opposite side of this court, but it faces toward the river rather than the court (Fig. 59). The northwest, or third, court of this group is long and narrow and is bounded on the southwest end by a platform situated at right angles to the long axis of the plaza. The northwest side of this court is marked only by a narrowing of plaza which opens up into a large, rectilinear court just beyond the second ball court. This courtyard was also of some importance, since five masonry buildings and a number of stelae and altars are associated with it. The ball court at the northwest end of this courtyard has one back court defined by a platform at the edge of the terrace along the river.

The third subgroup of the main complex is situated at the northwest end of the long plaza. It is bounded at the northwest end by a series of rising terraces, culminating in a large pyramidal structure which is oriented toward the long axis of the plaza. Once again, there are a series of platforms along the riverside together with two well-shaped pyramidal structures on the hillside, situated on a broad terrace high above the plaza. One of these structures supports a small temple building (Fig. 60). Another temple-type building faces southeast into the plaza at the point where it broadens out and rises slightly (Fig. 61). This group comes closer to assuming the typical plan arrangement found at most sites, where the major elements form a quadrilateral grouping around a level plaza.

In addition to the main complex, which has just been described, there are three other major groups situated on the higher ground to the southwest. Two of these are groups sited on the tops of hills, while the third follows partway up the crest of a ridge which ultimately leads to the highest group within the site. A few scattered mounds

141

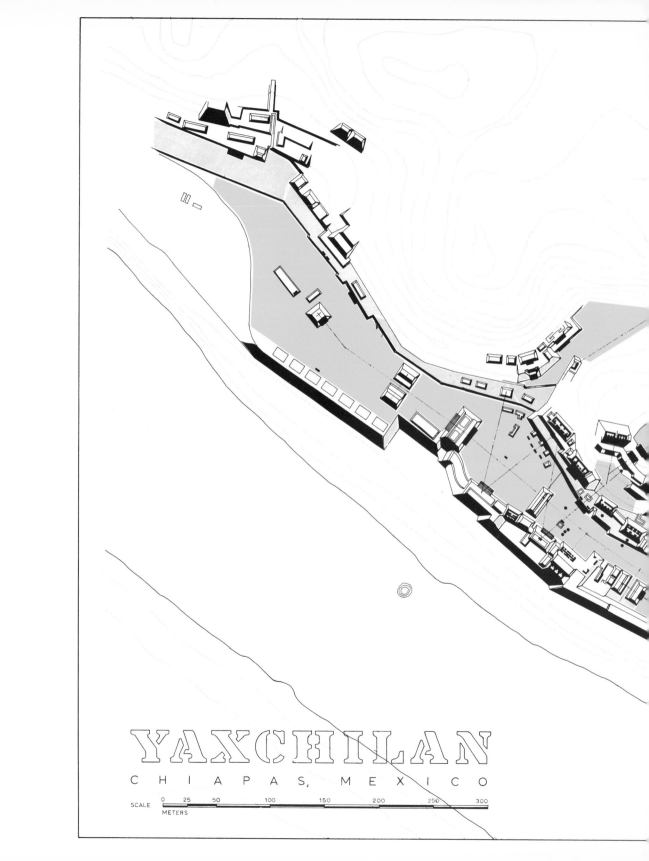

YAXCHILAN
CHIAPAS, MEXICO

SCALE |0 25   50   100   150   200   250   300|
METERS

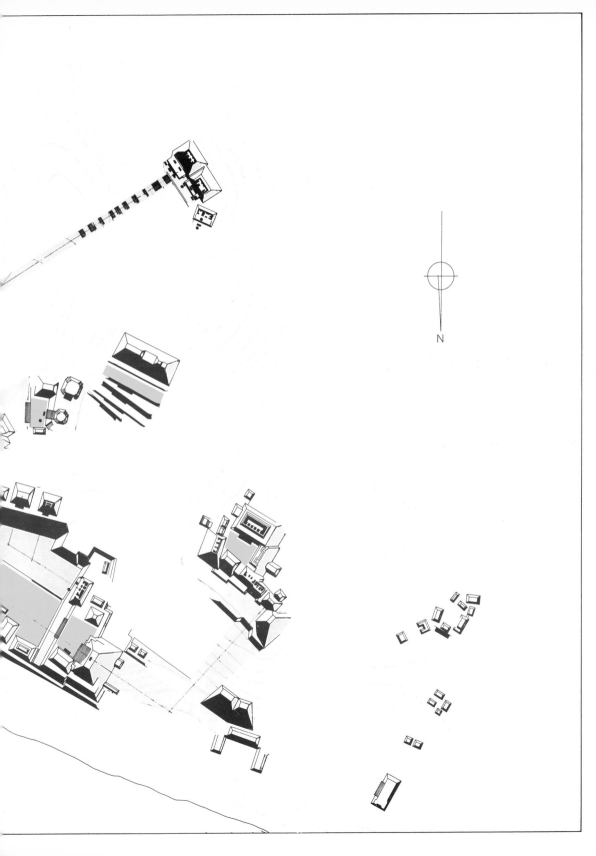

FIG. 57. Yaxchilan (after Bolles).

lie outside these groups, including a small cluster of low mounds at the western edge of the site which appear to be house mounds. Since the periphery of the site has never been thoroughly surveyed, it is likely there are many other house mounds which are not shown on the site map. The three major groups appear to be completely separate from one another and any circulation connections between them must have been by narrow trails, as has been postulated for other sites. It is clear, however, that two of these groups were intended to have some specific relationship to the main complex along the river front, particularly the linear group that moves up along the ridge running into the central plaza.

The westernmost of these peripheral groups is situated on the top of a small hill just above the northwest end of the main complex. It consists of a low terrace with a small pyramidal structure on its northwest side, above which is a quadrilateral group of platforms and buildings situated around a small plaza. Associated with this group are several large temple-type buildings, one of which is nearly 80 feet long. This building clearly dominates the group, both in size and position, and looks out to the river which lies nearly 180 feet below. Because of its dislocation from the main complex and the other major groupings, it is possible that this group was constructed early in the history of the site and played a minor role at the time the main complex was completed.

The second of these subsidiary groups stretches along the crest of a ridge which runs upward in a gentle S curve in a southwest direction from the northwest court of the central plaza. A stairway from this plaza leads into a small courtyard which gives access to three temple-type buildings situated on terraces above (Fig. 66). Behind the uppermost temple (Figs. 62, 63) is a small plaza with a broad stairway leading to a small terrace bounded on the north and south by pyramidal mounds. Just above is a second terrace supporting two highly articulated platforms, one of which is connected by a stairway to the lower terrace. A series of narrow terraces continues up the ridge beyond

this group, terminating in a long pyramidal structure with no exposed building remains. Conceptually, this rather strung-out group of elements bears little relationship to the Acropolis Group at Piedras Negras, aside from the fact that both involve a sequential series of events moving up a hillside. At Yaxchilan, this appears to be the accidental consequence of utilizing existing topography in the most direct way, while at Piedras Negras a very monumental scheme has been developed based on a predetermined hierarchy of spaces and enclosures. Given time, this group of structures might have evolved into something approaching the acropolis notion, but it has not yet reached that point.

The third of these subsidiary major groups is situated on the top of a hill nearly a quarter of a mile away from the main complex. This grouping consists of a pair of pyramid-temple structures which face toward the central court of the main plaza in a northeasterly direction, together with a small temple-type building, situated on a low platform, which faces in a more northerly direction (Fig. 67). Remnants of stepped walkways can be seen leading down from the shallow platform in front of the largest temple of the group in the general direction of the main complex, but it does not lead directly to any other group of structures. In spite of the fact that the pair of temples is some distance away from the main center, their importance is attested to by the fact that they are situated at the highest point within the site and enjoy a commanding view of the balance of the center as well as a good portion of the surrounding terrain, including the river. There are also a rather large number of stelae and altars associated with this group, which further attests to its importance (Figs. 64, 65). The difference in orientation between the small building on the low platform and the pair of temples just above is hard to explain on the basis of topography and appears to be a deliberate effort to establish two different sets of axial relationships with structures below.

Taken as a whole, the site of Yaxchilan makes a good case study for the theory that the organization of many

Maya cities was based on fortuitous features of existing topography rather than formal conceptions at a scale larger than the individual groups of structures, which collectively make up larger centers or cities. Certainly the great mall-like plaza just above the river, with its long rows of structures extending along either side, would have made an imposing sight when viewed from the river. But the effect is created by size rather than specific order and does not result in true monumentality, which is dependent on conceptual relationships rather than dimension. It can also be noted that, in spite of the fact that the greater part of the city lies immediately adjacent to the river, there is no apparent entry from the river into the main plaza. To be sure, the plaza does open toward the river at the southeast end, but there is no formal entrance at this point. The only real concession made to the river, in terms of a specific architectural commitment, is the small circular mound situated in the river opposite the central court of the main plaza. This structure was obviously meant to serve as some kind of marker and may have originally supported a monument which has since been washed away during a flood.

The lack of any strong relationships between the river and various parts of the center, both here and at Piedras Negras, is a curious circumstance, since the river must have been a source of food as well as an important means of communication between centers. It is navigable during a good part of the year and materials for making small boats or rafts are found in abundance along its banks. Perhaps the fact that large river-front sites are extremely rare prevented the builders of both Yaxchilan and Piedras Negras from establishing a new tradition involving both natural and man-made features. Traditionally, Maya builders were more concerned with transcending nature than creating dramatic vistas and views of natural features such as rivers or mountains. The generic ceremonial groups are inner-oriented and attention is focused on the open spaces of man-made plazas and courtyards. Nevertheless, the planning is highly organic in the same sense that the layout of Piedras Negras is organic; part of the natural environment has been reorganized but not obliterated, and a viable ecological balance is achieved.

FIG. 58. Yaxchilan—Structure No. 20
(photograph by T. Maler).

FIG. 59. Yaxchilan—Structure No. 6
(photograph by T. Maler).

FIG. 60. Yaxchilan—Structure No. 30
(photograph by T. Maler).

FIG. 61. Yaxchilan—Structure No. 19
(photograph by T. Maler).

FIG. 62. Yaxchilan—Structure No. 33 (photograph by T. Maler).

FIG. 63. Yaxchilan—Structure No. 33, Plan and Elevation.

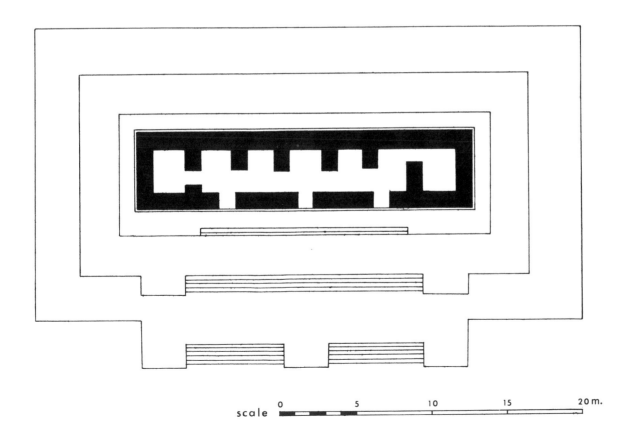

scale   0   5   10   15   20 m.

FIG. 64. Yaxchilan—Structure No. 40 and Stela No. 11 (photograph by T. Maler).

FIG. 65. Yaxchilan—detail of Stela No. 11 (photograph by T. Maler).

FIG. 66. Yaxchilan—Structure No. 25
(photograph by T. Maler).

FIG. 67. Yaxchilan—Structure No. 39
(photograph by T. Maler).

Bonampak is a small ceremonial center located on the north side of the Lacanha Valley in the state of Chiapas, Mexico. It is about thirty-six air miles southeast of Yaxchilan, the closest major site of which we have any extensive knowledge. Because of their proximity to each other and because Yaxchilan is a large center with many imposing buildings, it would be reasonable to assume that Bonampak was a provincial town, dominated by, or even founded by, a group from Yaxchilan. (We have suggested earlier that Yaxchilan might well be a major urban center.) Unfortunately, the physical evidence for this relationship is fairly scant. Some similarities in details may be noted between buildings at the two sites, but for the most part each retains its own distinctive character.

The topography at the two sites is significantly different so that no logical comparisons may be drawn between the site plans. At Yaxchilan, many of the more important buildings lie on a shelf which runs parallel to the river, and these same structures are associated with a series of interconnected courtyards and plazas. Behind this shelf, the ground rises steeply and other structures are situated on the higher points of ground. In contrast, there is only one large plaza at Bonampak and all of the standing structures are situated on several levels of a natural hill which has been artificially terraced and leveled (Fig. 68). It is also hard to draw comparisons between individual buildings at these two sites. At Yaxchilan, the standing buildings are large and elaborate, while at Bonampak they are small, single-chambered structures (with one exception which will be described later), with little elaboration (Figs. 69, 70). Regardless of any relationships which Bonampak might have had with Yaxchilan or other larger centers, it is an extremely interesting site in its own right, as it illustrates the concept of the ceremonial center in its simplest physical form.

As can be seen in the site plan (Fig. 68), Bonampak is a compact and well-organized center in which all the structures are related to a single large plaza measuring about 300 feet from east to west and 350 feet from north to south. The plaza was paved and generally leveled, although it slopes slightly toward the southwest corner. Surrounding the plaza on three sides are low mounds and terraces, while the south side is defined by a small hill which has been artificially terraced, forming a rough stepped pyramid which serves as the supporting base for a number of small structures. The remains of nine buildings are found at various levels on this terraced mound, five of them in a somewhat irregular row near the top (Figs. 71, 72). All but one of these buildings face north toward the main plaza and there is a surprising coincidence of alignment of the axes through the doorways of these buildings with the stelae in the plaza and those on the surrounding mounds or terraces. The significance of these alignments is certainly debatable, but it is difficult to account for the variation in orientations of these structures, particularly the five small structures near the top of the mound, except in terms of some special relationship to elements such as the stelae in the plaza below.

Three of these stelae are outstanding examples of the sculptor's art and because of their assumed significance in relation to building alignments are worthy of special notice. Stela No. 1, which is located near the center of the main plaza (Fig. 73), is too badly damaged to be reassembled, but some of the individual pieces are well preserved and the details of the carving are extremely delicate (Figs. 74, 75). Stela No. 2 and Stela No. 3, which are positioned on either side of the main stairway near the bottom of the terraced mound, are also noteworthy examples of Late Classic art (Figs. 76, 77). Stela No. 2 is dated at approximately A.D. 783 and Stela No. 3 at A.D. 785. These dates are

Bonampak

153

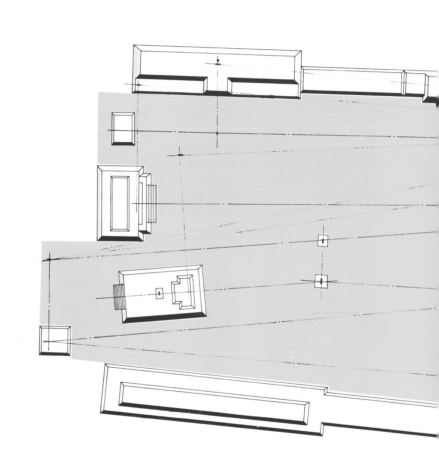

FIG. 68. Bonampak (after Ruppert).

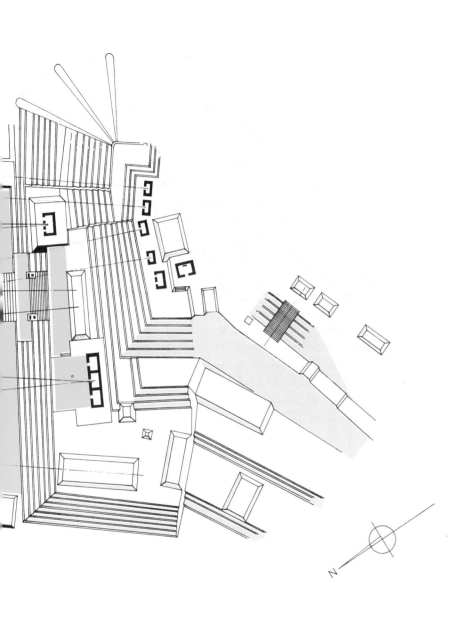

BONAMPAK

C H I A P A S ,   M E X I C O

SCALE ·

METERS

0   10   20   30   40   50   100

based on the style of the glyphs and sculptural details, as the calendar glyphs are too badly eroded to be translated directly. The position of these latter stelae, at the head of the main stairway which gives access to the upper terraces, would suggest that they commemorate some important events in the life of Bonampak beyond the mere recording of dates, but the meaning of many of the glyphs inscribed on these monuments is still not known, so we can only guess at their importance in terms of their positions.

In chapter 4 it was suggested that the ceremonial center in its generic form consisted of a single plaza and its associated structures. In this ideal form, the complex would consist of three pyramid-temple structures arranged around three sides of a large plaza. The fourth side was normally open, suggesting that movement into the plaza was by means of this open side, thus giving emphasis to the structure which terminated this axial approach. In its general spatial outlines Bonampak conforms to this pattern, even though the terraced hill on the south side cannot be said to be a pyramid and the terraces which flank the plaza to the east and west do not appear to have supported buildings. The basic relationships of solids and voids are maintained, however, and to this extent the archetypical form notion is retained. Other small mounds can be found in the areas to the north, east, and west of the main plaza, but their specific relationships to the ceremonial area are unknown. Some of these mounds undoubtedly represent house remains, but their number and character cannot be determined without extensive surveying.

Perhaps the greatest deviation from traditional ideas is found in the positioning of the nine structures on the terraced hill. These do not in any way suggest an Acropolis Group, nor do the temples, if indeed they are temples, conform to the tradition of groupings around a central plaza or courtyard. In most of the literature the hill and its associated structures is called an acropolis, but this is clearly a misnomer, since there is no hierarchical ordering of the various elements and there are no enclosed courtyards

which form the semiprivate spaces so necessary to the ordered sequence of an Acropolis Group as defined in chapter 5. All of the structures on the hill face directly onto the main plaza (with one exception) and the two lower structures (Structures No. 2 and No. 3) can be reached by separate stairways which connect them directly to the plaza (Figs. 71, 72). The most obvious explanation for this lack of adherence to tradition would be that the hill was exploited for its unique potential which allowed for views outward rather than internally oriented courtyards which are characteristic of Temple and Acropolis Groups. It is also likely that the terracing of the hill took place over an extended period of time and that buildings were added without regard for a preconceived scheme. Still, the break with tradition is very pronounced and some other explanation seems to be required.

Tentative dates obtained from stelae and carved lintels in several buildings indicate that much of the construction we now see exposed took place toward the very end of the Classic period. This might suggest that some significant alterations to the traditional pattern of ceremonial activity had begun to take place, leading to the replacement of the formal spatial ideas of the earlier Classic period with the more casual siting of buildings as noted here. There is no reason to believe that Bonampak was anything more than a minor ceremonial center within a region boasting several large urban centers and was likely to be out of the mainstream of events as far as architecture was concerned.

In spite of its seeming provincial status, Bonampak is an extremely important site in terms of our knowledge of Maya life because of the murals which cover the walls on the interior of Structure No. 2, the three-room building located on the lower terrace near the southwest corner of the terraced hill. It is not possible to include a photograph of this structure, since it has been entirely covered over with a wood-and-tin shed as a means of protecting the murals from further damage by the elements. The building containing the murals is the largest standing structure at Bonampak and is made up of three vaulted rooms, each about 8½ feet wide by 15 feet long and 17 feet high. Murals of any sort from the Classic period are extremely rare, and full-color murals such as are found here are almost unknown elsewhere. Aside from their unquestioned artistic value, they are probably the most important source of information in regard to the actual nature of activities in the ceremonial center presently available to the researcher. The murals are extremely realistic in that they depict scenes from real life, and the figures of the individuals represented appear to be portraits rather than the stylized or symbolic representations which are normally found on stelae (Fig. 78).

It does not seem appropriate to describe these murals in any great detail, as they have been thoroughly documented elsewhere (Ruppert, Thompson, and Proskouriakoff: 1955). What is of importance to us, however, is the fact that all of the scenes depict some aspect of ceremonial activity as it must have actually taken place at Bonampak during the period of its occupation. The backgrounds of the paintings show only the stepped sides of pyramids or terraces and it is clear that the stepped form of these structures had some functional as well as symbolic value. The stepped pyramids or terraces are also shown as being painted, and it is likely that much of the large terraced mound on which this building rests was painted in the same colors shown in the murals. It is also interesting to note that the paintings contain no direct references to nature; the environment in which the action takes place is entirely man-made. Not a single tree shows on the skyline and the omnipresent jungle might as well not exist. The paintings are perhaps the best evidence available in support of one of the notions advanced earlier in this study to the effect that the humanization of the natural environment tends to lead to a complete denial of nature. Thus, the ceremonial center as a human place becomes the most visible expression of man's symbolic detachment from his fortuitous surroundings.

FIG. 69. Bonampak—Main Plaza and Acropolis mound.

FIG. 70. Bonampak—Main Plaza and Acropolis (restoration).

FIG. 71. Bonampak—Main Plaza and Acropolis.

FIG. 73. Bonampak—
Main Plaza
and Stela No. 1 (right).

FIG. 72. Bonampak—Acropolis, Structure No. 2
in foreground.

FIG. 74. Bonampak—detail of Stela No. 1.

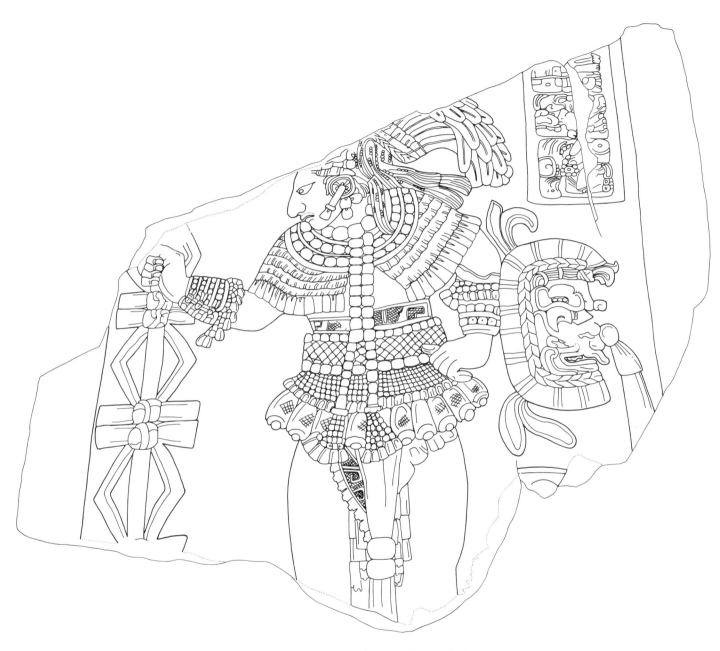

FIG. 75. Bonampak—Stela No. 1 (restoration).

FIG. 76. Bonampak—Stela No. 2 (dated A.D. 783).

FIG. 77. Bonampak—Stela No. 3 (dated A.D. 785).

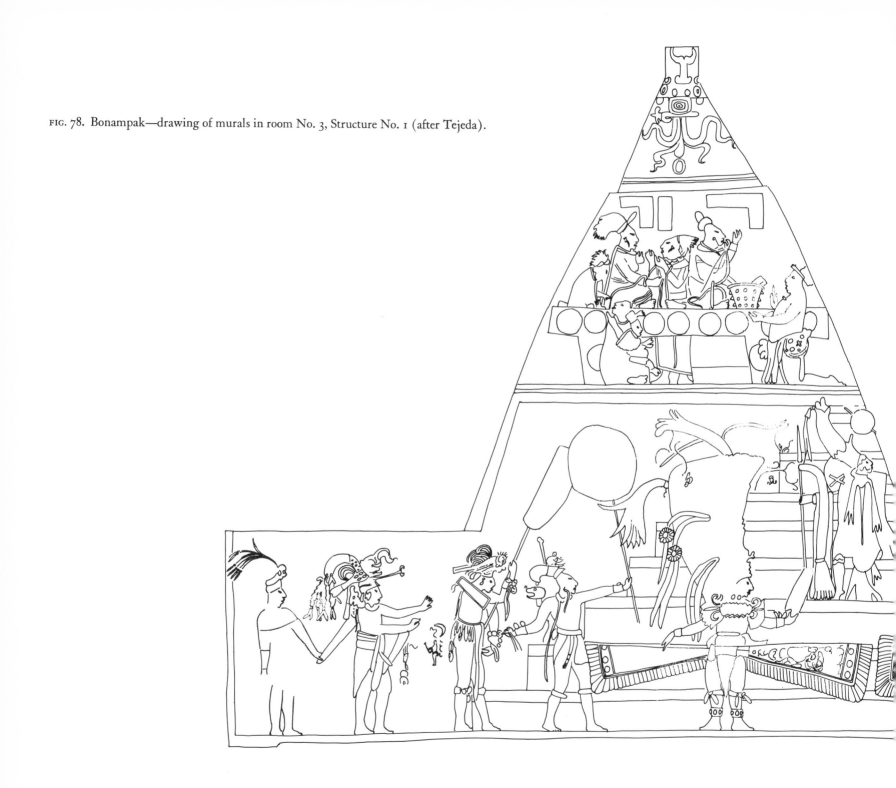

FIG. 78. Bonampak—drawing of murals in room No. 3, Structure No. 1 (after Tejeda).

Palenque

The ruins of the city of Palenque are located in the state of Chiapas, Mexico, at the base of a range of hills which limit the wooded plain of the states of Tabasco and southern Campeche. The principal section of the city lies on a natural platform about two hundred feet above the plain, which has been further developed into a series of smaller terraces. That part of the city which has been excavated and partially restored covers an area roughly twelve hundred by eighteen hundred feet (Fig. 79). Other structures are found to the east and west of the central area extending outward two kilometers to the east and six kilometers to the west. All along this plateau are a series of pyramids, situated on the tops of hills; the lower areas are occupied with smaller mounds. In all, the city must have covered at least sixteen square kilometers, making it comparable in size with Tikal. Thus, we have good reason to believe that it was a large urban center as characterized by Tikal, rather than a small ceremonial center as suggested by the restricted portion of the total city shown in the site plan.

It is not hard to understand why this particular site was chosen as the location for an important city. Its strategic position at the edge of an escarpment between the low-lying plain and the hills behind symbolizes the duality of its relationships with these two distinct areas. The fertile plains were the source of physical sustenance while the hills and mountains beyond were the abode of gods of the forest. Because of its height, the site offers commanding views out over the plain, which extends fifty miles northward to the Gulf of Mexico. On a clear day, the temples and the tower of the palace can be seen from below for a distance of six or seven miles. One can easily visualize the elaborately decorated stucco surfaces of these structures standing out in sharp relief against the dark green of the rain forest which clothes the hills behind. The site is crossed by several small streams and these, together with the irregular existing terrain, caused some problems for its builders, who were forced to do a considerable amount of reshaping of the existing ground form in order to maintain any semblance of visual order in the over-all layout of the city.

The central area of the city is made up of several well-defined groups of structures, all of which seem to be organized around the large Palace Group which occupies a dominant position in the main plaza (Figs. 80, 81). The Temple of the Inscriptions is situated near the southwest corner of the Palace Group, and the pyramid which supports it is in part a natural hill which has been reshaped to form the familiar stepped pyramidal substructure (Figs. 82, 83). The hill continues to rise behind this temple, and traces of other structures are found near the top. The areas north and northwest of the Palace Group have been shaped into a series of rectangular terraces, which support several other groups of structures. This side of the site is abruptly terminated by a nearly vertical cliff which drops abruptly down to the level of the plain below. Southeast of the Palace Group the natural terrain is very irregular but has been substantially reshaped in order to form another series of terraces surrounded by temple buildings (Figs. 84, 85). Here again, the existing hills have been modified into pyramidal substructures which support the temples.

All in all, the resulting scheme can be called highly organic on the basis that the natural ground form has been maintained in spite of the cutting and filling and it is obvious that the siting of buildings has been determined more on the basis of existing opportunities afforded by the site than abstract, or formal, notions of order. Natural elements have been modified but not completely overpowered. Perhaps this is one of the reasons why Palenque exerts such a powerful hold over nearly every visitor; it seems entirely at home with nature and the man-made elements exert their influence on the basis of sophistication of form and detail rather than pretentious monumentality.

The Palace Group sits on a large artificial mound 300 feet long, 240 feet wide, and 30 feet high (Figs. 86, 87). The complex of structures which make up this group are organized around a series of interior courtyards of varying sizes (Figs. 89, 90, 91). The relationships among these elements conform very closely to those which have been described as basic to the Palace Group concept. The inner courtyards are screened from view from the plaza below, but there are a large number of doorways in the buildings on the periphery which offer ready access from the plazas below (Fig. 88). These doorways lead into long galleries which form a continuous passageway around three sides of the structure (Fig. 92). A dividing wall, with several vaulted openings, separates these outer galleries from three parallel inner galleries oriented to the enclosed courtyards. While a certain degree of order is obtained from these galleries, the balance of the scheme is very confused and no clear internal paths of circulation can be observed. It is apparent that various buildings in the southern section were added from time to time without regard for any large system of organization. It also seems likely that the platform was extended northward at a later date and the outer ring of galleries added as a means of bringing some order to an otherwise chaotic collection of building elements.

The most unique element of the palace complex is a four-story tower that rises in the southeast courtyard (Figs. 88, 89). Towers have been reported at one or two other sites, which have yet to be fully documented, but this one represents a unique feature as far as most Classic sites are concerned. It is tempting to think that the tower was used for astronomical observations, since the Mayas had recorded movements of the planets over long periods of time and had succeeded in measuring the true length of the year. It is oriented more nearly to the cardinal points than most other buildings in the center, but this is not sufficient proof of its use as an observatory. It would have served equally well as a watchtower, since it provides a commanding view of the entire city and the surrounding countryside. In any event, it serves visually as a marker, reinforcing the Palace Group as the central element of the main ceremonial area, which can be visualized as a very irregular pinwheel with the tower as its center.

In this connection, it should be noted that the Palace can be thought of as an independent element which stands alone in a central position in the main plaza or as a supporting element belonging to several different groups. For example, the west side of the palace can be seen as an integral part of the group which includes the Temple of the Inscriptions and Temple XI (Fig. 93). At the same time, the north gallery of the Palace becomes part of a grouping which includes the ball court and Temple X. A major stairway from the terrace at the northern end of the Palace leads to the north gallery, and the center of this stairway is directly in line with the Temple of the Count (Figs. 95, 96). The duality of internal-external relationships has already been pointed out as one of the distinguishing characteristics of Palace Groups in general, and these are particularly striking at Palenque.

The plaza north of the palace is divided into two sections by a change in level near the center (Figs. 79, 86, 87). The lower level contains the remains of an open-ended ball court together with a temple-type building on a very low platform. This building is directly on axis with the Temple of the Inscriptions and the central doorways of the two buildings face one another. Despite this axiality, the low temple seems too detached from the upper plaza to function effectively as part of a typical Temple Group, which might be implied by its position with respect to the Temple of the Inscriptions and Temple X. The alignment and positioning of the ball court is also rather curious, as it is perpendicular to the north building of the Palace but its axis is not effectively terminated at either end. It is possible that the ball court was constructed earlier than the north end of the Palace and could not be effectively re-

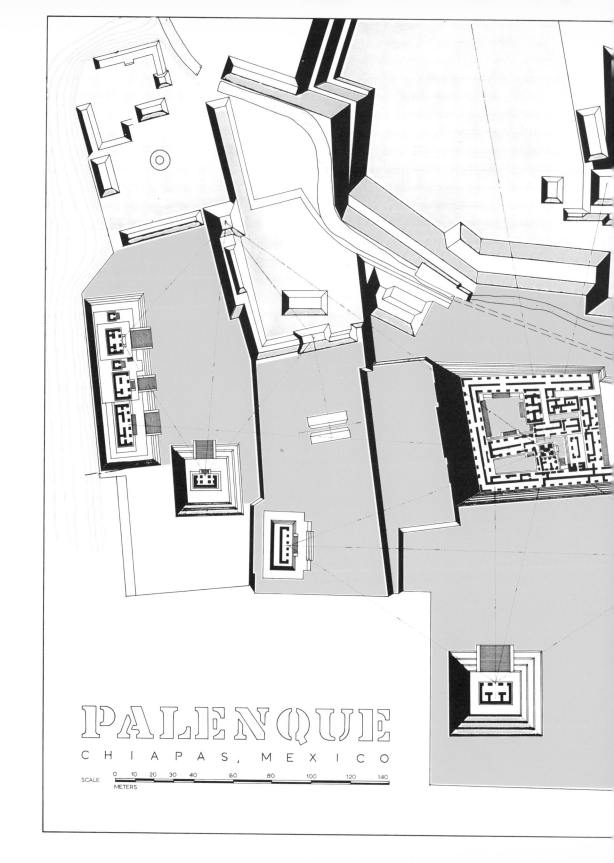

PALENQUE
CHIAPAS, MEXICO

SCALE
0 10 20 30 40   60   80   100   120   140
METERS

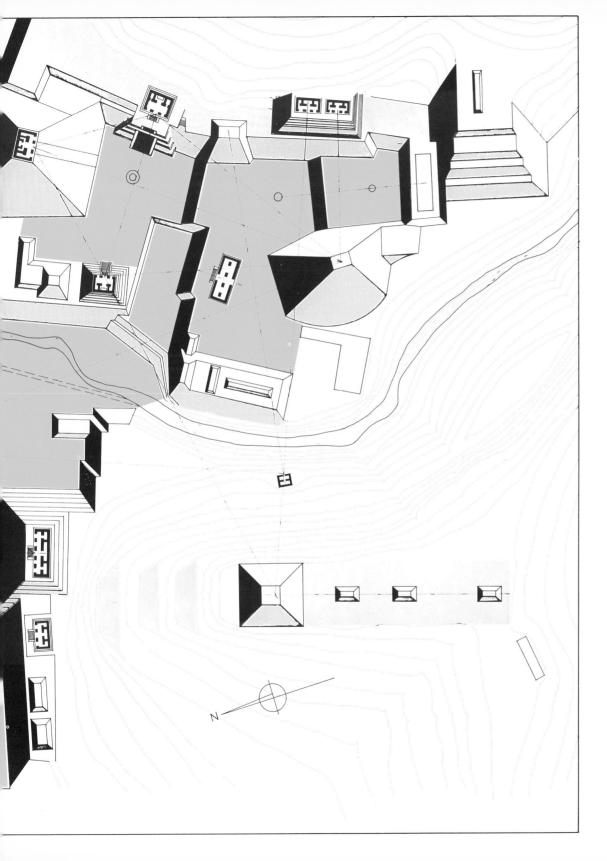

FIG. 79. Palenque (after Marquina).

lated to the palace stairway at the time it was enlarged and extended.

Beyond the plaza containing the ball court is another plaza, again at a lower level. This plaza is bounded on its northern side by the North Group and to the west by the Temple of the Count (Fig. 95). The other two sides are defined by low mounds which appear to be the remains of narrow platforms rather than buildings. The North Group consists of a rather disorderly row of five buildings situated on a low platform at the edge of the escarpment above the plains. The buildings are of different sizes and the platform itself is at several levels. This group, like the Palace, is an accretion and the platform has been extended on several occasions in order to accommodate additional structures. The Temple of the Count, which faces the plaza at a right angle to the North Group, is similar in form to the temples on the east terrace, although it lacks the refinement of proportions of these structures (Fig. 96). Its height suggests that it is the most important element of the larger group and this is further borne out by the fact that it is a singular, isolated structure in contrast to the undifferentiated collection of five temples of the North Group. It may not be too far-fetched to suggest that this sector of the city dates back to an earlier period than the eastern temples and the Temple of the Inscriptions. The concern for delicately scaled proportions and the greater degree of conceptual order which is evident in these latter structures is a good indication of the kind of refinement which is usually developed in a mature culture which has worked its way through a series of cruder models. Confirmation of this theory will have to wait for more accurate dating methods for the structures in question.

We have already noted that the irregularity of the existing ground form presented many problems for the architects of Palenque. Traditionally, plazas were laid out in fairly precise rectangles, and buildings were carefully disposed in the same manner. Axial alignments were important and major buildings did not vary a great deal in orientation from the cardinal points of the compass. In order to take advantage of existing shelves which could be made into level plazas and, simultaneously, utilize the lower hills as part of the substructures for temples, the builders were forced to accept certain irregularities in plan, and deviations from normal compass orientations are very pronounced. The basic forms of generic building groupings are maintained, but their relationships to one another are more tenuous than would be the case on a level site.

For example, the group of three temples which includes the Temple of the Sun, the Temple of the Cross, and the Temple of the Foliated Cross is situated on a terrace southeast of the main plaza (Figs. 84, 85). This triangular grouping of three temples is the most archetypical form to be found in any ceremonial center. The Temple of the Cross (Fig. 97) is built on a hillside which has been reshaped into a stepped pyramid on one side, and the Temple of the Foliated Cross is likewise situated on a pyramidal mound which is only partially artificial (Fig. 98). The plaza in front of these temples opens to a higher plaza to the south, but no stairway can be found which connects it to the main plaza to the west. It is apparent that great effort was made to establish a strong relationship between this Temple Group and the main plaza, as the stream which divides the main plaza from the upper terrace to the east has been covered over and is channeled through an aqueduct for a distance of several hundred feet in order to extend the plaza as an unbroken surface. The edge of this terrace has been reshaped, but generally follows the existing contours, producing a very irregular outline in plan. The terrace itself is very level and the ordering of elements vertically is very pronounced in contrast to the more casual plan relationships.

While this study is devoted to considerations of spatial organization rather than building details, some mention must be made of the unique features of the Temple of the Inscriptions (Figs. 93, 94), as well as the details of architectural style which distinguish the structures at Palenque from other regional styles. It has been emphasized many times that the pyramidal substructures which are used to support temples are solid masses of rubble and masonry whose sole function is to remove the temple to a position high above the general plaza level. The Temple of the Inscriptions is a striking exception to this rule, as its supporting substructure also served as a protective covering for a crypt which is directly below the temple at the natural grade of the plaza. This tomb, which is reached by a flight of stairs originating in the floor of the temple, is a typical corbeled-vault room about 30 feet long, 13 feet wide, and 23 feet high. It was obviously built prior to the construction of the pyramidal substructure and the stairway which connects it to the upper temple was filled in after the interment of an important personage in a large stone sarcophagus which takes up most of the floor space of the tomb.

When opened, the sarcophagus was found to contain the skeleton of a man whose limbs were covered with an elaborate collection of jade ornaments. In addition, the skull of the corpse had been covered with a jade mosaic mask which had subsequently come apart as the cement holding it together deteriorated with time. When fitted together, this mask appears to be a lifelike portrait of a Maya priest and may be the death mask of the individual interred. The presence of this tomb, in an unlikely location as far as Maya traditions are concerned, provides us with one more chapter in the evolution of Maya notions of placemaking, a rare exception to a long tradition, which involves a new concept of function and form.

The architectural style of the buildings at Palenque is noteworthy in two respects. First, that portion of the exterior wall above the doorways which is normally continued up as vertical plane at most other sites has become a sloping surface which is roughly parallel to the slope of the vaults on the interior (Figs. 101, 102). This sloping surface is joined to the vertical lower wall by means of a projecting cornice just above door height. This distinction between what might be called roof and wall is further heightened by the presence of roof combs which are po-

sitioned on the central axis of the building when viewed from the side (Figs. 99, 100). The roof combs are pierced with openings in a geometrical pattern and taper from bottom to top.

Secondly, in place of the stone mosaics which fill the upper part of the vertical walls in Puuc-style buildings in the Yucatan, these sloping roof surfaces were covered with stucco relief elements in the form of masks and human figures (Figs. 99, 100). The pillars between the doorways below were also covered with relief figures in stucco and many traces of color can be found where parts of the stucco reliefs are still in place (Fig. 103). The art of modeling in stucco seems to have been centered at Palenque and hundreds of hieroglyphic inscriptions as well as a large number of realistic human figures and heads made in stucco or plaster have been found in tombs and on the walls of buildings. Examples of this technique are found throughout the Maya area, but its more extensive use at Palenque, plus the high artistic and technical quality of the surviving examples, suggests that the artists seized on this medium as being the most flexible and expressive means available for adding a further touch of refinement to the small-scale buildings which depend on gracefulness rather than monumentality for their impact.

It is difficult to compare Palenque with the closest major sites which can be considered to be part of the same geographical region. Piedras Negras and Yaxchilan, both of which are within a radius of seventy-five miles from Palenque, are sited adjacent to the Usumacinta River and their plan organizations are partly governed by this unique physical feature of the landscape. Some similarities in architectural style can be observed between the three, but Piedras Negras and Yaxchilan appear to belong to a region of their own which is established along the course of the river. Strangely enough, the site which has the most marked affinities with Palenque is Comalcalco, near the gulf coast in the state of Tabasco, nearly one hundred miles to the northwest. There is no similarity of geography, as Comalcalco is situated on the level plains of Tabasco

which terminate at the base of the hills on which Palenque is built. (The particulars of these affinities will be discussed in detail in the description of Comalcalco.) In spite of this association, Palenque appears as a somewhat unique development within the general traditions of Maya notions of placemaking and architecture. The extent of its variations from basic themes is a measure of the vitality of its builders, who were not content to make carbon copies of older or traditional models but proceeded to establish their own identity through specialization and refinement. Thus, its characterization as a regional urban center seems fully justified, even though firm evidence of its political or administrative control over this region has yet to be found.

Note: A considerable amount of additional excavation and restoration has been carried out at Palenque by archaeologists representing the I.N.A.H. of Mexico since the above description was written. A large section of the stairway on the west side of the Palace Group has been restored (Fig. 88), and a small temple building adjacent to the Temple of the Sun has been excavated and partially restored (Fig. 101). The remnants of a beautifully carved stone tablet from the sanctuary of this temple were recovered and have been reassembled as shown in Figure 104.

FIG. 80. Palenque—the Palace
(before restoration of stairway) (top).

FIG. 81. Palenque—the Palace
(after partial restoration of stairway) (bottom).

FIG. 82. Palenque—Temple of the Inscriptions.

FIG. 83. Palenque—Temple of the Inscriptions
(from tower of Palace).

FIG. 84. Palenque—Temple Group: Temple of the Sun, Temple of the Cross, and Temple of the Foliated Cross

FIG. 85. Palenque—Temple Group (restoration).

FIG. 86. Palenque—the Palace, north end.

FIG. 87. Palenque—the Palace, north end (restoration).

FIG. 88. Palenque—the Palace, west side (after restoration of stairway).

FIG. 89. Palenque—the Palace, east court and tower.

FIG. 90. Palenque—the Palace, east court.

FIG. 91. Palenque—the Palace, east court from above.

FIG. 92. Palenque—the Palace, interior of gallery.

FIG. 93. Palenque—Temple of the Inscriptions and Temple XIII.

FIG. 94. Palenque—Temple of the Inscriptions and Temple XIII (restoration).

FIG. 95. Palenque—North Group and Temple of the Count as seen from the Palace.

FIG. 96. Palenque—Temple of the Count.

FIG. 97. Palenque—Temple of the Cross.

FIG. 98. Palenque—Temple of the Foliated Cross.

FIG. 99. Palenque—Temple of the Sun.

FIG. 100. Palenque—Temple of the Sun (restoration).

FIG. 101. Palenque—Temple of the Sun and Temple XIV.

FIG. 103. Palenque—detail of
stucco sculpture on pilaster (right).

FIG. 102. Palenque—Temple of the Sun
as seen from Temple of the Cross.

The site of Comalcalco is situated in the state of Tabasco, about forty miles northwest of Villahermosa, the state capital and fifteen miles due south of the Gulf of Mexico. Although lying on the banks of an extinct tributary of the Grijalva River, the site is presently some forty miles north of the main branch of this same river. The terrain is essentially flat, but differences in topographical relief, although small in terms of elevation, have had an important effect on the growth pattern of the site. Many parts of the site are inundated during the long rainy season, and both ceremonial groups and residential structures were situated on the higher rises of ground. House mounds in particular tend to be located on the higher ridges surrounding *bajos* or *aguadas*. This pattern is consistent with settlements at other Maya sites wherever *bajos* and shallow lakes are characteristic of the terrain. Most of the land which comprises the site is presently under cultivation or is used for grazing of cattle. Cacao is the major cash crop, but a variety of citrus fruits are grown, together with bananas, coconuts, coffee, and avocados. The modern town of Comalcalco, which has given this site its name, is situated about two and a half miles southwest of the ruins and serves as the main commercial center for the surrounding *fincas* and plantations.

While Comalcalco is a rather small center, particularly in terms of number of standing masonry buildings, and must have played a minor role in terms of the development of Maya culture as a whole, it is important to the present study in several ways. First, it marks the easternmost point in the spread of Maya culture along the Gulf of Mexico and was therefore subject to considerable pressure from adjoining cultures. Second, it was constructed and occupied shortly before the general collapse of Maya civilization and thus provides us with a good example of a Late Classic city. Third, it is the only Maya city of any

consequence, which is presently known, in which vaulted masonry buildings were constructed of burned-clay bricks instead of limestone. Finally, there is considerable evidence to substantiate the theory that Comalcalco was a provincial center dominated by, and perhaps even peopled by, *émigrés* from the more important city of Palenque, which is situated some one hundred air miles to the southeast in the state of Chiapas. This presumed relationship, which is based largely on architectural and sculptural evidence, will be more carefully documented later in the discussion.

The central portion of the site was carefully surveyed by a team of architects and archaeologists during the summer of 1966. The area surveyed covers a section of 3,000 by 3,500 feet, and extends outward from the three major ceremonial groupings approximately 1,000 feet in all directions (Fig. 105). Beyond these limits, mound density decreased very rapidly, and reconnaissances made up to a half-mile beyond the limits of the site map revealed no important structures with the exception of two well-shaped pyramidal mounds, lying approximately one and two miles respectively southeast of the Great Acropolis. As can be noted in the site map, the orientation of the major structures and complexes of structures is consistently within ten degrees of the cardinal points of the compass. The only major exceptions to this rule are a number of low-lying mounds which were tentatively identified as house mounds.

For purposes of description and analysis, the main features within the area mapped can be divided into three categories. The most important groupings of structures consist of the three major ceremonial complexes: the Great Acropolis, the North Group, and the East Acropolis. The second category consists of a number of well-shaped structures, with terraces and platforms at different levels, in-

Comalcalco

193

FIG. 104. Palenque—sculptured tablet
     from sanctuary of Temple XIV.

cluding two unusual and complicated structural configurations. The third category, low-lying earth mounds that are randomly dispersed on higher elevations around *bajos*, are assumed to be house mounds. The relationship among these categories is somewhat ambiguous and no evidence was found which would indicate specific circulation routes between the various elements. The lack of formalized circulation elements outside the systems of plazas and stairways among the most important ceremonial complexes is consistent with conditions at most other sites, where it is assumed that traffic among the various outlying groupings was conducted along irregular trails following the higher ridges of ground. There is some evidence to indicate that the Great Acropolis was connected to the North Group by means of a paved plaza which extended from the north side of the acropolis into the main plaza of the North Group. A small section of this plaza floor was located near the base of the northern leg of the acropolis, indicating that the paving consisted of three courses of fired-clay bricks topped with a thick coating of lime cement. There was no evidence of similar paving in other parts of the site.

The first category of structures, which includes the three major ceremonial groupings, forms the central portion of the ceremonial center. These three groupings are distinguished from the balance of the city by their high degree of formal organization, by their careful orientation to the cardinal points of the compass, by the elaboration and geometrical precision of their basic forms, and by the presence, in two of them, of vaulted masonry buildings. Each of these groups forms a discrete subcenter within the larger center, which is lacking in any strong over-all formal order. This condition, as we have seen, is typical for most Maya ceremonial centers, where various subgroups exhibit a high degree of internal order but appear to be only loosely related to one another. At a few sites, some larger ordering scheme is discernible which binds the individual groups together into a more coherent whole, but the general patterning suggests that the city

is an accretion of elements which is more dependent on fortuitous geographical features for its layout than formal notions of architectural organization.

The North Group, which is situated very close to the Great Acropolis, exhibits the strongest internal order, based on axial alignments. All of the structures associated with this group are situated around a large plaza which stretches some five hundred feet on an east-west line. The western end of this plaza is bounded by three pyramidal substructures, each of which supports the remains of a temple building. Temple I, which is the largest and highest of the three, faces east down the long axis of the plaza (Figs. 106, 107), while the two smaller temples face each other across the shorter dimension (Figs. 108, 109). The plaza is further bounded on the north and south sides by long platforms which are joined directly to the two pyramidal substructures supporting Temple II and Temple III and is terminated at its eastern end by a low platform running the full width of the plaza. Three small platforms are positioned along the central axis of the plaza, which runs from the central doorway of Temple I to the center of the platform at the eastern end. There is a large opening on the south side of the plaza near the eastern end which gives access from the North Group to the Great Acropolis, but the exact nature of this relationship is not clear, since there are no visible remains of stairways on the north side of the acropolis mound.

The Great Acropolis is a complex of structures which consists of two major parts: the Main Acropolis, which supports all of the remaining masonry buildings within the ceremonial precinct, and the group of structures which are situated west of the Acropolis Plaza. The acropolis mound is a huge mass of earth measuring approximately 700 feet from east to west, 680 feet from north to south, and 116 feet high at its highest point (Fig. 112). Stripped of its details, this mound can be visualized as a single large pyramid with two spurs projecting out from its western side. On the other hand, it might also be viewed as a U-shaped platform with sloping sides, with a smaller

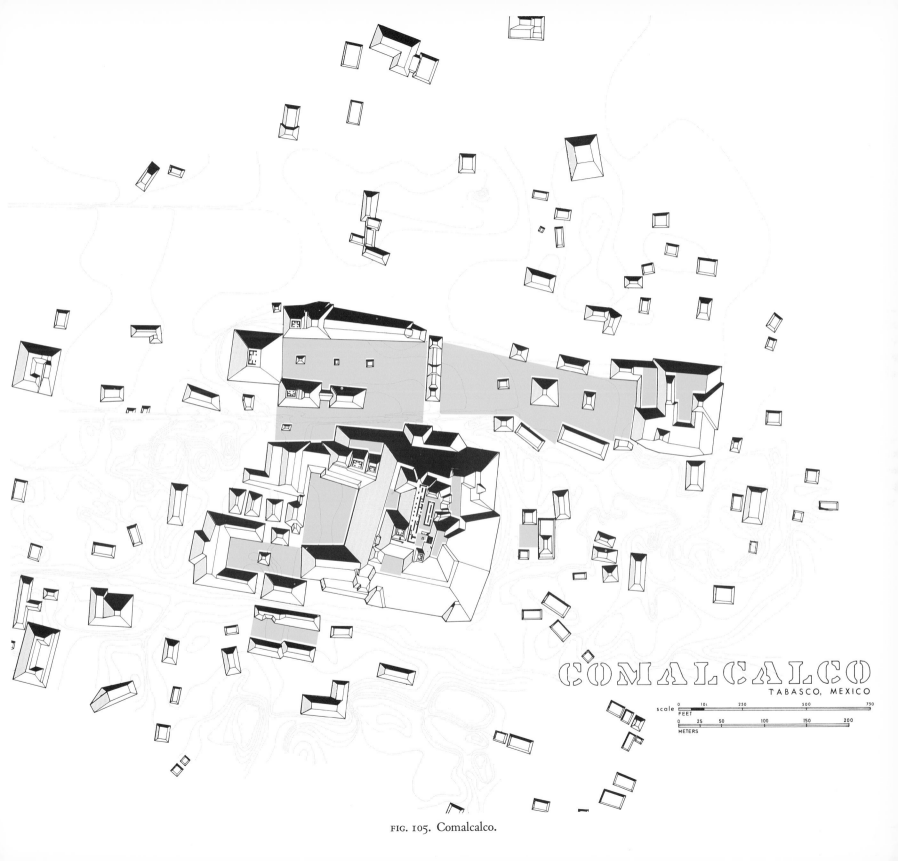

COMALCALCO

TABASCO, MEXICO

scale
0 10c 250 500 750
FEET
0 25 50 100 150 200
METERS

FIG. 105. Comalcalco.

pyramidal structure on top of that part of the platform which forms the base of the U. Neither of these simplified descriptions is entirely correct, since the acropolis is a fairly complex form and should be examined in greater detail in order to appreciate the particulars of its organization (Figs. 110, 111).

It can be noted in the site plan (Fig. 105) that the main mass of the acropolis consists of four distinct levels or layers, with a few small plazas or terraces interspersed at intermediate levels. The lowest major level is represented by the tops of the two spurs which project westward from the main mass forming a small plaza at the base of the mound on the west side. Three temples are situated on top of the northern spur, while the southern spur is lacking in any exposed building remains (Fig. 113). The level of the two spurs is approximately the same, about thirty-five feet above the level of the plaza. The basic form of the main mass suggests that these spurs were not part of the original construction, since there is no place for a logical circulation connection between the upper level of the spurs and the next higher level of the main mass. The temples on the northern spur appear to be related to the plaza below and it is likely that a stairway connected these temples to the plaza, although there are no remains of such a stairway presently visible. The same proposition holds true for the southern spur, although there are no exposed building remains which, in themselves, would have necessitated a stairway. It can also be noted from the map drawing that the northern spur has been further extended with a series of platforms which appear to have been added at a later date.

The stairways and stucco sculptures on the pyramidal substructures on the northern spur which are presently exposed are actually the remnants of earlier structures which were completely covered over when the substructures were enlarged at a later date (Figs. 114, 115). The mask on the stair of Temple VI is worthy of special notice, as it is an outstanding example of Maya art and craftsmanship (Fig. 116). The sculptures on the face of

the stepped pyramid supporting Temple VII are much smaller in size but are equally sophisticated examples of the art of modeling in stucco (Figs. 117, 118). The ground plans of Temple VI and Temple VII are so similar to the plans of the Temple of the Cross, the Temple of the Foliated Cross, and the Temple of the Sun at Palenque that they could easily be carbon copies of these latter, and better-known, structures. It is unfortunate that the temple structures themselves are so badly ruined, since they included inner sanctuaries of the sort found in the temples at Palenque and were likely decorated much in the same manner. (See Figure 104 for an example of the sculptured panel from the interior of a sanctuary at Palenque.)

The next highest level of the Main Acropolis mound is represented by a series of terraces or plazas, connected by a narrow ledge which runs almost continuously around all four sides of the mound. It has already been suggested that this level can be interpreted as representing the top of a large platform in the form of a truncated pyramid which supports a smaller pyramidal structure constructed at a later date. Excavations in the western side of this upper mass indicate clearly that it was enlarged in plan and raised in height on more than one occasion. The small plaza at this level, situated just below the long palace-type building, appears to be the remnant of a larger plaza which was connected to the main plaza below by means of a stairway which has long since disappeared. The third level of the acropolis appears to have been the main level in its final form, since five masonry buildings including the large palace-type structure are situated on this level and form the densest concentration of building remains within the entire center. These five buildings form an integrated complex, with the palace building as its focal point.

Within this complex three subgroups can be identified, each of which is related to the palace. One of these groups is formed by the palace and the small temple on its western side (Fig. 119). A second subgroup includes the palace and the long building situated on its eastern side, and the third subgroup is organized around a small courtyard immediately east of the southern end of the palace. This courtyard is bounded on the north side by a small masonry building of an indeterminate type (Fig. 120), on the east by a large platform with a stairway on its western side (Fig. 121), and on the south by a small pyramid-temple structure which faces west rather than into the courtyard (Figs. 122, 123). The upper level of the platform to the east of the courtyard is the highest point within the site, approximately 116 feet above the level of the plaza below (Fig. 120). There are no exposed building remains on this platform, which would have been an ideal location for an important temple, and it is possible that the site was abandoned before such a temple could be constructed. The whole complex of buildings which has just been described involves a complicated network of relationships, but it is apparent that the palace building was intended to be the most important element of the whole, whether viewed from within the complex or from the ground below (Figs. 119, 124, 125).

On the west side of the Great Acropolis mound, and at the same level as the plaza below the palace building, is a small brick vaulted tomb. Vaulted masonry tombs are fairly rare and the tomb in question is of particular importance, since three of its walls are covered with well-preserved stucco figures and hieroglyphic inscriptions. There are nine figures in all, three on each of the walls. Unfortunately, the figures have suffered considerable deterioration since they were first discovered in 1925, but enough still remains to give a good idea of their original appearance (Fig. 126). Both the sculptures and the walls of the tomb were painted red and traces of this color still remain. The high artistic quality of these sculptures cannot be denied and indicates that the art of modeling in stucco had developed to the point where it rivaled that of Palenque. A full description of the tomb and its contents may be found in the report by Frans Blom and Oliver La Farge (Blom and La Farge: 1926, 115–30).

The group of mounds situated west of the Main Acropolis mass must be considered as an integral part of the acropolis complex, even though they are clearly subordinate to the main group by virtue of their size and position (Fig. 105). A large U-shaped mound is on axis with the southern arm of the Main Acropolis mass and it is clear that some specific relationship existed between them. Other platforms are joined directly to the northern arm, and one of these platforms extends in a southerly direction, forming the fourth side of the Acropolis Plaza. In addition to this, the pair of mounds on the far west side of this extension are highly reminiscent of the typical ball-court form. Unfortunately, these structures are in an advanced state of ruin and it is impossible to verify this function without extensive excavation. Without further supporting data, it is difficult to tell if these subsidiary mounds were constructed before or after the Main Acropolis mound, but it is apparent that considerable effort was made to incorporate them into the larger scheme of the Great Acropolis complex.

The East Acropolis, which is situated about five hundred feet northeast of the Great Acropolis, can be considered as a small-scale version of the latter, although it contains no remains of masonry buildings. The form of the main mound of this group is similar in many respects to the main mound of the Great Acropolis, even though it is considerably smaller in size and less complex in configuration. The main mound is oriented toward a large plaza, which is bounded on two sides by low platforms and on the west side by a pyramidal structure. A small mound is situated near the center of the plaza. Several smaller platforms are situated on all sides of the main group of structures, but it is difficult to tell if they should be considered as part of this complex. It is very apparent, however, that some effort was made to establish certain visual relationships between this secondary acropolis and the North Group by means of axial alignments. A line drawn from the central doorway of Temple I in the North Group through the highest point of the East

197

Acropolis comes very close to passing through the center of the platform at the east end of the North Group, as well as the center of the pyramidal structure on the east side of the East Acropolis plaza. This alignment appears to be deliberate, and in a sense the two groups form a continuous mall-like grouping terminated at either end by the highest structures within this larger complex. It is not possible to check the significance of these relationships today, since a large cacao orchard blocks the view between the two groups.

The second category of structures referred to earlier includes those mounds which by virtue of their size, form, and location appear to be ceremonial structures. They are situated adjacent to the main ceremonial groups and tend to be positioned toward the outer periphery of the central area. Such structures are easily differentiated from the surrounding mounds on the basis of size, height, and complexity of organization. In ground plan, they appear as intermediate elements in relation to the structures which form the three major ceremonial groupings. Their most prominent features consist of a number of terraces or platforms situated at different levels on well-shaped pyramidal forms. They are generally oriented to the cardinal points of the compass, and in terms of general location appear to be functionally related to the main center, though no specific physical connections are observable. There is no evidence that any of these structures supported brick masonry buildings, nor was any brick masonry used in their construction for facings or floors, but it is possible that they supported wood-and-thatch buildings which have long since disappeared. There is some evidence from other sites that wood-and-thatch structures continued to be built alongside of masonry vaulted structures; this may suggest a significant difference in function.

The third category of mounds, which consist for the most part of low-lying, rather shapeless mounds of earth, are assumed to be house mounds, although none of them was excavated. However, their general size and shape, together with their disposition around the edges of *bajos*,

are indicative of their residential function and they are similar in all respects to house mounds found elsewhere. In general, the highest concentration of these smaller mounds is found in the areas immediately adjacent to the main ceremonial complexes and the density drops off sharply as one moves away from the center of the site. This is not always the case, however, as the greatest density of occupation is near the periphery of the site in the southeast quadrant. This latter condition is consistent with conditions at other sites, where clusters of residences are found in association with suburban ceremonial centers. A total of one hundred and eleven of these smaller mounds was located in an area approximately .72 square kilometers, which gives an average density of one hundred and fifty-four mounds per square kilometer. In comparison, the densities of house mounds at Uaxactun were eighty-two per square kilometers and two hundred and eighty per square kilometers at Tikal. Since each mound may represent several houses, a total population of one thousand to fifteen hundred can be postulated, using an average figure of five persons per house. Obviously, Comalcalco was not a large city by any stretch of the imagination, but it must have been an important ceremonial center with a sizable resident population.

The use of fired-clay bricks for the construction of vaulted masonry buildings at Comalcalco in place of limestone, which is typical at all other Maya sites, raises several interesting questions (Figs. 124, 125). Excavations in the Great Acropolis and other parts of the site indicate that the earliest building technology consisted of large earthen platforms which were surfaced with several coats of lime plaster. Very late in the history of the site, fired-clay bricks made their appearance; brick masonry was substituted for facings of substructures and vaulted masonry buildings were constructed in place of wood-and-thatch buildings.

It might be argued that the introduction of fired-brick masonry is evidence of the intrusion of ideas from an adjoining culture. This possibility is suggested by the location of the site, which is close to the Gulf of Mexico and at the very edge of the area occupied by the Mayas, and by the fact that brick masonry does not appear at any other documented Maya site. Unfortunately, there is no evidence to back up this theory, since there are no building remains associated with adjoining cultures where brick masonry was employed as a construction material. Neither is there any significant change in the basic form or style of building elements constructed of bricks, which should be the case if the use of brick is the result of outside influence. The buildings at Comalcalco are typically Classic Maya in all respects and are very similar in style and detail to the limestone buildings at Palenque. For these reasons, it seems much more probable that the development of brick masonry was a logical adaptation to a localized condition where there was a very limited choice of indigenous building materials. In reality, it is not a large step to move from fired-clay pottery to fired-clay bricks, and it seems inevitable that such a step would be taken when the city developed to a point where permanent structures were desired. Similar adaptations to local conditions are characteristic in most preindustrial cultures throughout the world.

Earlier in the discussion, it was suggested that Comalcalco might be considered as a provincial outpost of the city of Palenque and may well have been founded and governed by missionaries or immigrants from this larger and more important center. The evidence for this assertion is found in certain architectural and sculptural aspects of the buildings at Comalcalco.

First, it can be noted that there is no fundamental difference among the eight temple buildings in the main ceremonial center, which indicates quite strongly that they were built in a relatively short period of time. At other sites where there is clear evidence for a long sequence of masonry buildings of the same type, there is also evidence of the evolution of the basic form from simple to more complex, in addition to some change in the technology of building construction. At Comalcalco, there

is no evolutionary sequence of any kind as far as masonry buildings are concerned. The building types appear fully developed and there are no significant differences in construction techniques from one to the other. This suggests that the basic concepts for these structures must have been imported fully developed from elsewhere. Since the architecture is typical Classic Maya, there are no grounds for assuming the intrusion of ideas from a foreign culture. The closest Maya site of any importance is Palenque, and an examination of the architectural remains at both sites suggests that the buildings at Comalcalco are copies of similar structures at Palenque, modified only slightly by local stylistic mannerisms. The similarity between structures at the two sites is too great to be accidental and the evidence is overwhelming in favor of the development of masonry buildings at Palenque prior to the construction of the brick-masonry buildings at Comalcalco. From this we must conclude that the movement of ideas was from Palenque to Comalcalco and not the reverse.

Second, it can be noted that the ground plans of temple buildings and palace buildings at both sites are similar in small details as well as over-all form. In both cases the ground plans of temples consist of two rooms with small sanctuaries centered on the back wall of the inner room. This plan is not followed at most other sites, though there are variations of it at several sites. In addition, one of the unique features of the buildings at Palenque is found in the sloping face of the upper walls above the cornice line, which is roughly parallel to the sloped face of the inner vault. At most other sites these walls are carried up vertically to the full height of the building. While none of these upper walls is still in place in any of the buildings at Comalcalco, it is quite clear, from the examination of several large pieces of these upper walls which are among the exposed debris associated with several temples, that the same pattern of sloping upper walls was followed here. In addition, these remnants of upper walls contain traces of stucco ornamentation which is quite similar to the stucco ornamentation found on the temples at Palenque. 199

Finally, it is readily observable that there is a considerable likeness in the sculptural style of stucco-modeled figures and decorative motifs at both sites. The figures on the walls on the tomb at Comalcalco are very similar to the figures in the tomb and sanctuary panels of temples at Palenque, and great similarities can be noted in the basic techniques of modeling in stucco (Fig. 126). This technique had been developed at Palenque long before any of the masonry buildings had been constructed at Comalcalco. It can hardly be argued that a similar technique and style was developed independently at two sites which were so close together, and the origin must be assumed to be Palenque.

On these grounds, the weight of evidence is very strongly in favor of the provincial status of Comalcalco in relation to Palenque. To some extent, this tends to substantiate the theory advanced in chapter 4 that the Maya area was made up of a number of large regions, each of which contained a regional center surrounded by a number of secondary, or provincial, centers. It was also suggested that specific styles made their way from the larger centers to the smaller centers and that some time might elapse be-

FIG. 106. Comalcalco—Temple I, side view (top).

FIG. 107. Comalcalco—Temple I, from North Plaza (bottom).

fore the smaller centers caught up with the latest style emanating from the capital. This would account for the late development of Comalcalco in relation to Palenque and points to a relatively short period of occupation at Comalcalco as compared with Palenque. While all of this is consistent with the limited data which is presently available from this region, much more definitive data from a wide range of sources is required in order to fully substantiate the relationships as outlined here.

Note: A full description of the survey of Comalcalco carried out in the summer of 1966 can be found in the monograph entitled *Comalcalco, Tabasco, Mexico—an Architectonic Survey*, by George F. Andrews with D. Hardesty, C. Kerr, F. E. Miller, and R. Mogel (1967). This report contains a detailed description of all features of the site together with photographs and drawings of all buildings in the North Group and Great Acropolis. In addition, the report contains large-scale map drawings of the area surveyed which indicate contours as well as all exposed cultural features, both pre-Columbian and modern.

FIG. 108. Comalcalco—Temple II, elevation (top).

FIG. 109. Comalcalco—Temple III, elevation (bottom).

FIG. 110. Comalcalco—Main Acropolis as seen from Temple III.

FIG. III. Comalcalco—Main Acropolis and northern spur (restoration).

FIG. 112. Comalcalco—Main Acropolis
as seen from North Group.

FIG. 113. Comalcalco—northern spur, Main Acropolis.

FIG. 114. Comalcalco—Temple VI and Temple VII.

FIG. 115. Comalcalco—Temple VI, stairway with mask on substructure.

FIG. 116. Comalcalco—Temple VI,
detail of stucco mask on stairway.

FIG. 117. Comalcalco—Temple VII, detail
of stucco sculpture on substructure.

FIG. 118. Comalcalco—Temple VII,
detail of stucco figure (right).

FIG. 120. Comalcalco—Main Acropolis, courtyard at upper level.

FIG. 119. Comalcalco—Main Acropolis, upper level, with remains of palace and Temple IV (left).

FIG. 121. Comalcalco—Main Acropolis, courtyard and stair leading to highest point of acropolis mound (126 feet high).

FIG. 122. Comalcalco—Temple V, side view.

FIG. 123. Comalcalco—Temple V,
front view showing entry
to lower chamber.

FIG. 124. Comalcalco—
palace structure, Main Acropolis (right).

FIG. 125. Comalcalco—palace structure,
Main Acropolis, detail of brick vault.

FIG. 126. Comalcalco—
stucco figures in tomb, Main Acropolis (right).

Copan

The site of Copan is located in Honduras, about twelve miles from the border of Guatemala. The city lies in a beautiful valley, about two thousand feet above sea level, which is ringed by mountains rising another thousand feet higher. The Copan River runs through this valley, and it can be seen from the site plan (Fig. 127) that part of the acropolis on the eastern side was washed away by the river during a series of floods. Fortunately, this does not represent a total loss, as a complete cross section of the acropolis was exposed by this washout, making it possible to visualize the various stages of the construction of this mass. From this cross section it is evident that the acropolis underwent many reconstructions and that the whole mass is largely a man-made construction.

Attention was first drawn to Copan through the efforts of John Lloyd Stephens and Frederick Catherwood, who spent several days there in 1839. Stephens' descriptions and Catherwood's drawings made it clear that the monuments of Copan were of special interest, even though the bulk of its buildings were in an advanced state of decay (Stephens: 1843). Alfred Maudslay spent a considerable amount of time at the site in 1888 and compiled a magnificent record of the monuments and inscriptions, which still serves as one of the major sources of information regarding the site, in spite of the mass of material which was forthcoming following its partial excavation and restoration in subsequent years (Maudslay: 1889–1902).

The main group shown in the site plan (Fig. 127) covers an area of approximately seventy-five acres, but there are sixteen subgroups extending outward from this nucleus to a distance of seven miles. As early as 1889, Maudslay pointed out that this peripheral area contained large numbers of small mounds, so it seems likely that the general pattern as observed elsewhere, where a large ceremonial complex is surrounded with houses or clusters of houses which, in turn, have reference to smaller, or suburban, ceremonial areas, is the case at Copan. The map, then, shows only a small portion of a larger urban area whose specific pattern is still unknown. Nevertheless, the spatial structure of the main center is clearly revealed.

Copan is undoubtedly one of the most highly organized architectural complexes to be found anywhere in the Maya area. It is obvious that a clear conceptual order has been maintained throughout its evolution, in spite of the fact that the city underwent many reconstructions over a period of several hundred years. It is impossible to trace the specific course of this evolution, but it is possible that the basic scheme was not altered appreciably, if the development of the ball court is indicative of the site as a whole. Careful excavations have revealed that while the ball court was rebuilt on several occasions, the changes were minor and it retained its basic form throughout these several alterations. The orientation of buildings and plazas at Copan conforms very closely to the cardinal points of the compass, and the deviations from these axes seem more deliberate than accidental. It is generally conceded that Copan was an important center in the field of astronomy, as the hieroglyphic inscriptions found on the stelae and buildings indicate that the priests at Copan had measured the true length of the year and the intervals between eclipses of the moon more accurately than at most other centers. This emphasis on measurement and accuracy is reflected in the general ordering of the site, which suggests few accidental relationships or fortuitous forms.

There are two major parts to the center: the Great Plaza and the Acropolis Group. These, in turn, are subdivided into smaller groupings which are organized around five open plazas or courtyard spaces. Beyond these two major areas are several subordinate groupings which are peripheral to the basic scheme. To borrow a current phrase, they appear as "happenings" in relation to the pristine order of the Great Plaza-Acropolis Group complex.

The Great Plaza is a level, and at one time paved, area measuring approximately 800 feet from north to south and 350 feet from east to west. The northern end of the plaza is defined by a low stepped terrace extending around three sides, while the southern end is marked by the base of the huge platform supporting the acropolis (Figs. 128, 129). Two small temple buildings are centered on top of the terraces on the west and south sides of the northern end of the plaza and their presence is indicated by stelae which stand at the base of the stairways leading from the plaza to these temples. There are large openings between the structures on the east and west sides of the plaza which must have served as major entry points into the plaza from the surrounding terrain.

The plaza is initially divided into two smaller areas by virtue of a small pyramidal platform toward its northern end which is roughly centered on the north-south axis of the plaza. Within the space defined by this structure and the low terraces described above are found a large number of elaborately carved stelae for which Copan is justly famous. (These will be discussed in greater detail later.) The southern part of the Great Plaza is further differentiated into two major areas by the position of the ball court, which projects into the plaza from the eastern side. One of these spaces, that which is called the Court of the Hieroglyphic Stairway, is defined on the east by the Hieroglyphic Stairway (Fig. 130), to the south by the stepped face of the acropolis mass and to the north by one end of the ball court (Figs. 131, 132). To the west are the remains of a small structure on top of a stepped terrace which faces the Hieroglyphic Stairway across the courtyard. Several other partially defined spaces can be noted within the Great Plaza, and the subtle manner of definition and complexity of the overlapping spatial divisions are indicative of the high degree of sophistication of placemaking ideas which characterizes Copan.

Some of these notions can be seen in the manner in which the ball court establishes an inner domain, which is represented by the space of the playing alley, and simultaneously creates several subordinate spaces within the Great Plaza (Figs. 131, 132). This duality, or inner-outer set of relationships, is emphasized by the two structures which flank the playing alley of the ball court to the east and west. On one hand, they form an integral part of the ball court and it must be assumed that their function was associated with the game or ceremony conducted in the ball court. On the other hand, each of these buildings has doorways on all four sides so that three of the doorways face outward toward other parts of the main plaza. In the case of the building on the west side of the ball court, these doorways connect to stairways leading directly to subordinate spaces within the main plaza. It must also be noted that the playing alley itself opens to the main plaza at its northwest corner, while the southern end opens directly to the Court of the Hieroglyphic Stairway. This court obtains its name from the stairway on the eastern side, which contains nearly two thousand hieroglyphic inscriptions on the faces of the risers which form the stairway (Fig. 130). This stairway leads to a small temple which adjoins the acropolis, but it is evident that it did not serve as an entry to the acropolis itself.

Earlier in this book we gave a general definition of acropolis as being "a settlement on an eminence," but further defined the Maya notion of acropolis as a linear series of rising courts or plazas, surrounded by palace or temple structures, culminating in a temple structure at the highest point of the complex. The acropolis at Copan does not conform precisely to this definition, but it does manifest the general form notions which we associate with this idea. As indicated earlier, the acropolis is a huge artificial mound, supporting a number of pyramidal substructures, temples, terraces, and courtyards. The whole complex is dominated by a large pyramid which rises to a height of 125 feet above the level of the Great Plaza. Entrance into the acropolis is effected by means of a broad stairway lead-

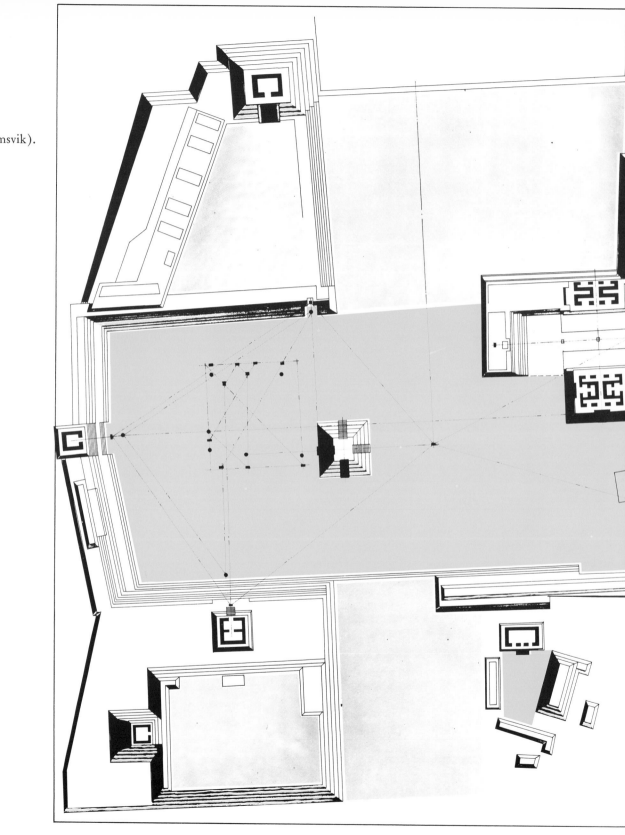

FIG. 127. Copan (after Strömsvik).

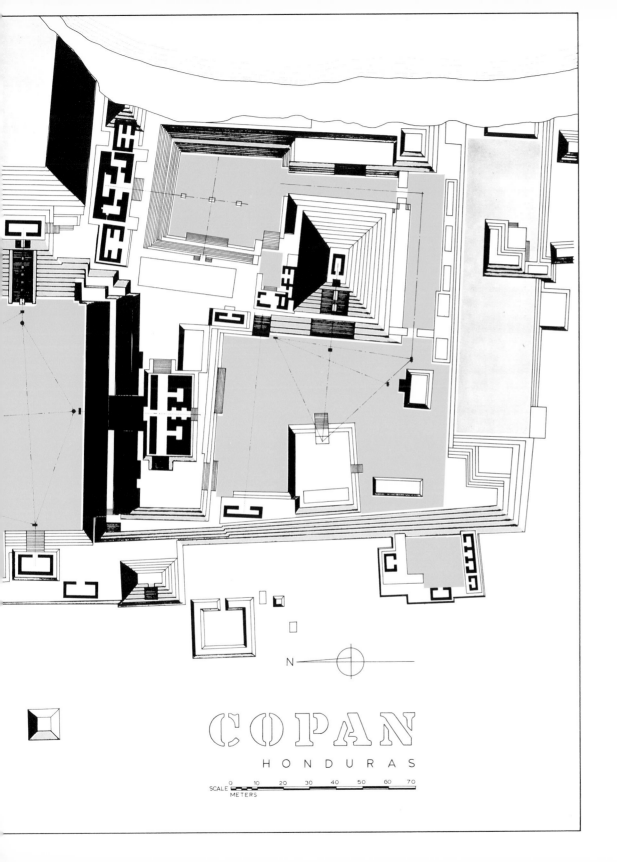

COPAN

H O N D U R A S

SCALE 0 10 20 30 40 50 60 70
METERS

N

ing from the Court of the Hieroglyphic Stairway to a large building which dominates the northern side of the acropolis. It is necessary to pass through this building in order to reach the more private spaces of the acropolis; this method of entrance is commonly used in other Acropolis Groups.

There are two large courtyards, or plazas, within the acropolis which have the appearance of being cut into the mass of the mound supporting the whole complex (Fig. 133). These two courtyards are connected to each other by means of two narrow alleyways along the base of the large pyramid which is the dominant element of the whole (Fig. 134). As is the case with other Acropolis Groups, the path of movement between the individual courtyards is quite clear, as it is fairly difficult to pass from one of these courts to the other except by means of the alleyways. This circling movement gives added emphasis to the large pyramid, which must have supported an important temple, even though the temple building appears to have been very small. The northern courtyard of the acropolis is defined on three sides by a stepped terrace, similar to the stepped terrace at the northern end of the Great Plaza (Fig. 135). The north side of this court is further delimited by a large temple building which faces south into the courtyard (Fig. 136). Around the inner doorway of this temple are some splendid examples of the lifelike sculpture which is found only at Copan (Fig. 137).

If we pass through this courtyard and along the two alleyways at the base of the Great Pyramid, we enter the eastern court at its southwest corner. To the right is the Great Pyramid, while ahead is the structure through which we first entered, called the Reviewing Stand (Figs. 138, 139). This is actually a series of superimposed structures which culminates in a single temple building at the highest point. The combined effect of these "hidden" courtyards and the surrounding temples on top of stepped terraces is one of great repose and tranquillity. Stelae and altars punctuate the open spaces near the bottoms of stairways, and hieroglyphic inscriptions, relief carvings, and

sculptural elements enliven the risers of stairways and façades of buildings (Figs. 140, 141). The courtyards are visually and physically removed from the plazas below and it is easy to imagine that the acropolis was reserved for the most important ceremonies involving only the high priests, while the more public activities took place in the open space of the Great Plaza below.

Mention was made earlier of the large number of carved stelae which are found in the northern end of the Great Plaza.[3] These stelae are unusual both by virtue of their location and the unique quality of the relief sculpture which covers nearly every square inch of their surfaces (Figs. 142, 143). As has been noted elsewhere, the general tendency at many sites was to position stelae and altars in association with important stairways. There are a number of examples of this relationship at Copan, both around the edges of the Great Plaza and in the Acropolis Group (Fig. 138), but the large number of stelae in the open space of the plaza and the obvious care lavished on their design suggests that their position had some symbolic significance and that their alignments with doorways of buildings or among themselves were of some importance.

The artistic quality of these stelae is unique in that they are considerably more three-dimensional than typical Maya stone carving, which is done in flat, shallow relief, and the forms are much more exuberant, or Baroque, in character when compared with the more static stylized figures which have come to be accepted as part of the Maya tradition.[4] Apparently the sculptors at Copan were sufficiently emboldened to break with the tradition or were simply far enough removed geographically from other centers to develop a regional style and technique which moved further and further away from the norm

---

[3] It should be pointed out that this part of the plaza is very similar in its basic organizations to the south end of the large plaza at Quirigua; i.e., it is bounded on three sides by a series of low terraces and focuses on a small pyramid which is centered on the fourth side. (See Figure 32 for plan of Quirigua.) Quirigua is one of the few known sites where large stelae are also found in abundance in the open spaces of plazas.

as it was passed on from generation to generation. Copan is located very near the southeast edge of the territory occupied by the Mayas and it seems quite reasonable to assume that pronounced regional variations would most likely occur in such a peripheral location. This notion is reinforced by the character of the individual buildings and the over-all plan as well, both of which suggest a distinctive regional development in which traditional forms have been modified in response to local conditions of environment or cultural evolution.

[4] It has been pointed out, however, that the elaborateness of the carvings on stelae, particularly those at Copan, is due to the nature of the ideas being presented and their method of presentation. Each element of the sculpture is an ideogram with a specific message to convey rather than a superfluous bit of decoration used to fill in blank space. (Proskouriakoff: 1965.) The problem for the viewer today is that he has no way of understanding the message and tends to react only to the "exotic" aspects of the sculptures.

FIG. 128. Copan—view of Main Plaza
looking south toward
ball court and acropolis.

FIG. 129. Copan—Main Plaza and ball court.

FIG. 130. Copan—hieroglyphic stairway, stela and altar in foreground.

FIG. 131. Copan—ball court, view looking south.

FIG. 132. Copan—ball court as seen from upper level of acropolis.

FIG. 134. Copan—Temple XXII as seen from alleyway.

FIG. 133. Copan—sunken courtyard
and alleyway at upper level of acropolis (left).

FIG. 135. Copan—courtyard and Temple XXII.

FIG. 136. Copan—Temple XXII.

FIG. 137. Copan—Temple XXII, detail of sculpture around interior doorway.

FIG. 138. Copan—Temple II and reviewing stand, acropolis.

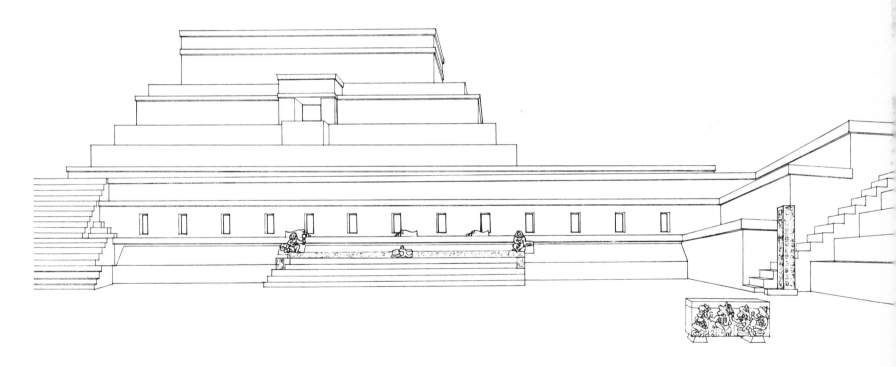

FIG. 139. Copan—Temple II and reviewing stand (restoration).

FIG. 140. Copan—Temple II.

FIG. 141. Copan—Temple II, detail of sculpture.

FIG. 142. Copan—Stela "C," Main Plaza (dated A.D. 782).

FIG. 143. Copan—Stela "C," side view
showing hieroglyphic inscriptions.

Quirigua

The site of Quirigua is located on the northern side of the Motagua Valley, about sixty miles from the Gulf of Honduras in the Republic of Guatemala. The ruins are over half a mile from the banks of the Motagua River and it is likely that this location was chosen in order to avoid inundation by the river, which sometimes overflows its banks during the rainy season. The closest major site to Quirigua is Copan, which is situated some thirty miles to the south. There is reason to suppose that Quirigua was founded by missionaries or settlers from this larger and more important center because of the remarkable similarities in plan form and in sculptural and architectural styles at the two sites. Quirigua has been the subject of several extended studies and was partially excavated some forty years ago by a group representing the Carnegie Institution of Washington.[5] At the same time, many of the fallen monuments were reset and cleaned, and the site has now been set aside as a national park by the government of Guatemala.

The main group of structures at Quirigua occupies an area approximately 1,000 feet from east to west and 2,500 feet from north to south. Several other smaller groups of ceremonial structures are located nearby, but they do not seem specifically related to the main group shown in the site map (Fig. 144). If the general pattern of a main center supported by suburban centers holds here, we can assume that these secondary ceremonial groups were associated with groups of houses which have left little or no trace of their existence. Within the main ceremonial area, the various plazas and their associated structures form several distinct groupings of elements which make a kind of pinwheel, with the Temple Group or Acropolis at the center of the pinwheel. Three major plaza spaces can be observed, each of which has a distinctive character. These plazas are shown in yellow on the site plan.

The Temple Plaza, which forms the nucleus of the acropolis, appears to have been the most important place within the center, partly because of its central position in the scheme and partly because it is surrounded by the only large temple or palace buildings to be found within the site. This plaza is defined by low stepped platforms upon which are located six structures. Two of these structures, Temple I and Temple II, are shown in Figure 145. These structures are all different in size and shape and do not show any strong axial alignments with one another. In spite of this, the general outlines of a Quadrangle Group can be discerned, even though the idea is not fully developed. Nevertheless, it can be argued that the whole mound and its subordinate elements could be considered as an Acropolis Group. In some ways this latter idea seems more appropriate, but the acropolis concept is only partially realized as compared with other Acropolis Groups. It can be noted that the axes of the Temple Plaza are nearly fifteen degrees from the cardinal points of the compass, which is greater than the deviation found at most sites.

Associated with this Acropolis Group and Temple Group is a small plaza, at the same level as the Great Plaza, which is defined on three sides by arms extending out from the main mass of the acropolis and on the fourth side by a small, free-standing pyramid. There are no remains of a building on top of this pyramid and it must be assumed to be a ceremonial platform rather than the substructure for a temple building. It has already been noted in the discussion of Copan that this free-standing

---

[5] At the time of the author's last visit to the site in 1971, a new road had been built to the site and work had begun on clearing the acropolis, which was once more overgrown with trees after being neglected for over forty years. New data should be forthcoming in the next few years which might verify some of the assumptions presented here.

pyramid is organized in relation to the surrounding terraces in the same fashion as the pyramid and terraces at the north end of the Great Plaza at Copan. This might be considered as additional evidence of some connection between the two sites. It is tempting to suggest that these stepped terraces formed a sort of grandstand where ranges of celebrants could watch the ceremonies in the plaza below from a desirable vantage point. This is actually more than a tentative hypothesis, since the murals at Bonampak clearly show stepped terraces being used for this purpose.

Near the south end of this plaza are found two zoomorph-altar combinations which are unique to Quirigua. The name *zoomorph* has been given to several huge egg-shaped stone monuments which are almost completely covered with intricate relief carvings. The largest of these monuments is a single piece of sandstone nearly 12 feet long, 10 feet wide, and over 7 feet high (Figs. 146, 147). Why such grotesque monuments should have been created in addition to the traditional and more familiar stelae is hard to imagine, but the effort which went into their making suggests that they had great symbolic value. The altars associated with these zoomorphs are nearly as large in size and equal to them in the intricacy and quality of the relief carving. Two smaller zoomorphic figures are found on the east side of this plaza close to the base of the stepped terrace.

The Main Plaza lies between one arm of the acropolis and the low mound at the north end of the site. The plaza is further bounded on its eastern side by seven somewhat irregularly spaced mounds but is open on the west side. This configuration corresponds in most ways to quadrilateral groupings found at many sites, where plazas are bounded along three sides with one or more structures while the fourth side is left open. In many cases the west side is the open side, but this is not consistently the case. The Ceremonial Plaza, which was described above, can be considered as a secondary space within the Great Plaza as well as a primary space associated with the acropolis.

Within the Great Plaza are located most of the large stelae and altars for which Quirigua is noted (Figs. 148, 149). The two stelae which together with a large zoomorph form a triangular group near the northern end of the plaza are the largest ever found at a Maya site (Figs. 150, 151, 152, 153). The largest of these extends over 26 feet above ground and with its butt extending another 8 feet below ground has a total height of over 35 feet. This is a single piece of stone weighing about 65 tons, intricately carved with hieroglyphic inscriptions and human figures, representing a significant technical as well as aesthetic achievement (Figs. 150, 151, 152). Many of the other stelae are considerably smaller, but all of them attest to the superb skill of the stone masons and sculptors of Quirigua, who brought the art of stela carving to the highest degree of perfection ever attained by the Mayas (Figs. 154, 155, 156, 157). The question as to why this should have happened at a minor site, as far as size and architectural development is concerned, must be turned aside in favor of a closer examination of the spatial arrangement of these monuments.

It is difficult to believe that the position and grouping of these great stelae and their associated monuments did not have some importance beyond their calendric function. Individual stelae are commonly found in association with stairways leading to temple or palace structures at other sites, and it is generally assumed that the dates recorded on the stelae refer to the dates on which these buildings were dedicated. Occasionally a number of stelae are found in a long row, again usually in association with a stairway or building. At Quirigua, there is a row of three stelae at the base of the mound at the northern end which conforms to this pattern, but the larger stelae stand in the open space of the plaza with no obvious relationships to any structures. This arrangement is similar to the condition at Copan, where many of the large stelae are situated in the open space of the Great Plaza, well away from any buildings. This is further reason to assume some connection between the two sites in addition to the simi-

235

larity of plan organization. It can be noted that the stelae form two larger groupings, not including the single stela on the western side of the plaza, and these clusters serve to mark out particularized places within the larger space of the plaza. It seems logical to assume that very special ceremonies took place in relation to these smaller precincts which are so carefully marked out. Since they do not appear to be associated with buildings, the locations of these stelae seem fairly arbitrary, but this would not be the case if they played some specific role in ceremonial activity.

In addition to the elements which have just been described, there are two small groups of mounds lying east and south of the acropolis (Fig. 144). The East Group consists of three low mounds arranged around a small courtyard. These appear to have been terraces as there is insufficient debris to suggest that they might have supported superstructures. One side of the acropolis opens toward this group and there is the suggestion of a plaza lying between the acropolis and these mounds. South of the acropolis is a larger group of mounds which are somewhat irregularly disposed. Three of these mounds define a small courtyard, but the largest mound, which is pyramidal in form, bears no observable relationship to this court. It is possible that these constructions represent the earliest efforts by the builders of Quirigua and were abandoned by the time the acropolis and the structures surrounding the Main Plaza were built and the center took on its final form. This assumption is based on the fact that there are no stelae associated with this group of structures and the entire center appears to have been abandoned shortly after the last stela was put up in the main plaza. One would assume that some stelae would have been erected in association with this group had it played an important part in the life of the city at the same time as the structures surrounding the main plaza were being used.

In spite of the beauty and importance of the stone monuments which have brought Quirigua to a position of

236

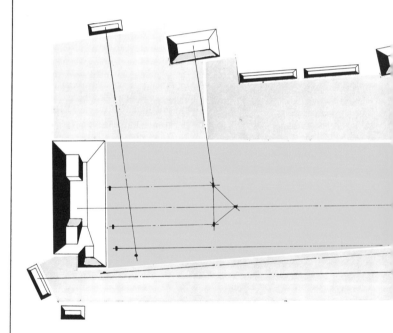

FIG. 144. Quirigua (after Adams).

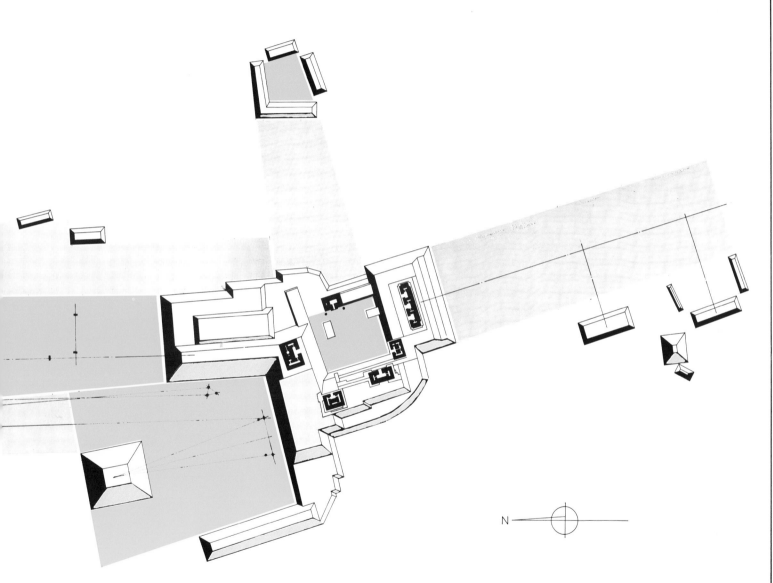

QUIRIGUA

GUATEMALA

SCALE 10 0   25   50   75   100   150   250
       METERS

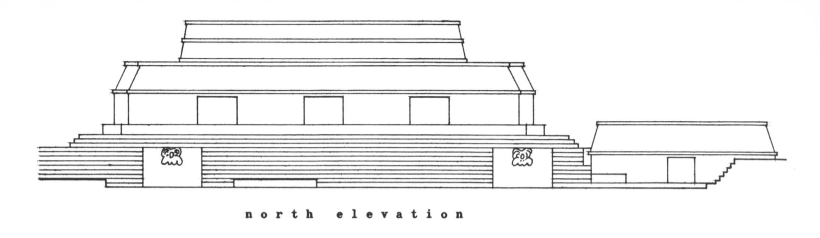

north elevation

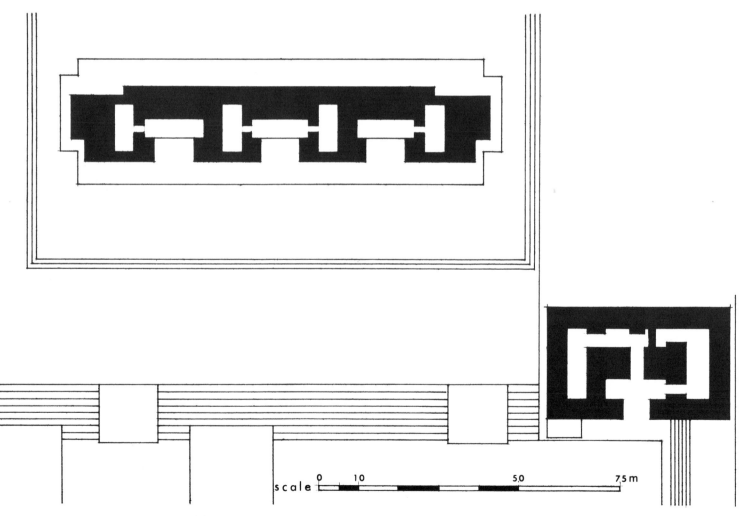

scale | 0 | 10 | | 50 | 75 m

FIG. 145. Quirigua—plans of Temple I and Temple II, upper level of acropolis.

eminence among Maya scholars, it is obvious that it cannot be considered a major site as far as architecture is concerned. Quirigua has particular value to this study, however, as it serves to illustrate the concept of ceremonial center in one of its simpler forms. In spite of its proximity to Copan, it is more comparable to Bonampak than to Copan in that both Quirigua and Bonampak consist essentially of one large plaza which is dominated by a very large mound or acropolis. The main difference between them is found in the manner in which the temple or palace buildings of each site are related to the main plaza. At Bonampak, the buildings all face onto the main plaza from various levels of the mound, while at Quirigua the buildings all face inward toward an open court. This latter arrangement is the normal condition for most of the archetypical building groupings which we have previously identified; the emphasis is on the contained space of the courtyard and the surrounding buildings serve to define this space. The combination of open plaza, which served as the gathering place for the bulk of the population, and the courtyard, raised above ground level and hidden from view below by its surrounding structures, contains the two basic ingredients of the ceremonial center: an "inner sanctum," or sacred place, where only the initiated could enter, and a larger, more open space where the people could gather and pay homage to the gods. This polarity is clearly expressed at Quirigua, and what it may lack in grandeur and complexity is partially made up by the clarity of this conception.

FIG. 146. Quirigua—Zoomorph "p" (top).

FIG. 147. Quirigua—Zoomorph "p" (dated A.D. 795) (bottom).

FIG. 148. Quirigua—view of Main Plaza looking north, Stela "E" in background.

FIG. 149. Quirigua—Stela "E."

FIG. 150. Quirigua—
Stela "E," south side
(left).

FIG. 151. Quirigua—
Stela "E" (center).

FIG. 152. Quirigua—
Stela "E," west side
(dated A.D. 771)
(right).

FIG. 153. Quirigua—
Stela "F," east side
(dated A.D. 761)
(left).

FIG. 154. Quirigua—
Stela "D," north side
(dated A.D. 766)
(center).

FIG. 155. Quirigua—
Stela "J," east side
(dated A.D. 756)
(right).

FIG. 156. Quirigua—Stela "J," west side (dated A.D. 756).

FIG. 157. Quirigua—Stela "I," east side
(dated A.D. 800).

Edzna

The ruins of Edzna are located some thirty miles southeast of the city of Campeche, the capital of the state of Campeche, Mexico. The site is situated near the northern end of a roughly oval basin that extends about nine miles from east to west and approximately twelve miles from north to south. The basin is bounded on its northern and eastern sides by a relatively continuous range of hills, while the other sides are also bounded by hills with broader valleys between the hills. Thus, the site is located between the lowland plains to the north and the river basins to the south on what must have been an ancient transportation route through the central hill region between the Rio Bec centers farther south and the Puuc area to the north. It also seems plausible that an east-west route from the Chenes area to the Gulf coast would have passed near Edzna en route to the ancient center of Akinpech, located at, or near, the present city of Campeche. One of the most extraordinary features of the site is a uniform and relatively straight, obviously man-made channel that begins near the Main Acropolis of Edzna, runs southeast to a large moat-surrounded quadrangle, and then cuts south across the basin for a distance of nearly eight miles, where it terminates in a savanna area that may be the remains of an old lake bed (Fig. 158). Similar features have not been reported from any other part of the Maya area and it may well be that the channel dates from the Spanish colonial period, but at the present time it remains an enigma.

Until very recently, Edzna has been one of the lesser known Maya sites and it was generally thought of as being a minor site, even though the Main Acropolis Group, which was partially excavated and restored between 1958 and 1962 by R. Pavon Abreu of the I.N.A.H. of Mexico, proved to be a very large and imposing acropolis structure. In the summer of 1968, a group from the University of Oregon made an extensive surface survey of the main ceremonial area together with some of the peripheral areas, and their maps show clearly that Edzna was a very large and important center with definite "urban" characteristics. The description and discussion which follows is largely an abstract of the monograph on Edzna which describes this survey in detail (G. F. Andrews: 1969).

Within the area mapped, Edzna appears to have consisted of two major sectors: a ceremonial center, covering an area approximately four thousand feet square, and a suburban "residential" area of approximately the same size, which is situated to the west and slightly north of the ceremonial area as shown in Figure 159. In order to avoid any possible misinterpretation of this map, it must be made clear that, while the main ceremonial area was very thoroughly mapped and shows all but the most minor or difficult-to-discern mounds, the so-called suburban area was only partly mapped and the shaded areas represent unmapped areas rather than areas where no mounds were found. Some exploration was undertaken within these areas, and other mounds are known to exist, so it is very likely that the residential zone was much more extensive than the map would seem to indicate. Keeping this in mind, it appears that the general settlement pattern at Edzna is similar in many respects to the pattern of Dzibilchaltun to the north or Tikal to the south.

Dzibilchaltun is now known to have covered an area of approximately fifty square kilometers, of which twenty square kilometers have been carefully mapped. These maps show that the city consisted of one massive ceremonial center and what may have been several smaller ones. Beyond the main center, the city is characterized by concentrated clusters of house mounds, usually centered around one or more vaulted or unvaulted multichamber structures. A similar condition is found at Tikal. The areas between the suburban clusters were too small to have contributed substantially to the agricultural needs of the community but may well have been used for this purpose. Within the ceremonial area are numerous smaller platforms and vaulted structures which might represent religious, administrative, or residential structures for the ruling class or classes. (See map of Dzibilchaltun, Fig. 272.)

The general pattern described above is repeated in almost all respects at Edzna. In addition to the main ceremonial center, two smaller ceremonial centers were located. One of these focuses around a very large pyramidal structure, situated about one-half mile northwest of the Main Acropolis, which has been called the Northwest Pyramid. Further to the west is another small ceremonial complex called the Far West Group. This group lies nearly two miles west of the Main Acropolis and there is some doubt as to whether it should be considered as being part of Edzna proper (G. F. Andrews: 1969). As at Dzibilchaltun, the house mounds are found in somewhat concentrated clusters which include at least one large pyramidal structure, clearly distinguishable from the smaller and lower house mounds, although they do not include multichamber stone buildings as at Dzibilchaltun. While the number of house mounds at Edzna is appreciably smaller than at Dzibilchaltun (the densities are roughly comparable), if our assumptions are correct in regard to the existence of larger numbers of mounds in the unmapped areas, a large resident population can be postulated. As indicated earlier in chapter 4, the pattern at Dzibilchaltun points toward urbanization in its fullest sense, and the same must be said for Edzna. The full outlines of the form and nature of this latter "city" have yet to be filled in, but we can begin to outline some of its main characteristics.

If we turn our attention to the large-scale map of the main ceremonial area (Fig. 160), we see that the whole center appears to focus on a large complex of structures in the form of an Acropolis Group. The general form characteristics of Acropolis Groups have been discussed in detail in chapter 5, and it can be noted that while the acropolis at Edzna is less complex than those at Uxmal and Piedras Negras, the essential form characteristics are all present and the degree of monumentality achieved is in no way lessened by its simpler organization (Fig. 17).

The buildings of the Acropolis Group are situated on a very large man-made platform which measures approximately 500 feet along its base on all sides and approximately 22 feet high (Figs. 161, 163). Access to the upper level of the platform is by means of a broad stairway on the western side (Figs. 163, 164). Two long palace-type buildings are situated just beyond the top of the stairway, with a narrow opening giving access to the Acropolis Plaza beyond (Fig. 162). The plaza measures 150 feet from east to west and 250 feet from north to south; a low platform is roughly centered in the open space of the plaza (Fig. 162). The north and south sides of the plaza are bounded by large pyramidal mounds and traces of low platforms with stairways extending into the plaza at the base of the mounds can still be found.[6] The east side of the plaza is bounded by a five-story pyramid-temple which is also called the *Templo Mayor* (Figs. 165, 166). The balance of the acropolis platform is occupied by a series of plazas, courtyards, and structures which are clearly subordinate to the main pyramid temple.

The multilevel pyramid with its crowning temple is the dominant element of the acropolis; the top of the roof comb of the temple measures 126 feet in height above the general level of the ground below (Figs. 171, 175). Because of its great height and mass, it also dominates the entire ceremonial area and can even be seen clearly from

[6] During 1970–1971, several additional structures within the acropolis complex were excavated and partially restored by R. Pavon Abrey of the I.N.A.H. of Mexico (Figs. 169, 170). Unfortunately, it was not possible to make a sufficiently detailed assessment of these buildings in time to include them in this discussion. The building on the south side of the main plaza is particularly noteworthy, as it is one of the few restored examples of a major structure with a pole-and-thatch roof (Figs. 167, 168). The structure on the northwest corner of the acropolis platform has a base molding in the typical Puuc style, indicating that it was a very late addition to the complex.

the Far West Group, which is two miles to the west (Fig. 173). The pyramid itself, which acts as a supporting structure for the superimposed temple, is of considerable interest, since it is composed of four stories of rooms arranged in a pyramidal form (Fig. 174). It is not clear if the rooms extended around all four sides of the pyramid or if they were confined to the west side, as appears to be the case. As has been pointed out in chapter 5, the stepped pyramids or superimposed terraces which serve as the supporting substructures for temples are normally solid masses of masonry and rubble and do not contain rooms on their outer surfaces. As far as is presently known, there are no comparable structures anywhere within the Maya area, although the three-story palace structures at Sayil and Santa Rosa Xtampak show some affinities in that they are made up of several stories of superimposed rooms. Neither of them, however, has the same pyramid-temple configuration. (See Figs. 266, 267 for the palace at Sayil.)

It can be noted in Figure 174 that the pyramid proper rests on a platform about six feet high and access to the first level of the pyramid is by means of a broad stairway projecting westward into the Acropolis Plaza. A large number of the stones which form the risers of the stairway are covered with hieroglyphic inscriptions, many of them in good state of preservation. From the top of the platform, another stairway extends the full height of the pyramid, giving access to the upper platform and the main temple.

The main temple consists of five rooms, one on the east side in addition to four interconnected rooms on the west side. The room on the east side has a single exterior doorway, while there are three doorways on the west side all giving access to the same room. A large doorway in the east side of this room gives access into a somewhat smaller room which is flanked on either side by very small vaulted chambers. A very high roof comb is situated over the dividing wall between the two main rooms of the temple (Fig. 175). The roof comb is divided into horizontal bands by several rows of slightly projecting stones

and is divided vertically by narrow slots, making a symmetrical over-all pattern. A number of small stones are tenoned into the face of the roof comb which undoubtedly supported plaster sculptures which have long since disappeared. (See chapter 5 for a more detailed discussion of roof combs.)

Perhaps the most unusual feature of the temple is the fact that it has exterior doorways on two opposite sides. The general pattern, as we have already pointed out in chapter 5, is one where doorways in temples are found on only one side, making them unidirectional. This deviation from the norm appears even more curious when it is noted that there is no corresponding stairway on the east side of the pyramid in front of this doorway. There is some reason to believe that the temple is an Early Classic construction, but there is no way at the present time of relating this assumption to a firm constructional sequence for the balance of the site.

Beyond the fact that it marks the highest point within the ceremonial center and is the dominant structural element within the entire city, it is also clear that the temple was intended to have some special relationship to several large structures situated east, west, and north of the acropolis platform. The doorway on the east side faces directly on axis with a large pyramidal mound about seven hundred feet to the east. This mound is part of a larger complex of structures which can be seen as a small-scale version of the Main Acropolis complex. The central doorway on the front, or west side, of the temple is on axis with the opening between the long palace-type structures which border the west side of the main plaza, and this axis terminates in a large pyramidal mound with the remains of a round building on its top. Immediately south of the Main Acropolis is a large platform which supports four small structures centered along the edges of each of its four sides. The central north-south axis of this complex falls on the center line of the Main Acropolis plaza. These axial configurations are too precise and too pronounced to be accidental, and a further examination of the balance

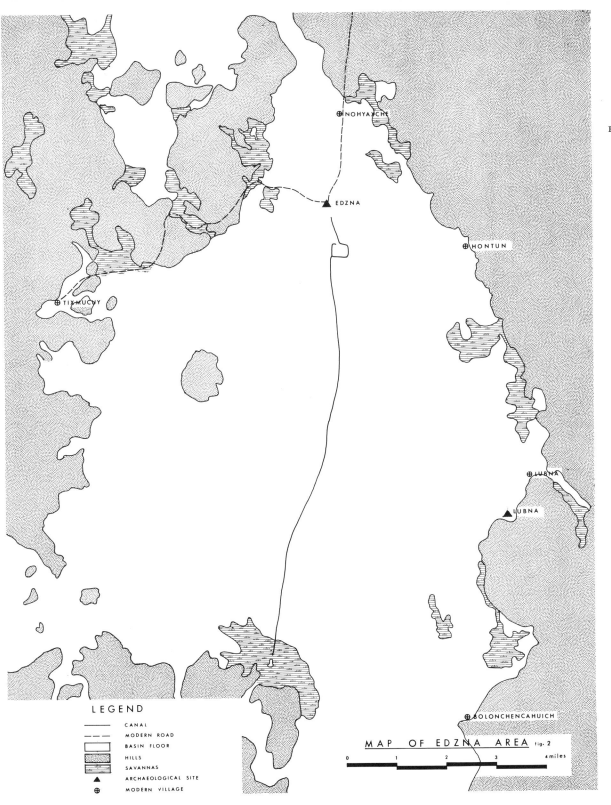

FIG. 158. Edzna area.

NOHYAXCHE

EDZNA

HONTUN

TIX MUCHY

LUBNA

LUBNA

BOLONCHENCAHUICH

LEGEND

————— CANAL
— — — MODERN ROAD
⬜ BASIN FLOOR
▨ HILLS
⬜ SAVANNAS
▲ ARCHAEOLOGICAL SITE
⊕ MODERN VILLAGE

MAP OF EDZNA AREA fig. 2

0   1   2   3   4 miles

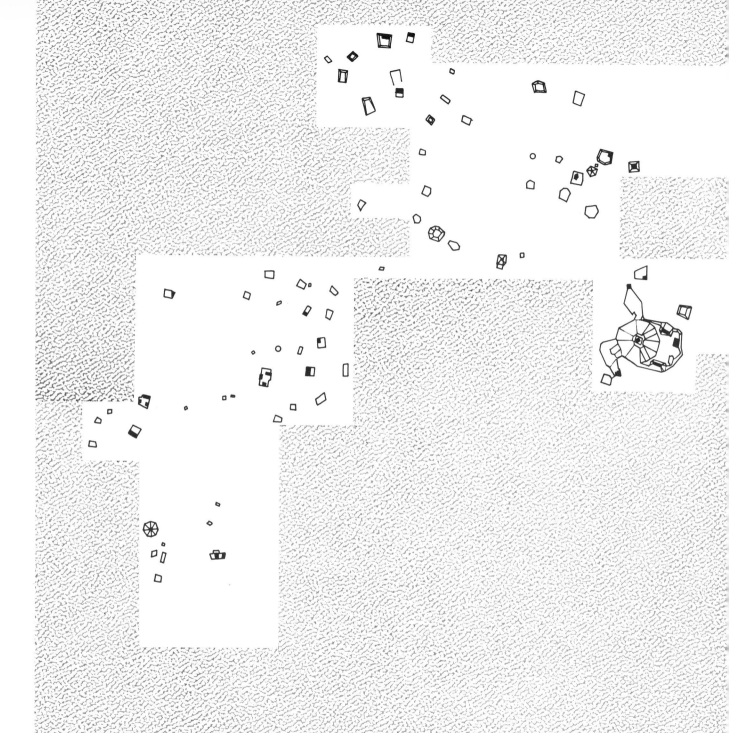

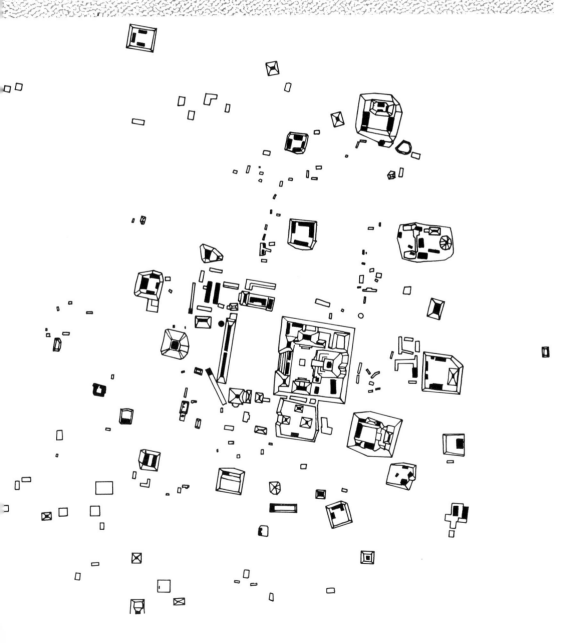
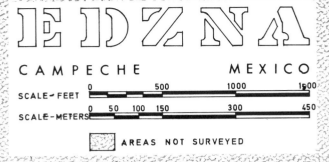

E D Z N A

CAMPECHE   MEXICO

SCALE—FEET 0   500   1000   1500

SCALE—METERS 0 50 100 150   300   450

AREAS NOT SURVEYED

FIG. 159. Edzna.

EDZNA

CAMPECHE   MEXICO

SCALE
0   100   200   300   400   500   600   700   800
Feet

SCALE
40   0   50   100   150   200
Meters

of the ceremonial zone shows that similar axial alignments and arrangements are the dominant ordering notions used in the organization of the center as a whole and can be observed at several scales.

In order to demonstrate this, a closer look at the map of the ceremonial zone is required (Fig. 160). From this map it can be noted that the various constructions within the center fall into three main categories: (1) low platforms lacking masonry superstructures; (2) low platforms supporting masonry superstructures, vaulted and unvaulted but not in combination with a definable substructure; (3) superstructures on platforms supported by primary or secondary substructures. Each of these main categories can be broken down into subcategories, but our purpose at the moment is only to talk about large relationships and not details. (All of the mounds within the ceremonial area have been carefully classified and indexed. [G. F. Andrews: 1969.]) It seems likely that many, or perhaps even most, of the small mounds in the first category are the remnants of house mounds. This assumption is supported by the fact that they are not consistently oriented, as is the case for the large ceremonial complexes in the third category, plus the fact that they are generally situated along the edges of the *bajos*, a primary location for house mounds at many other sites. Since no excavation has been undertaken as a means of testing out this assertion, we can only be guided by the general form similarity between this category of mounds and similar forms elsewhere which have actually proved to be house mounds.

The second category of mounds, which includes masonry superstructures on top of masonry substructures, presents even more difficulties of interpretation than the first category. There is considerable variation in size and shape among the structures falling into this category and their spatial distribution is not very consistent. All of the vaulted buildings in this category are found either as integral parts of specific spatial assemblages or are located immediately adjacent to other ceremonial structures. On the other hand, the platforms supporting unvaulted structures tend to be found in association with *chultunes* and low platforms or are located along the edges of the *bajos* in a manner reminiscent of these platforms. This suggests that a further distinction should be made between vaulted and unvaulted structures. We are inclined to paraphrase E. W. Andrews in his description of similar structures at Dzibilchaltun and suggest that this category consists of various religious, administrative, and residential structures.

The third category of structures is a different matter; there is every reason to believe that they all represent religious or ceremonial structures of some sort. The symbolic expressions of height, size, symmetry, order, and spatial definition and the consistent orientation and interrelationships between these elements reflect an ideology and commitment that far exceeds the demands of the commonplace or utilitarian aspects of life. Again, this is not consistently the case, but whatever larger order can be observed within the ceremonial area is due to the positioning and spatial organization of these imposing and sometimes very complex elements.

As indicated earlier, the primary distinguishing feature of this class of constructions, which sets them apart from the other two, is the use of large elevated substructures upon which are located one or more superstructures and platforms. The substructures were all constructed with rough-cut-stone retaining walls filled with earth and rubble. It did not appear that veneer stones were used as facings for these substructures, but it is possible that such veneer facings have been covered over with debris from above. Positive evidence for substructures with stepped sides is also lacking in most cases, but perhaps for the same reason as suggested above. This class of constructions includes three subcategories as follows: (1) single buildings resting on platforms supported by pyramidal substructures; (2) multiple buildings in a linear arrangement supported by rectangular substructures; and (3) large, relatively square substructures supporting a complex of structures defining a central courtyard or plaza. For purposes

253

FIG. 160. Edzna—main ceremonial area.

of discussion this latter subcategory will be called a ceremonial complex.

There are twenty-eight constructions in the third category and seventeen of these are large complexes as defined above. The Main Acropolis Group belongs to this category, and several of the other large complexes might be considered as representing secondary Acropolis Groups. Whatever we choose to call them, they are impressive constructions and the massive substructures which support them range in size from two hundred to five hundred feet square. Seven of the ceremonial complexes were crowned with temples as the dominant feature, although only the temple of the main acropolis is still standing.

The previous discussion of construction types referred to discrete groups or complexes of structures in that they consist of physically isolated masses of material elevated above the natural ground level. It can be noted from the map, however, that there are larger assemblages of structures which also form integrated spatial organizations, even though they are made up of several disparate parts. The same spatial concept, or mental template, has been applied to these larger assemblages and to the smaller individual complexes. In both instances, one structural unit dominates the others and is located on the eastern side of a large plaza. In both cases this element faces the west.

The most outstanding example of this is the Main Acropolis Group and its subordinate elements. A glance at the map shows that the main acropolis complex faces west toward a large plaza which measures about 600 feet from north to south and 400 feet from east to west. The west side of this plaza is bounded by a long rectangular platform which supports the remains of two palace-type buildings, each of which is about 180 feet long (Fig. 176). These two structures are separated from one another by a narrow opening about twelve feet wide. The south side of the plaza is bounded by several pyramidal mounds, one of which supports the remains of a small temple building on top. The north side of the plaza is bounded by a large rectangular platform with the remains of several

masonry structures along the top (Fig. 177). This larger configuration is obviously based on the same spatial concept as the main acropolis itself and argues strongly for a generic concept after which both were modeled. The same idea is repeated throughout the center at various scales and with various degrees of conformity to the ideal or generic model.

Beyond this there is no larger discernible order anywhere within the city. Many of the larger complexes are isolated from one another by intervening *bajos* and there is no trace of any causeways or other circulation elements which might have served to connect them. As appears to be the case at most sites, the actual positioning of individual buildings or complexes is dependent in part on the fortuitous configuration of the existing terrain and the highest points of ground have been selected for building purposes. The contours show that the ceremonial area was laced with *bajos*, but whether this represents a natural condition or is the result of repeated mining of these areas to obtain material for construction purposes is a matter of conjecture. My own guess would be that the *bajos* represent a combination of both factors, i.e., that existing small *bajos* were widened and deepened. This would avoid excessive transport of building materials from one part of the site to another and would simultaneously create basins where water could be collected from the higher surrounding areas.

One of the most vexing questions in connection with Edzna has to do with the temporal sequence of construction within the main ceremonial area. There is every reason to believe that the site was occupied for a period of at least several hundred years and that during this time older constructions were modified or enlarged, others were completely abandoned, and new constructions were continuously added. At the present time, we have no way of assigning dates to any of the different structures. All that can be said for sure is that what we see exposed on the surface represents the last state in the development of the site prior to its abandonment, but this does not tell us if all

254

the structures were still in use at that time or which are new and which are old. It also does not tell us whether or not our assumptions about the "residential" character of the smaller mounds is correct or whether they were early or late, even if they should prove to be house mounds as assumed.

At Dzibilchaltun, it has been shown that during what Andrews calls the Early period (A.D. 0 to 600) the architecture is significantly different from that of the Florescent period (A.D. 600 to 900). During the Early period, buildings were constructed of rough-cut-stone blocks laid up in courses, and vaults were of the true corbeled type. Veneer construction, utilizing a concrete core for both walls and vaults, did not make its appearance until the Florescent period, and buildings erected in this period are significantly different from the Early period both in construction and details. (E. W. Andrews: 1965.) Both of these construction types can be found at Edzna and it is tempting to work out a temporal sequence based on veneer versus masonry-block construction. Unfortunately, this appears to be a risky proposition, since one of the rooms in the five-story pyramid of the main acropolis which is behind the outermost set of rooms on the second level has both veneer-type vaults and walls while the outer room, which must be assumed to be from a later date, has a corbeled vault of rough stones. While this anomaly may be only an isolated case, it serves to reinforce the notion that only large-scale excavation will establish an accurate temporal sequence for the main ceremonial area.

Thus far our discussion has been confined primarily to the main ceremonial area of the site, but it is clear that the city extended some distance to the west of this area. While some exploration was undertaken in the areas immediately north, south, and east of the ceremonial area, no large mounds of any sort were found and very few small mounds were observed, due in part to the heavy undergrowth which forced this search to be very superficial. Thus, we cannot speak about these areas with any degree of certainty. Fortunately, the landscape is some-

what more open toward the west and a fairly large area of this sector was surveyed.

As shown on the small-scale map (Fig. 159), there is a gap of about one thousand feet between the concentration of structures in the main ceremonial area and the eastern edge of the concentration of smaller mounds which represents a residential zone. The eastern edge of this suburban zone is further distinguished by the presence of a very large pyramidal structure, surrounded by smaller mounds, called the Northwest Pyramid (Figs. 178, 179). Because of the lack of building remains between this pyramid and the main center, it appears that this complex is a secondary ceremonial area, associated with the residential area lying west and north, rather than an adjunct of the main ceremonial area. This pattern is consistent with the conditions at both Tikal in the Peten and Dzibilchaltun to the north, where outlying ceremonial centers are found beyond the main center.

The large pyramid which forms the focus of this group is a massive structure measuring seventy-five feet in height and three hundred feet in diameter at the base. (It is more octagonal or roundish in plan than square.) The remains of a small temple are found on top of this pyramid, but almost nothing can be made of its ground plan. There are faint traces of stairways on the northeast and southeast sides of the large pyramid, indicating that its orientation was significantly different from the structures in the main ceremonial area which are consistently oriented seven to eight degrees east of magnetic north. This gives added weight to the assumption that it was not directly associated with the main center.

The large pyramid is situated on a low platform which also supports a number of smaller structures. These structures are also lacking in consistent orientation, and the impression is created that they were sited in regard to the existing ground contours, which are rather irregular. Just north of the main complex of structures are two low platforms with smaller mounds on their upper terraces, but these are positioned in such a way that no clearly defined

255

plaza or courtyard is created between them and the large pyramid. On almost all counts this ceremonial complex fails to show either the conceptual order or the geometrical precision of the complexes in the main ceremonial area, and it may not be too far-fetched to suggest that this is an indication that it was not contemporary with the structures in the main ceremonial area, even though there is presently no archaeological evidence for this.

The mounds lying northwest, west, and southwest of the Northwest Pyramid consist for the most part of low rectilinear platforms together with several larger pyramidal mounds which are assumed to represent the remains of community or ceremonial structures in contrast to the smaller mounds which are assumed to represent house mounds. The pattern of distribution of these mounds is not very definitive, although it can be seen that they form several rough clusters with anywhere from three to seven mounds in each cluster. Most of the clusters contain one of the larger pyramidal mounds just referred to. The mounds themselves have no dominant orientation and many of them are so badly deteriorated that they cannot be said to have any orientation at all. The natural ground form is very flat in the west and southwest sectors, while it is gently rolling in the northwest sector. In this latter sector the mounds tend to follow the higher ground elevations, while in the other sectors the ground is extremely flat and the positioning of mounds must have been determined on some other basis. In all sectors, *aguadas* are found next to the larger mounds and it may be assumed that these basins were created when material was excavated to construct the adjacent mounds.

All of these smaller mounds were classified and typed and could be put into six distinct categories (G. F. Andrews: 1969). Two of these categories appear to represent structures of a nonresidential type, which might be called either community or ceremonial structures, while the balance appear to have been house mounds (Fig. 180). While none of these mounds was excavated, the assertion that they were actually house mounds rests on their marked similarity in size and form to similar mounds at Tikal and Barton Ramie, which were carefully excavated and proved to be house mounds. Without going into unnecessary detail, it can be said that there is such a close correspondence between the mound types at Edzna and those at Tikal and Barton Ramie that it seems perfectly appropriate to refer to them as house mounds with no further qualification. The best-preserved mounds have edges clearly defined by rows of stones forming retaining walls, and in several instances these stones include *metates* which were too worn to be of further use and thus became building stone. The existence of this residential area is a strong argument in favor of the urbanization of Edzna. There is some open space between the mound clusters, but it is too small to have been useful as *milpa* plots and it must be assumed that the major agricultural zone lay beyond this particular sector. If the general pattern observed elsewhere holds true for Edzna, we would expect that the residential area would gradually give way to more rural areas with no sharp break in between. Without further mapping, this assumption cannot be verified, but all the indications point in this direction.

The general picture that begins to emerge from the foregoing description and discussion is one where Edzna can be viewed as an "urban agglomerate" with a well-defined center made up of numerous large and imposing ceremonial structures interspersed with smaller structures representing nonceremonial, or nonreligious, functions. Beyond this center at least one residential zone can be identified, which also contains a minor ceremonial center. Assuming the existence of other residential areas in those parts of the site that were not mapped, we get a pattern which is analogous to present-day cities. That is to say, the city has a center, subcenters, and suburban zones. The main community facilities are concentrated in the center; in the case of modern cities, these are commercial rather than religious in character, but the analogy still holds. Interspersed among the commercial buildings in a modern city we find everything from houses to schools to churches and hospitals. Beyond the center are residential neighborhoods, and each of these neighborhoods has its own local center, where commercial and other facilities are found. This again is analogous to the Maya residential area, which contains structures other than houses.

It obviously would not pay to try to carry the analogy too far; the point is that, rather than being viewed as an "empty ceremonial center," Edzna must be seen as an urban place, a city of a special kind, perhaps, but a city nonetheless. Taken together with Tikal and Dzibilchaltun, it forms another link in the chain of evidence which is gradually accumulating in regard to the urbanized character of the larger Maya settlements. This, in turn, suggests a new direction in Maya archaeology where inquiry will be directed toward questions of social organization and city life rather than calendrics and decorative styles.

Note: Interested readers are referred to the monograph entitled *Edzna, Campeche, Mexico—Settlement Patterns and Monumental Architecture* (G.F. Andrews: 1969) for a detailed description of the various structures at Edzna. This report also includes large-scale maps which show the main ceremonial center in considerable detail.

FIG. 161. Edzna—Main Acropolis,
        west side (before restoration) (top).

FIG. 162. Edzna—Main Acropolis,
        main entry and upper plaza (bottom).

FIG. 163. Edzna—Main Acropolis (after partial restoration, 1970–71).

FIG. 164. Edzna—Main Acropolis, monumental stairway and entry to upper plaza.

FIG. 165. Edzna—Main Acropolis, five-story pyramid (*Templo Mayor*).

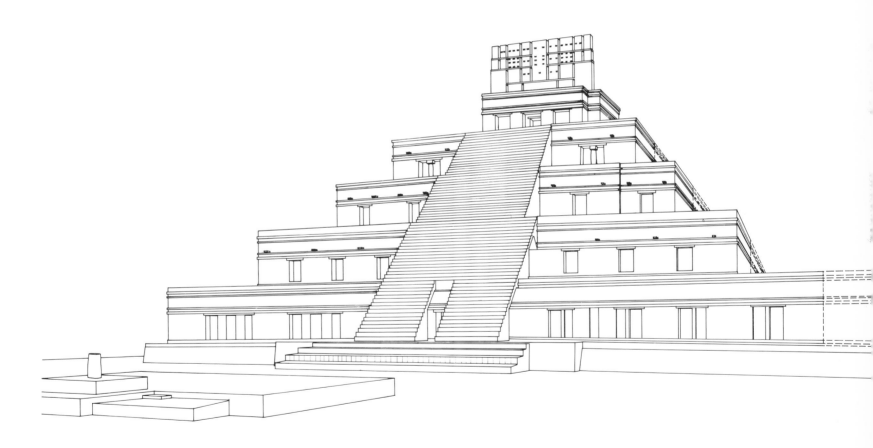

FIG. 166.   Edzna—Main Acropolis, five-story pyramid (restoration).

FIG. 169. Edzna—Main Acropolis,
building with thatch roof, Structure No. 21
(after recent restoration).

FIG. 167. Edzna—
Main Acropolis,
Structure No. 21 and
Structure No. 23
(after recent restoration) (top left).

FIG. 168. Edzna—
Main Acropolis,
Structure No. 21 (bottom left).

FIG. 170. Edzna—Main Acropolis,
Structure No. 12 (northwest
corner of upper plaza).

FIG. 171. Edzna—Main Acropolis, five-story pyramid and Structure No. 23.

FIG. 172. Edzna—Main Acropolis, Structure No. 21.

FIG. 173. Edzna—Main Acropolis
and northwest pyramid
as seen from Far West Group.

FIG. 174. Edzna—Main Acropolis,
five-story pyramid, west elevation.

FIG. 175. Edzna—Main Acropolis,
detail of roof comb on temple
of five-story pyramid.

FIG. 176. Edzna—palace mound, west side of Main Plaza.

FIG. 177. Edzna—Structure No. 15, north side of Main Plaza (after recent restoration).

FIG. 178. Edzna—northwest pyramid
as seen from Main Acropolis.

FIG. 179. Edzna—northwest pyramid
as seen from residential sector.

Because of the remarkable homogeneity of the building remains at the five Puuc centers considered in the present study, as well as their close physical proximity, it seems desirable to treat them initially as a group, in order to avoid unnecessary duplication in the discussions of the individual sites. The five centers referred to are Oxkintok, Uxmal, Kabah, Labna, and Sayil, and these centers, together with another thirty or more nearby archaeological sites, can all be found within a restricted physiographic area which is commonly called the Puuc region. The Puuc region, or hill country, is a vaguely defined geographical area which includes the southernmost parts of the state of Yucatan, Mexico, as well as an adjoining section of the northern part of the state of Campeche. The hills, which are characteristic of most of this region, rise abruptly from the level northern plain and run in a northwesterly direction from a point near the border between the state of Yucatan and the territory of Quintana Roo until they terminate just this side of the coastal plains of western Yucatan.

Judging from the large number of sites with extensive architectural remains which are found in this area, it must have been one of the most densely populated districts within the entire Maya expanse during its peak period of occupation. This anomaly, together with the distinctive architectural style which characterizes the Puuc centers, indicates that the Puuc development is somewhat unique in terms of the Yucatan Peninsula as a whole and thus is worthy of special attention. Our present knowledge of the salient features of this development can be summarized as follows.

The sudden flowering of the Puuc style is a Late Classic manifestation which appears to have been restricted to the very limited geographical area described above. The total number of Puuc centers is still not known, but there are at least thirty sites of varying size with building remains in the pure Puuc style. These centers form an almost unbroken chain of settlements from one end of the Puuc area to the other, although the concentration seems heaviest in the area just southeast of Uxmal. The evidence at hand indicates that, with a few notable exceptions, all of the Puuc centers were built and occupied during the latter part of the Classic period (A.D. 600 to 900), which gives them a very short life span in relation to the known period of Maya history, which covers upwards of two thousand years.

While intensive stratigraphic excavation of the kind that has recently been completed at Dzibilchaltun and Tikal has never been attempted at any of the Puuc sites, there is little reason to assume any extensive occupation of these same sites prior to the Puuc florescence in the eighth and ninth centuries. In contrast to other large centers just outside the Puuc area which are represented by ceramic collections showing two or more clearly differentiated stages, the Puuc collections are limited to a single stage, i.e., Late Classic. With the exception of Oxkintok and Uxmal, the architectural remains are also limited to a single stage, which has likewise been dated by several methods to the Late Classic period. Thus, everything points to a sudden outburst of activity in an area which was only lightly inhabited during its earlier and late periods. This has led some scholars to believe that it can be thought of as a subcultural region which is coincident with the geographical region which gives it its name. We will return to this latter proposition a little later.

Physically, the Puuc area is marked by low hills and ridges interspersed with valleys and flat basins and is covered for the most part with a dense growth of scrub forest. The soil is fairly rich, but there are no natural sources of water other than rainfall, and the Maya in-

The Puuc Cities

FIG. 180. Edzna—house mound in main residential sector.

habitants were completely dependent on artificial water-storage elements of their own making in order to sustain themselves during the long dry season. Elsewhere in the peninsula, particularly in the north, *cenotes*, or natural wells, are found, but there are none in the Puuc hills. In contrast to the Peten area, where the highest points of ground were sought out as the location of ceremonial groupings, the Puuc centers tend to be located in well-drained valleys or basins, near the bases and lower slopes of hills rather than on the tops of the hills themselves. This may account in some measure for the more dispersed quality of the Puuc centers in relation to the tighter clustering which characterizes the Peten area, since the relatively flat sites offered better opportunities for spreading out horizontally.

Both the ceramic and architectural remains from the Puuc sites suggest that this late, but very intense, development was guided by a highly organized elite class or power group, since both are very conservative in terms of change during the two- to three-hundred-year life span of the style and both seem to be conceived in terms of mass production.[7] The decoration of pottery is fairly simple compared to the elaboration of buildings, but it is remarkably uniform and so is the architecture. The dominant characteristics of Puuc-style architecture are rather high and elaborate base moldings, generally plain lower walls, large and elaborate cornice moldings just above the plain lower walls, and upper cornices of the same kind. The space between the lower and upper cornices is filled with very detailed cut-stone mosaics. Puuc-style buildings also make frequent use of mosaic masks over doorways and on the corners of the upper friezes, decorated roof combs, and small columns with square capitals centered in doorways. The stonework employed in Puuc buildings is of the highest order in terms of precision of cutting and fitting, and stucco decoration, which is easier to manipulate, was used only in rare instances. The vocabulary of motifs employed in the decorative mosaic work varied between simple geometric patterns and stylized human and animal figures and tends to be repetitive, thus making it very adaptable to mass production techniques.

Some of the particulars of the Puuc development, as outlined above, leave us with several questions which are important in terms of our general understanding of the cultural history of the Yucatan Peninsula as a whole. First, is there any validity to the notion of a Puuc culture region, and, if so, does it coincide with the geographical region as described earlier? Second, how can we account for such a dense concentration of centers in a region which does not contain any natural water resources? Third, why should the construction of the Puuc centers be confined to such a short period of time (two hundred and fifty to three hundred years)? Fourth, to what extent had urbanization taken place within the Puuc area and what range of settlement types are represented by the various sites? Fifth, where was the administrative or political power for the Puuc area centered, assuming that authority was centralized? Finally, what is the source of the Puuc style and where did it originate, if not within the Puuc area itself? It is clear that there is no way at the present time to give definitive answers to these questions on the basis of firm archaeological evidence, but it is possible to indulge in some speculation based on what little evidence is available.

In reference to the first question, we have already suggested in chapter 4 that style, in itself, is not a good indicator of specific cultural regions. Styles are associated with time periods and it is clear that the Puuc style is confined to the latter part of the Classic period. Therefore, it is possible that the Puuc area can be thought of as a province within a larger region which includes sites with non-Puuc

[7] The relationship between conservatism in art styles and an entrenched power structure can be challenged, but the "establishment" tends to resist innovations and welcomes mass production techniques which will enable it to leave its stamp of authority on everything in sight. The Puuc development is startling in terms of the energy expended in building monumental structures on such a vast scale, but it is relatively static as far as change is concerned.

architecture. This would be the case if it could be demonstrated that there was a larger cultural region within which the Puuc style was only one of several closely allied styles. There is some reason to suspect this might be the case, since the Chenes, Rio Bec, and Edzna area styles all have something in common with the Puuc. At the same time, individual buildings in the Chenes style are found at sites which are otherwise pure Puuc, and vice versa, and this overlapping of styles is a further indication of the close cultural affiliations between these two areas.

Beyond this, we would expect that any site within the Puuc area which was occupied prior to the emergence of the Puuc style would also have buildings of a different style which were associated with the earlier period. This turns out to be the case; the site of Oxkintok, which is near the northwest extremity of the Puuc area, is represented by two distinct architectural styles. One style can be dated from the Early Classic period and is much more akin to Early Classic remains in the Southern Lowlands area than to the Puuc style which later replaced it. It is also possible that the Chenes style was developed earlier than the Puuc style; this would account for the presence of Chenes-style buildings at Uxmal as well as at other so-called Puuc sites. Thus, the only thing we can say for certain about the Puuc area in terms of its regional implications is that by definition it is an area where Puuc-style buildings are found, and these are confined to the limited geographical region as noted. It can only be considered as a valid cultural region in terms of the Late Classic period, and even then it may have been only a subregion within a larger region which included both the Chenes and Edzna areas.

The question in regard to the density of occupation of the Puuc area is extremely important, as it has several implications. We have already noted that the Puuc centers form a very dense cluster where many large centers are no more than a few miles from one another. For example, Uxmal, Kabah, Labna, and Sayil all fall within a circle with a radius of approximately five miles. The total population within this circle (urban and rural) must have been measured in tens of thousands. This same area is only lightly populated today and there is no reason to suppose that the basic ecological conditions have changed substantially in the intervening years. We have also noted that the Puuc area has no natural water resources and the inhabitants were thus forced to find some means of storing rain water for use during the long dry season. Given the density of population, this must have constituted an immense problem. Since the Puuc sites were occupied at the same time, there is no possibility of a small population moving from place to place, building new cities as they went along.

On the surface, everything seems to mitigate against such a dense concentration of people in a small area with a questionable ecological base, but several alternatives can be suggested as to how it came about. One possibility would be that there was a general northward drift of population from the southern areas toward the middle of the Classic period and that these people settled in the Puuc area for reasons unknown. This would account, in part, for the late development of the Puuc area in relation to the rest of the Maya area as a whole. It would not account for the Puuc style, however, since it has no known antecedents in the south.

A second explanation would be that the Puuc area was ideally suited to *milpa* farming as practiced by the Mayas and could therefore support a larger population than could be expected in other areas. The soil is rich and the annual rainfall is higher than in the northern parts of the peninsula. This would not account for the late development of the Puuc area, however, as we would expect that prime land would have been sought out during the earliest explorations of the peninsula by the ancestors of the Classic Mayas.

A third explanation would be that the development of *chultunes* for the purpose of storing water was a more important achievement than has previously been recognized and led to an explosive increase in population, once it proved to be workable. *Chultunes* are found in abundance in nearly every Puuc site and there is little question as to their water-storage function. Once sufficient water was available, the density of population could increase up to the point where the full agricultural potential of the Puuc area could be realized. The higher density of occupation of this area compared with areas to the north and south is then a function of the basic differences in agricultural possibilities between these areas, even though there was a long period of time when this advantage could not be turned to account. This latter explanation seems much more plausible than the other two, as the lack of population at the present time is largely due to lack of adequate water resources during the dry season.

The late development of the Puuc area can also be explained as a consequence of the late development of the *chultunes*. Prior to the time when these water-storage devices came into widespread use, the Mayas could not have lived in this area in any great numbers, as they would have been eitirely dependent on fortuitous water resources, which were almost nonexistent. It must be kept in mind that we are talking about water used for domestic purposes rather than water required for agriculture. *Milpa* farming depends entirely on rainfall, which is more than adequate during the period when crops are grown. But a considerable amount of water is required on a year-round basis for domestic purposes, which can be collected and stored during the rainy season for later use providing the technology is available for accomplishing this. The invention of the *chultun* solved this problem, and we are forced to assume that this took place some time around the middle of the Classic period, since this is the point in time when building activity within the Puuc area began in earnest. Whether the invention of the *chultun* represents a stroke of genius on the part of a very thirsty Maya peasant or resulted from a long series of experiments carried out consciously in response to the problem of storing water may never be known. However it came about, it must be ranked high on the list of accomplishments of

the Mayas, since their descendents, who presumably have access to modern technology, have yet to find an adequate solution to the same problem.

The question in regard to urbanization and settlement types is extremely difficult to deal with. Most of the Puuc sites have never been mapped so we know next to nothing about their physical structure, and those maps which are available for the better-known sites show little more than the central ceremonial areas of these cities; the peripheral areas are ignored. Thus, there is no basis for determining the size or extent to which any of the Puuc sites were urbanized, as we know very little about the patterns of housing in relation to the ceremonial areas. House mounds have been located at all of the well-known Puuc sites and the basic house types are similar to those found elsewhere, but there is no definitive data in regard to their over-all distribution. It has been assumed by many writers that Uxmal was a larger and more important center than its closest neighbors, but there is little real evidence to support this view, which seems to be based on the fact that the buildings at Uxmal are more imposing and better preserved than structures at other sites. Actually, the structures at Kabah are equally large and imposing and cover a larger ground area than the equivalent structures at Uxmal, but they are not as well preserved. Labna appears to have been much smaller than either Uxmal or Kabah, and Sayil seems to fall somewhere in between. There are a large number of structures shown on the map of Sayil, but most of them are quite small and many of them are likely to represent house mounds.

On the basis of present knowledge, Oxkintok appears to be the largest center within the Puuc area, but it has received almost no attention in relation to the better-known sites such as Uxmal and Kabah. Oxkintok consists of a large central area, about one square kilometer in extent, and many suburban or satellite groups are situated east, west, and south of this central nucleus. We have already postulated that the presence of suburban or satellite centers is an indication of advanced urbanism, as these secondary ceremonial groupings have been found to be the focus of large residential areas. The main ceremonial center itself is marked by a network of *sacbes*, or roadways, which connect various temple and palace complexes together, and a larger causeway connects the main center with one of the outlying groups. House mounds are also found in and near the main center, which further reinforces its urban character. While the over-all density and distribution of housing at Oxkintok is not known, all of the above data indicates that it was an urban center of some importance and might well have been the largest center in the Puuc area. Whether it functioned as an administrative center in relation to the other Puuc centers is debatable. It is still possible that this kind of control was somewhat dispersed, with Uxmal and Kabah both playing an important role in terms of the development of the area as a whole.

The question in regard to the source of the Puuc style is perhaps the most troublesome. If we are correct in our assumption that the larger regional centers would most likely be the places where new styles originated, then it is necessary to identify this singular site among the thirty-odd sites within the Puuc area. As was pointed out in the preceding paragraph, this cannot be done with the data presently available; what is required is a very detailed chronology for the whole Puuc area that would tell where buildings in the Puuc style first made their appearance. Lacking this, we can only reiterate that Oxkintok shows more of the characteristics which have been outlined for the larger regional centers and is thus the most likely candidate for this exalted position within the Puuc area itself. If we look elsewhere for the beginnings of the Puuc style, the situation is equally obscure, since buildings in all of the surrounding areas share some traits in common with the Puuc style, but they are clearly different in some important respects. The suggestion that the style evident at Edzna represents an intermediate stage between the Peten style and the Puuc style is not tenable, since many of the buildings at Edzna are contemporary with those in the Puuc area and are clearly not in the Puuc style.[8] Thus, the question in regard to the origins of the Puuc style must be left unanswered pending the development of a more definitive chronology for both the Puuc area and the areas surrounding it, particularly the Chenes and Edzna areas, which are even less well known than the Puuc.

In spite of the many questions which still remain to be answered in regard to the Puuc area as a whole, Oxkintok, Uxmal, Kabah, Labna, and Sayil stand as large-scale symbols of the inventiveness of the Mayas in terms of their ability to develop a viable regional culture in the face of extremely difficult environmental conditions which have resulted in the same area being almost deserted today. This inventiveness is expressed not only in terms of a pronounced regional architectural style, which is reflected in other art forms as well, but in technological advances of some importance. The invention of the *chultun* as a device for storing water was clearly the most important technological accomplishment within the Puuc area, since the entire development was predicated on a reliable year-round source of water for domestic and building purposes. In addition, the veneer-over-concrete construction technique was brought to its highest peak of refinement within the Puuc area, and the richness and delicacy of the mosaic stonework in the friezes of Puuc-style buildings is unmatched anywhere within the larger Maya area. Thus, in spite of their short life span, the Puuc cities must be seen as worthy successors to the long heritage of place-making ideas which appear to have been initiated in the more favored areas to the south.

8 In 1971 a small building on the northwest corner of the main acropolis at Edzna was excavated and partially restored. The base moldings of this building are clearly in the Puuc style, which raises some questions in regard to the chronology of the different structures in this Acropolis Group. The position of this building at one edge of the acropolis mound suggests that it was a very late addition, but there is no proof of this.

The Puuc Cities: Oxkintok

The ruins of Oxkintok are located about three and one-half miles east of the present-day town of Maxcanu and about nineteen miles northwest of the better-known site of Uxmal. The central portion of the site lies on the edge of a gently rolling and fertile plain which terminates in the Puuc hills to the north. Oxkintok marks the westernmost extension of the Puuc architectural region, as the hills turn just beyond Oxkintok and run in a southwesterly direction toward Campeche. There is a distinct possibility that Oxkintok may have been connected to Uxmal by a *sacbe*, or causeway, much in the same manner that Uxmal was connected to Kabah by a similar roadway. A network of artificial causeways connects various buildings and plazas within the site and one well-built road runs in a southeasterly direction from the center of the site to an outlying group approximately one-third of a mile beyond the eastern edge of the area shown on the map (Fig. 181).

The map, which covers an area of 1.3 square kilometers, shows only the central portion of the city, which extended some distance to the east, south, and west. Many other groups of structures are found in these outlying areas, which leads us to believe that Oxkintok was an urban center of considerable size. The detailed characteristics of these outlying areas have not been mapped out, but their general character suggests that they represent the kind of suburban residential areas which have been postulated for the larger urban centers.

Two great pyramids, both of which are associated with acropolislike complexes, face toward each other from the northern and southern extremities of the site (Fig. 182). A third, and somewhat smaller, pyramid-temple, is centered between these complexes at the western edge of the central area, completing a monumental triangular arrangement which is highly reminiscent of the great trian-gular configuration at Uxmal, where the Pyramid of the Magician is similarly centered between two large Acropolis Groups (Fig. 183). The bulk of the other structures at Oxkintok lie east of the north-south axis running between the two large pyramids, and, as can be noted on the site map, most of these are associated with large complexes of structures situated on the tops of raised platforms (Figs. 181, 183, 184). Included among these structures are eight other high pyramid-temples, several smaller pyramids, many palace-type buildings, a ball court, a portal vault similar to those at Uxmal and Labna, and a variety of smaller structures including numerous house mounds, which are shown as low, rectangular platforms. In addition, there are circular and rectangular altar platforms and specialized drainage basins built around a series of *chultunes*.

With the exception of the great triangular configuration involving three large pyramid-temples, as noted above, there is no large-scale organizational scheme observable among the numerous building complexes in the central area. As is the case at most other sites, the higher points of ground have been selected for building purposes and the fortuitous ground form does not lend itself to any preconceived arrangement of buildings. It can be noted, however, that individual buildings as well as complexes of buildings have been carefully sited with respect to compass orientation, which has been consistently maintained throughout the site. It can also be noted that several of the larger complexes exhibit the hierarchical ordering along a central axis which characterizes Acropolis Groups. In addition, some effort has been made to link the larger complexes with one another by a system of raised causeways, or roadways, but for the most part these appear to be afterthoughts and serve no organizational purpose.

In spite of the lack of formal order at the largest scale,

FIG. 181. Oxkintok (after Shook).

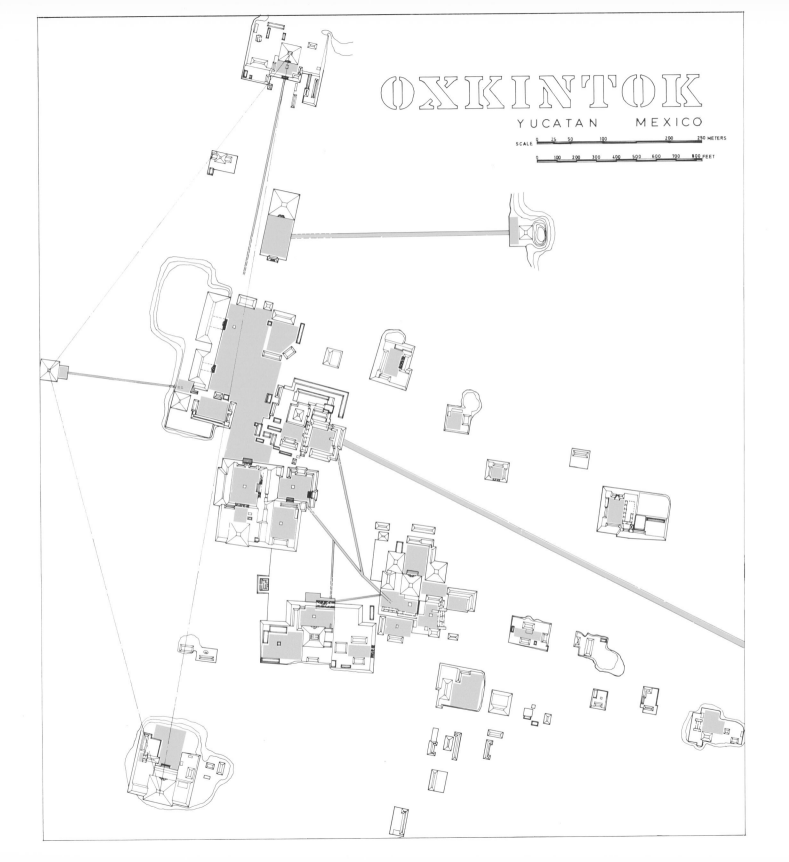

OXKINTOK

YUCATAN   MEXICO

SCALE 0 25 50 100   200   250 METERS

0   100 200 300 400 500 600 700 800 FEET

a certain degree of monumentality is achieved by the sheer size and mass of the eight large complexes of structures which dominate the site. Several of these complexes are over 500 feet square along the base, and the platforms supporting the uppermost structures are 20 to 30 feet high (Fig. 183). The similarity between these large complexes and those at Edzna is too great to be accidental, suggesting that the earlier constructions at Oxkintok and Edzna are contemporary in time and based on models preceding from the Southern Lowlands area.

As indicated in the general discussion of the Puuc cities, two distinct types of building remains are found in Oxkintok which can be associated with two different periods in its history. The earlier buildings differ from the later in terms of assemblage, style of architecture, details of construction, and the association of stelae with hieroglyphic inscriptions (one of these stelae carries the date 9.2.0.0.0, which makes it the earliest initial-series date presently known from the northern Yucatan area). There is also a high incidence of pyramid-temple structures among the earlier buildings, while the later remains consist largely of palace-type buildings. In connection with this, it must be remembered that the appearance of large numbers of palace-type buildings, which occurs consistently toward the end of the Late Classic period, is indicative of a general change from purely religious to more secular activity. The earlier buildings are most easily distinguishable from the later structures on the basis of construction details. The wall masonry of the early buildings consists of roughly cut-and-dressed blocks set in irregular courses against a crude concrete hearting, and small stones are used abundantly for leveling purposes. The vaults are made of roughly shaped slabs laid in horizontal courses and the irregular face of the vault was covered with a thick layer of plaster (Figs. 185, 186, 187). Façade decoration seems to have been limited to simple panels or painted stucco (Shook: 1940).

The second type of building remains is in the typical Puuc tradition. This style of architecture, which is found in its most fully developed form at sites such as Uxmal, Kabah, Labna, and Sayil, is characterized by structures with walls built of well-cut and dressed veneer stones laid in regular courses and smooth-faced vault stones tenoned into the hearting of the upper walls (Fig. 188). It also includes decorated moldings and cornices and features large masks and cutstone mosaics in the upper wall zone. A sculptured doorway column and carved stone lintel in the typical Puuc style were found in the debris of the building shown in Figures 189, 190. At the time of the author's visit to the site in the summer of 1971, a number of trenches had been dug around the lower walls of this building by natives looking for buried treasure, revealing several perfectly preserved walls faced with beautifully cut and dressed Puuc-type veneer stones.

One of the major differences between the later, or Puuc-style, remains and those in the earlier style can be seen in the way in which complexes of buildings were formed. The earlier structures, which make up the bulk of the exposed remains in the central area, generally occur in compact and orderly complexes on raised platforms (Figs. 182, 183). In terms of size and spatial organization, these groupings are similar to the large acropolislike complexes which are found in abundance at Edzna as well as at a number of sites in the Southern Lowlands area. (A detailed description and analysis of this kind of complex can be found in the section on Edzna.) It should also be noted that, while the outlying groups (not shown on the map) include mostly Puuc remains, buildings in the Puuc style are found infrequently in the central area. The Puuc remains are scattered in amongst the earlier structures in the central area and for the most part do not occur in highly organized configurations. An exception to this can be noted in the quadrilateral grouping of structures near the center of the site, which includes a Puuc-style building with a portal vault. This rectilinear form is very characteristic of Puuc remains at other sites. (See maps of Uxmal, Kabah, and Sayil.)

From what little is presently known of Oxkintok, it

seems to meet the general criteria we have established for urban centers as opposed to ceremonial centers. First, it appears to have been built and occupied over a long period of time. The evidence for this assertion is found in the two types of structures with distinctly different architectural styles, which obviously belong to two different time periods and are associated with two different kinds of pottery. In 1940 Dr. George W. Brainerd dug several trenches in different parts of the site, one to a depth of two and one-half meters. Brainerd found that the top layers of all trenches produced nothing but typical Puuc pottery, while the lower levels produced sherds that were similar, but not identical, to the Tzakol ware found at Uaxactun and Tikal, which is associated with the Early Classic period. (Brainerd: 1958.) The two main pottery divisions give added weight to the architectural sequence as outlined, since all pottery found at pure Puuc sites such as Uxmal and Kabah belong to the Late Classic period.

Second, the extent and character of the architectural remains in themselves attest to the urban character of Oxkintok. The central area contains a large variety of building types, including houses, and this central area is surrounded by suburban areas which contain both houses and ceremonial structures. The presence of these suburban residential districts was postulated as one of the dominant characteristics of urban centers. While these outlying areas are not shown on the map, they are known to exist, and their presence supports the thesis of urbanization. Finally, most of the other elements which have been established for urban centers are present, including a stable year-round water supply (*chultunes*), dated monuments (twenty-three stelae have been located), a ball court, raised causeways, and "satellite" centers (X'mil and La Esperanza). While there is no way of measuring the density of house mounds either in the main center or in the outlying areas, it is clear from the size and number of the buildings in the central area that a sizable population must have been involved if all the structures were in use at one time.

It is difficult to assess the position of Oxkintok in rela- tion to the Puuc development as a whole, but it must have been a center of some importance long before the bulk of the Puuc cities came into existence. The evidence at present indicates a very brief life span (two hundred to three hundred years) and a very late development for the Puuc area as a whole. E. W. Andrews (1967) has even suggested that Puuc development occurred after the collapse of the Late Classic centers in the southern area. The thing that is still not clear is whether the early period buildings were still in use during the time the Puuc-style buildings were constructed. If so, Oxkintok would easily have been the largest and most important city within the Puuc region. The case for this kind of dominance would be further strengthened if it could be shown that Puuc style was developed at Oxkintok and then spread to the rest of the region. It may well be, however, that the earlier buildings had already been abandoned at the time of the Puuc florescence, and, if this is the case, Oxkintok might well have been only a provincial center, attempting to maintain some of its former glory in the face of its eclipse by its more important neighbors such as Uxmal, Kabah, and Sayil.

We earnestly hope that major excavation and restoration will be forthcoming at Oxkintok some time in the near future as a means of settling these questions. Such an effort would also halt the depredations of treasure hunters who are destroying what little archaeological evidence the forces of nature have still left intact.

Note: In 1971 much of the site was cleared of trees and a good part was put under cultivation by natives from Maxacanu. Unfortunately, it was not possible to add any details to the base map made by Edwin M. Shook in 1940, since the bulk of the exposed structures were in an advanced state of ruin. Loose building stone has been used by the natives to construct walls around their pastures and *milpa* plots, and the frequent clearing and burning of the jungle in conjunction with planting has accounted for even further destruction of the architectural remains.

FIG. 182. Oxkintok—view of
southwest sector of site,
southernmost pyramid in background.

FIG. 184. Oxkintok—
view of western sector of site (right).

FIG. 183. Oxkintok—view looking north
from southern edge of site.

FIG. 185. Oxkintok—view of large ceremonial complex, central area.

FIG. 186. Oxkintok—detail of Early Period structure.

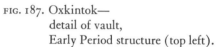

FIG. 189. Oxkintok—
   view of southeast sector
   of site, Puuc-style structure
   in foreground (top right).

FIG. 187. Oxkintok—
   detail of vault,
   Early Period structure (top left).

FIG. 188. Oxkintok—
   detail of vault,
   Puuc-style structure (bottom left).

FIG. 190. Oxkintok—
   Puuc-style structure,
   central ceremonial area
   (bottom right).

The Puuc Cities: Uxmal

The site of Uxmal is located about fifty miles south of the present-day city of Merida, the capital of the state of Yucatan, Mexico. Together with Kabah, Sayil, Xlabpak, and Labna, it forms the nucleus of a region which is characterized by Puuc-style architecture. The principal part of the city covers an area well over a half mile from north to south and some seven hundred yards from east to west (Fig. 191). Other structures lie scattered outside this area, principally to the south, including the remains of a free-standing archway which is similar in size and form to the archway at Kabah.[9]

The natural terrain surrounding the center is relatively flat and there is little about the over-all plan to suggest that existing topography played an important role in determining its physical organization, as is the case for many cities in the Usumacinta and Peten areas further south. It is possible that the huge platform which supports the Governor's Palace may be partly a natural hill, but, if so, it has been completely reshaped to conform to the requirements of the urban scheme. It is extremely unfortunate that the site map of Uxmal shows only the main ceremonial precinct, as this makes it appear to be limited to the groups of monumental structures now in view. It is, in fact, considerably larger and the peripheral areas are known to contain many house mounds.

From the site plan, it can be observed that the central ceremonial precinct consists of a number of discrete groupings of structures, and, with the exception of a few scattered buildings, these groups form a larger organization based on common orientation, axial alignments, and interconnected plazas (Fig 191). It is impossible today to determine the full extent of plaza areas, as the paving which once differentiated the space of the "city" from the surrounding landscape has long since disappeared; they may be inferred, however, wherever the ground has been carefully leveled. With the exception of Copan, the plan of Uxmal exhibits the most precise geometry of any well-known Maya city. Most of the buildings are consistently oriented about seventeen degrees from the true cardinal points of the compass, and deviations from right-angular relationships within the over-all plan, or within individual groups of structures, appear to be deliberate rather than accidental. It is clear from the design and execution of individual buildings that the builders of Uxmal were capable of producing precise right-angular relationships whenever this suited their purpose.

But it is also clear that at the scale of the whole center this kind of geometric precision is unnecessary, since our ability to perceive or comprehend large-scale forms is not dependent on precise mathematical relationships. We perceive the spatial organization of the city through the interplay of solids and voids, and the open spaces of plazas, terraces, and courtyards are the strongest organizing elements. Viewed in this light, buildings play a dual role. On one hand, they are perceived as objects or monuments which dominate the open spaces surrounding them. On the other hand, they act as walls, giving definition and form to the open spaces of plazas and courtyards. Perhaps we are inclined to read too much into the scheme and are merely reflecting our own ideas of order, but a closer look at some of the individual elements of the center reveals that the designers of Uxmal fully understood the subtleties of spatial manipulation which provides the framework for a complex and monumental architecture.

[9] The archway is located about one-half mile south of the acropolis and is assumed to mark the end of a causeway leading to Kabah, although this has not yet been fully verified. In common with Kabah, the position of this archway is very curious, as it is not associated with any important buildings of the central area, and its function as an important entryway is debatable.

We can test out the above proposition by looking first at the complex of buildings which includes the Pyramid of the Magician, the Nunnery, the Ball Court, the House of the Turtles, and the Governor's Palace, since all of these structures have been partially restored, making it easier to see the relationships among them. The Pyramid of the Magician is situated on the eastern side of the Nunnery Quadrangle, nearly centered with respect to the two groups of structures which mark the southern and northern boundaries of the map. Its shape is somewhat unusual for a Maya pyramid, as it is elliptical in plan rather than square or rectangular, but in other respects it conforms closely to the traditional pyramid-temple form (Figs. 192, 193). Like so many other pyramids or substructures, it has been enlarged on several occasions and the existing structure represents five distinct superimpositions, the uppermost temple representing the latest addition. The two upper temples can be reached by means of stairways on the east and west sides of the pyramidal substructure, but the stairway on the east side does not connect with a well-defined plaza or court. On the west side, the stairway is associated with a small courtyard adjacent to the Nunnery (Fig. 194).

The position of this pyramid with respect to the Nunnery Quadrangle leaves some room for doubt as to the designers' intentions. Had the pyramid been centered on the east-west axis of the courtyard of the Nunnery, it would have dominated the open space of the quadrangle. As it stands, the stairway and temple on the west side of the pyramid are centered on the central axis of the south building of the Nunnery and this balancing act diverts some attention away from the Nunnery Quadrangle toward the large plaza containing the Ball Court. The simplest explanation for this apparent imbalance would be that the original pyramid was constructed before the south range of the Nunnery was built; the Nunnery is obviously part of a larger conception which includes the Ball Court and Governor's Palace, but its relationship with the Pyramid of the Magician is ambivilent.

The so-called Nunnery Quadrangle has already been cited earlier in general text as one of the most outstanding examples of this form to be found at any Maya site. The refinement of the individual buildings, each of which is different in its details from the others, is indicative of the high degree of architectural sensibility which has made Uxmal the best-known city in the Puuc region. For our purpose, however, it is more important to recognize that the Nunnery is part of a larger spatial concept which is worth examining in some detail.

It can be noted that the four buildings of the Nunnery are at different levels (Figs. 195, 196). The north building is at the highest elevation, the east and west buildings at a somewhat lower elevation, and the south building is at the same level as the inner courtyard. These differences in elevation are not fundamental to the concept of the quadrangle, but the reason for the differences in height becomes readily apparent when this complex is viewed from the terrace supporting the Governor's Palace or from the playing alley of the Ball Court. If we take a position next to the House of the Turtles and look across the plaza toward the Nunnery complex, it appears at first glance that the south building is a two-story structure, since the north building has been raised to a height where its whole façade can be seen just above the roof line of the south building (Figs. 197, 198). But a closer look tells us that there is actually some void space between the two elements, since we can also see the decorated upper walls of the east and west buildings in sharp perspective, revealing the presence of the void space in between. To the right of the Nunnery sits the great mass of the Pyramid of the Magician, higher by far than any part of the Nunnery, but secondary to it from this position, as it is near the edge of our vision (Fig. 199). The doorways of the south building, which give access to small hutlike spaces behind, are dark and uninviting, but the large open archway in the center of the façade provides a glimpse of the courtyard beyond (Fig. 200).

If we now move down into the plaza and take a posi-

287

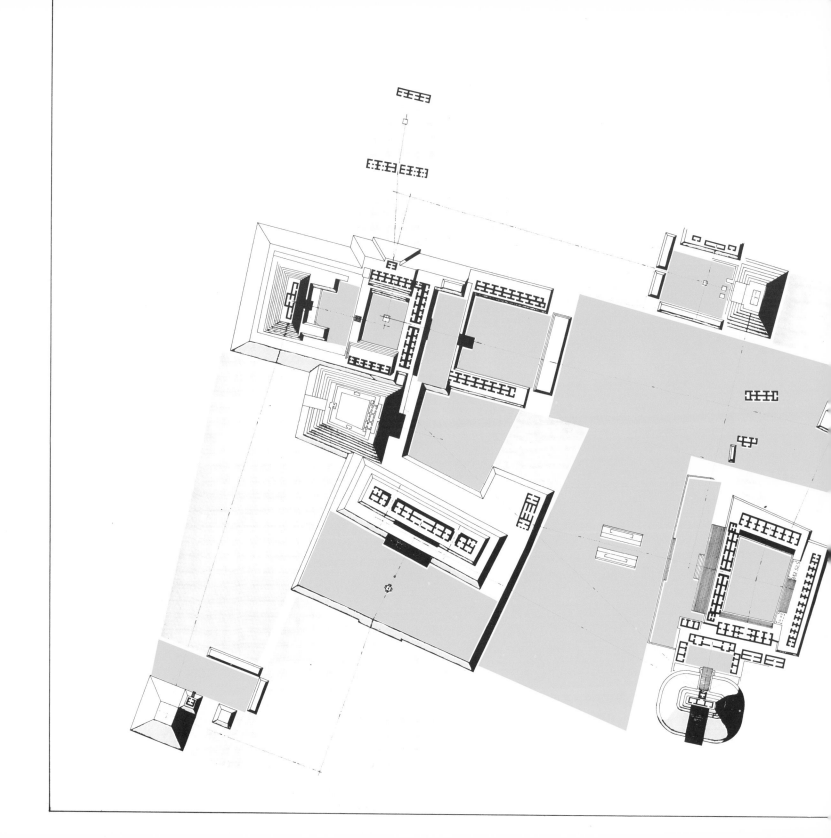

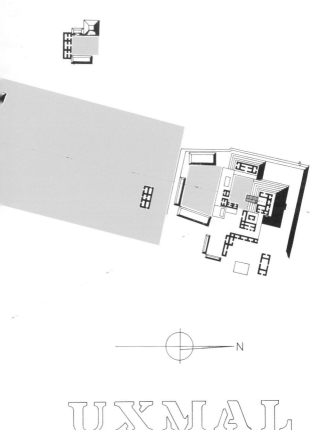

UXMAL
YUCATAN MEXICO

SCALE 20 10 0   50   100   150
METERS

tion in the center of the Ball Court, a different set of relationships appears. The mass of the north building has entirely disappeared behind the façade of the south building, but its presence is still revealed by the projecting masks, which make a sawtooth pattern against the sky (Fig. 200). The east and west buildings have almost disappeared, but we still get a glimpse of their stone mosaic friezes. Since we are now at a lower level than the terrace on which the Nunnery stands, nothing can be seen of the inner courtyard itself, but through the archway we can see a small section of the stairway leading to the north building, together with one of its doorways, which is not, however, the central doorway. A short flight of stairs just north of the Ball Court takes us from the plaza to a low terrace at the base of the Nunnery, and beyond, a broad flight of stairs, nearly the full width of the south building, leads to the top of the terrace on which the buildings of the Nunnery stand. It takes very little imagination to envision a great ceremonial procession moving through the Ball Court, up the stairs, through the archway, and into the hidden space of the inner courtyard (Fig. 201).

Having passed through the archway, a new kind of open space is revealed. The large plaza through which we have just passed is only partially defined and leads to other plazas which, in turn, connect to other open spaces. But the courtyard of the quadrangle is a finite space, closed both to nature and to the surrounding man-made world except for a single entry. To the left and right are long palace-type buildings, raised on low platforms with stairs running the full width of the court (Figs. 202, 203). Ahead, on a higher platform, the north building rises up majestically, flanked by two small temples on either side of a broad stairway (Figs. 205, 206). In the center of the courtyard is a small altar, and the central doorways of the four surrounding buildings are aligned with this monument. This axiality might suggest that the quadrangle is a static space, based on a simple scheme of double symmetry, but this is far from being the case. The

289

FIG. 191. Uxmal (after Marquina).

differences in height of the four buildings plus the limited access provided by the single entryway through the south building produce a scheme which is highly directional, and it is clear that the north building has been carefully positioned in order to effectively terminate the axial movement which began in the plaza below to the south. The potential symmetry of the quadrangle is further destroyed by the fact that the façades of the individual buildings are significantly different, and in plan it is deliberately opened slightly to the south.

Proceeding up the stairway leading to the north building, we come to the highest platform of the ensemble. In front of us the doorways of the north building invite us to enter, but the actual experience is anticlimactic. The rooms are small and dark, the air close, and the bare walls tell us nothing of their purpose. Once again we are forcefully reminded that the important spaces of the city are the open plazas and courtyards rather than the inner spaces of buildings, which never succeed in becoming anything more than stone-and-plaster versions of the interiors of simple wood-and-thatch huts. Their value as places is more symbolic than real, and the repetition of these symbolic rooms throughout the buildings of the Nunnery provides no real clue as to their actual use.

If we turn around and look back along the path we have traveled, it becomes apparent that the height of the platform on which we are now standing was carefully chosen to provide a dramatic reversal of the previous experience, which was concerned primarily with the open spaces of plaza, terrace, ball court, and courtyard. Immediately below is the open space of the courtyard, giving us an anchor to the ground but no longer providing an enclosure. Beyond, the south building cuts off all view of the surrounding ground plane and the city is seen as a series of pyramidal masses, divorced from the earth. On the far left the great mass of the Pyramid of the Magician looms up over the roof of the east building. Then a succession of masses—the Pyramid of the Old Woman, the Governor's Palace and its supporting platform, the Great Pyra-

mid, and finally the acropolis, with the roof comb on the structure called the Dove Cotes forming a gigantic sawtooth pattern against the green of the jungle behind (Figs. 209, 210). It is difficult to place these great masses in space, but the effect of being entirely surrounded by huge man-made elements is overwhelming. Nature has been overpowered and man has asserted his own importance, while at the same time paying homage to the gods.

The final act in this drama takes place when we move back down into the courtyard and proceed toward the single archway which gives access to the inner space of the quadrangle. The great pyramids disappear from view and we are once more surrounded by the buildings of the Nunnery. At the point of entry through the archway, a framed view is presented which has been carefully conceived. At the bottom of this composition is the Ball Court, its long playing alley on axis with the archway. Just above are the long horizontal banks of the stepped face of the terrace supporting the House of the Turtles and the Governor's Palace. The House of the Turtles appears just to the right of the central axis of the composition, which is culminated by the Governor's Palace seen in perspective against the sky (Figs. 211, 212). The role of the House of the Turtles (Figs. 213, 214) in this sequence of events is somewhat ambiguous. As seen from the archway, it occupies a subordinate position with respect to both the Governor's Palace and the Great Pyramid. At the same time, the central doorways on its northern and southern sides have been carefully aligned to focus directly on the archway and central doorway of the north building of the Nunnery (Fig. 208). As shown in Figure 208, the House of the Turtles is an integral part of the complex axial composition which includes the Ball Court and the Nunnery, but it is also clear that from the archway the Governor's Palace is the center of attention. It seems almost redundant to point out that this kind of duality, or ambiguity, is the hallmark of a mature and truly sophisticated art.

We can better understand the significance of the composition described above by comparing it with the Acropolis in Athens. It has been pointed out by many writers that the temples of the Greek Acropolis contained no important enclosed spaces and were designed and positioned to be seen in perspective rather than in elevation. The same proposition holds true for the Governor's Palace, and the success of the composition seen through the archway is due in large measure to the fact that this great mass is seen in perspective from below, giving a good indication of its true size and form. Passing through the archway, the open space of the Great Plaza is once more in view. From this vantage point the Ball Court now assumes more importance, since it is the only man-made element within the open expanse of the plaza (Fig. 215). At the same time, other sectors of the city begin to assert themselves and the directionality which has marked our course thus far gives way in favor of the larger order of the city.

At this point, it is necessary to look more carefully at the site plan (Fig. 191). We have already noted the high degree of formal geometric order which characterizes Uxmal in contrast to the more organic schemes of Tikal, Uaxactun, Piedras Negras, and Yaxchilan. This order is based on a system of cross axes which are roughly oriented to the cardinal points of the compass. The longest of these axes, running on a north-south line, is terminated at both ends by large complexes of buildings, terraces, courtyards, and pyramids.

At the south end is the Acropolis Group, the largest single complex within the center; at the north end is a complex called the North Group, a smaller and greatly simplified version of the acropolis, now in an advanced state of ruin. Between these two groups stretches a long, mall-like plaza interrupted at several points by small buildings and a large platform. Centered on the north side of this mall is a group of structures called the Cemetery Group, which establishes the position of the major cross axis. This axis may be thought of as a line passing through the center of the Cemetery plaza and the center of the Ball Court. Most of the other elements of the site are or-

ganized in relation to secondary axes which are roughly parallel to the major axes just described. For example, the axis which runs through the Nunnery, Ball Court, House of the Turtles, and Governor's Palace is parallel to the main north-south axis, and the cross axis of the Nunnery Quadrangle is parallel to the major east-west axis as defined by the Ball Court and the Cemetery Group. The only major exception to the orientation of buildings and building groupings to these axes is the Governor's Palace, but it has already been suggested that this was the result of a conscious effort to provide a more dramatic view of this building from the vaulted entrance into the Nunnery. With this introduction, we can examine each of the three groups just mentioned in greater detail.

The acropolis has already been described and analyzed earlier in the text under the heading of Acropolis Groups (chapter 5) and will receive only cursory treatment here. In terms of size and complexity of organization, it is the most important group of structures at Uxmal, but whether it was the most important functionally is debatable (Figs. 215, 216, 217, 218). In any event, the hierarchial sequence of spaces and structures which culminates in the temple at the top of the acropolis suggests that this temple played a unique role in the life of the city, since it is situated at the highest point within the entire site (Figs. 219, 220, 221, 222). This temple together with the temple atop the Pyramid of the Magician and the temple situated at the top of the largest pyramid of the North Group form a great triangle which marks the extremities of the main ceremonial center. This particular goemetry, which occurs so frequently in Maya cities, appears to be derived from the basic Temple Group, which is a small-scale version of the same triangular form. Again, this may be reading too much into the scheme, but the positioning of these three temples seems carefully calculated rather than accidental.

The Great Pyramid is situated between the acropolis and the southern end of the large terrace supporting the Governor's Palace (Figs. 215, 216). It is actually joined physically to both of these structures and its northern side rises from a terrace at the base of the platform supporting the palace. The remains of a broad stairway lead from this terrace to a very narrow platform near the top of the pyramid, giving access to a palace-type building with a double range of rooms opening onto the upper platform. The basic form of this pyramid is similar to all Maya pyramids; i.e., it is a truncated pyramid with stepped sides, but, unlike the typical pyramidal structure, it does not support a temple on the upper level. Instead, long palace-type buildings are arranged around four sides of the uppermost level of the pyramid and the roofs of these buildings are level with the top of the mass of the whole structure. The buildings on the east, west, and south sides consist of a single small room centered in a long wall, while the multichambered palace-type building referred to earlier occupies the north side.

This pyramid is a most unusual configuration and represents an intermediate stage between the typical pyramid-temple form and the pyramid-palace forms found at Sayil and Edzna. There do not appear to be any important formal relationships between this structure and the Acropolis Group or the Governor's Palace, in spite of the fact that it is contiguous to both of them. While its function is unknown and its relationships to other structures is ambiguous, it is the largest single building mass at Uxmal and its huge bulk looms large against the sky from almost any point within the entire city.

The complex of buildings called the North Group terminates the long mall stretching northward in front of the acropolis (Fig. 223). To some extent the components of this group are organized in the same manner as the main acropolis, but it cannot be properly considered as an Acropolis Group as defined earlier in the text. The whole complex is situated on a low platform, and that part of the platform facing the long plaza is further bounded by three additional structures forming a small courtyard. The southernmost of these structures is decorated in the Chenes style, which suggests that this particular complex should not be thought of as part of the North Group, which consists of pure

Puuc-style buildings. Behind this courtyard, at a higher level, is an even smaller court which can be entered by means of a vaulted opening which passes through a small building on the south side of the inner court. This vaulted entryway is similar in all respects to the archways which pass through the south building of the Nunnery and the Dove Cotes building of the acropolis (Fig. 224). The upper courtyard is bounded on the east and west by small palace-type buildings, and on the north side by a pyramidal structure supporting a temple-type building.

In a limited way, this series of courtyards and structures involves the same notions of hierarchy and sequence which characterizes the acropolis, but the effect is partially negated by the small size of the elements involved and by the positioning of other structures which are irrelevant to this sequence. For example, a small group of buildings is situated on the east side of the large pyramid in a rather casual fashion, and another group of palace-type buildings is situated around a small courtyard just below. It should also be noted that the pyramid supporting the main temple has stairways on both the north and south sides and several of the rooms face north rather than into the courtyard on the south side. This ambivalence in direction takes something away from the strength of the implied sequence which initiates in the long mall to the south. It must be said, however, that these relationships can only be made clear after large-scale excavations of the whole group have been undertaken. The advanced state of ruin of the buildings and the large amount of fallen debris filling the courtyards has made it impossible to reconstruct an accurate plan or to determine the exact heights of the various elements in relation to one another.

The Cemetery Group, which is situated on the west side of the long mall, forms the terminus of the major east-west axis which bisects the plaza lying between the Nunnery and the platform supporting the Governor's Palace (Fig. 225). In one sense, this same plaza can be said to continue on to the east side of the Cemetery Group, making a larger L-shaped plaza when combined with the north-south mall. This group takes its name from two altars situated in the central plaza, or court, which are covered with skull-and-crossbone symbols (Fig. 226). This symbol is most commonly associated with the Toltec culture, which suggests that this group was constructed in the Postclassic period when the Toltecs were in power at Chichen Itza. The architectural remains do not bear out this theory, however, as they are built in the typical Puuc style which is characteristic of other buildings at the site.

The grouping itself is Classic Maya in form, i.e., a group of structures arranged around a rectilinear plaza, dominated by a large pyramidal structure which normally supports a temple. In this case there are no exposed building remains on top of the pyramid and the lack of debris suggests that it should be considered as a ceremonial platform. The east and south sides of the plaza are bounded by long mounds which may actually represent buildings in an advanced state of ruin. The west side of the plaza is bounded by a low platform which supports three small, one-room buildings. There is some suggestion of a long plaza extending southward from this group along the western base of the acropolis, leading to a long palace-type building at the southwest end of the plaza. Another palace-type building is situated west of this structure, giving partial definition to an additional plaza. Aside from the altars, with their rather ominous symbols, there is nothing particularly outstanding about this group as far as architecture or planning is concerned. It appears to be a secondary element with respect to the total scheme but provides a firm anchor for one of the cross axes which is fundamental to the large-scale ordering of the center.

While our main concern is with the physical structure of the city rather than details of individual buildings, some mention must be made of the Governor's Palace, since it is the most imposing building at Uxmal and may well be the most outstanding example of Puuc-style architecture to be found in the Yucatan Peninsula. This structure, which is nearly 340 feet long, is situated on the uppermost level of two superimposed platforms which, in

turn, rest on a broad terrace raised some 50 feet above the general level of the plazas below (Fig. 215). It faces east toward the open expanse of the terrace, which measures approximately 560 feet by 230 feet in size. A small altar is centered in the open space of the terrace on axis with the central doorway of the palace building (Fig. 228). Access from the terrace level to the upper platform is by means of two broad stairways, nearly 150 feet wide (Figs. 227, 228). The building was originally divided into three sections by means of vaulted openings about 60 feet in from either end which passed through the full width of the structure. Later on, these openings were filled in, but the façade is still composed of three distinct parts due to the recesses which occur at the points where the vaulted openings were located (Fig. 229).

The basic components of this building, which are characteristic of all buildings in the Puuc style, are as follows: The building proper rests on a base, about two feet high, and above this the lower walls rise vertically to the height of the lintels over the doorways. The doorways are recessed into this wall, which forms a smooth, continuous surface running the entire length of the building. This wall was undoubtedly covered with stucco in its original state, but this has long since disappeared. Above the lintels, a stone cornice projects out nearly two feet, and above this is an elaborate sculptured frieze, framed at the top by a larger projecting cornice. The frieze itself is composed of a combination of abstract geometrical motifs and stylized naturalistic forms, including gigantic masks over each doorway. The frieze continues on all four sides of the building, and at each corner masks of Chac, the rain god, are set at a forty-five-degree angle, marking the end of each façade but helping the eye to turn the corner. Viewed from a distance, the main façade of this structure reveals the carefully considered proportions between the smooth lower wall, projecting cornices, and decorated upper frieze which is the hallmark of classic Puuc art (Fig. 227). In consistency and coherency of design, in the masterful way in which the play of light on projections and recesses   293

has been used to enrich the whole façade, and in the attention which has been given to the smallest details of decorative or symbolic motifs, it rivals anything built in Greece or Rome.

Aside from the many differences which can be noted in architectural style between the buildings at Uxmal and their counterparts in the Peten and Usumacinta areas, the more significant differences appear at the level of urban planning. Cities in the Peten and Usumacinta regions are characterized by organic planning, in which existing topographical forms are a strong generating force in determining the over-all layout of the city. Large hills were terraced and reshaped, large plazas were created by cutting and filling, and large structures were added at critical points, producing a scheme which is only roughly based on geometrical relationships. In spite of these alterations, the general form of the natural terrain was maintained, and the man-made elements establish a delicate balance between fortuitous irregularity and formal geometry.

At Uxmal, however, there is almost no trace of this organic quality at any scale. The rigid formalism of the city scheme is imposed on top of the natural environment with no apparent regard for existing conditions. The demands of axis and cross axis are not to be denied, nor are the compass directions which establish the specific orientations of the axes. The basis for this particular attitude remains obscure. On one hand, it can be argued that the existing topography was so featureless that it provided no organizing cues for the builders, who were then led to extend the same kind of geometrical ordering which was normally reserved for small subgroups up to the scale of the city as a whole. On the other hand, it might also be argued that the formalism of Uxmal is a logical outgrowth of a desire to express more forcefully the distinction between man-made elements and the balance of nature. At Uxmal the Mayas succeeded in creating a truly monumental architecture—that completely denies its dependence on nature by its insistence on conforming to abstract rules of order and form as determined by man.

FIG. 192. Uxmal—Pyramid of
the Magician (left).

FIG. 193. Uxmal—Pyramid of
the Magician, south side (top right).

FIG. 194. Uxmal—Pyramid of
the Magician, west side (bottom right).

FIG. 195. Uxmal—the Nunnery as seen from Pyramid of the Magician.

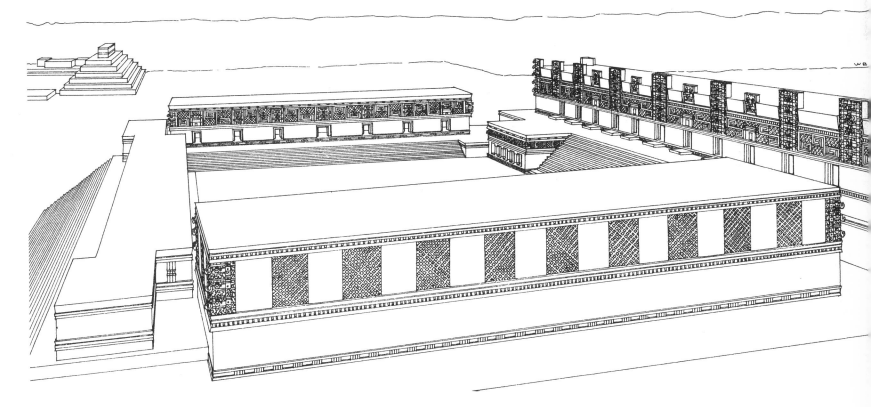

FIG. 196. Uxmal—the Nunnery (restoration).

FIG. 197. Uxmal—View looking north from terrace of Governor's Palace.

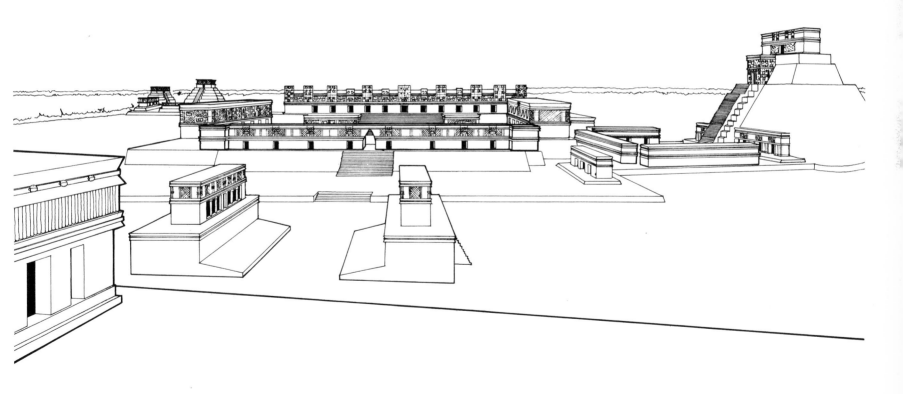

FIG. 198. Uxmal—View looking north from terrace of Governor's Palace (restoration).

FIG. 199. Uxmal—View of Ball Court and Nunnery from south side of Main Plaza.

FIG. 200. Uxmal—South building of Nunnery as seen from Main Plaza.

FIG. 201. Uxmal—the Nunnery, south building as seen from terrace in front of north building.

FIG. 202. Uxmal—the Nunnery, west building, from courtyard.

FIG. 203. Uxmal—the Nunnery, east building, Pyramid of the Magician in background.

FIG. 204. Uxmal—the Nunnery, detail of southeast corner from courtyard.

FIG. 205. Uxmal—the Nunnery, north building.

FIG. 206. Uxmal—the Nunnery,
temple next to stair of north building.

FIG. 207. Uxmal—House of the Turtles,
south side before restoration.

FIG. 208. Uxmal—House of the Turtles,
view of Nunnery through central doorways.

FIG. 209. Uxmal—view looking south from north building of Nunnery.

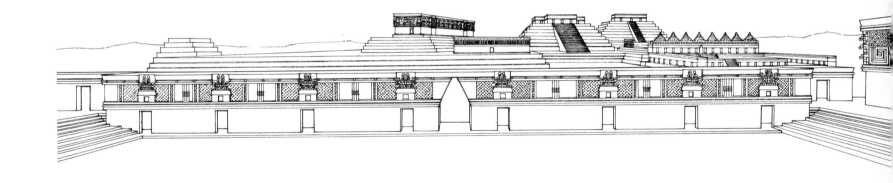

FIG. 210. Uxmal—view looking south from north building of Nunnery (restoration).

FIG. 211. Uxmal—
view through archway,
south building of Nunnery.

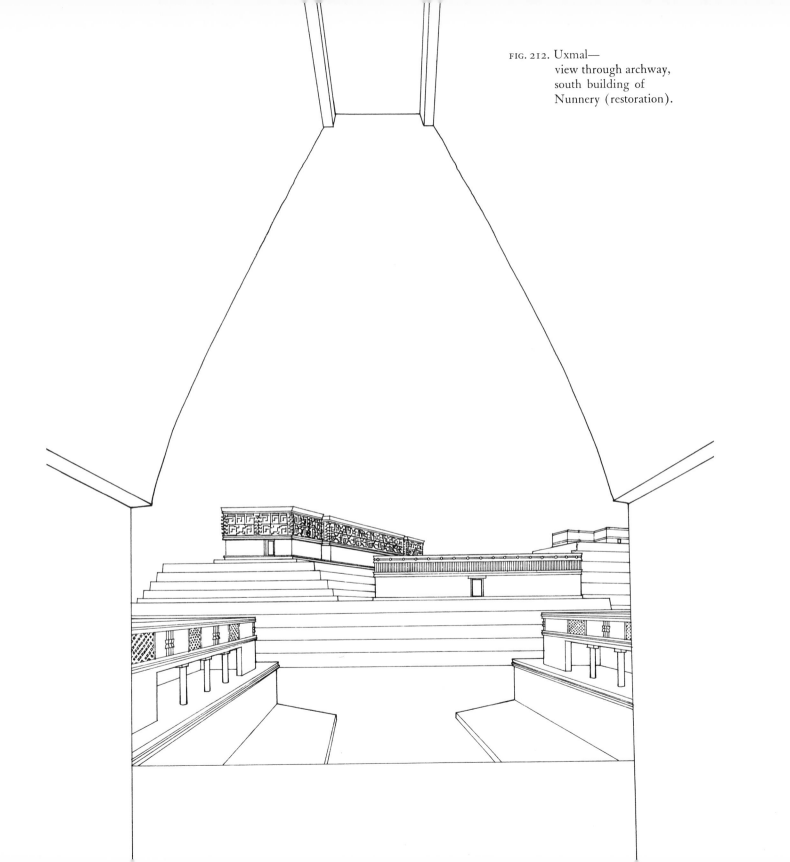

FIG. 212. Uxmal—
view through archway,
south building of
Nunnery (restoration).

FIG. 213. Uxmal—House of the Turtles.

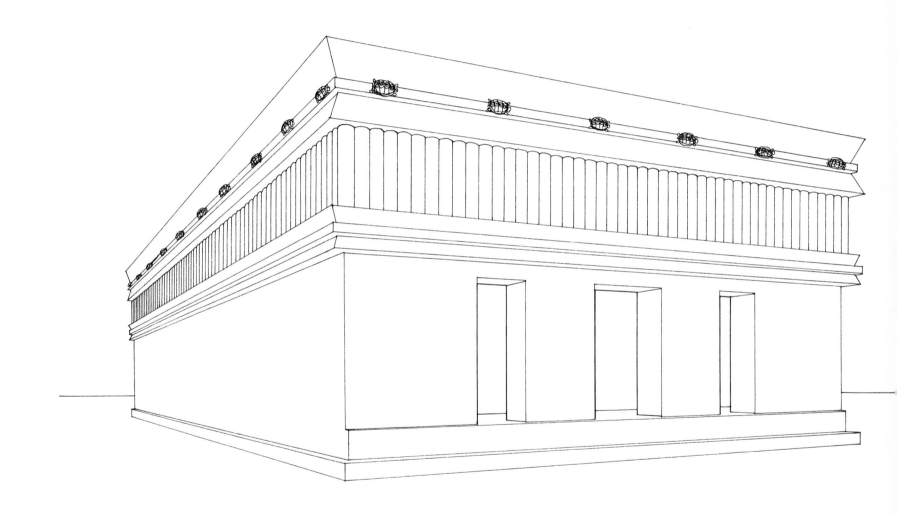

FIG. 214. Uxmal—House of the Turtles (restoration).

FIG. 215. Uxmal—platform and Governor's Palace
from Pyramid of the Magician.

FIG. 216. Uxmal—Governor's Palace,
Great Pyramid, and Acropolis.

FIG. 217. Uxmal—Dove Cotes building of Acropolis.

FIG. 218. Uxmal—Dove Cotes building
of Acropolis, south elevation.

FIG. 219. Uxmal—archway through Dove Cotes building of Acropolis.

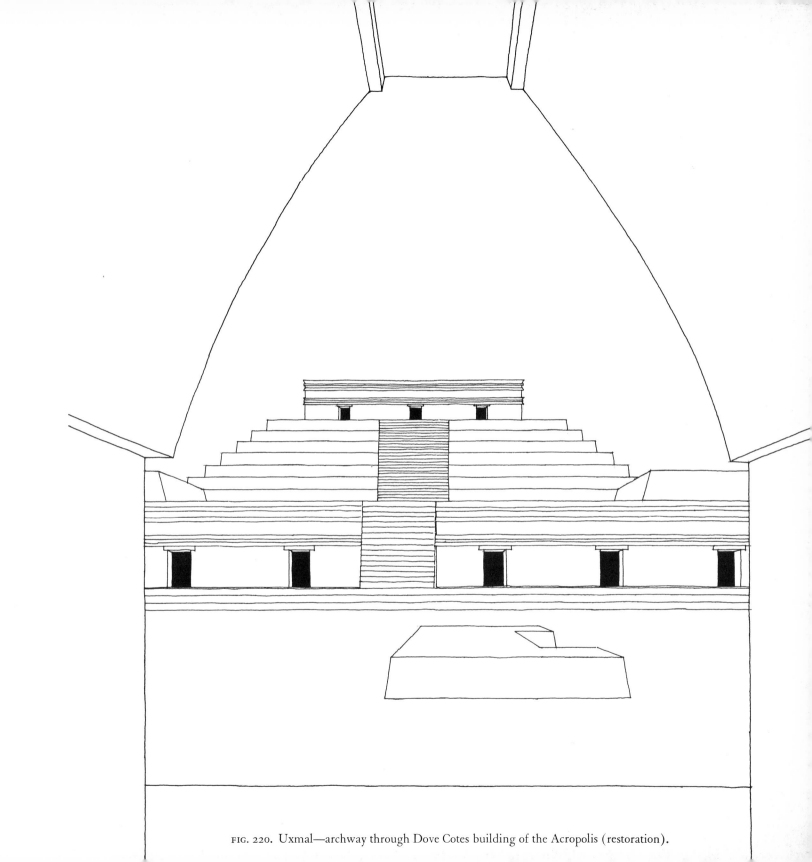

FIG. 220. Uxmal—archway through Dove Cotes building of the Acropolis (restoration).

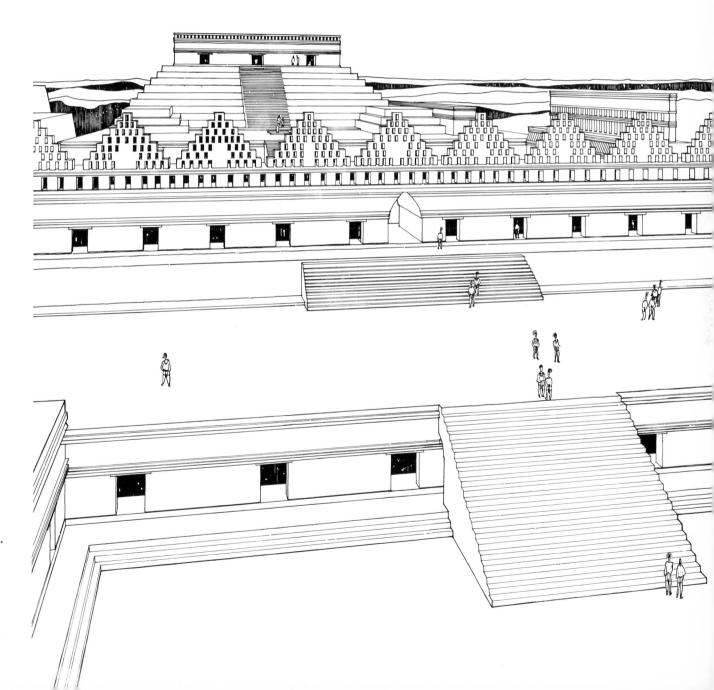

IG. 221. Uxmal—
  upper courtyard
  and Main Temple, Acropolis
  (left).

. 222. Uxmal—
  Acropolis (restoration)
  (after Proskouriakoff) (right).

FIG. 223. Uxmal—view looking north from upper level of Acropolis.

FIG. 224. Uxmal—archway, North Group.

FIG. 225. Uxmal—Cemetery Group as seen from terrace of Governor's Palace.

FIG. 226. Uxmal—altar in courtyard of Cemetery Group.

FIG. 227. Uxmal—
          Governor's Palace (top left).

FIG. 229. Uxmal—Governor's Palace,
          detail showing infilling of archway (right).

FIG. 228. Uxmal—Governor's Palace,
          west elevation (bottom left).

The Puuc Cities: Kabah

The ruins of Kabah are located about twelve miles south of Uxmal in the state of Yucatan, Mexico. Unfortunately, it has never received the attention it deserves, particularly in relation to Uxmal, and this is due in large measure to the fact that the western sector of the city, which contains the remains of many large structures, has never been cleared or restored. Thus, it appears to be a minor site when in fact its central area is larger than that of Uxmal. The area included within the site map is about 4,000 feet from east to west and 3,000 feet from north to south, about 1.2 square kilometers in all (Fig. 230). The natural ground configuration within the central ceremonial precinct is somewhat irregular and the structures in the western part of the site have been built on the side of a low hill which has been terraced and leveled in order to accommodate several large complexes of buildings. The ground to the east is fairly flat and most of the buildings in this sector have been constructed on large artificial platforms and terraces, raised well above the natural ground level.

The extent to which the city extended out beyond this nucleus is unknown, so there is no real basis upon which it can be classified in terms of size and population. Judging from its somewhat dispersed character, it can hardly be classified as an urban center, but it is clear that it must be considered as a major ceremonial center, and as such would have had a sizable resident population who lived just outside the central precinct. A number of houses have been found in the peripheral areas, but they represent only a random sampling, since these suburban zones have never been carefully studied. It is also possible that some of the smaller palace-type buildings which make up the bulk of the exposed remains were used as residences by the elite class and, if this was the case, the total area which can be thought of as belonging to Kabah proper might not have been very great. Readers must be tired by now of continued references to inadequate mapping, but the fact is that without more comprehensive maps we are put in the position of having to guess at the real nature and extent of centers such as Kabah. In spite of this, what we are able to see is of considerable interest, as some of the standing structures are in a good state of preservation and represent unusual variations on traditional themes.

Kabah was apparently connected to Uxmal by means of a *sacbe*, or causeway, which is shown on the site map generally leading northward in the direction of Uxmal (Fig. 230). The presence of this causeway has given rise to the theory that Kabah was a satellite center, dominated by Uxmal in the same way that Uaxactun is thought to have been subordinate to Tikal. (Actually, the notion that Uxmal was larger or more important than Kabah has yet to be proved.) The point where the causeway gives entrance into the central precinct of Kabah is marked by a large free-standing archway (Figs. 231, 232, 233). The arch is built on a low platform and it is necessary to climb a low stairway before passing through the portal of the vaulted opening. It might be expected that once having passed through the archway one would arrive at a major plaza, or that an important vista would open up on axis with the causeway, but such is not the case. The causeway continues on for some distance, passing between two low platforms in an angular fashion, and then enters a small courtyard which appears to be a relatively minor space within the center. Just beyond this courtyard, the causeway picks up again and continues south until it terminates in a small plaza in front of a good-sized pyramid. Aside from its connection to the causeway, this pyramid is very isolated from the rest of the center and may well have been the focus of a suburban residential area which is not shown on the map.

The function of the causeway and its associated archway is not really clear when its relationships to the various sectors of the city are considered. The causeway itself must have served as an important means of communication with Uxmal, but conceptually it does not appear to play an important role in the spatial organization of Kabah. The elements which are most directly related to the causeway appear as minor events and there are few, if any, junction points along its length. In a like manner, the archway seems badly placed in terms of marking the entrance to the city. Perhaps we are misled by the image of the archways or gateways which marked the entrances to so many medieval cities in Europe. The design and position of these letter elements were based more on problems relating to defense than on abstract notions involving "entrance." At Kabah, the archway might well have served solely as a symbol for a special ceremony which did not lead to any further sequence of events. In spite of its lack of sculptural elaboration, the archway is an impressive monument and it serves adequately as a symbol for the city, even though its specific entrance function remains questionable (Fig. 233).

The causeway divides Kabah into two distinct parts which do not evidence any strong relationships to one another except in terms of the general orientation of the major structures in both areas, which is very consistent (Fig. 230). The over-all scheme for the city appears to arise from the utilization of high points of ground as locations for important building groupings rather than any formal organizational notions. This is particularly noticeable in the western sector, where the largest buildings are situated on a series of rising terraces which conform more to the natural contours of the land than they do to any abstract conceptual scheme (Figs. 234, 235). Each of the individual complexes of structures presents an orderly appearance and several of the terraces containing these complexes are linked together in an effort to make a more coherent whole, but the effect is still one of fortuitous relationships rather than preconceived order.

It is apparent that orientation played a major role in the siting of these particular complexes, as the plazas and courtyards all open toward the east. Most of the larger buildings also face east, and it must be assumed that this direction had some special significance. The same pattern of orientation can be observed at many other sites, although we have already pointed out that there is no preferred orientation when a large number of sites is considered. At Edzna, a major center some eighty miles to the south, the preferred orientation was west, which leaves us in doubt as to the symbolic significance attached to particular orientations. Most of the buildings in this sector of the city are in an advanced state of ruin, but those parts which are still standing indicate that in terms of size, construction, and details they were very similar to the better-preserved buildings in the eastern sector (Fig. 236).

Four major complexes of structures are found on the east side of the causeway plus several smaller clusters of mounds. The largest complexes form two larger groupings separated from one another by a large plaza. Unfortunately, the modern highway between Merida and Campeche runs through the center of this plaza, making the two large groupings appear more separated than is actually the case. The structures closest to the causeway consist of a small guadrangle, now in a very advanced state of ruin, and a temple-plaza group, just to the north, which is dominated by the largest pyramid-temple structure within the entire site (Fig. 239). The temple supported by this large pyramid faces south, and it is interesting to note that, in contrast, nearly all of the other major structures, which are palace-type buildings rather than temples, face either east or west. Because of its strategic position at the northern edge of the center, midway between the elements on either side of the causeway, it undoubtedly was the most important visual element in the center; from the doorway of the temple the high priests would have enjoyed a commanding view of the entire city (Fig. 240).

Southeast of the two groups adjacent to the causeway

323

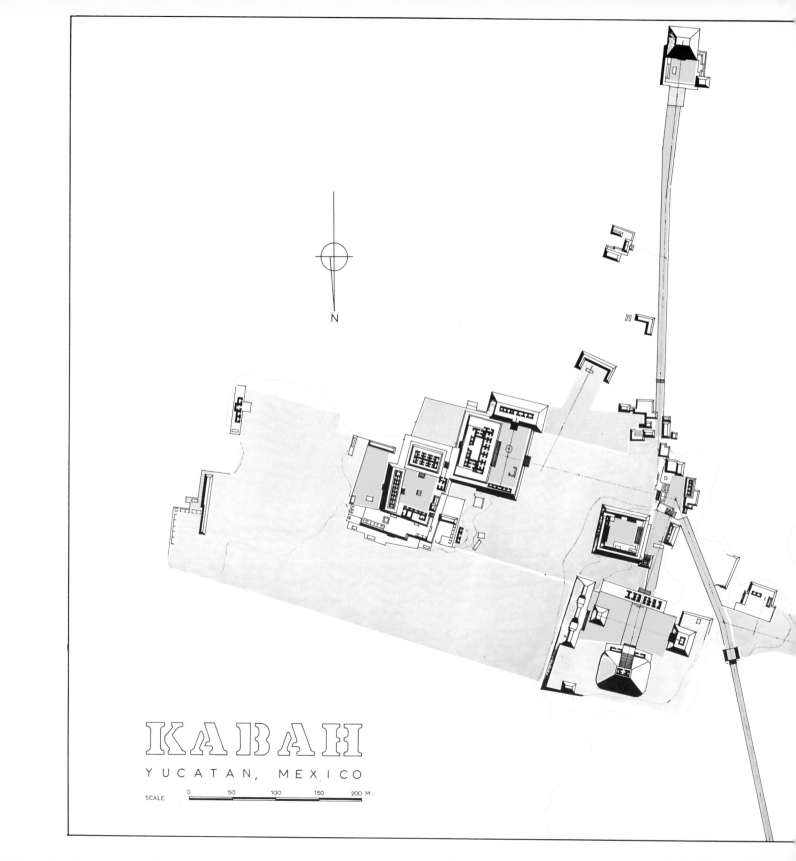

KABAH
YUCATAN, MEXICO

SCALE 0   50   100   150   200 M.

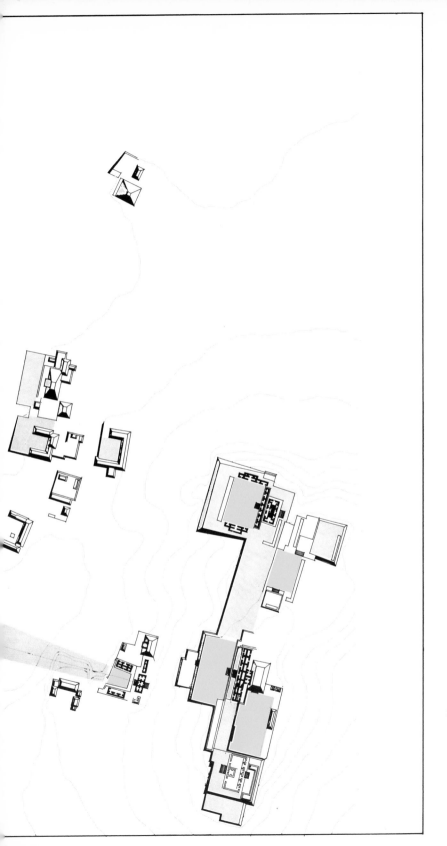

FIG. 230. Kabah (after Ponciano Salazar).

are two contiguous groups of palace-type structures which are the best-preserved buildings in the center. Both of these groups are situated on large platforms and the buildings are ranged on three sides of the platform, leaving the western side open (Figs. 237, 238). Thus, the open sides of major plazas or terraces on either side of the causeway face toward one another, but there are no observable axial alignments between the buildings in these two sectors. In spite of this, it is apparent that careful orientation of all structures on both sides of the causeway gave order to the whole assemblage, and the view looking from east to west, or vice versa, where individual buildings could be seen rising higher and higher behind one another, must have been an impressive sight. The southernmost of the adjoining groups described above includes the most unusual building in the city, called the Codz-Poop. This is a large palace-type building, nearly one hundred and sixty feet long, with its principal façade completely covered with masks of Chac, the rain god (Figs. 241, 242). Seen at close range, the individual masks are striking examples of the sculptor's art, but the over-all effect is blurred by the endless repetition of the same motif and the basic form of the building is lost in the profusion of detail (Figs. 243, 244). This loss through exaggeration and meaningless repetition brings to mind a current architectural dictum which states that "less is more": So be it.

The second group of structures, just northeast of the group which includes the Codz-Poop, is much more complex in organization and appears to be the result of a number of superimpositions which took place over a long period of time. The buildings at the upper levels of this group form a large quadrangle, and there is a second set of structures around its periphery on three sides, situated on a series of lower terraces or platforms. The two largest buildings in this group have parallel ranges of rooms with doorways on either side of the long façades, which is characteristic of Palace Groups, so it is not clear whether this complex should be classified as a Palace or a Quadrangle

Group (Fig. 245). It is evident that there is no single, clear concept involved, as the nature of the superimposed constructions suggest that the builders were continuously striving for a more monumental appearance as the complex grew in size. This concern for visual effect is evident throughout the city and the building called Codz-Poop is the most exaggerated case in point.

At the far eastern edge of the area shown on the site map is a long palace-type building which is separated from the main group of structures by a distance of nearly eight hundred feet. About three hundred and fifty feet southwest of this structure is a building of similar size, although its floor plan is significantly different (Fig. 230). These two structures are very isolated from the rest of the major structures, indicating that they represent a zone of activity which was functionally different from the main center, even though the buildings themselves are very typical palace-type structures and do not show any marked differences from similar structures in other parts of the site (Fig. 246). The upper façade of the building illustrated consists of a simple repetition of the fluted colonnette motif which is found so frequently in Puuc-style structures (Fig. 247).

Because of the close connection which is implied by the causeway connecting Kabah to Uxmal, we might expect to find great similarities between them in terms of architecture and over-all planning. The same thing might be said for Labna and Sayil, both of which are closer to Kabah than Uxmal. A glance at the site plans of these four sites reveals that there is almost no consistency in their general configurations. The building types and architectural style are nearly identical, but this similarity does not carry over into their over-all spatial organizations. This is certainly due in part to the difference in natural topography at the various sites, but topography in itself would not account for the great disparity among them, since we have found that the Mayas were willing to go to great lengths to modify the natural terrain in order to achieve their ends. The differences in layout might also be attrib-

326

uted to a difference in function among centers, but this cannot be demonstrated with the data on hand. There is a high incidence of multichamber palace-type buildings in relation to temple-type structures at all Puuc sites, and this is particularly noticeable at Kabah and Uxmal. Any number of different functions might be represented by individual buildings at different sites, but there is presently no way of knowing exactly what they might be.

All of the above suggests that many of the differences in plan organization between Kabah and Uxmal which cannot be charged to differences in topography or function might represent nothing more than an inevitable difference in interpretation of traditional forms which seems to arise between different segments of any given culture. The same kind of differences are apparent among present-day cities within the same culture. Thus, the provincial status of Kabah in relation to Uxmal is not really the issue; they were separate, distinct places, built by different individuals with different ideas, and each tended to develop along a different path. The essential difference between them lies in the degree to which large-scale space-ordering ideas are present. Uxmal exhibits a clear visual order which is based on formal geometric configurations at the largest possible scale, while Kabah seems disjointed and no central organizing concept is observable. On this basis, Uxmal can be assigned a dominant role in relation to Kabah only to the extent that this large-scale ordering is indicative of a more highly organized power group at work. This relationship, which is still very evident today in contemporary societies, puts a premium on monumentality and downgrades the individual. In some measure both Kabah and Uxmal suffer from this kind of pretentiousness which marks all top-heavy societies.

FIG. 231. Kabah—the arch, north side.

FIG. 232. Kabah—the arch, south side.

FIG. 233. Kabah—the arch and *sacbe* leading to Uxmal.

FIG. 234. Kabah—western sector
as seen from Codz-Poop.

FIG. 236. Kabah—
small temple
in western sector (right).

FIG. 235. Kabah—western sector
and Great Pyramid.

FIG. 237. Kabah—view of Codz-Poop and Palace Group.

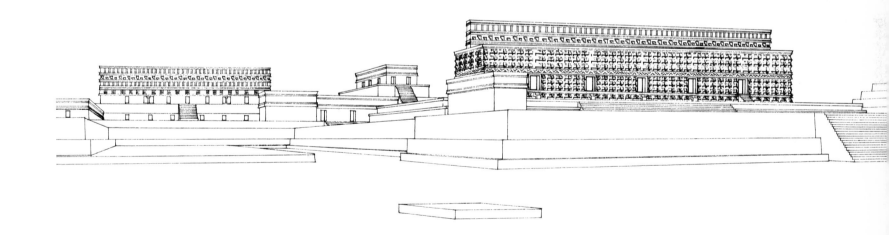

FIG. 238. Kabah—view of Codz-Poop and Palace Group (restoration).

FIG. 239. Kabah—Great Pyramid
from doorway of palace building
in eastern sector.

FIG. 241. Kabah—
Upper plaza level, Codz-Poop
(top right).

FIG. 242. Kabah—
Codz-Poop, west elevation
(bottom right).

FIG. 240. Kabah—Great Pyramid, south side.

FIG. 243. Kabah—detail of west elevation, Codz-Poop.

FIG. 244. Kabah—detail of Chac masks, Codz-Poop.

FIG. 246. Kabah—palace structure, western sector.

FIG. 245. Kabah—
        palace structure adjacent
        to Codz-Poop (left).

FIG. 247. Kabah—detail of palace structure
        showing typical fluted columns of Puuc style.

The Puuc Cities: Labna

The ruins of Labna are situated in the southern part of the state of Yucatan, Mexico, only a few miles from the neighboring cities of Kabah, Sayil, Xlabpak, and Uxmal. Like its neighbors, Labna is notable for its Puuc-style architectural remains and there is every reason to believe that the majority of the standing structures date from the end of the Classic period. The topography in the immediate vicinity of the central ceremonial area is generally very flat, but there is a ring of low hills just beyond this central area. The tops of these hills have been artificially leveled and the sides cut into a series of terraces. The area between the base of these hills and the main group of structures is covered with numerous mounds and terraces, many of which are undoubtedly house mounds.

A large number of *chultunes* are found in association with these mounds and terraces and others are cut into the terraces on the adjacent hills. The *chultunes*, which are bottle-shaped containers cut into bedrock, were used as containers for storing water for use during the dry season. Further to the north, natural wells, or *cenotes*, served the same purpose, but there are few, if any, *cenotes* in this part of the peninsula. These *chultunes* can be used as a basis for projecting population, since it has been calculated that, on an average, each *chultun* holds enough water to meet the needs of fifty people during the six-month dry period.[10] Since there are at least sixty *chultunes*

in the area that can be considered as belonging to Lagna proper, a resident population of three thousand can be postulated who lived entirely within the confines of the city.

On this basis, Labna should be classified as a major ceremonial center, even though it is normally considered to be a very minor site. It is extremely unfortunate that Labna has never been thoroughly explored and mapped, as an accurate map showing the small mounds and terraces (house mounds) in relation to the *chultunes* would provide a more realistic basis for projecting population.[11] The map shown in Figure 248 is based on a sketch map made by E. H. Thompson in 1898 which is now hopelessly out of date.

We have already noted that the central portion of the site is extremely flat and it must be assumed that any order which can be observed among the several elements present is the result of a conscious effort to maintain formal relationships which are part of the cultural tradition rather than fortuitous relationships due to existing geographical features. If this is actually the case, it may be a good indication that Labna was a fairly provincial center, since the plan organization seems to lack the kind of refinement we would associate with a more important center such as Uxmal. This lack of refinement, or formal order, is fairly evident in the rather casual relationships which can be observed between the three major complexes of structures which form the central nucleus of the city.

The three groups referred to lie at opposite ends of a

[10] In connection with his study of the ceramics of Yucatan, George Brainerd calculated the number of people who could be supported by one *chultun* holding 7,500 gallons of water, an average size for the *chultunes* at Labna. As a maxium, 25 families, or 125 people, could be served from a single *chultun* over a 190-day period, but he concluded that 10 families of 50 people would be a more realistic figure. The *chultunes* would then be of a size to accommodate an extended family of the sort which has been postulated for the typical house groups as found throughout the Maya area. He also suggested that a *chultun* could be kept filled by collecting rainwater from an area of 540 square feet, which would have

to be paved. The plaza or courtyard areas around which the house clusters were built undoubtedly served this function. (Brainerd: 1958.)

[11] See footnote 2 in chapter 4 for a detailed discussion of how house mounds can be used for estimating population. The presence of *chultunes* in connection with the house clusters would add considerable weight to the estimates based on houses alone.

large, level plaza measuring five hundred and fifty feet from east to west and six hundred feet from north to south (Fig. 248). The north end of the plaza is bounded by a large Palace Group constructed on two levels (Figs. 249, 250). The south end of this plaza is terminated by two unusual complexes, one centered around a pyramid-temple structure called El Mirador (Fig. 251) and the other on a large archway which serves as the connecting element between two small courtyards (Fig. 252). A narrow raised causeway running the full length of the plaza connects the two main groups, but the connection is stronger physically than visually, as the long axis of the causeway is not satisfactorily resolved at either end (Figs. 249, 251). Another small platform supporting two small structures of the palace type is located on the east side of the main plaza, but no large buildings have been noted on the west side (Fig. 253). Further to the south, beyond the complex containing the large pyramid-temple, is another group of buildings and platforms in an advanced state of ruin. This part of the site is so overgrown with brush that the relationships of these structures to the other elements of the main area cannot be ascertained. It has already been noted that other small mounds and terraces extend outward from the main nucleus on all sides.

The presence of the raised causeway, or *sacbe*, in the center of the plaza is something of a puzzle, since elements of this sort are generally used to connect sectors of cities which would otherwise be isolated from one another due to the irregularity of the terrain lying between them. In other cases, such as Dzibilchaltun, *sacbes* are used to connect suburban ceremonial areas with the main center which lies some distance away. Neither of these conditions is represented at Labna. Here, the causeway splits a major plaza into two sections and the plaza itself is perfectly level. The reasoning behind the introduction of the causeway in this case is very obscure, unless it was recognized that the visual relationships between the structures at either end of the plaza were unsatisfactory and the causeway was introduced as a means of making a stronger tie

between them. If this is so, the result is not especially convincing, as the major axis of the causeway seems very arbitrary in relation to the elements it is supposed to connect.

The Palace Group, which limits the north side of the Main Plaza, includes some interesting variations on the basic Palace Group concept. Perhaps it would be more appropriate to say aberrations rather than variations, as this group is almost totally lacking in the kind of cloistered internal order which is characteristic of Palace Groups at other sites. This cannot be attributed to the fact that the individual buildings at Labna were constructed at different times, since we have already noted that this appears to be the case in all groups of this kind. Rather, it appears to be a lack of ability or concern on the part of the builders to conceive ideas of order at a large enough scale to achieve much more than a superficial degree of unity through the use of similar decorative details.

The lower level of the palace platform is divided into three distinct courtyards or plazas. A long palace-type building faces each of these open spaces (Figs. 255, 256, 257) and two of the plazas are further separated from each other by a fourth building which juts out at approximately a right angle between them (Fig. 254). The mound behind the three lower palace structures rises to the same height as the roofs of these buildings, making a second level which supports several other structures, again of the palace type. Two of these structures form a pair which is centered on the central axis of the lower group, but the whole effect is still one of imbalance (Figs. 249, 250). Behind the paired structures on the upper level are the remains of several smaller structures, and the platform itself appears to be uncompleted. Apparently work was still in progress when the site was abandoned at the end of the Classic period. A further feature of this upper level is a round collecting basin connected to a *chultun* located near the center of the plaza in front of the pair of palace buildings. The body of the *chultun* lies directly behind the palace structure on the lower level and must   341

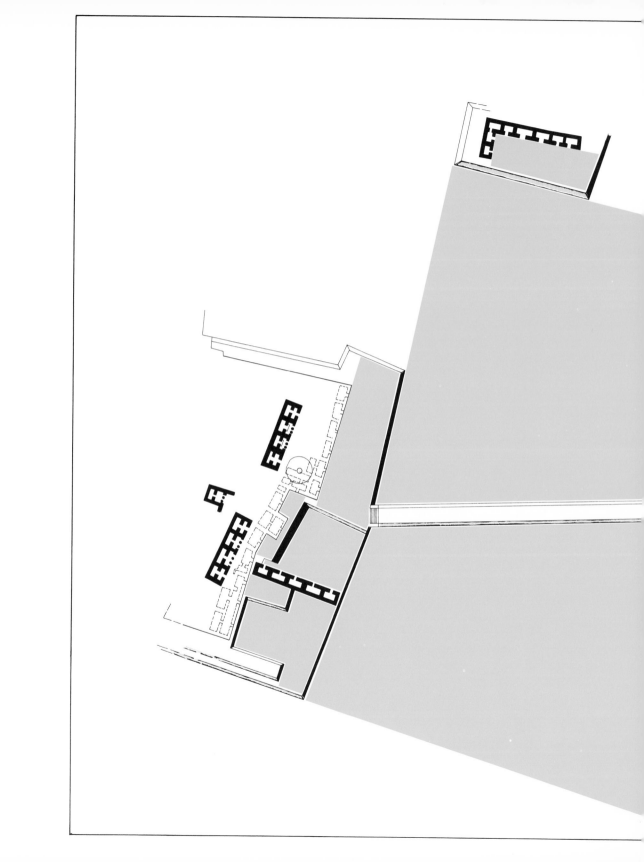

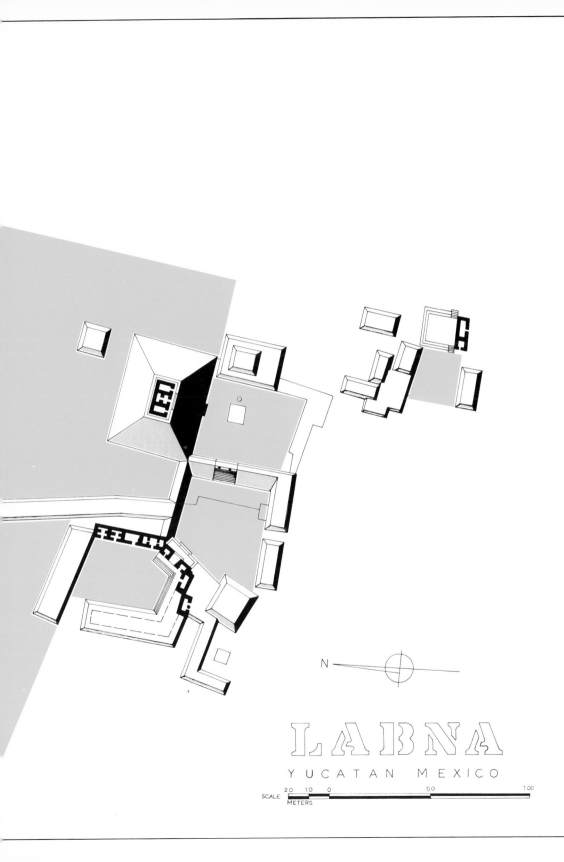

LABNA

YUCATAN MEXICO

SCALE 20 10 0   50   100
METERS

N

FIG. 248. Labna (after *Thompson*).

have been a constant source of concern due to the possibility of water seepage which might have destroyed the lower rooms.

From the Palace Group, the causeway runs in a southerly direction, beginning on a line which bisects the space between the two groups of structures at the south end of the plaza. As it nears the end of the plaza, it veers slightly to the west and terminates in a small courtyard which is associated with the group of buildings containing the arch (Figs. 260, 261). This courtyard gives access to the plaza in front of the large pyramid-temple called El Mirador by means of a broad stairway on the east side of the courtyard. The archway on the northwest side of this court gives access to a smaller court surrounded by platforms and the remains of long palace-type buildings. The axis through the archway cuts through the two courtyards on a diagonal line and there are no building elements which act as a terminus for this axis at either end.

It seems fairly certain that the archway was a freestanding structure at one time and that the buildings now connected to it were added at a later date. This suggests that the archway might originally have connected to a *sacbe* leading to another part of the city or to another site, but no remains of such a roadway can be observed. The archway itself is a very fine example of Puuc-style architecture, and the details of the upper frieze are very refined (Figs. 252, 261). The palace-type buildings connected to the archway on either side form a rough quadrangle, but the positioning of these buildings is such that the basic spatial relationships pertaining to this form are almost completely lost. The courtyard which connects to the causeway is also somewhat quadrangular in form, but the structures surrounding it are so badly destroyed that it is almost impossible to visualize their internal relationships in any detail.

The stairway leading from this latter courtyard to the raised terrace in front of the main temple is at right angles to the front of the temple which faces south. The grouping of elements around this terrace is suggestive of the typical Temple Group, but here again the form has been distorted and there is only one flanking temple on the east side of the plaza in place of the usual pair on opposite sides. The substructure of the main temple rises to a height of about fifty-five feet above the plaza and is crowned with a fairly large temple building containing four rooms (Fig. 258). The central portion of the temple has two rooms, one behind the other, with a single small room on either side. The front wall of the building is continued upward to form a roof comb about fifteen feet high (Fig. 259). The roof comb must have been a very elaborate affair, as there are a number of stones still projecting out beyond the surface of the wall which at one time supported large masks made in stucco.[12] This structure dominates the entire site by virtue of its height, but turns its back to the main plaza. This anomaly suggests that its orientation to the south had important symbolic significance which became the overriding consideration in determining its relationships to other elements of the center.

Above all, we are struck by the singularity of this temple; it appears to be the only temple of any consequence within the main ceremonial area and indicates a sharp break from the traditions of the earlier part of the Classic period, where large numbers of temples and Temple Groups were the order of the day, particularly in the southern area. This gives us one further indication that Labna was a minor center, constructed fairly late in the Classic period when the generating force which earlier led to the conceptualization of the temple-oriented ceremonial center was already on the wane. The stylistic elements which are part of the local tradition are maintained almost intact

[12] At the time John Lloyd Stephens visited Labna in 1841, much of the stucco ornamentation was still in place. According to his description, the front of the roof comb was completely covered with stucco relief sculptures, including a row of death's heads at the top, two lines of human figures just below, and a colossal seated figure over the central doorway. Above the central figure was a large ball with a human figure beside it and another below. The figures and ornaments on the wall were painted, as traces of bright color were still visible. In all respects, it was an extraordinary example of Classic Maya art. (Stephens: 1843.)

and in some cases even elaborated on, but no new space-organizing ideas were forthcoming which might have stirred the imagination of the visitor who came to pay homage to the gods. For this reason, Labna must be relegated to the position of a minor outpost attempting to live on fading glory of its predecessors.

FIG. 249. Labna—Main Plaza and Palace Group.

FIG. 250. Labna—Main Plaza and Palace Group (restoration).

FIG. 251. Labna—view of Main Plaza looking south.

FIG. 252. Labna—the arch.

FIG. 254. Labna—Palace Group, building on lower level.

FIG. 253. Labna—
palace building, east sector (left).

FIG. 255. Labna—Palace Group, buildings on lower level.

FIG. 256. Labna—Palace Group, detail of buildings on lower level.

FIG. 257. Labna—Palace Group, detail of mask on corner.

FIG. 258. Labna—pyramid and temple El Mirador.

FIG. 259. Labna—detail of roof comb on temple El Mirador (note projecting stones which supported stucco sculptures).

FIG. 260. Labna—view of structure adjoining the arch.

FIG. 261. Labna—the arch and pyramid-temple El Mirador.

The site of Sayil is located only a few miles east of Kabah and is generally thought of as a relatively unimportant member of the group of smaller centers which cluster around Uxmal in the manner of provincial towns in relation to a larger capital. It must be kept in mind, however, that this relationship has been assumed on the basis of the size and number of exposed monumental structures at the various Puuc centers and may not be indicative of the actual character or importance of the communities represented. While very few standing buildings are presently visible at Sayil, it is actually a fairly large site and the remains of several hundred structures can be found in the areas surrounding the large three-story palace complex which occupies a central position toward the northern edge of the site (Fig. 262). The map covers an area measuring 5,600 feet north and south by 4,800 feet east and west, which is four times larger than the area shown on the map of Uxmal. Several large hills in the northern sector have been partially leveled and terraced in order to accommodate clusters of palace-type buildings, and the same practice was followed in the western sector, where smaller hills are crowned by complexes of buildings. While most of the buildings are consistently oriented about ten degrees east of magnetic north, there is more deviation from this general pattern than is the case at either Uxmal or Kabah.

Even though the map is incomplete and lacks the accuracy of maps made with plane table and alidade surveying methods, it is clear that Sayil was a center of considerable importance, as it included a number of large complexes of structures situated on platforms built up above the general ground level in addition to the multistory palace complex which has been cleared and partially restored. These large complexes are positioned in the more level part of the site and several very large groupings are connected by a long causeway which runs in a southerly direction from the palace until it terminates in a ball court near the southern edge of the area mapped. In 1841, John Lloyd Stephens discovered the well-preserved remains of the large building on the terrace west of the ball court, but this part of the site is now completely overgrown and its present condition is unknown. There is no obvious explanation for the presence of this causeway in terms of the over-all distribution of structures, even though it does establish a special connection among some of the larger building groupings.

Lacking any definitive date in regard to these complexes, it is difficult to say if they correspond to any of the archetypical groups which we have postulated earlier in chapter 5. The general pattern of distribution of the major structures is somewhat reminiscent of Oxkintok and Edzna, where many large complexes of structures are found in close proximity to one another together with more isolated structures which do not form ordered groupings. The pattern is also fairly random, which again seems to be the consequence of choosing the higher portions of ground as the locations for buildings. It can be noted that many of the smaller complexes are clustered on the higher portions of ground on either side of the spine of structures along the causeway. In this sense, the over-all pattern is very similar to the pattern within the suburban areas of Tikal, which is equally random and dispersed. In contrast, the main structures at Uxmal and Kabah are much more compactly grouped and greater attention has been paid to compass orientation.

At the present time, only the multistory palace and a small temple structure situated several hundred yards to the south are sufficiently cleared and restored to give any clear idea of the character of the main ceremonial area. Both of these structures are of considerable interest, how-

The Puuc
Cities:
Sayil

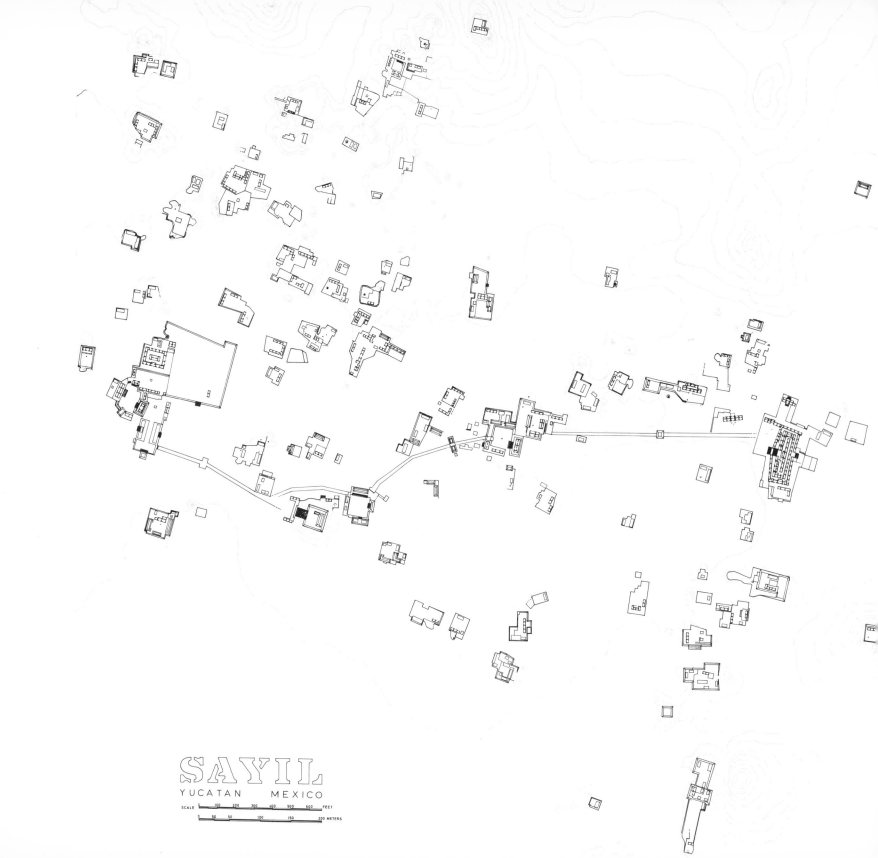

SAYIL

YUCATAN   MEXICO

SCALE 0 100 200 300 400 500 600 FEET

0 50 50 100 150 200 METERS

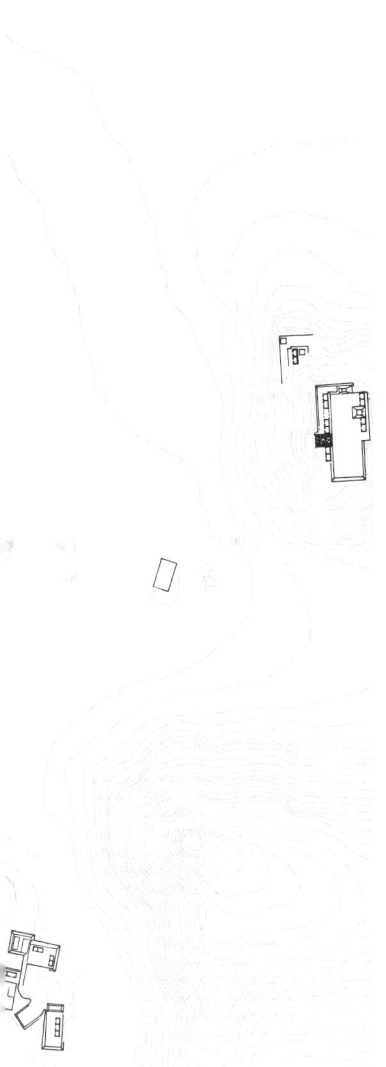

ever, as they tend to verify the proposition advanced in chapter 5 to the effect that pronounced regional styles can be superimposed on structures which continue to retain the basic forms which are part of the larger Maya tradition; multichamber palace-type structures and temples situated on pyramidal substructures are well-established basic forms that are found at all Maya sites. In this case they are in Puuc style, but this represents only a superficial change in the details of the exterior treatment; the underlying form remains unchanged. This relationship holds true even though the palace at Sayil is a very elaborate version of the basic palace form and might even be thought of as a new variety of the basic form. This elaboration of form has nothing to do with style, however, as the form would remain the same if it were treated in the Usumacinta, Chenes, or Rio Bec style. The same proposition holds true for the temple building called El Mirador. Its form is part of a long tradition, but it is treated in a local style (Fig. 263).

As indicated earlier, the structure commonly called the palace is a three-story structure in which each of the three stories is stepped back from the lower story (Figs. 266, 267). Because of its great length in relation to its height, it does not have a pyramidal shape and might better be described as a series of three superinposed terraces with rooms along the edges. An additional one-story structure projects out at a right angle at the western end of the main level, helping to define a large plaza on the southern side. The two lower stories consist of long ranges of rooms on opposite sides of the terraced substructure, while the uppermost story is represented by a single range of rooms with doorways facing south toward the main plaza. A broad central stairway leads from this plaza to the upper levels of the complex, giving access to the terraces in front of each range of rooms (Figs. 264, 265). The north side of the building has not been restored and it is impossible to ascertain if there was a second stairway on this side.

As is the case with so many Maya structures, the palace

FIG. 262. Sayil (after Shook).

359

represents an accretion of elements over a long period of time and each of the individual elements is different in its details from the others. The three wings of the lowest story were obviously built at different times, as the two buildings flanking the central stairway are considerably different in decorative detail and are positioned at a slight angle to one another. The structure to the left of the stairway has a fairly plain upper zone while the same space in the building to the right is filled with a simple repetition of halfround column shapes which are one of the characteristic features of the Puuc style (Fig. 265).

The second story consists of two long multichamber structures which are symmetrically disposed on either side of the main stairway, and these are much more elaborate in their details than the lower stories. The upper zones of these façades contain a number of stylized masks and the lower walls are elaborated with colonnettes on either side of the doorways (Figs. 268, 269). The doorways themselves are much wider than normal and are divided into several smaller openings by means of round columns with square capitals which support the lintels above. The use of these columns in doorways is another feature of Puuc-style architecture.

The upper story consists of a single long structure with the room at the center pushed forward in recognition of the stairway. This makes it appear to be three separate buildings, but they are obviously all part of a single conception and were built at the same time. At this level, the façades are rather plain, but each doorway was marked by a large stucco mask which projected above the normal roof line, giving added emphasis to these entranceways.

In contrast to Labna, where the large Palace Group is a rather confused collection of badly related elements, the palace at Sayil is a well-organized and imposing structure. The individual components of which it is composed are different in size and detail and it was added to on several occasions before attaining its present form, but there is no confusion as far as the ultimate result is concerned. This argues very much in favor of the creative ability of its builders, who recognized that many different decorative details could be incorporated into the same structure as long as they did not overpower the basic form (Figs. 269, 270, 271). This brings to mind one of the theories that was advanced early in our discussion to the effect that evidence for chronological development could be obtained from architectural remains alone, i.e., that complex architectural forms are generated from simpler models. The palace at Sayil seems to offer some proof of this thesis.

A single palace-type building by itself is not necessarily imposing nor it is necessarily monumental just because of its size. The notion of monumentality depends on establishing a relationship between the observer and the building in which the apparent size of the structure is greater than its actual size. In addition, the individual parts of the building must be subordinate to a larger conception which creates the whole. Thus, a random collection of large elements fails to achieve monumentality, since they do not form a comprehensible whole. The monumentality of the palace complex at Sayil can be seen as the final stage of an evolutionary process which initiated in the construction of a single-story structure with no special features and culminated in an extraordinary aggregation of structures involving complex notions of hierarchy and order. This level of sophistication can be gained only through the cumulative experience of several generations of builders, each of whom projects a new and expanded image of the "ideal" environment. True monumentality, as evident in the palace structure here, is the end product of a long series of separate, but related, concepts and it is not surprising that this imposing form appears very late in the history of Maya placemaking. Unfortunately, it seems to mark the beginning of the end of Maya creativity as well, since Sayil was abandoned not long after the palace was completed.

The temple building which is called El Mirador lies about twelve hundred feet south of the multistory palace and the two structures are connected by a raised causeway, as shown on the site map (Fig. 262). The temple, if it can rightly be called that, is part of a larger complex of structures which are situated on a series of raised platforms. Most of the structure is in an advanced state of collapse and it is noteworthy only for the remnants of a large roof comb, pierced by a series of window-like openings (Fig. 263). A number of projecting stones can also be noted, which indicate that the surface was covered with stucco ornamentation. Traces of stucco figures can be found in the debris of the superstructure and it is likely that the decorative elements were similar to those on the roof comb at Labna, since the façades are strikingly similar.[13] The doorway shown in the photograph is actually in an interior wall, as the entire front of the building has fallen away. The balance of the structures associated with this building are now so ruined and so overgrown with brush that nothing can presently be made out regarding the character of the larger grouping.

From all outward appearances, Sayil does not seem to embody any unique urban concepts, nor does it present building types that are not found at other Puuc sites. Still, it is unfortunate that it has been relegated to the position of a minor site in terms of the Puuc area as a whole, since this is largely an accident due to the lack of large-scale excavation and restoration at a large enough scale to reveal its real character. This makes it appear to be smaller than its neighbors to the west, but it is doubtful if this is actually the case. The jungle still hides most of its monuments, and the present-day visitor is hard-pressed to make out even the faint traces of its former grandeur. Future work at Sayil may well show that it played a more important role in the history of the Puuc area than is presently suspected, and certainly more data is required before it can be put in its proper perspective in relation to the sequence of events which led to the former concentration of population in this now deserted area. As it stands, Sayil can best serve to remind us that the ancient Mayas were far more adept at turning the jungle to account than their present-day counterparts, who have been unable to sustain even a small village in the same place that was once the scene of a great ceremonial center replete with hundreds of stone structures of all descriptions. Today, a single hut belonging to the caretaker stands at the base of the palace, a pathetic reminder of its past glories.

[13] The use of stucco for decorative purposes is rather limited in Puuc-style buildings due to the extensive use of cut-stone mosaics and carved stone sculpture. It has been suggested that stucco ornamentation was used whenever human figures were desired, since they would be quite difficult to execute as a veneered mosaic. The use of stucco also increased the possibility of adding color, which way well have been the case at Sayil. A small structure located midway between Uxmal and Kabah has recently been discovered which has remnants of large-scale murals in color on its interior walls. This discovery gives added weight to the notion that the use of color on buildings in the Puuc region was more widespread than had previously been believed.

FIG. 266. Sayil—the palace.

FIG. 267. Sayil—the palace (restoration).

FIG. 268. Sayil—the palace, doorways to rooms on second level.

FIG. 269. Sayil—detail of mask over doorways on second level.

FIG. 270. Sayil—the palace, northeast corner.

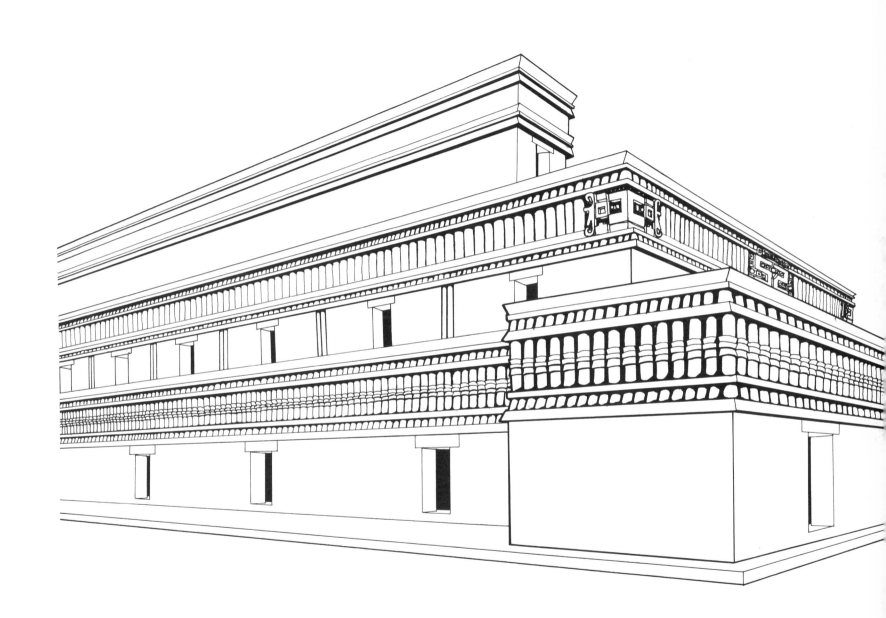

FIG. 271. Sayil—the palace, northeast corner (restoration).

Dzibilchaltun

The site of Dzibilchaltun is located about seven miles north of the city of Merida in the state of Yucatan, Mexico. In spite of its close proximity to the capital city of Yucatan, its existence was not known until 1941 when E. Wyllys Andrews and George W. Brainerd first began to investigate a series of previously unreported mounds near the hacienda of Dzibilchaltun. Preliminary investigations indicated that the site was extraordinary both in extent and age, but World War II forced postponement of any further investigation until 1956, when the Middle America Research Institute of Tulane University in cooperation with the I.N.A.H. of Mexico and *National Geographic Magazine* undertook an extensive program of excavation and restoration which subsequently brought to light the largest Maya city which is presently known. An extensive survey of the site indicates that it covered an area of nearly fifty square kilometers, although only the central area, which covers about twenty square kilometers, has been mapped in detail.

The city as a whole appears to have consisted of a densely built-up central area surrounded by a number of suburban centers (Fig. 272). The central core included numerous pyramid-temples, palaces, and other stone vaulted structures together with smaller thatched-roof dwellings which are assumed to be the residences of the priests or ruling class. The suburban centers consist of six or more vaulted stone buildings situated on a raised platform, surrounded by groups of houses numbering anywhere from one hundred to one hundred and fifty. The houses are frequently found in clusters of three or four which center on a multichamber structure of stone, roofed with thatch. Many of these outlying centers were connected to the main center by means of *sacbeob*, or paved roadways. The space between the main center and the suburban centers was less densely occupied, but, as the city continued to grow, more houses were added and the divisions between the various sectors became less pronounced. Within the central area of twenty square kilometers, over eighty-five hundred structures were mapped and of these 72.5 per cent were house mounds. From this, it has been computed that the population within the main sector was upwards of fifty thousand, making it the largest city anywhere in the New World.

From what is presently known of Dzibilchaltun, it appears to have a history of continuous occupation for a period of over three thousand years. This places its origin somewhere around 1500 B.C. In contrast to most Classic Maya sites to the south, which are assumed to have been abandoned by the year A.D. 900, Dzibilchaltun continued to flourish on a somewhat reduced scale throughout the entire pre-Columbian period and the evidence points to its continued occupation up through the early part of the Spanish occupation. If these dates prove to be correct, the building remains should include traces of the earliest known Preclassic Maya culture as well as the latest Postclassic culture. This now appears to be the case; the latest findings at Dzibilchaltun suggest that the earliest structures erected could well be called pre-Maya rather than Preclassic in that they show very few of the characteristics that we have come to associate with Maya art and architecture. This, in turn, suggests that while the city was more or less continuously occupied for a very long period of time, at least two, and perhaps three, separate cultures are represented: a pre-Maya culture, the Classic Maya, and a Postclassic culture with strong overtones of Mexican or Toltec influence.

The bulk of the exposed building remains date from the Classic period, or what Andrews calls the Early and Florescent periods. Most of the early, or pre-Maya, buildings have disappeared under the constant rebuilding of the city and thus are brought to light only with intensive excavation. In addition, there are relatively few structures that can be assigned to the Postclassic period (Mexican or Decadent), and it appears that the population was greatly reduced over what it had been earlier. While the vast size of the city has prevented reconstruction on anything but a minor scale, those buildings which have been uncovered give some impression of the grandeur of the city during its prime.

The heart of the central area appears to have been organized around a great causeway which runs for about a mile and a half on an east-west line (Figs. 273, 274). At some points this causeway is nearly sixty feet wide and eight feet high. Connected to the causeway are numerous terraces which supported pyramids and palaces (Figs. 275, 276), and at intervals smaller causeways lead off at right angles to other complexes of palaces and ceremonial structures. Throughout its length it was marked by carved stone monuments showing sculptured figures and hieroglyphic inscriptions (Fig. 274). This causeway and its associated structures is truly a monumental conception. In contrast to most causeways at other sites, which served primarily as a connecting link between otherwise isolated groups of structures, it is used here as a kind of grand boulevard, as it is lined for most of its length with what must have been the most important buildings of the center. For example, one of the Palace Groups which adjoins the causeway covers an area of nearly twelve acres. The only causeway construction comparable to this is found at Teotihuacan just north of Mexico City, where the so-called Avenue of the Dead extends for an even greater length.

The site map (Fig. 272) shows an area of 3,000 meters east and west by 2,000 meters north and south. This is only a portion of the total area which has been mapped, which covers an area 13 kilometers by 31 kilometers (14 square miles). This area was selected for illustration because it includes the large concentration of ceremonial structures centered around the long east-west causeway and the *cenote* Xlacah as well as some of the suburban areas which are typical of the balance of the site. It can be noted that the general organization of the central area is not substantially different from many of the other large centers which have been described earlier. That is to say, this area includes a number of well-organized large complexes of structures which are uniformly oriented with respect to the cardinal points of the compass. As is the case at many of the centers in the Southern Lowlands, these complexes are connected together by a series of causeways in an apparent effort to bring some order to an otherwise scattered arrangement.

While the ground is relatively flat, the higher portions of ground have been selected as sites for the largest complexes, which is characteristic of Maya planning. The generic groups which we have described earlier (Acropolis Groups, Temple Groups, Quadrangle Groups, and Palace Groups) are not clearly represented among these complexes, but there is the same tendency toward rectilinear groupings around large plazas which is the hallmark of all Maya building complexes. It must also be recognized that most of the structures shown are in a very advanced state of ruin and it is extremely difficult to make a detailed analysis of the rather amorphous mounds of rubble which remain.

It can also be noted that much of the space around the central area is filled in with small mounds, most of which represent houses or groups of houses. Interspersed among the houses are somewhat larger structures which may represent very local ceremonial elements (Figs. 277, 278). Other suburban ceremonial centers lay outside the area shown and one of these is connected to the main center by a causeway which runs in a southerly direction from the great mass of structures surrounding the *cenote* Xlacah (Fig. 279). It should be fairly clear from the map that the amount of open space between the houses is not sufficient to allow for *milpa* plots, although small garden plots of the kind that have been postulated for Tikal could easily be accommodated.

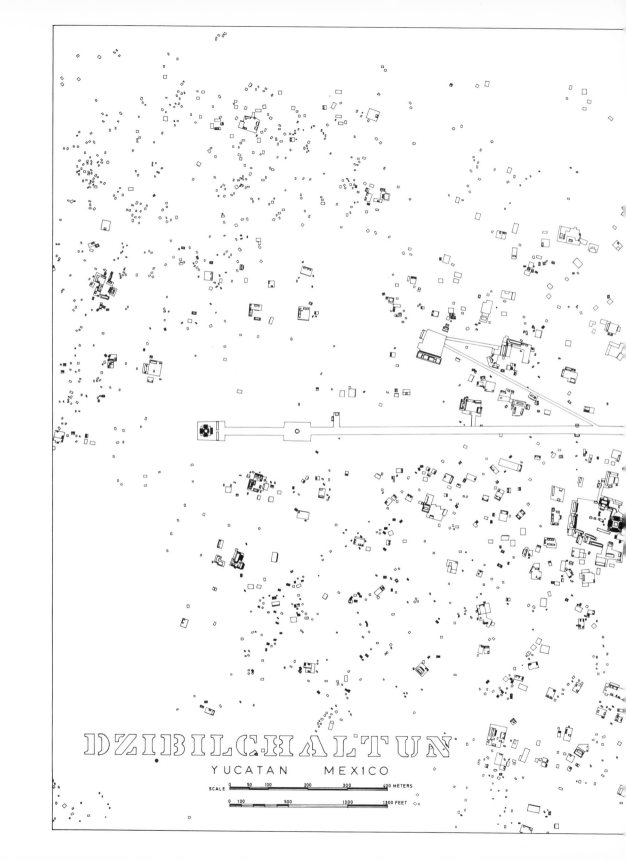

DZIBILCHALTUN

YUCATAN   MEXICO

SCALE 0   50   100   200   300   400 METERS

0   100   500   1300   1300 FEET

FIG. 272. Dzibilchaltun (after Stuart et al.).

Returning to the central area, we find that the eastern end of the main causeway is terminated by a group of fifteen structures centered on a pyramid-temple structure called the Temple of the Seven Dolls (Fig. 280). This name is derived from a cache of seven clay dolls, or figures, which were found buried under the floor of the temple. Carbon dates obtained from samples of the wooden beams in this structure indicate a construction date of approximately A.D. 500. This makes is contemporary with many of the earlier buildings in the Peten and Usumacinta areas and, because of some significant differences in its form and construction when compared with buildings from these latter regions, raises some interesting questions in regard to the amount of contact between the northern and southern regions during the Early Classic period. In its general outlines the Temple of the Seven Dolls conforms to the basic pyramid-temple form which has already been described in some detail; i.e., it consists of a substructure in the form of a truncated and stepped pyramid which supports a single temple building which, in turn, is surmounted by a roof comb (Fig. 280). The details of these elements vary considerably from those found elsewhere in the Maya area—so much so, in fact, that we are led to believe that it represents a somewhat independent regional development. At this point, a closer look at these details seems in order.

The typical temple building, as found in either the northern or southern area, consists of a single vaulted room or a series of two or three such rooms ranged from front to back which can be entered from a single doorway at the front of the temple. There are many exceptions to this, and buildings which are commonly accepted as representing temples may have up to five doorways, but in almost all cases these doorways are located on a single side which must be considered as the front side. Because the rooms are vaulted, they tend to be narrow from front to back, producing a rectangular ground plan. Thus, the temple is highly directional and we can easily identify the front, sides, and rear. This directionality is continued into the supporting pyramidal substructure, which generally has a single stairway on the front side. In contrast to this, the Temple of the Seven Dolls is square in plan and consists of a large vaulted room with doorways on all four sides and a small inner room centered within the larger room. In addition, two of the walls of the outer building are pierced with openings which have the appearance, if not the function, of windows (Fig. 281). This kind of opening in the outer walls is entirely unknown at other Classic sites.

The temple is also surmounted with a superstructure which might be called a room comb, here again its form is significantly different from the typical roof comb, which is a wall-like element, many times pierced with openings, which is always parallel to the front of the temple. Here the superstructure is square in plan and has the shape of a truncated pyramid. This superstructure rests directly over the small chamber in the center of the building below. The pyramidal substructure also varies from the typical form, since it is symmetrical on both axes and has stairways on all four sides. Similar substructures are occasionally found elsewhere, the outstanding examples being Structure E-sub VII at Uaxactun, the twin pyramid complexes at Tikal, and the Castillo at Chichen Itza.

The façades of the Temple of the Seven Dolls generally follow the traditional pattern, in that the lower walls to the base of the vaults are plain while the upper walls are decorated with masks over the doorways and at the corners, with other stucco ornamentation in between; but here again the details of the elements vary sharply from the well-known Puuc or Chenes styles found in other parts of the Yucatan Peninsula (Fig. 282). The whole of the façade was covered with a thick coating of stucco, which is normal for all Maya buildings. The details of the construction of this temple indicate that it should be classified as Early Classic or even Archaic, since it is formed of large stone slabs laid in somewhat regular courses rather than veneer stones imbedded in a rubble-concrete inner hearting, which is commonly found in the Late Classic period. The remarkable state of preservation of the exposed remains is due to the fact that it was covered over by a later structure, which unfortunately was so badly destroyed that no real impression of its form and details could be determined. Structure E-sub VII at Uaxactun had similarly been covered over, but in both cases the loss of the latter structures was more than compensated for by the gain in knowledge of Early Classic forms.

Turning aside from the question of details to the question of organization, it can also be argued that the multi-directionality which is implicit in the double symmetry of the temple and its pyramidal substructure indicates some ambivalence with respect to the relationships between the temple and its associated structures. This condition is also nontypical as far as temples are concerned, since we have already suggested that the basic concept of temple and plaza is both axial and directional. Its axiality is due to the single stairway leading from the plaza to the temple, which establishes a strong direction of movement both horizontally and vertically. The equivalence of the four sides of the Temple of the Seven Dolls leaves the question of movement open, as there is no order of importance among the various sides.

Thus, the whole ensemble does not fit any of our established categories of groupings and leaves open the question as to whether it should be considered as an archaic version of the Classic Temple Group, without its distinctive order, or as a unique concept based on a local version of ceremonial activity which did not require any ordered sequence of events. There is some support for the first of these theories, as Structure E-sub VII at Uaxactun, which is the earliest dated structure from that site, also has stairways on four sides (Fig. 3), while the later buildings have single stairs and typical unidirectional temples.

It is difficult to draw useful comparisons between Dzibilchaltun and some of its closest neighbors in the northern part of the Yucatan Peninsula. Mayapan, which is located some forty miles to the south, is entirely Postclassic in construction and was built at a time when Dzibilchaltun was well past its peak and only sparsely populated. Other nearby sites such as Acanceh, Ake, and Izamal are either too small for meaningful comparison or have been largely destroyed by the overlay of modern settlements. Chichen Itza, which is around seventy-five miles to the east, reached its peak during the Toltec, or Mexican, period (A.D. 900 to 1200) when Dzibilchaltun was in a period of decline. It is perhaps most easily compared with Coba, a large city near the east coast of the peninsula, or with the larger cities in the central and southern areas. Coba is known to be contemporary with Dzibilchaltun during the time when Dzibilchaltun enjoyed its greatest prosperity and, on the basis of the size and complexity of its main ceremonial area, was probably similar in its larger settlement pattern as well. Thus, we find two great contemporary cities in the northern part of the peninsula whose spheres of influence overlapped somewhere in the neighborhood of Chichen Itza.

Dzibilchaltun is probably best compared with Tikal, which is situated several hundred miles to the south in the Peten area of Guatemala. In almost every respect, these two sites show parallel developments up through the end of the Late Classic period. Tikal is now known to be a city, or a *large urban center*, to use our terminology, even though its population may have been substantially less than Dzibilchaltun's. Its physical organization is very similar to that of Dzibilchaltun in that it consists of a very large central ceremonial area surrounded by suburban ceremonial areas which include large numbers of houses. Both are marked by huge ceremonial, or civic, complexes which cover anywhere from four to twelve acres of ground. Both were occupied for very long periods of time and there is no reason to suppose that their similarities are not due in part to continuous exchange of ideas throughout their histories. Most certainly they are part of the same cultural heritage, which in its later stages brought forth true urbanization on a large scale. Reference was made in chapter 4 to the possibility of at least a dozen large urban centers which were contemporary in time and

undoubtedly shared the same essential characteristics of advanced urbanism. Thus, Dzibilchaltun is not unique, except perhaps for its great size. Its importance to this study lies in the fact that it demonstrates conclusively that the Mayas ran the full course of placemaking ideas from thatched-roof hut in the wilderness to great cities much as we know them today.

Note: Dzibilchaltun was the subject of an extensive program to excavation and restoration during the years 1956 to 1964 under the direction of E. W. Andrews. A number of preliminary reports have been published covering various phases of this work, but the final reports are still in press. (See bibliography under Dzibilchaltun for preliminary reports.) Interested readers are referred to these early reports for more detailed descriptions of various aspects of Dzibilchaltun, including architecture and planning.

FIG. 273. Dzibilchaltun—view on
main causeway, looking west.

FIG. 274. Dzibilchaltun—platform and stela
near western end of main causeway.

FIG. 275. Dzibilchaltun—pyramid
adjacent to main causeway.

FIG. 276. Dzibilchaltun—platform and
small ceremonial structure
adjacent to main causeway.

FIG. 277. Dzibilchaltun—
small ceremonial structure
near causeway in central area.

FIG. 279. Dzibilchaltun—
cenote Xlacah, near main causeway,
central ceremonial area (right).

FIG. 278. Dzibilchaltun—
small ceremonial structure
in central area
(note veneer-type vaults).

FIG. 280. Dzibilchaltun—Temple of the Seven Dolls.

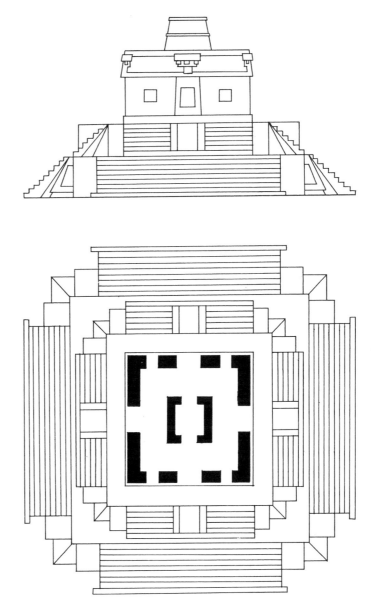

FIG. 281. Dzibilchaltun—Temple of the Seven Dolls,
plan and elevation.

The site of Chichen Itza is situated about seventy-five miles east of Merida, the capital of the state of Yucatan, on the main highway which connects Merida with Valladolid. It is probably the best known and most frequently visited Maya city in Yucatan, due to the extensive work of excavation and restoration which was carried out over a period of twenty-five years through the combined efforts of the Carnegie Institution of Washington and the I.N.A.H. of Mexico, making it the showplace of this region. For our purposes, Chichen Itza is particularly noteworthy, since various parts of the city can be assigned to different periods of time which are represented by Late Classic, Mexican, or Toltec, and Post-Toltec building remains.

Buildings constructed during the Late Classic Maya period are in the Puuc or Chenes style which is typical for this part of the peninsula, and these are similar in many respects to structures at Uxmal and Kabah. The Mexican, or Toltec, period is represented by a change in architectural style as well as a change in building types and spatial arrangement. The architecture shows striking similarities to that found at Tula, in the Valley of Mexico, which is presumed to have been the early capital of the Toltecs before they migrated to the Yucatan Peninsula near the end of the first millenium A.D. The salient features of Toltec architecture include serpent columns, feathered serpent balustrades, Atlantean figures used as supports, wooden lintels and beams, and large colonnaded interior spaces. Buildings from the Post-Taltec period are less easy to identify, as there is no definable architectural style and they are not found in specific groupings. There are, however, a number of fairly crudely constructed buildings scattered throughout the site which should be assigned to this later period.

The area included within the map of Chichen Itza covers approximately one and a half square miles and several hundred structures can be included within its boundaries (Fig. 283). Some of these are found in well-defined groups on large terraces, in arrangements which are typical of the Classic Maya period. Others form less well-defined groupings associated with level plaza areas, while some appear in isolated positions with no observable relationship to other elements. Some groups are connected to one another by means of a *sacbe*, or roadway, and the large group of Toltec-period structures at the northern end of the site is connected to the Sacred *Cenote* by a well-preserved causeway.

In spite of the presence of a few groupings which show evidence of preplanning or conceptual order, the over-all scheme is very fragmented and there is little evidence indicating the application of ordering principles at a scale large enough to bind the disparate elements into a cohesive whole. This may be due in part to the rather uneven terrain, which does not lend itself easily to formal organizations, and in part to the disruption and partial reconstruction of the city after the Toltec invasion. It is also entirely possible that the earlier structures were no longer in use during the Toltec period and no necessity was felt to include them as integral parts of later developments. This possibility is suggested by the presence of a low stone wall which surrounds most of the larger structures erected during the Toltec period. The Classic Maya structures lie outside this precinct and no strong relationships can be noted between them and the later Toltec constructions.

In spite of its large area, the extent to which Chichen Itza might be considered as an urban center during any of its three periods of occupation is debatable. That it was the most important political center in the northern part of the peninsula during the Toltec period cannot be doubted; both the archaeological record and the written records from the early part of the Conquest period bear

383

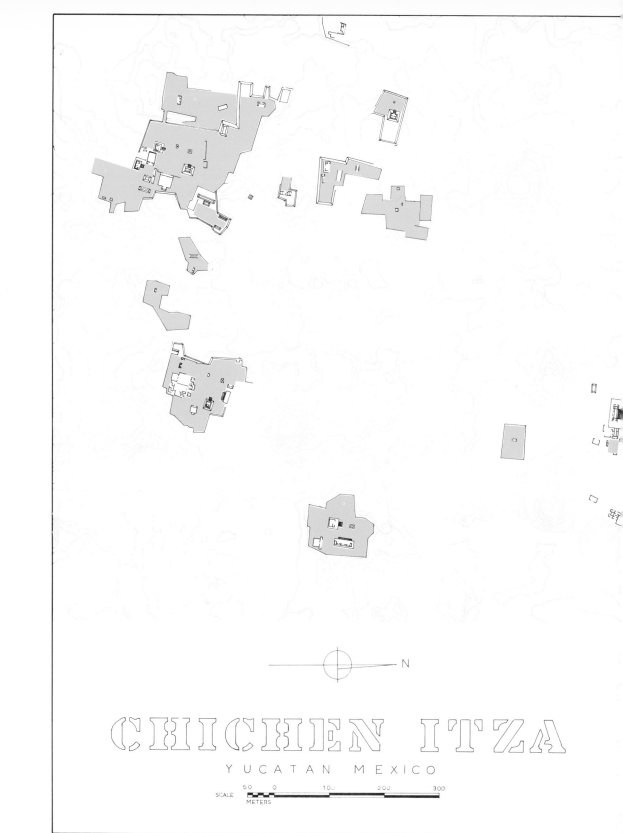

CHICHEN ITZA

Y U C A T A N   M E X I C O

SCALE
50   0   100   200   300
METERS

N

FIG. 283. Chichen Itza (after Kilmartin and O'Niel).

this out. During this same period, the great urban center of Dzibilchaltun was in a state of decline, and Mayapan had not yet come into existence. As the seat of power for this region, we have reason to believe that it should have been a major urban center, but the presence of house mounds in densities approaching those at Dzibilchaltun or Tikal has not yet been established. This may be due, in part at least, to the techniques of mapping employed at Chichen Itza some years ago as compared with the extremely detailed maps which have been made elsewhere in recent years (Dzibilchaltun, Tikal, Edzna, Comalcalco, Barton Ramie, etc.). At the present time there is much more concern for locating and recording the existence of the low, formless mounds of earth and rubble which mark the presence of house platforms. At the time the map of Chichen Itza was made, the emphasis was on monumental architecture and most of the data recorded was in reference to masonry, ceremonial-type structures.

Some house-type mounds can be seen on the map (Fig. 283), but these appear to be more scattered than is the case of Tikal and Dzibilchaltun, where clusters of one hundred and fifty to two hundred houses can be found in close association with suburban ceremonial groups. It is also possible that the Toltecs introduced a new pattern of housing during their period of ascendency, but there is no real evidence for this. Since the general pattern of urbanization as evident at both Dzibilchaltun and Coba had been established long before the Toltec invasion, it is reasonable to assume that this same pattern would have been continued at Chichen Itza during the time it was a major seat of power under the Toltecs, even though the city might not have been large in terms of numbers of permanent residents. The environs of the main ceremonial area will have to be searched more carefully for the remains of houses before any definitive image of its assumed urban character can be substantiated.

The differences between Maya and Toltec notions of placemaking can be readily observed by comparing the two groups of structures which lie just on either side of the highway which presently cuts through the site (Fig. 284). The group immediately north of this road includes the Castillo (Figs. 285, 286), the Great Ball Court (Figs. 289, 290), the Temple of the Warriors (Figs. 287, 288), the Court of the Thousand Columns (Fig. 291), the Market (Fig. 292), the Platform of the Jaguars and Eagles (Figs. 293, 294), the Platform of the Skulls, and several other major structures of the Toltec period. South of the highway are a large number of Classic Maya structures, including the Red House (Fig. 295), the Deer House, the Akabdzib, the Nunnery (Figs. 296, 297), the Church (Fig. 300), and the Observatory (Figs. 301, 302). The Observatory (Caracol) is presumed to belong to an intermediate period between the Late Classic and Early Toltec. Farther to the south are a number of other major groups of structures which include both Maya and Toltec elements, but these will not be included in the present discussion, since most of them are in an advanced state of ruin. An exception to this is the Temple of the Three Lintels, a small building in the Puuc style which has been completely restored. It is well removed from the two groups under consideration, however, and is not part of any spatial scheme relating to them.

The main group of Classic Maya structures is unusual in two respects. First, there is no large pyramid-temple combination of the sort which we have identified elsewhere as being the most basic element of the ceremonial center during the Classic period. Those buildings which have been identified as temples rest on large platforms with smooth sloping sides rather than on a stepped pyramid (Fig. 295). Second, the individual buildings are not organized clearly into the kind of groupings which have been shown to be typical at most other Classic sites. For example, there are no Temple Groups, no Palace Groups, no Quadrangle Groups, and no Acropolis Groups. In place of these well-defined formal arrangements, we find various elements associated with raised terraces or level plazas but not in recognizable patterns. The building called the Nunnery bears little resemblance to the Nunnery at Uxmal, which is a pure quadrangular form. Here, the Nunnery is a disjointed collection of unrelated elements (Figs. 298, 299).

These two variations from the traditions of the Classic Maya period are so great as to suggest that Maya Chichen represents a distinct regional development which was separated both in space and time from the main current of events during the height of the Classic period. Its geographical position on the northern periphery of the Maya area supports this notion, and the dates obtained from hieroglyphic inscriptions associated with buildings indicate that the construction of these buildings occurred near the very end of the Classic period. By this time, the driving force which gave rise to Maya civilization had nearly spent itself and the signs of decay were already present. Perhaps these variations from traditional themes are actually indicative of outside influences at work prior to the larger-scale invasion which resulted in Toltec Chichen.

The Caracol, or Observatory, which dominates this group of Classic Maya structures by virtue of its great height is further evidence of the transitional nature of Maya Chichen. The whole structure consists of two superimposed terraces which support a round tower nearly fifty feet high (Fig. 303). Stylistically, these elements belong both to the Maya and Toltec periods, but the round tower form is almost completely unknown at other Classic Maya sites.[14] Round buildings appear at Mayapan (again, not towers), but these have been assigned to a much later time period. It has also been assumed that Mayapan was built to *émigrés* from Chichen Itza, so it is necessary to look elsewhere for round-tower precedents. Unfortu-

nately, these have not yet been found, so it might be argued that the round tower was generated as a form solution to a specific problem associated with making astronomical observations. This requires considerable stretching of the imagination, but it is not impossible; new forms do come into being on this basis. It cannot be proved that the tower was actually used for purposes of observation, but it is the only logical explanation which can be advanced in support of its unusual form and details with respect to "window" openings.

It can be noted that the Observatory forms a visual link between the older Maya structures which lie to the south and west and the later Toltec structures to the north (Fig. 306). It cannot, however, be said to belong to either of these groups on the basis of implicit spatial relationships, though some effort was made to use it as a boundary for the plaza in front of the Nunnery. This plaza is not well defined and the elements which actually pertain to it are in doubt. The lack of formal groupings among the Classic Maya structures has already been commented on and this is readily apparent when an effort is made to differentiate out specific areas and their associated buildings in this part of the site. The various structures are scattered about in a haphazard fashion and it is difficult to tell exactly where plazas began or ended. The lack of order is so pronounced that we are led to wonder if some elements, which might well have made more unified assemblages if they were present, were destroyed during the Toltec period and the materials incorporated into the later buildings to the north.

Turning to the northern, or Toltec, group, we find that it is made up of two distinct subgroups. One of these consists of the structures associated with the Great Plaza, which is dominated by the largest pyramid-temple building in the entire site, called the Castillo (Figs. 285, 286). The basic form and construction of this building is typical of the Classic Maya period, but the decorative details are Toltec. At the west end of this plaza is the Great Ball Court (Figs. 305, 306), the largest such court yet discov-

[14] A round, free-standing masonry tower was found in 1967 at a site in southern Campeche called Puerto Rico. This tower is a solid mass of masonry raised up on a conical base. The upper part of this tower is pierced by several very small horizontal openings, but they do not seem to have any astronomical significance. (*Boletin*, I.N.A.H., Mexico, No. 31 March 1968.) More recently, the lower parts of the walls of two round structures were found at Edzna, Campeche. There is no reason to assume that these structures were towers, however, and they may not have had masonry roofs. (G. F. Andrews: 1969.)

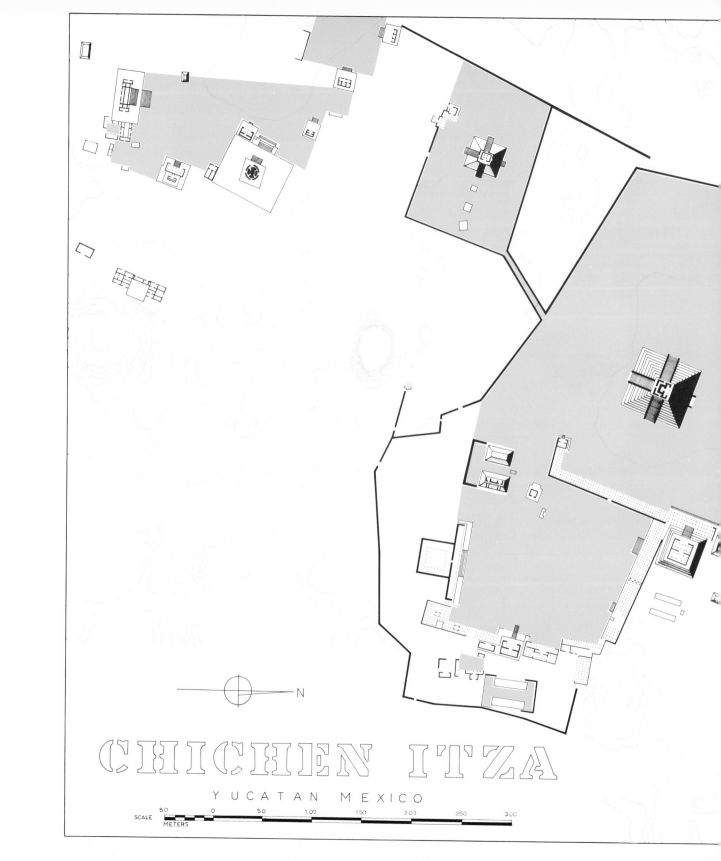

CHICHEN ITZA

YUCATAN MEXICO

SCALE
METERS
50 0 50 100 150 200 250 300

N

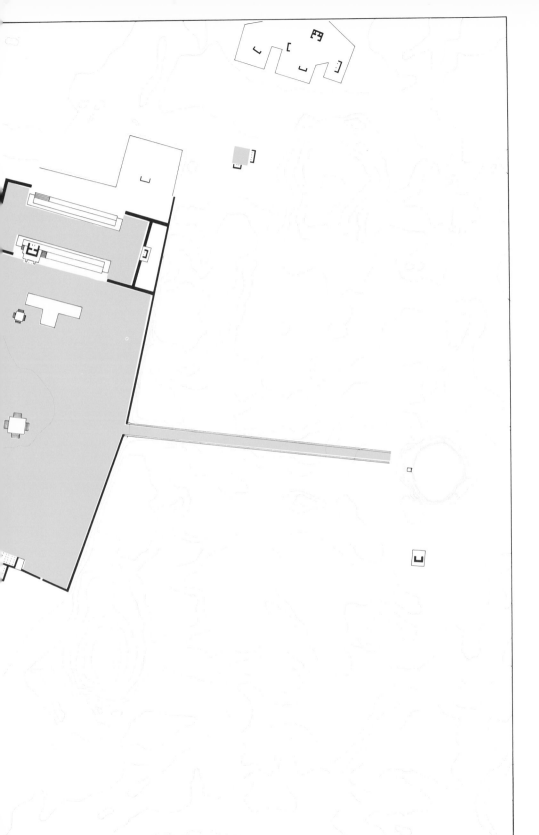

FIG. 284. Chichen Itza—central area
(after Kilmartin and O'Niel).

ered, while the east side is founded by the Temple of the Warriors (Figs. 287, 308, 309) and a long colonnaded hall which extends southward from this temple for a distance of four hundred and fifty feet (Fig. 291). Three altars or low platforms are situated in the plaza between the Ball Court and the Temple of the Warriors, one directly north of the Castillo and the other two close to the Ball Court (Figs. 293, 294).

A *sacbe*, or causeway, leads from the center of the north side of the plaza to the sacred *Cenote*, which is also called the sacrificial well (Fig. 310). When this *cenote* was dredged in 1923, a number of skeletons and a large collection of valuable ritual objects were recovered, which tends to substantiate the theory that it was used for ritual sacrifices.[15] It is interesting to note that this causeway is only roughly aligned with the central axis of the Castillo, which can hardly be called an accident, since the causeway is an artificial construction for its entire length.

East of the Great Plaza and separated from it by the long colonnaded hall which connects to the Temple of the Warriors, is a second plaza which is surrounded by other colonnaded halls on three sides and on the fourth side by a ball court and the building called the Mercado, or Market (Fig. 292). These colonnaded halls represent a new building type which is not found in Classic Maya sites. The round column as a supporting member is found in Puuc-style buildings, but only as a support for the lintels of doorways. It was rarely, if ever, used to support beams or vaults in the interior of buildings. Here, the buildings consist entirely of enclosed spaces formed by the use of columns and beams as supports for wooden roofs in place of the stone vaults of Classic Maya architecture.

The advantage of this construction system over the corbeled or concrete vault is quite apparent when the size and character of the spaces produced by post-and-beam methods are compared with those roofed over with corbeled vaults. The latter is limited to a single gallery, the width of one vault, while the former can be extended endlessly in both directions, forming larger spaces of almost any size and shape. Some of the wooden beams appear to have supported the usual stone vaults, which seriously limits the advantages of post-and beam-construction, but later the roofs were made entirely of wood, which reduced the weight sufficiently to allow greater spans and larger open spaces.

The function of the colonnaded hall is very debatable; it may well be a variation of the earlier multichambered palace structure, but could equally well represent a logical response to a new but still undetermined ritual activity which supplanted the older Maya traditions under the Toltecs. Colonnaded halls are found at Tula, and these were undoubtedly the original source of the halls here, but it is not clear if they served the same functions at both sites. Their widespread use in Toltec Chichen indicates that they played an important role in specific activities associated with the ceremonial center, even though these may have been secular in nature. The structures associated with the East Plaza are clearly differentiated from those surrounding the Great Plaza, which suggests a significant difference in function between the two areas. This difference is further reinforced by the fact that nearly all of the colonnaded halls are found around the East Plaza.

Some mention must also be made of the pyramid-temple structure called the Ossuary, which is located southwest of the Great Plaza. This structure is very similar in form and details to the Castillo, although smaller in size. Visually, it appears as an isolated element standing on its own plaza, which is bounded by a low wall but connected to the south side of the Great Plaza by a short causeway. It is clearly subordinate to the Castillo both in size and position, but this may not always have been the case, as the Castillo in its present form is an addition to a smaller pyramid-temple which is now completely buried inside the later addition.

[15] The well was dredged on two other occasions, 1961 and 1967–68, and many additional artifacts were recovered. A good description of the work conducted in 1961 can be found in the October, 1961, issue of *National Geographic*.

The manner in which the Ossuary is connected to the Great Plaza is indicative of the rather naïve decisions which were generally made by the Toltec builders whenever they were confronted with the problem of linking various sectors of the city visually as well as physically. In the case of the Ossuary, the physical link is clear, but the result is not satisfactory visually; it remains detached, but the result is not satisfactory visually; it remains detached, as it cannot be recognized as part of any larger form idea. The other structures associated with the Great Plaza are also handled as isolated elements, with the result that each tends to suffer by comparison with the others.

The distinction between true monumentality and mere pretentiousness was not really understood by the Toltecs, and this is made clear by the lack of form consciousness in this part of the city at a scale larger than a single building. The conscious striving for effect is clear, based on size in the case of the Ball Court and the Castillo, or based on area and numbers in the case of the great colonnaded halls, but any unifying force is lost in the conflict of visual interest between individual elements. The generalized brutalization of art forms, including architecture, and the resultant pretentiousness are characteristic of any society which depends for its existence on force of arms rather than the efficacy of its ideals and aspirations for the common good. This notion is clearly demonstrated at Chichen Itza, where the Toltec invaders swept away the refinements of a culture devoted largely to intellectual and artistic achievements and replaced it with a crude distortion based on ideas of power and authority. This kind of change carries with it the potential for technological advancement, which certainly must be credited to the Toltecs, but this is a poor substitute for the humanizing qualities of Classic Maya art and architecture, which brought its originators so close to lasting greatness.

Reports covering the excavation and restoration of various buildings at Chichen Itza are so numerous and so well documented that no effort has been made to give a complete description of any individual structures in this analysis. See bibliography by site for a list of these publications. Likewise, the dredging of the Well of Sacrifice in 1923 and the description of the material thus recovered is best covered in the book by Edward Thompson and thus has been given only cursory treatment here. (Thompson: 1932)

FIG. 285. Chichen Itza—the Castillo.

FIG. 286. Chichen Itza—the Castillo showing restored and unrestored stairways.

FIG. 287. Chichen Itza—Temple of the Warriors.

FIG. 288. Chichen Itza—Temple of the Warriors, detail of columns with Toltec motifs.

FIG. 289. Chichen Itza—Great Ball Court,
looking north down playing alley.

FIG. 290. Chichen Itza—Great Ball Court,
looking south down playing alley.

FIG. 291. Chichen Itza—Court of the Thousand Columns as seen from above.

FIG. 292. Chichen Itza—the Market (note tall columns which supported pole-and-thatch roof).

FIG. 293. Chichen Itza—
view of main plaza in Toltec sector.

FIG. 295. Chichen Itza—
the Red House (Maya sector) (right).

FIG. 294. Chichen Itza—
Platform of the Jaguars and Eagles.

FIG. 296. Chichen Itza—the Nunnery (Maya sector).

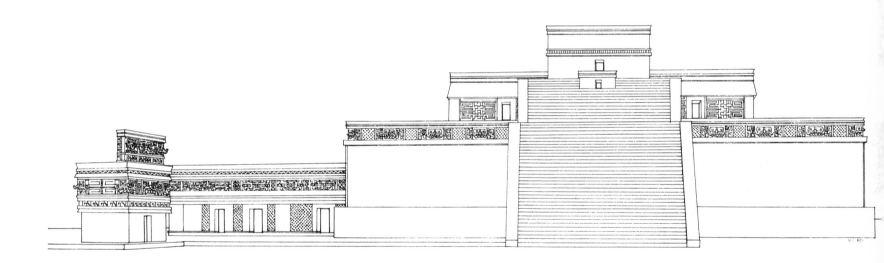

FIG. 297. Chichen Itza—the Nunnery (restoration).

FIG. 298. Chichen Itza—the Nunnery and the Church, east side.

FIG. 299. Chichen Itza—the Nunnery, detail of doorway and sculpture.

FIG. 300. Chichen Itza—the Church, east side.

FIG. 301. Chichen Itza—the Observatory (Caracol), south side.

FIG. 302. Chichen Itza.—the Observatory, west side.

FIG. 303. Chichen Itza—
the Observatory, view from plaza.

FIG. 304. Chichen Itza—the Observatory, Toltec sector in background.

FIG. 305. Chichen Itza—main plaza in Toltec sector from Temple of the Warriors.

FIG. 306. Chichen Itza—main plaza and Great Ball Court, Toltec sector.

FIG. 307. Chichen Itza—Temple at north end of Great Ball Court.

FIG. 308. Chichen Itza—Temple of the Warriors,
serpent columns flanking doorways.

FIG. 309. Chichen Itza—Temple of the Warriors,
serpent columns and Chac Mool.

The site of Mayapan is located about thirty miles southwest of the present city of Merida, the capital of the state of Yucatan. It appears to have been built and occupied during the three centuries just preceding the Spanish invasion, and this falls well beyond the Classic period which has been the concern of this study. It has been included as a postscript to the main discussion, together with Tulum, which is also a Postclassic site, as it gives us some basis for comparing the effects of internal disintegration coupled with outside invasion on the basic ideas of place-making which were developed and sustained during the six hundred years of the Classic period. Some of these ideas are still present at Mayapan but have degenerated to the point where the main ceremonial center has become a mishmash of conflicting ideas of order, further obscured by an overlay of symbols and details borrowed from neighboring regions. Compared with the quiet dignity of Copan or the geometrical precision of Uxmal, the fragmentation and disorder of Mayapan is very pronounced and its interest lies in its contribution to incipient notions of a new kind of urbanism rather than the character of its monuments.

The city of Mayapan figures prominently in the Maya chronicles which were written shortly after the Spanish conquest. Together with Uxmal and Chichen Itza, it was supposed to have formed a triumvirate which exercised control over most of the Yucatan Peninsula following the period of Mexican invasion. This assumption is no longer tenable, however, as Uxmal now appears to have been abandoned at least three hundred years before Mayapan was founded, and Chichen Itza was reduced to the status of a minor center during the time Mayapan flourished. Bishop Landa, in *Relacion de Cosas de Yucatan*, gives a lengthy description of a Maya city and describes it as having temples and plazas in the center, the houses of lords and priests around this center, then those of the most important people, and finally the houses of the lowest classes. He also describes the founding of Mayapan on the order of Kukulcan, the Toltec god who had previously reigned at Chichen Itza, and told how it was surrounded by a low stone wall within which were located the temples and houses for the lords and high priests. Other houses were supposed to be located outside the wall.

What remains of Mayapan fits fairly well to these descriptions; it represents a dense urban agglomeration as we understand it today in contrast to the more dispersed urban patterns of the Classic period. This change to walled city from the open city of the earlier period suggests a change in the basic conditions of life as well as a change in the form of government. Evidently this new form of government was even less successful than the oligarchy of Classic times, and the city appears to have been partially destroyed and then abandoned somewhere around the year 1440, giving it a life span of only two hundred to two hundred and fifty years. However, the stage had already been set for the Old World brand of urbanism which was to come with the Spanish invaders a hundred years later.

The city of Mayapan covers an area of more than four square kilometers and was enclosed by a very thick wall. The area thus enclosed has the plan form of a crudely drawn ellipse (Fig. 311). Within the wall were over four thousand structures, of which only one hundred and forty can be called ceremonial buildings, the rest being either houses or structures associated with houses. The size and shape of the enclosing wall and the presence of the houses within the wall raise several interesting questions. Was the wall supposed to offer protection for the inhabitants and, if so, why was the wall so low and thus easily breached? Was the wall only a visible expression of the

Mayapan

411

FIG. 310. Chichen Itza—*Cenote* of Sacrifice (usually called sacrifical well).

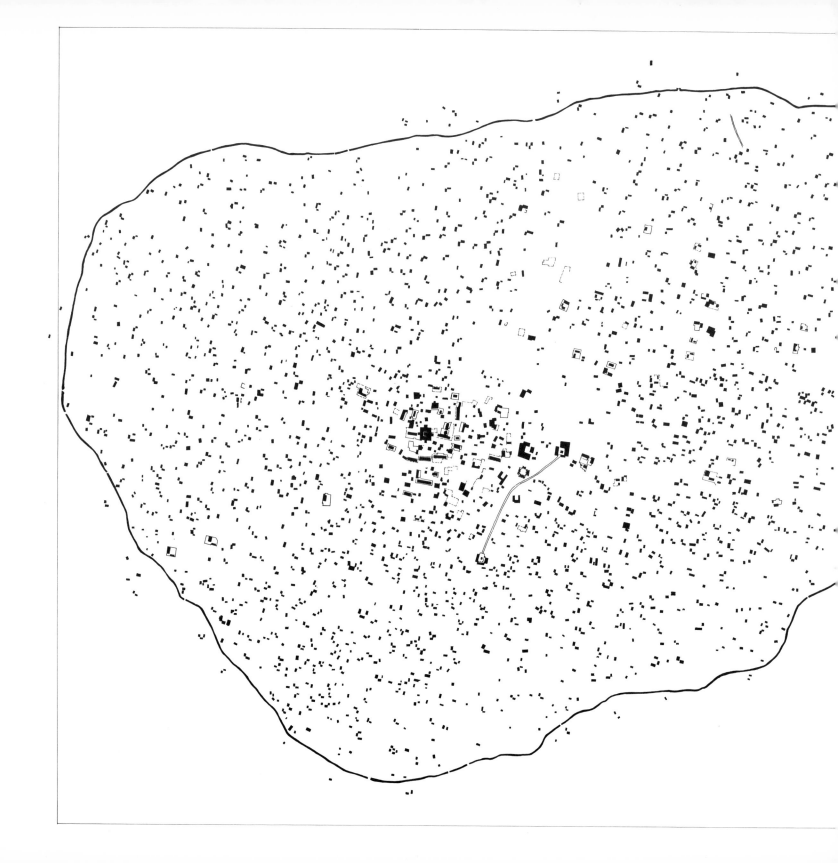

SCALE

| 0 | 200 | 400 | 600 | 800 | 1000 | 1000 | 1400 | 1600 FEET |

| 0 | 50 | 100 | 200 | 300 | 400 | 500 METERS |

MAYAPAN

YUCATAN   MEXICO

notion of a "community" which was so disassociated from other communities that its boundaries had to be described so forcefully? Why was the earlier pattern of small clusters of houses located close to farmsteads abandoned in favor of town living, which required much travel back and forth from the town in order to tend the cornfields? Why are there no other examples of walled cities in the same region?

Other vexing questions might be asked, but it is almost impossible to give any definitive answers. The Old World concept of town made discrete by an enclosing wall is clearly visible, even though in an embryo form, but there is no evidence to confirm it as a logical extension of earlier prototypical forms and no clear evidence of a change in conditions of life which would bring it into existence, despite a lack of precedents. Tulum and Xcaret, on the coast of Quintana Roo, also have enclosing walls, but cannot be proved to be earlier than Mayapan, and there are few, if any, houses within the walls. Thus, the problem of the origin of the walled-city concept must be left open for the moment.

The greater part of the ceremonial structures are clustered together in a small area near the center of the site (Fig. 312). The balance are found in several smaller groups away from this center. The ceremonial structures occupy 15 per cent of the total site, the rest being used for houses or unidentified structures. Since we are mainly concerned with changes in the spatial organization of a Postclassic city in relation to the earlier Classic Maya urban centers, particularly in regard to the relationships between dwellings and the balance of the city, a brief description of the residential quarters of Mayapan is in order.

The houses, or house groups, appear to be spread at random throughout the entire site. In most cases, houses occur in groups of two or more and these are surrounded by a low wall which defines a court, or yard, which belongs to these dwellings. They are more densely packed near the main ceremonial area, but there is no apparent pattern to their positions. An examination of the contours

413

FIG. 311. Mayapan (after Jones).

discloses that the higher rises of ground were preferred for dwellings as well as most other structures, and the apparent randomness of plan is largely due to the selection of these elevated positions. Whatever space was left between the house groups had to serve for circulation purposes, and these paths are also random. There are twelve gates through the enclosing walls, but these do not connect to major thoroughfares, due to the accidental character of the circulation scheme. The whole configuration is a gigantic maze of winding streets and alleyways, which is particularly confusing to the visitor who has just come from Merida, where the streets are laid out in a gridiron and numbered consecutively from the main square.

While it is not useful to our purposes to attempt to describe in detail the various kinds of house groups or house types found at Mayapan, several aspects of these houses are noteworthy, as they tend to duplicate known house types and house groupings at Classic centers elsewhere and thus lend support to the notion of urbanism at these latter centers. The houses range in size and form from small one-room houses made of perishable materials to fairly imposing housing groups with multichamber masonry residences adjacent to private ceremonial buildings. The vast majority of the more imposing house groups are located in the vicinity of the main ceremonial center, while the smaller ones are scattered around the balance of the site in more remote positions. The smallest houses were relegated to the worst locations, since they occupy the lower ground levels where water tends to collect.

It seems likely, then, that many of the nonceremonial structures which lie within, or close to, the ceremonial sectors of the larger Classic sites may also represent the remains of the larger and more important dwellings of officials and priests, while the houses of the general populace were further away from the center of things. House mounds are also found in the peripheral areas of most Classic sites, but most of them have not been carefully surveyed, so there is no way of knowing how many house

mounds might actually exist. Where house mounds have been located, they are not substantially different from the mounds at Mayapan, although the density is lower. Many of the house-mound groups at Classic sites include one or more ceremonial structures, which also duplicates the conditions at Mayapan. Thus, Mayapan is unique only in terms of the density of houses represented rather than the fact that it included houses.

The same kind of randomness, or lack of structural order, which characterizes the residential zones can also be observed within the limits of the main ceremonial center. Unlike the Classic centers in Yucatan such as Uxmal or Kabah, which consist of a number of discrete groups of buildings in specific formal arrangements, the main ceremonial buildings of Mayapan are tightly clustered around a single pyramid-temple building called the Castillo. This is the largest and highest structure in the city and is quite similar in many respects to the Castillo at Chichen Itza, which is assumed to be its precursor (Figs. 313, 314, 315, 316). Within this agglomerate are a number of identifiable subgroups, but this is more the result of similarity of building types than spatial arrangements. These subgroups are arranged in two concentric rings around the Castillo in a fairly irregular fashion. Two major classes of subgroups have been identified which have been called Temple Assemblages and Basic Ceremonial Groups. In both of these, the specific arrangement and number of elements varies considerably, but the repetition of certain building types within each group leads to the supposition that each was limited to a specific function or set of functions.

A typical Temple Assemblage consists of a pyramid-temple in conjunction with several other distinctive building types, which at Mayapan have been given the names of Colonnaded Hall (Figs. 317, 318), Shrine (Figs. 319, 320), and Oratory (Fig. 321). There are no exact equivalents of these three building types of Classic sites, which further supports the notion that significant changes had taken place in the structure and organization of Maya society following the Classic period. These structures are grouped around a level plaza and the general pattern is one in which the Colonnaded Hall stands at a right angle to the Temple and the Oratory faces the Temple across the plaza. Unfortunately, the clarity of these relationships are mostly obscured by the presence of other colonnaded halls and shrines which occur in seemingly arbitrary positions in various groups.

The Basic Ceremonial Group consists of the same elements as the Temple Assemblage minus the pyramid-temple. Since there are only a few structures which can properly be considered temples in the entire center, most subgroups fall into this latter type. In the Basic Ceremonial Group, the Raised Shrine generally faces and is centered on the Colonnaded Hall. The Oratory is away from this pair in one of several positions. There is considerable confusion involved in separating the individual subgroups and in determining which structures belong to which groups. The groups tend to overlap and the boundaries are not clearly defined. In the plan of the main ceremonial area which accompanies this description, the individual plazas with which the subgroups are associated are shown in yellow (Fig. 312). The decisions in regard to the makeup of the groups thus indicated is admittedly somewhat arbitrary, but the basic organization represented by the two concentric rings of elements is clearly demonstrated.

A number of theories can be advanced as a means of accounting for this particular organization, but one stands out as being the most logical if we accept the proposition advanced by Landa and others who tell us that Mayapan was founded by the Itza under the leadership of a priest or god who was called Kukulcan. The great pyramid at Chichen Itza and its counterpart at Mayapan are both presumed to be dedicated to this same Kukulcan. If this is so, then the organization of the center, which clearly recognizes the one large pyramid-temple as its focal point, makes good sense in spite of the irregularity of its geometry. If all other gods were subordinate to Kukulcan, the arrangement of the lesser temples in a ring around the main temple is a logical expression of this idea. The fact that there are two rings may indicate the order of importance among the lesser gods, who were relegated to the outer ring, or may simply indicate a needed expansion of the center when the first ring was filled in. In this kind of concentric organization, it is the position of elements with regard to the center point which is most important; the relationships of these lesser elements among themselves is less important and therefore tends to become confused.

Since we have already noted that higher points of ground were favored as locations for important structures, it would also follow that any formal plan would tend to be distorted in order to utilize these vantage points, even though they were not in the best locations as far as formal spatial organization was concerned. This is a far cry from the Classic period, when great masses of earth and rock were moved in order to maintain certain archetypical organizational ideas; in comparison, the organization of Mayapan can best be described as naïve. Aspects of the Classic period are present, but in a degenerate form, and the grandiose quality of the Mexican, or Toltec, constructions at Chichen Itza has also been lost.

The lack of spatial coherence of the ceremonial center is mute evidence that the conflict between Classic Maya and Toltec traditions was not fully resolved and Mayapan must be seen as an abortive effort to set up a new order of ritual and community activity within a physical framework that had not found its own logical expression. It is useless to speculate on what this might ultimately have become had not the Spaniards arrived shortly after the demise of Mayapan and thus changed the whole course of events in the Yucatan. As it stands, Mayapan represents a rather unique effort at urbanization, which is all the more striking as it seems to stand alone with no known precedent which might have served as a model. It is not appropriate to suggest Dzibilchaltun as the model, even though Dzibilchaltun was nearly and, most certainly, a

415

densely populated urban center long before Mayapan came into existence. The enclosing wall at Mayapan sets it apart, and it represents a distinctive spatial concept more analogous to medieval cities in the Old World than anything in the New World.

Note: The ruins of Mayapan were carefully explored, mapped, and partially excavated during the period 1951 to 1955 by a team of archaeologists and various specialists representing the Carnegie Institution of Washington. Their report, *Mayapan, Yucatan, Mexico*, covers all phases of the work undertaken there. The maps used in the present study are based on the more detailed maps which appear in the publication cited above, and readers with more than a casual interest in Postclassic Maya architecture will find detailed drawings of both ceremonial and residential structures. (Pollock, Roys, Proskouriakoff, and Smith: 1962.)

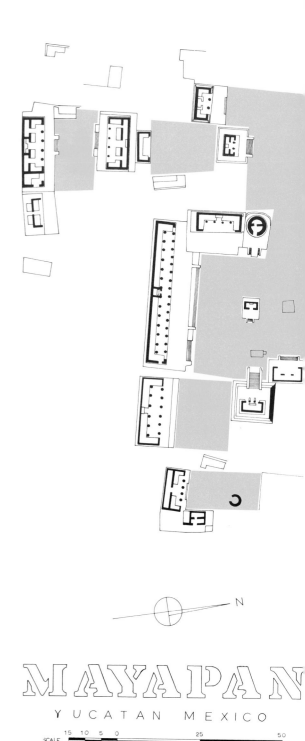

MAYAPAN

YUCATAN MEXICO

SCALE 15 10 5 0 25 50
METERS

416   FIG. 312. Mayapan—main ceremonial area (after Proskouriakoff).

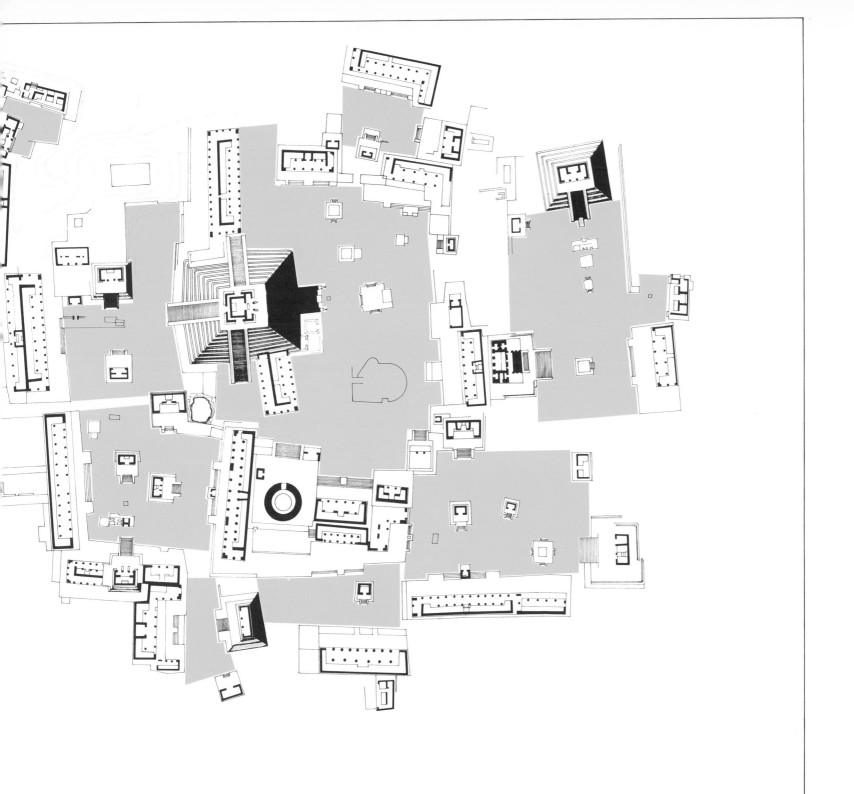

FIG. 313. Mayapan—the Castillo,
showing stair and balustrade.

FIG. 314. Mayapan—the Castillo, detail of rounded corner of pyramid.

FIG. 315. Mayapan—the Castillo and Colonnade Hall.

FIG. 316. Mayapan—the Castillo and Colonnade Hall (restoration).

FIG. 317. Mayapan—Colonnaded Hall, front elevation.

FIG. 318. Mayapan—detail of Chac mask on Colonnaded Hall.

FIG. 319. Mayapan—Shrine, rear view.

FIG. 320. Mayapan—Shrine, front view.

FIG. 321. Mayapan—Oratory (note serpent head on balustrade).

FIG. 322. Mayapan—Round Temple.

The ruins of Tulum are located in the territory of Quintana Roo, Mexico, on the east coast of the Yucatan Peninsula. The ruins of other cities are found to the north and south along the coast, but Tulum appears to have been the largest and most important city in this region. The best evidence available at the present time places the earliest construction at Tulum some time during the Mexican period (A.D. 900 to 1200), but the bulk of the standing remains appear to have been built after 1200, and there is some reason to suppose that the city was still occupied at the time of the arrival of the Spaniards in the early part of the sixteenth century. Tulum has been included in this study as a means of tracing the course of Maya ideas of placemaking up to the time when the invasion of the Spaniards put the final *coup-de-grâce* to a civilization which had long since passed its apogee and had suffered through a series of internal struggles for a period of nearly six hundred years. In a very real sense, both geographically and temporally, Tulum represents the last outpost of a crumbling civilization, but its builders managed to retain some vestige of the old order, even though we shall see that they were only crude approximations of the sophisticated conceptions which characterized the Classic period.

The central portion of Tulum is located on the summit of a limestone cliff some 40 feet high, which faces on the Caribbean Sea (Figs. 324, 325). The ground slopes downward from the edge of the cliff and then rises again, forming a ridge which roughly parallels the sea. The central portion of Tulum is enclosed by a great wall about 20 feet wide and 15 feet high. The wall follows the ridge for a distance of nearly 1,270 feet, and two arms roughly 550 feet long connect this longer wall with the edge of the cliffs. Within the rectangle formed by the walls and the cliff edge stand the principal buildings of the city (Fig.

323). From the southwestern angle of the great wall a lower wall runs to the sea, forming an additional triangular enclosure. Traces of platforms and mounds are found within this enclosure, but there are no standing buildings. The large enclosing wall is pierced with five gateways, and small temples, or guard buildings, are found on the two inland corners (Figs. 326, 327).

It has already been noted in our discussion of Mayapan that the use of enclosing walls either for purposes of defense or spatial definition is extremely rare in any part of the Maya area. Traces of low walls are found at a limited number of sites, but a true enclosing wall of the dimensions found at Tulum is unknown except at Mayapan. The site of Xcaret, which is some distance north of Tulum, is reported to have enclosing walls, but as of now no survey has been made. It has been argued by many writers that the function of the wall was protection from attack, but this argument has several serious flaws. In the first place, it can be noted that the wall stops short of the edge of the cliff, making it easy for any attackers to enter the city from these exposed flanks. Secondly, while the wall is very massive, it is not very high and could have been scaled hand over hand with no difficulty. Finally, one might ask why the concept of fortifications should develop at a provincial center when there were larger and more important centers further inland which would surely have been protected in a similar manner if this were necessary.

On the other hand, the wall does exist, and some explanation must be advanced if the notion of fortifications is rejected. Since the bulk of the masonry buildings within the wall appear to be either ceremonial structures such as temples, altars, oratories, and shrines or small palace-type structures which could have been the living quarters for the priests and nobles, it might be argued that the wall is

Tulum

a symbolic representation marking the boundary of the inner sanctum, or sacred place, making it distinct from the balance of the surrounding suburban area, which contained the living quarters of the bulk of the population. This image is somewhat muddied by the fact that the low platforms in the northwest and southeast quadrants of the site appear to represent substructures which at one time supported pole-and-thatch houses of the type normally associated with the working class. If the houses were tightly clustered together, a total population of nearly four hundred could have lived in these two sectors.

This could not have been the entire population of Tulum, however, as beyond the wall in every direction are traces of low walls which appear to have marked out the boundaries of plots of land. This suggests that the specific location and positioning of houses in the suburban zone corresponds closely to the situation at Mayapan, where house clusters were invariably surrounded by similar low walls, leaving narrow, irregular alleys or streets in between. In the case of Mayapan, as we have already noted, the houses were inside the large enclosing wall and the area outside was very lightly populated. Thus we come back to the notion that the real purpose of the wall was to differentiate the ceremonial area from the suburban and rural areas; the wall simply formalizes this distinction. This notion is further reinforced by the fact that much of the space within the enclosing wall is apparently devoid of buildings of any kind, held in reserve perhaps for additional ceremonial structures as the need arose.

As can be seen in the site map (Fig. 323), the main group of buildings at Tulum form a compact, highly organized complex (dominated by a structure called the Castillo (Figs. 328, 329, 330). This is the highest building in the whole city and from the doorway of the upper temple one has a commanding view of the entire city as well as a large area of the surrounding countryside (Figs. 331, 332). The Castillo is also an important landmark when seen from the sea and is still included on many

426

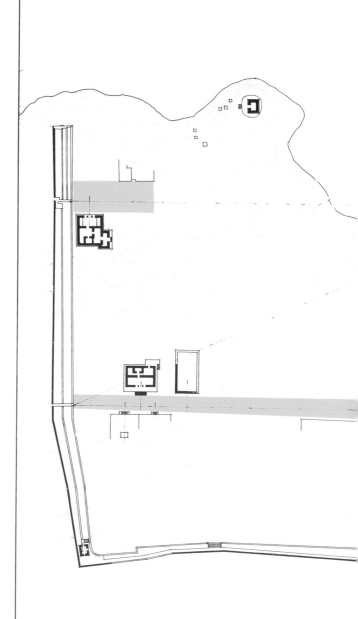

FIG. 323. Tulum (after Lothrop).

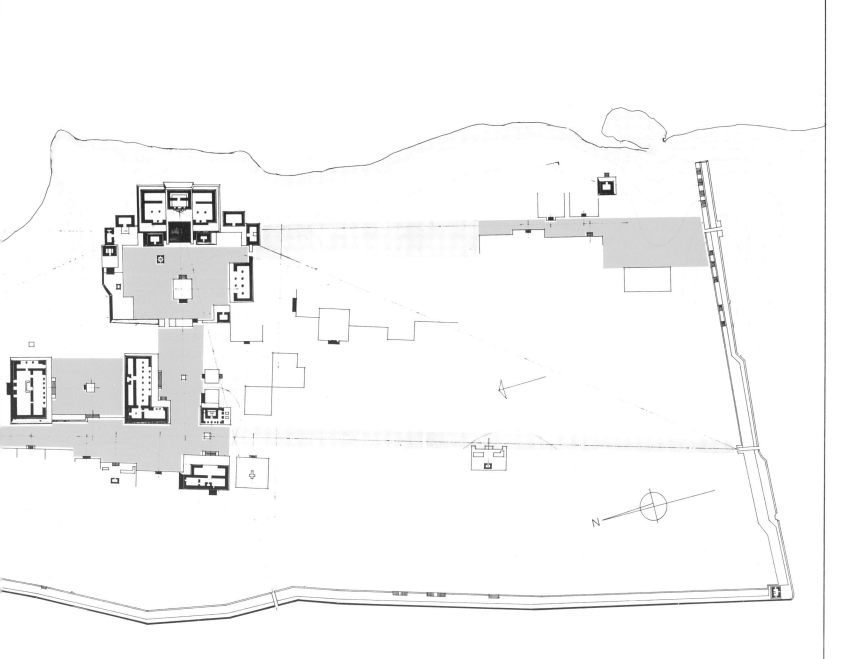

TULUM
QUINTANA ROO, MEXICO

SCALE 0   50   100   150   200 FT

N

maps as a navagational guide. Numerous other structures lie outside this main plaza area; these, for the most part, seem to be associated with streets or roadways, which connect the central area with the entrances through the north and south walls.

The main plaza is defined on two of its sides by smaller structures and the plaza itself is raised several feet above the natural ground level. The main plaza connects to a somewhat less well-defined plaza or court to the west, which in turn becomes the focus of the north-south street. The entrances through the north and south enclosing walls which lie closest to the Caribbean focus on the main plaza and Castillo, but there is little evidence to suggest that there was actually a street on the north side (Figs. 333, 334). There is also no indication of a street leading from the single entrance through the west wall (Fig. 335), but there is a dramatic view of the main plaza and Castillo once you have passed through the narrow opening in the wall (Fig. 336). It can hardly be accidental that the axis of this opening focuses directly on the temple structure which is the most important feature of the Castillo.

Further attention must be drawn to the so-called streets which lead from the entries through the north and south walls to the central groups. It has been pointed out earlier that the typical classic city or ceremonial center was not organized around streets. Plazas were connected in various ways to other plazas, courtyards, or terraces, in many cases with broad flights of stairs where the levels change, but, with the exception of raised causeways, which connected otherwise isolated parts of larger centers, the notion of a street within the precincts of the ceremonial center appears to have been unknown.[16] Any linear organization such as a street system implies a sequential set of relationships among the parts, with the events taking place one after another in an orderly succession along a predetermined path. The lack of any such street systems at classic centers suggests that the nature of the ceremonies was such that each identifiable grouping of elements acted as a semiautonomous part of the whole, with no fixed or sequential relationships to other areas. Patterns of movement within earlier centers appear to have been generalized rather than specific, and there is little reason to assume that streets would have served any particular purpose.

If this reasoning is correct, we are left with two alternate explanations for the streets at Tulum; either they represent a change in the pattern of civic activity which has now become structured in a sequential manner, or else the street can be seen as an inevitable consequence of fixed entry points through a boundary, which quite naturally promote linear movement patterns from these entries to specific places within the boundaries. Given further time, is it possible that the street and plaza concept within a gridiron organization, which the Spaniards later imposed over the old order, would have developed *in situ* from this embryonic example?

The general character of the architecture at Tulum is similar to that found at other sites along the east coast, but in many respects it appears to be closely linked with the Mexican period at Chichen Itza. From this it might be reasoned that Tulum occupied the position of a provincial capital in relation to the larger and more important center located some seventy miles to the northwest. Evidence supporting this position is found, for example, in the serpent columns in the doorway of the Castillo at Tulum, which are similar to the serpent columns of the Temple of the Warriors at Chichen Itza (Fig. 331). Many of the structures at Tulum also utilze the stone-post and wooden-beam roof construction which is characteristic of the Mexican period at Chichen Itza. Details such as moldings, sculptural and decorative elements over doorways and on corners of buildings, and certain symbolic ele-

[16] There is some evidence that streets, or paved areas akin to streets, may have existed at some Classic Maya sites, though they are hard to recognize. Recent work at the site of Yaxha, which is not far from Tikal, has disclosed a number of streetlike elements which are significantly different from *sacbes*. At Yaxha, the "streets" are like grand avenues, lined with important buildings on both sides. (Hellmuth: 1971.)

ments are different at the two sites, but the general similarity of architectural features is unmistakable (Figs. 337, 338). Structures which are essentially colonnaded halls are found at both sites, and these belong exclusively to the Mexican period. Curiously, vaulted roofs were used at Tulum in addition to the flat post-and-beam roofs, but some of these can be assigned to its later phase of development, which is the reverse of the chronology at Chichen Itza, where the vaulted spaces of the Classic period were later replaced by flat-roof column-and-beam systems.

In spite of this anomaly, the widespread use of Mexican-inspired architectural elements at Tulum clearly connects it with Chichen Itza and other parts of Yucutan, although the nature of the relationship is not clear. The relationship between Tulum and Coba, its closest inland neighbor to the west, is also not clear. Coba is assumed to be a Classic period site, but a small temple on a huge pyramid at Coba has the same figure of the Diving God over its doorway as the temple at Tulum shown in Figure 339.

In certain respects, Tulum presents a more orderly arrangement of buildings than is found in other parts of Yucutan, but the individual structures are almost entirely lacking in the richness of ornamentation and refinement of proportion which generally characterizes Classic Maya architecture. The stucco bas-reliefs over the doorways and the profile faces on the corners of many of the structures at Tulum are almost cartoons when compared with the elegant reliefs at Palenque, for example (Figs. 339, 340, 341). Also missing are the complex stone-mosaic friezes which enliven the upper walls of the façades of countless Puuc- or Chenes-style buildings scattered throughout the peninsula. One building, called the Temple of the Frescoes, does contain the remains of well-preserved wall paintings similar to frescoes found at Chichen Itza (Fig. 342). These are a far cry from the Classic scenes at Bonampak. The art of stonecutting and building construction had indeed reached a low ebb at Tulum and this lack of technical proficiency is matched by the lack of artistic merit in the architecture. The simplification of façades through the elimination of ornamentation does not lead in this instance to a corresponding gain in appreciation of mass or profile. Perhaps it is unfair to characterize these features as evidence of decadance, but, aside from the highly romantic quality of its setting, Tulum remains thoroughly provincial.

Note: Tulum was explored and mapped by members of the Carnegie Institution of Washington Expedition of 1923. A detailed record of their work was published under the title *Tulum, an Archaeological Study of the East Coast of Yucatan*. Interested readers are referred to this monograph for details of buildings and decorative features. (Lothrop: 1924.)

FIG. 324. Tulum—east edge of site and Caribbean Sea.

FIG. 325. Tulum—steep cliffs behind Castillo.

FIG. 326. Tulum—north enclosing wall
(note entry near right end).

FIG. 327. Tulum—watch tower on corner of enclosing wall.

FIG. 328. Tulum—the Castillo and Temple of the Frescoes.

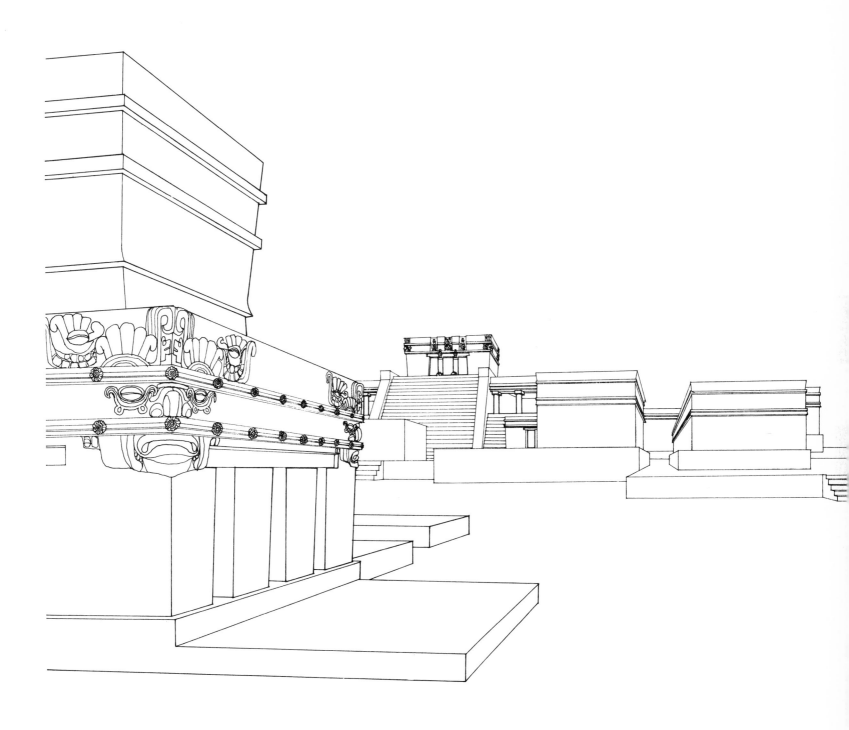

FIG. 329. Tulum—the Castillo and Temple of the Frescoes (restoration).

FIG. 331. Tulum—the Castillo,
doorways with serpent columns
similar to columns on
Temple of the Warriors
at Chichen Itza.

FIG. 330. Tulum—the Castillo (left).

FIG. 332. Tulum—
view looking west
from doorway of Castillo
(note enclosing wall
in background).

FIG. 333. Tulum—view from entry through north wall.

FIG. 334. Tulum—view from entry through south wall (note traces of low platforms in foreground).

FIG. 335. Tulum—view showing west wall and entry.

FIG. 336. Tulum—view from entry through west wall.

FIG. 337. Tulum—Temple of the Frescoes.

FIG. 338. Tulum—detail, Temple of the Frescoes.

FIG. 339. Tulum—Temple of the Diving God.

FIG. 340. Tulum—Temple of the Diving God seen from entry to main plaza.

FIG. 341. Tulum—stucco mask
on corner of small temple.

FIG. 342. Tulum—detail of frescoes,
Temple of the Frescoes.

Zaculeu

The ruins of Zaculeu are located high in the mountains of central Guatemala about three miles from the modern town of Huehuetenango. The valley in which the city was located is relatively flat with mountains rising on all sides. The elevation in the valley near the ruins is about sixty-five hundred feet, which produces a temperate and invigorating climate. The area to which the ceremonial center was confined is a small peninsulalike spur bounded on three sides by deeply eroded barrancas. Two of these ravines converge to form a narrow neck of land, about five hundred feet wide, which gives access to the site. Approach to the site from any other side is extremely difficult because of the steeply sloped sides of the barrancas. The terrain within the center is relatively flat with some slope to the west and southwest. The area enclosed by the barrancas covers about three and one-third acres, within which the ceremonial structures form a very compact group (Fig. 343). A case can be made that this particular site was selected because of its natural defensive possibilities, but it seems just as likely that its relative isolation from the immediate surrounding area gives it the prominence required of an important religious or ceremonial center.

The present study is confined to a study of lowland Maya ceremonial centers, but Zaculeu has been included in order to illustrate certain contrasts, as well as similarities, between highland and lowland sites. It is generally conceded that the highland sites in Guatemala belong to a separate culture from that of the lowlands.[17] Excavations at Zaculeu have produced considerable evidence showing that some communication took place between the two areas, and tentative dating indicates that Zaculeu was established somewhere around A.D. 500 to 600, which makes it contemporary with many Classic lowland sites. However, most of the lowland sites, with the exception of the Yucatan Peninsula area, were abandoned around A.D. 900, while Zaculeu continued to be occupied until its final overthrow by the Spaniards in 1525, and many of the structures now visible date from the Postclassic period.

In spite of the fact that the two cultures existed simultaneously and maintained some contact with each other, the architectural development in the two areas was significantly different, even though certain general characteristics are common to both. The most widespread feature among lowland Maya sites is the presence of vaulted stone buildings with high roof combs; at Zaculeu, and other highland sites, these are entirely lacking. In place of the high stone vaults, the buildings at Zaculeu had low wood-framed roofs supported on columns. While none of these roofs remains standing, it is not difficult to reconstruct the general form of the roof from existing remains, and it is obvious that wooden roofs could not have supported masonry roof combs. Another feature of buildings at lowland sites is the extensive use of sculptural elements, in some cases extremely elaborate, on the upper portions of buildings and on the roof combs. At Zaculeu the façades of buildings have only smooth plaster surfaces with no traces of decorative elements (Figs. 344, 345). In addition, no carved stelae are found at highland sites, nor are there any hieroglyphic inscriptions on, or in association with, the buildings.

In spite of these differences, the same basic elements of the ceremonial center are found in both areas. The structures at Zaculeu include stepped pyramids which served as the supporting elements for temples (Figs. 346, 347), platforms, terraces, ball courts, plazas, altars, and court-

[17] Various aspects of the highland Maya culture, including architecture and civic planning, are fully presented in Vol. 2 of *Handbook of Middle American Indians* (Wauchope: 1965.)

yards, which are also found in profusion at lowland sites. Perhaps it would be more accurate to say that while similar building types and spatial elements are found in both areas, the details of the buildings are considerably different and the organization of building groupings and their relationships to each other are different. This difference in spatial order can be seen by looking at the site plan.

As previously noted, the site is very compact and there are a large number of structures in close physical proximity to one another (Fig. 343). In contrast to many lowland sites where a high degree of order can be observed among building groupings, particularly where the natural terrain is relatively flat, Zaculeu exhibits a surprising lack of conceptual organization. Several distinct groupings are to be found within the total, but these do not bear any clear relationships to each other. Several courts and plazas are fairly well defined by adjacent terraces and platforms, but they are not connected with one another in any consistent way and it is almost impossible to discern specific paths of movement between the various sectors of the city. Irregularity in varying degrees is characteristic of the entire complex and any instances of axial alignment appear to be accidental rather than deliberate. Buildings on opposite sides of a plaza are not on a common axis and altars are not in alignment with the doorways of temples. The orientation of buildings in no way conforms to the cardinal points of the compass, although there is a general deviation of thirty to forty degrees from true north. It is possible that the siting of buildings was influenced by the location of the river, which is to the northeast of the site, but even this is debatable, since the river cannot be seen from most points within the site.

Perhaps the most significant difference between highland and lowland sites, in terms of civic planning, is the total absence at highland sites of the sophisticated building complexes developed by the lowland Maya which we have called Palace Groups, Quadrangle Groups, and Acropolis Groups. Embodied in these groupings are sets of relationships involving ideas of direction, progression, hierarchies, or orders of importance, subtle distinctions between inside and outside, shadings of openness or enclosure, and a host of other formal considerations which are evidence of a mature architectural development. At Zaculeu, on the other hand, the building groupings are limited to variations on a single theme—quadrilateral groupings of structures around a plaza or courtyard.

We have noted that at lowland sites, the quadrilateral Temple Group represents the first stage in a long evolutionary sequence of placemaking ideas which became more complex as time went on. By more complex is meant a condition where more elements can be resolved into a larger unified whole. Thus, while the quadrilateral groups can be used in a variety of ways, they tend to remain static and their inherent self-containment makes it difficult to establish larger relationships with contiguous elements. Under these conditions, it is not surprising that Zaculeu tends to be a collection of disparate elements, with no larger ordering ideas present which might give it greater coherence. While Zaculeu can scarcely be said to represent the total architectural development in the highlands, it seems fairly typical with regard to notions of planning, which for the most part are limited to the making of numbers of discrete, but unrelated, assemblages of structures whose proximity to one another only emphasizes their separateness.

Special mention should be made of the ball court which occupies a central position within the site (Figs. 346, 348). It is surprisingly well ordered and more strongly defined than ball courts at many lowland sites. The two ends of the court beyond the playing alley are closed by a low wall which completely differentiates the ball court from the surrounding space (Figs. 349, 350). At many lowland sites this back-court area is lacking in definition and it is questionable as to just how much space was actually used as part of the playing area of the court. It must be recognized, however, that it is this same overlapping, or interdependence, of spaces that gives many of the lowland sites their special character.

445

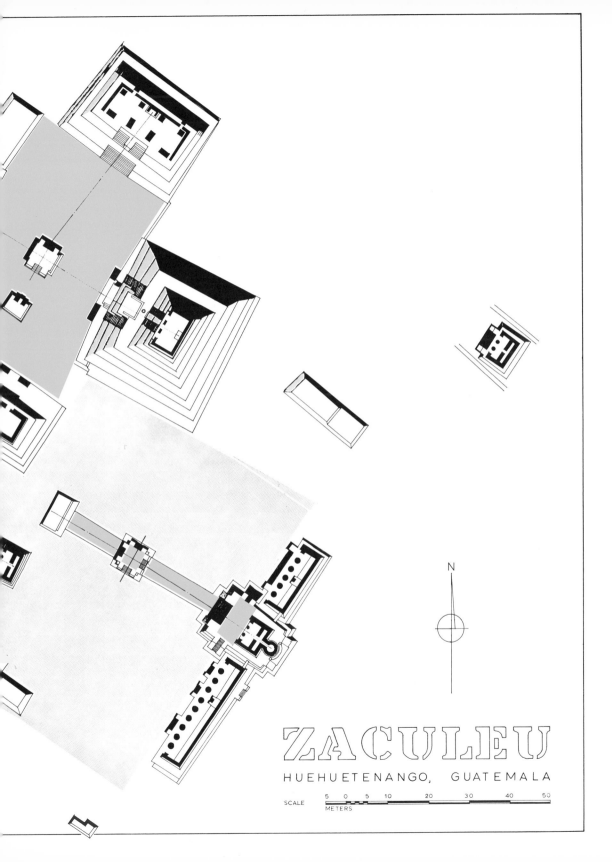

ZACULEU

HUEHUETENANGO, GUATEMALA

SCALE

5 0 5 10   20   30   40   50

METERS

FIG. 343. Zaculeu (after Dimick).

The ball court at Zaculeu is a clear conception in itself, but its failure to fit to a larger conception within the whole center is indicative of the incipient nature of large-scale organizational ideas in the highlands as contrasted with the highly sophisticated ideas developed in the lowlands at the height of the Classic period. It is certainly not accurate to imply that all buildings and building groupings at lowland sites fit into well-organized over-all schemes, and this has already been noted in connection with certain structures at specific lowland centers. Nevertheless, it can be seen from the site plans that a typical lowland site exhibits a degree of organization that is lacking at Zaculeu and that some effort was made to conceptualize ideas of order at the scale of the over-all scheme at these sites even though the center was continuously rebuilt and expanded. At Zaculeu it must be assumed that the builders were not concerned with hierarchical sequences or precise axial relationships, as the irregularity appears to be almost deliberate. Since Zaculeu is one of the very few highland sites that has been extensively excavated and restored, it is not possible to generalize about generic spatial forms in the highlands as we have done for the lowland sites.

The discussion of Zaculeu and the comparisons drawn with lowland sites would not be complete without some mention of the differences in technological development which further distinguish the two areas. It has already been pointed out that buildings at Zaculeu were roofed with flat or gently sloping wood-framed structures rather than the stone vaulting which was consistently employed at lowland sites (Fig. 351). This does not imply that stone vaults are better than wooden roofs, but they are certainly more permanent and require a more advanced technology to execute than the crude pole-and-rubble roofs which are used in Zaculeu and other highland sites. During the course of excavation and restoration it was discovered that the basic construction of all structures at Zaculeu was rough stone slabs, cemented together with mortar and covered with a thick coating of plaster on the outer surface.

FIG. 344. Zaculeu—view looking southeast from Temple No. 9.

FIG. 345. Zaculeu—Temple 1, front elevation.

FIG. 346. Zaculeu—ball court and Temple 1.

FIG. 347. Zaculeu—platforms in center of plaza, Temple No. 6 in background.

FIG. 348. Zaculeu—Plaza No. 2, ball court in background.

It can be noted that not only is the over-all site scheme somewhat irregular but the ground plans of individual buildings and details such as edges of terraces and stairways are also very irregular (Fig. 351). This seems to suggest a lack of technical ability or reliance on primitive construction techniques, as these irregularities are glaring even to the naked eye. Similar irregularities can be noted at lowland sites in structures erected during the Preclassic and Early Classic periods before the technique of erecting rough concrete heartings faced with cut-stone veneers had been fully developed.

The many differences which have been noted in both planning and architecture between highland and lowland Maya sites suggests some difference in cultural affinities. It has already been noted that the ties between the two Maya cultures is tenuous, particularly in terms of architectural development. There appears to be a much stronger link between the highland Maya and cultures in central Mexico, if the architectural evidence is a good indicator. These affinities show up in the direct importation of stylistic and decorative elements from Teotihuacan as well as building forms and plan arrangements that have their counterparts in later cultures from the same area.

The movement of ideas appears to have been from central Mexico to the Guatemalan Highlands rather than the reverse, and this may help to explain the nature of architectural development in the highland area. Following the general collapse of the lowland Maya culture near the end of the ninth century A.D., groups from central Mexico penetrated the lowland area in the northern part of the Yucatan Peninsula, and the Toltec-Mexican architecture at Chichen Itza from the Postclassic period shows much greater similarity to the architecture at Zaculeu and other highland sites than anything from the Classic period. Aside from this tenuous connection, the lowland and highland Maya cultures represent two distinctive and divergent lines of placemaking ideas, even though they began with the same basic vocabulary of temple, pyramid, and plaza.

FIG. 349. Zaculeu—view looking northeast from Temple No. 2.

FIG. 350. Zaculeu—ball court (note enclosing walls at both ends).

FIG. 351. Zaculeu—Temple No. 4 (note irregularity of stairway).

8.
Epilogue

We began this discussion of Maya architecture and Maya cities with the proposition that architecture in general is concerned with the self-conscious making of "places" which mark out the specific domain of man as something distinct from the balance of nature. This process initiates with an abstract concept, conceived in the mind, and leads to a physical realization of the concept in the form of architecture, or man-made places. To its creators, the open space of a plaza or courtyard says, in effect, "This is the place; this is a unique domain which I have marked out as something essentially human." The solid mass of a pyramid or substructure is seen as an object which occupies or takes possession of part of the earth, declaring, "Here I am; I have taken occupancy of this place, now and forevermore."

Maya cities, as we have seen, consist in essence of these two kinds of places. The open spaces of plazas, terraces, platforms, and courtyards, leveled and paved with lime-stone cement, mark out the places where the idea of "a community of man" is given visible form. The great pyramidal substructures, which serve as support for temples or palaces, take possession of the earth, their great mass and dead weight alone attesting to their immobility and seeming permanence. To the Maya peasant, bound to his cornfield and wooden hut and never more than a few steps removed from nature in its most primordial form, the city must have been a magnificent and truly magical place, its great plazas more extensive than any field he could conceive of and its huge pyramids more impressive than any mountain seen in the distance. That all this should eventually come to naught is still almost incomprehensible.

The combination of these two kinds of places into the plaza-pyramid-temple configuration which seems to mark the initial conception of the ceremonial center, and later

blossomed into the larger complex of the city, does not, in itself, argue for the independent creation of the notion of architecture by the Maya. It is possible that the generic ideas proceeded from elsewhere, although the evidence is strongly in favor of an independent development *in situ* which parallels similar developments in other parts of the world. We have tried to show how the open space of a field cleared for planting can be formalized into a plaza or square and how the simple wooden hut was transposed into the monumental stone temple. Even if these transformations were initiated by neighbors or by predecessors of the Mayas who lived in the same area during an earlier period, this takes nothing away from the accomplishments of the Mayas, who expanded the germinal seeds of architecture into an amazingly broad range of space-ordering ideas that far exceeded the efforts of their contemporaries in other parts of Mesoamerica, both in terms of complexity and degree of refnement.

The importance of these complex notions of placemaking, as evidenced in the remains of Maya cities, rests in the manner in which they evolved from a single prototype consisting of only three basic elements (plaza, platform, temple) into very elaborate spatial conceptions which included many of the fundamental form ideas which still remain current in those parts of the contemporary world where monumentality and hierarchical ordering continue to find a place. It is readily apparent that the terms *temple, palace, nunnery, observatory, shrine, acropolis*, etc., as used within historical or contemporary societies, can be applied to the basic elements of Maya cities without losing too much of their meaning. The formal aspects of these spatial configurations are identical wherever they are used, even though there may be no similarity in function or details of design when transposed to another culture. By the same token, we can apply contemporary terms such as *roadway, colonnade, courtyard, plaza,* and *square* to the open spaces in Maya cities without creating an entirely false impression of what they are like.

In a very real sense, the Mayas visualized all of the basic spatial concepts which are necessary to construct anything from the smallest dwelling to a fairly large city, complete with everything we ourselves might need in the way of specialized spaces for a broad range of activities; its only drawback might stem from a lack of those mechanical services and gadgets which we now take for granted. The rural Maya Indian of today, living in certain extremely isolated parts of the jungles in Chiapas, Peten, and Quintana Roo, is faced with a very primitive existence in comparison to the civilized urban life of his ancestors, who tamed the same jungles over fifteen centuries earlier.

The growth and expansion of Maya settlements during the latter part of the Classic period is marked by an increase in the degree of complexity and sophistication of the basic forms which constituted the physical substance of the city, together with an increase in the variety of building types represented. At the same time, the nature of the city also was changing, and by the end of the Classic period the processes of urbanization had advanced to the point where it is probable that nonreligious structures accounted for the bulk of new construction. New temples continued to be built and older temples were buried beneath larger versions in the latest style, but their total number was small in relation to the total building effort. The emerging city was no longer primarily a religious center, but a thriving commercial and administrative center as well, with a large resident population of non-farmers. The visible aspect of the city in terms of the exterior of its buildings shifted from naturalistic motifs to greater and greater abstraction, and large sections of important buildings were covered with stone-mosaic sculptures based on geometric patterns. Stelae were erected in greater profusion, and new structures were erected to mark the occasion of each new *katun*, ending

as described in glyphs on the stelae. At the same time, there was a tendency to indulge in seemingly endless repetitions of a limited palette of basic forms and motifs which have the quality of being mass-produced. Inventiveness apparently declined as quantities increased.

In short, we see the beginnings of what might be called decadence, and certain forms and details which have the superficial appearance of being more sophisticated are in reality only willful abstractions which exist solely for their own sake: symbols which have lost their meaning, since they no longer generate out of basic human needs or aspirations. The whole of the physical city—its buildings and plazas, its stelae with their sculptured figures and calendar inscriptions, the masks of gods everywhere present on walls and roof combs of buildings—give mute testimony to the implicit faith of the Mayas in the efficacy of symbols as a means of currying favor with the pantheon of gods who controlled their destinies.

The city as a single entity must be considered as an even larger symbol, a gigantic monument to man's faith in his ability to transcend nature; what had begun as a self-conscious assertion by the Mayas of their own importance in the scheme of things was ultimately elaborated into a monumental effort to embrace the whole cosmos by giving it visible form in their own terms. But this kind of blind faith in abstractions disassociated from realities ultimately leads to disaster, if we are to judge from the history of mankind as a whole, and the sudden collapse of Maya society at a time when building activity had reached its peak suggests that these same symbols became anathema to a civilization that had spent over six hundred years creating them. The power presumed to lie in the symbols actually lies in man himself.

By the beginning of the tenth century the great plazas were deserted, soon to be replaced by the omnipresent jungle, which had only been temporarily held in check. The temples and palaces, raised high above the earth on their massive substructures, held out a little longer before they too succumbed to the onslaught of the jungle

455

and collapsed on themselves, leaving only mounds of rubble to mark the fact that they had ever existed. The builders of the stone temples believed that they would last forever; hadn't these same stones been part of the earth since time immemorial? But in spite of this assumed permanence, the combined efforts of countless generations of builders and artists to dominate the natural environment ultimately led to failure, and the Maya peasant returned once more to the jungle with only his crude clearing and thatched-roof hut as visible reminders of a glorious past. To be sure, a few of the successors of the great city builders who lived in the northern part of the Yucatan Peninsula continued to erect monumental buildings and even took further steps in the direction of urbanization, but these were at best only ill-conceived and shoddily constructed imitations of the great Classic centers. Another four hundred years were to lapse before a city comparable to Dzibilchaltun in its prime was destined to wipe out all traces of the jungle and reassert the superiority of man.

Such is now the case, and the modern city of Merida, the capital of the state of Yucatan in Mexico, stands not far from Dzibilchaltun and the ruins of a score of other Maya cities, some of which have been partially restored to their former state of glory. Tourists arrive in Merida by plane, sleep in air-conditioned rooms in luxury hotels, and drive out to the ruins in the latest-model cars on paved highways that actually pass through the same plazas the Mayas had won from the jungle twelve hundred years earlier with only a few stone tools and an unbounded faith in their ability to transcend nature to assist them in the task. Such is the ultimate fate of nearly every early civilization of which we have a record. Their social institutions were destroyed either by enemies from without or collapse from within, while the remains of the great cities they created lie buried beneath the newer monuments erected by their successors. We assume that change means progress, but we still have no way of knowing the full extent of the losses entailed in the eclipse of a major civilization.

The last chapter of this story is still to be written. Aside from Merida and a few smaller cities scattered through other parts of the old Maya area, the jungles of the Peten and the Yucatan Peninsula are scarcely inhabited today and the ruins of hundreds of stone cities built by the Mayas are the only visible evidence of man's insatiable appetite to conquer the natural environment and convert it to his own purposes. The jungle continues to resist any further invasion by man in spite of the availability of modern technology, which has given us the capacity to convert deserts into oases and wastelands into thriving cities almost overnight. It may well be that there is simply nothing in the way of natural resources or other attractions within the bulk of the Maya expanse to make any such wholesale invasion and conversion worthwhile, but, even if this is true, the achievements of the Mayas, in an environment that remains almost totally inhospitable to twentieth-century man, must be laid alongside those of Egypt, Greece, or Rome. The development of a truly monumental architecture, and in turn large urban communities, starting with only a thatched-roof hut as a model, was surely the most remarkable architectural accomplishment of the New World.

Adams, R. E. W.

1970 "Suggested Classic Period Occupational Specialization in the Southern Maya Lowlands," *Papers of the Peabody Museum,* Harvard University, Vol. LXI, Part V, No. 4. Cambridge.

Andrews, E. W. IV

1943 "The Archaeology of Southwestern Campeche," *Carnegie Institution of Washington, Pub. 546,* Contrib. 40. Washington, D.C.

1965a "Archaeology and Prehistory in the Northern Maya Lowlands," *Handbook of Middle American Indians,* II, 288–330. Austin, University of Texas Press.

1965b See under Dzibilchaltun.

Blom, Frans, and Oliver La Farge

1926 *Tribes and Temples.* Middle American Research Institute, Tulane University, *Pub. 1.* 2 vols. New Orleans.

Brainerd, G. W.

1958 *The Archaeological Ceramics of Yucatan.* University of California *Anthropological Records,* No. 19. Berkeley.

Bullard, W. R.

1960 "Maya Settlement Patterns in Northeastern Peten, Guatemala," *American Antiquity,* Vol, XXV, pp. 355–72.

Childe, V. G.

1950 "The Urban Revolution," *Town Planning Review,* Vol. XXI, pp. 3–17. Liverpool.

Erasmus, C. J.

1965 "Monument Building: Some Field Experiments," *Southwestern Journal of Anthropology,* Vol. XXI, No. 4, pp. 277–301.

Graham, Ian

1967 *Archaeological Exploration in El Peten, Guatemala.* Middle American Research Institute, Tulane University, *Pub. 33.* New Orleans.

Haviland, W. A.

1966 "Maya Settlement Patterns: A Critical Review," Middle American Research Institute, *Archaeological Studies in Middle America, Pub. 26.* New Orleans.

1968 "Ancient Lowland Maya Social Organization," Middle American Research Institute, *Archaeological Studies in Middle America, Pub. 26.* New Orleans.

Hellmuth, N. M.

Ms. 1971 "Possible Streets at a Maya Site in Guatemala." Unpublished MS.

Jacobs, Jane

1970 *The Economy of Cities.* New York, Random House.

Jones, E.

1966 *Towns and Cities.* New York, Oxford University Press.

Landa, D. de

1941 *Relación de Cosas de Yucatán.* Translated and edited by A. M. Tozzer. *Papers of the Peabody Museum,* Harvard University, Vol. XVIII. Cambridge. *Southwestern Journal of Anthropology,* Vol. XXI,

Lundell, C. L.

1934 "Preliminary Sketch of the Phytogeography of the Yucatan Peninsula," *Carnegie Institution of Washington, Pub. 436,* No. 12. Washington, D.C.

Maler, T.

1901–1903 *Researches in the Central Portion of the Usumatsintla Valley. Memoirs of the Peabody Museum,* Harvard University, Vol. II, Nos. 1 and 2. Cambridge.

Mariscal, F.

1928 *Estudio Arquitectonico de las Ruinas Mayas: Yucatan y Campeche.* Mexico, Secretary of Public Education.

Marquina, I.

1951 *Arquitectura Prehispanica. Memorias* del Instituto Nacional de Antropologia y Historia. Mexico.

Maudslay, A. P.

1889–1902 "Biologia Centrali-Americana," *Archaeology,* Vols. I–IV. London.

Morley, S. G., and G. W. Brainerd

Bibliography,
General

1954 *The Ancient Maya.* Palo Alto, Stanford University Press.

Ortega y Gasset, J.
1961 *The Revolt of the Masses.* London, Unwin Books.

Pollock, H. E. D.
1965– "Architecture of the Maya Lowlands," *Handbook of Middle American Indians,* II, 378–439. Austin, University of Texas Press.
1966 "Architectural Notes on Some Chenes Ruins," *Papers of the Peabody Museum,* Harvard University, Vol. LXI, Part I. Cambridge.

Proskouriakoff, Tatiana
1946 *An Album of Maya Architecture.* Carnegie Institution of Washington, *Pub. 588.* Washington, D.C.; Norman, University of Oklahoma Press, 1963.
1960 *A Study of Classic Maya Sculpture.* Carnegie Institution of Washington, *Pub. 593.* Washington, D.C.
1963 "Historical Data in the Inscriptions of Yaxchilan (Part I)," *Estudios de Cultura Maya,* Vol. III, pp. 149–67.
1965– "Sculpture and Major Arts of the Maya Lowlands," *Handbook of Middle American Indians,* II, 465–97. Austin, University of Texas Press.

Puleston, D. E., and O. S. Puleston
1971 "An Ecological Approach to the Origins of Maya Civilization," *Archaeology,* Vol. XXIV, pp. 330–37. London.

Rapoport, A.
1969 *House Form and Culture.* Englewood Cliffs, N.J., Prentice-Hall, Inc.

Rivet, P.
1954 *Maya Cities.* Paris, Albert Guillot.

Roys, R. L.
1934 "The Engineering Knowledge of the Maya," Carnegie Institution of Washington, *Pub. 436,* Contrib. 6. Washington, D.C.

Ruppert, Karl, and John H. Denison, Jr.
1943 *Archaeological Reconnaissance in Campeche, Quintana Roo, and Peten.* Carnegie Institution of Washington, *Pub. 543.* Washington, D.C.

Ruz Lhuillier, A.
1945 *Campeche en la Arqueologia Maya. Acta Antropologica i Mexico.*

Sanders, W. T.
1960 "Prehistoric Ceramics and Settlement Patterns in Quintana Roo, Mexico," Carnegie Institution of Washington, *Pub. 606,* Contrib. 60. Washington, D.C.
1962 "Cultural Ecology of the Maya Lowlands," Part I, *Estudios de Cultura Maya,* Vol. II, Universidad Nacional Autonoma de Mexico, D.F.
———, and B. J. Price
1968 *Mesoamerica—The Evolution of a Civilization.* New York, Random House.

Sjoberg, G.
1960 *The Preindustrial City.* New York, The Free Press.

Spinden, H. J.
1957 *Maya Art and Civilization.* Indian Hills, Colorado, Falcon Press.

Stephens, J. L.
1841 *Incidents of Travel in Central America, Chiapas, and Yucatan.* 2 vols. New York.
1843 *Incidents of Travel in Yucatan.* 2 vols. New York; Norman, University of Oklahoma Press, 1962.

Thompson, E. H.
1932 *People of the Serpent.* Boston and New York, Houghton Mifflin Co.

Thompson, J. E. S.
1945 "A Survey of the Northern Maya Area," *American Antiquity,* Vol. I, pp. 2–24.
1954 *The Rise and Fall of Maya Civilization.* University of Oklahoma Press, Norman, 2nd ed., revised and enlarged, 1966.
1965– "Archaeological Synthesis of the Southern Maya Lowlands," *Handbook of Middle American Indians,* II, 331–59. Austin, University of Texas Press.
———, H. E. D. Pollock, and J. Charlot
1932 *A Preliminary Study of the Ruins of Coba, Quintana Roo, Mexico.* Carnegie Institution of Washington, *Pub. 424.* Washington, D.C.

Tozzer, A. M., trans.
1941 *Landa's Relacion de las Cosas de Yucatan. Papers of*

the Peabody Museum, Harvard University, Vol.
XVIII. Cambridge.

Wauchope, R., ed.

1965– *Handbook of Middle American Indians*. Austin,
University of Texas Press.

1965 *They Found the Buried Cities*. Chicago, University
of Chicago Press.

Willey, G. R., W. R. Bullard, J. B. Glass, and J. C. Clifford

1965 *Prehistoric Maya Settlements in the Celize Valley.
Papers of the Peabody Museum*, Harvard University, Vol. LIV. Cambridge.

————, and W. R. Bullard

1965– "Prehistoric Settlement Patterns in the Maya Lowlands," *Handbook of Middle American Indians*, II,
Part 1. Austin, University of Texas Press.

————, and D. B. Shimkin

1971 "The Collapse of Classic Maya Civilization in the
Southern Lowlands: A Symposium Summary State-
ment," *Southwest Journal of Anthropology*, Vol.
XXVII, pp. 1–18.

Bibliography, Cities

Bonampak

Ruppert, Karl, J. E. S. Thompson, and T. Proskouriakoff
1955 *Bonampak, Chiapas, Mexico.* Carnegie Institution of Washington, *Pub. 602.* Washington, D.C.

Chichen Itza

Maudslay, A. P.
1889–1902 "Biologia Centrali-Americana," *Archaeology,* Vol. I–IV. London.

Morris, E. H., J. Charlot, and A. A. Morris
1931 *The Temple of the Warriors at Chichen Itza.* Carnegie Institution of Washington, *Pub. 406,* 2 vols. Washington, D.C.

Pollock, H. E. D.
1936 "The Casa Redonda at Chichen Itza, Yucatan," Carnegie Institution of Washington, *Pub. 465,* Contrib. 17. Washington, D.C.

Ruppert, Karl
1931 "The Temple of the Wall Panels, Chichen Itza, Yucatan," Carnegie Institution of Washington, *Pub. 403,* Contrib. 3. Washington, D.C.
1935 *The Caracol at Chichen Itza,* Yucatan, Mexico. Carnegie Institution of Washington, *Pub. 546.* Washington, D.C.
1943 *The Mercado, Chichen Itza, Yucatan, Mexico.* Carnegie Institution of Washington, *Pub. 546.* Washington, D.C.
1952 *Chichen Itza: Architectural Notes and Plans.* Carnegie Institution of Washington, *Pub. 595.* Washington, D.C.

Tozzer, A. M.
1957 *Chichen Itza and its Well of Sacrifice. Memoirs of the Peabody Museum,* Harvard University, Vol. XI and XII. Cambridge.

Comalcalco

Andrews, G. F., D. Hardesty, C. Kerr, F. E. Miller, and R. Mogel
1967 *Comalcalco, Tabasco, Mexico—An Architectonic Survey.* Eugene, University of Oregon.

Blom, Frans, and Oliver La Farge
1926 *Tribes and Temples.* Tulane University, *Pub. 1.* New Orleans.

Copan

Gordon, G. B.
1902 "The Hieroglyphic Stairway, Ruins of Copan," *Memoirs of the Peabody Museum,* Harvard University, Vol. I, No. 6. Cambridge.

Maudslay, A. P.
1889–1902 "Biologia Centrali-Americana," *Archaeology,* Vol. I–IV. London.

Morley, S. G.
1920 *The Inscriptions at Copan.* Carnegie Institution of Washington, *Pub. 219.* Washington, D.C.

Stromsvik, G.
1952 "The Ball Courts at Copan," Carnegie Institution of Washington, *Contributions to American Anthropology and History,* Vol. XI, No. 55. Washington, D.C.

Trik, A. S.
1939 "Temple XXXII at Copan," Carnegie Institution of Washington, *Pub. 509,* Contrib. 27. Washington, D.C.

Dzibilchaltun

Andrews, E. W.
1959 "Dzibilchaltun: Lost City of the Maya," *National Geographic Magazine,* Vol. CXV, No. 1, pp. 90–109.
1959b *Progress Report on Two Seasons' Work at Dzibilchaltun, Northwest Yucatan, Mexico: 1956–57, 1957–58.* Washington, D.C., National Geographic Society.
1961 *Preliminary Report on the 1959–60 Season Dzibilchaltun Program.* Middle American Research Institute, Tulane University, Misc. Series No. 11. New Orleans.
1965a See General Bibliography.
1965b "Progress Report on the 1960–64 Field Seasons National Geographic Society—Tulane University Dzi-

bilchaltun Program," Middle American Research Institute, Tulane University, *Pub. 31*, pp. 23–67. New Orleans.

1968 "Dzibilchaltun—A Northern Maya Metropolis," *World Archaeology*, Vol. XXI, No. 1, pp. 36–47.

Edzna

Andrews, G. F.

1969 *Edzna, Campeche, Mexico—Settlement Patterns and Monumental Architecture.* Eugene, University of Oregon.

Ruz, Lhuillier, A.

1945 *Campeche en la Arqueologia Maya. Acta Antropologica i Mexico.*

Labna

Thompson, E. H.

1897 "The Chultuns of Labna," *Memoirs of the Peabody Museum*, Harvard University, Vol. I, No. 3. Cambridge.

Mayapan

Pollock, H. E. D., R. L. Roys, T. Proskouriakoff, and A. L. Smith

1962 *Mayapan, Yucatan, Mexico.* Carnegie Institution of Washington, *Pub. 619.* Washington, D.C.

Oxkintok

Shook, E. E.

1940 "The Ruins of Oxkintok," *Revisita Mexicana de Estudios Antropologicos*, Vol. IV, No. 3, pp. 165–71. Mexico, D. F.

Palenque

Blom, Frans, and Oliver La Farge

1926 *Tribes and Temples.* Tulane University, *Pub. 1.* New Orleans.

Maudslay, A. P.

1889–1902 "Biologia Centrali-Americana," *Archaeology*, Vols. I–IV. London.

Ruz Lhuillier, A.

1956 "Exploraciones Arquelogicas en Palenque," *Anales del Instituto Nacional de Antropologia y Historia*, Vol. X, No. 39. Mexico.

Piedras Negras

Satterthwaite, Linton, Jr.

1944 *Piedras Negras Archaeology: Architecture.* Part II—*Temples*; Part IV—*Ball Courts*; Part VI—*Unclassified Buildings and Substructures.* Philadelphia, University Museum, University of Pennsylvania.

Quirigua

Maudslay, A. P.

1889–1902 "Biologia Centrali-Americana," *Archaeology*, Vol. I–IV. London.

Morley, S. G.

1935 *Guide Book to the Ruins of Quirigua.* Carnegie Institution of Washington, *Supp. Pub. No. 16.* Washington, D.C.

Tikal

Carr, R. F., and J. E. Hazard

1961 *Tikal Report No. 11, Museum Monographs.* Philadelphia, University Museum, University of Pennsylvania.

Coe, W. R.

1965 "Tikal: Ten Years of Study of a Maya Ruins in the Lowlands of Guatemala," *Expedition*, Vol. VIII, No. 1, pp. 5–56. Philadelphia, University Museum, University of Pennsylvania.

1967 *Tikal: A Handbook of the Ancient Maya Ruins.* Philadelphia, University Museum, University of Pennsylvania.

Haviland, W. A.

1965 "Prehistoric Settlement at Tikal, Guatemala," *Expedition*, Vol. VII, No. 3, pp. 14–23. Philadelphia, University Museum, University of Pennsylvania.

1969 "A New Population Estimate for Tikal, Guatemala," *American Antiquity*, Vol. XXXIV, pp. 429–33.

1970 "Tikal, Guatemala, and Mesoamerican Urbanism," *World Archaeology*, Vol. II, No. 2, pp. 186–98.

Maler, T.

1911 *Explorations in the Department of Peten, Guatemala—Tikal. Memoirs of the Peabody Museum*, Harvard University, Vol. V, No. 1. Cambridge.

Maudslay, A. P.

1889–1902 "Biologia Centrali-Americana," *Archaeology*, Vols. I–IV. London.

Puleston, D. E.

1965 "The Chultuns of Tikal," *Expedition*, Vol. VII, No.

3. Philadelphia, University Museum, University of Pennsylvania.

Shook, Edwin, et al.

1958 *Tikal Reports, Nos. 1–4, Museum Monographs.* Philadelphia, University Museum, University of Pennsylvania.

Tozzer, A. M.

1911 "Prehistoric Ruins of Tikal, Guatemala," *Memoirs of the Peabody Museum,* Harvard University, Vol. V, No. 2. Cambridge.

Tulum

Lothrop, S. K.

1924 *Tulum: An Archaeological Study of the East Coast of Yucatan.* Carnegie Institution of Washington, *Pub. 335.* Washington, D.C.

Uaxactun

Ricketson, O. G., Jr., and E. B. Ricketson

1937 *Uaxactun, Guatemala, Group E, 1926–31.* Carnegie Institution of Washington, *Pub. 477.* Washington, D.C.

Smith, A. L.

1950 *Uaxactun, Guatemala: Excavations of 1931–1937.* Carnegie Institution of Washington, *Pub. 588.* Washington, D.C.

Smith, R. E.

1937 "A Study of Structure A–1 Complex at Uaxactun, Peten, Guatemala," Carnegie Institution of Washington, *Pub. 456,* Contrib. 19. Washington, D.C.

Wauchope, R.

1934 "House Mounds of Uaxactun, Guatemala," Carnegie Institution of Washington, *Pub. 436,* Contrib. 7. Washington, D.C.

Uxmal

Morley, S. G.

1910 "Uxmal—A Group of Related Structures," *American Journal of Archaeology,* Series 2, Vol. XIV, pp. 1–18.

Yaxchilan

Maler, T.

1903 *Researches in the Central Portion of the Usumatsintla Valley. Memoirs of the Peabody Museum,* Harvard University, Vol. II, No. 2. Cambridge.

Proskouriakoff, T.

1963 "Historical Data in the Inscriptions of Yaxchilan (Part I)," *Estudios de Cultura Maya,* Vol. III, pp. 149–67.

Zaculeu

Woodbury, R. B., and A. S. Trik

1953 *The Ruins of Zaculeu, Guatemala.* Richmond, Wm. Byrd Press.

Izamal: 375

Jacobs, Jane: 23

Kabah: 23, 271, 273–74, 278–79, 286 & n., 340, 357, 414; and regional culture, 274; location, 322; platforms, 322–23, 326; terraces, 322ff., 323, 326; major ceremonial center, 322; palaces, 322ff., 326–27; causeway, 322–23, 326; archway, 322–23; plazas, 322–23; courtyards, 323; orientation, 323; dwellings, 323; temples, 323, 326; quadrangle, 326; and power group, 327
Kerr, C.: 201
Kukulcan (Toltec god): 411, 415

Labna: 271, 273, 276, 278, 286, 361; and regional culture, 274; location, 340; ceremonial centers, 340, 344; *chultunes*, 340 & n., 341; *cenotes*, 340; as major ceremonial center, 340; house mounds, 340 & n.; as provincial center, 340, 345; plaza, 341, 344; palaces, 341, 344; raised causeway, 341, 344; platforms, 341, 344; temples, 341, 344; courtyards, 341, 344; arch, 344; quadrangle, 344; masks, 344
Lacanha Valley: 153
La Farge, Oliver: 18, 197
Landa, Bishop: 3, 411
Late Classic period: 33, 76, 94, 130–31, 153, 193, 271, 273, 278–79, 374–75, 383, 386
Late Development period: 130
Late Early period: 18
Lime cement: 194, 454; *see also* cement
Limestone: 72, 193, 198–99; *see also* stone
Lintels: 33, 42, 278, 360, 390; wood, 72, 79, 383; stone, 140; carved, 156; *see also* doorways

Maize: 9, 11, 72
Major ceremonial centers: 23; *see also* ceremonial centers
Maler, Teobert: 4, 22, 140
Marker: 145, 169
Masks: *337, 367, 422, 432*; as Maya art, 173, 196, 272, 278, 289, 344, 360, 374; of Chac, 293, 326
Masonry: 39, 42–43, 47, 72–73, 76, 173, 197–98, 200, 253–54, 278, 383, 425ff.; stone and mortar, 130, 255; fired brick, 193–94, 198–99; vaulted, 194, 198, 255; houses, 414
Maudslay, A. P.: 4, 18, 214
Maxcanu, Mexico: 276, 279
Maya Indian, rural: 455
Mayan culture, rise and decline of: 454–56
Mayapan: 17, 80–82, 375, 386–87; location, 411; ceremonial center, 411, 413–15; urbanism, 411, 414–15; and Spanish invasion, 411,

415; wall, 411, 413–14, 416, 425; house clusters, 413–14, 426; house mounds, 414; lack of order, 411, 414–15; platform, 414–15; temple, 414–15; plazas, 415; shrine, 415
Mayapan, Yucatan, Mexico: 416
Merida, Mexico: 286, 323, 370, 383, 411, 414, 456
Mexican invasion: 411
Mexican period: 370, 375, 411, 428–29, 452; *see also* Toltec
Mexico: 3–5, 9, 10, 23, 68, 452, 456
Mexico City, D.F.: 371
Middle America Research Institute of Tulane University: 370
Miller, F. E.: 201
Milpa farming: 10, 23, 82, 94, 132, 256, 273–74, 279, 371
Minor ceremonial centers: 23, 29; *see also* ceremonial centers
Mirador: 21–22, 83
Moat: 80, 246
Mogel, R.: 201
Montagua River: 234
Montagua Valley, Guatemala: 36, 80, 234
Monuments: 17, 51, 214, 234–36, 239, 279, 286ff., 371, 411ff.; *see also* zoomorphs *and* stelae
Morley, S. G.: 10
Mosaics: 73, 78, 173, 272, 275, 278, 289, 429
Motifs: human figures, 235, 272, 326ff.; geometric patterns, 272; animal figures, 272
Murals: *166*; *see also* Bonampak

Nakum: 132
Naranjo: 132
National Geographic Magazine: 370
Northern Lowlands: 25, 31, 43
Numeration: 60

Observatories: *see* astronomical assemblages
Oregon, University of, Eugene, Ore.: 246
Organic planning: 139–40, 145, 168
Orientation, building: 51–53, 323
Ortega y Gasset, Jose: 7
Oxkintok: 271; architectural styles, 273, 278–79; and regional culture, 274; largest Puuc center, 274–75; location, 276; urban center, 276, 279; plazas, 276; platforms, 276, 278; temple, 276, 278; acropolis groups, 276; palaces, 276, 278; ball court, 276, 279; portal vault, 276, 278; house mounds, 276, 279; *chultunes*, 276, 279; causeways, 276; stelae, 278–79; hieroglyphic inscriptions, 278; panels, stucco, 278; and pottery, 279; ceremonial structures, 279; monuments, 279

Palaces: *44, 59, 61, 62, 118, 119, 174, 178–83, 211–12, 268, 312,*

465

Walled cities: 81, 411, 413–14, 416, 425–26; *see also* Chichen Itza, Mayapan, *and* Tulum

Walls: *431*, *437*; 6, 33, 39, 47ff., 78, 173ff., 278, 286, 374; masonry, 74, 199; wooden, 74; Puuc style, 173; at Chichen Itza, 383; at Mayapan, 411, 413–14, 416

Watchtower: 169

Willey, Gordon: 17

Wood and thatch: 12, 72–73, 131, 290, 426; roofs, 76, 444, 448; huts, 12–13, 130; buildings, 198

Xcaret: 413, 425

Xlabpak: 286, 340

Yaxchilan: 36, 133, 153, 173, 291; location, 140; lintels, 140; stelae, 140–41, 144; plazas, 140–41, 144–45; river-oriented, 140; and organic planning, 140, 145; ball courts, 141; terraces, 141; temples, 141, 144; platforms, 141, 144; altars, 141, 144; house mounds, 144; walkways, 144; marker, 145; and communication, 145; ceremonial groups, 145

Yucatan, Mexico: 3, 25, 29, 43, 68, 173, 271, 278, 286, 322, 340, 370, 383, 411, 414, 429, 456

Yucatan Peninsula: 3, 5, 9, 11, 16, 25, 36, 80, 271, 374–75, 383, 411, 424, 444, 452, 456

Zaculeu: 81; location, 444; architecture, 444–45, 448, 452; ceremonial center, 444; communication, 444; cultures, 444–45, 448, 452; platforms, 444–45, 452ff.; temples, 444–45, 452ff.; terraces, 444–45; ball courts, 444–45, 448; plazas, 444–45; altars, 444–45; courtyards, 444–45; highland site, 444–45, 448, 452; compared with lowland sites, 444–45, 448, 452

Zoomorphs: 235; *see also* monuments